NEHRU

'For too long Nehru has been presented as a limited historical figure, as someone through whom we learn only about India. Now Dr Zachariah's exciting book gives us new means of understanding the international opportunities and pressures that confronted this intriguing man, and the remarkable ways in which he responded to them.'
Robert Anderson, Simon Fraser University, Vancouver

' . . . there is an urgent need to reassess the life and work of Jawaharlal Nehru. Benjamin Zachariah does this in an original and provocative way. This book is not merely a biography of Nehru, it is also an important account of the origins of contemporary India.'
Rajat Kanta Ray, Presidency College, Calcutta

How did Jawaharlal Nehru come to lead the Indian nationalist movement, and how did he sustain his leadership as the first Prime Minister of independent India? Nehru's vision of India, its roots in Indian politics and society, as well as its viability, have been central to historical and present-day views of India. This engaging new biography dispels many myths surrounding Nehru, and distinguishes between the icon he has become and the politician he actually was.

Benjamin Zachariah places Nehru in the context of the issues of his times, including the central theme of nationalism, the impact of Cold War pressures on India and the transition from colonial control to a precarious independence. Connecting the domestic and international aspects of his political life and ideology, this study provides a fascinating insight into Nehru, his times and his legacy. It is essential reading for students and all those with an interest in Indian history or international relations.

Benjamin Zachariah is Lecturer in International History at the University of Sheffield. His research focuses on the social and intellectual history of colonial south Asia, and the transition from colonial rule to the postcolonial Indian state.

ROUTLEDGE HISTORICAL BIOGRAPHIES

SERIES EDITOR: ROBERT PEARCE

Routledge Historical Biographies provide engaging, readable and academically credible biographies written from an explicitly historical perspective. These concise and accessible accounts will bring important historical figures to life for students and general readers alike.

In the same series:

NEHRU

Benjamin Zachariah

Routledge
Taylor & Francis Group

LONDON AND NEW YORK

First published 2004
by Routledge
11 New Fetter Lane, London EC4P 4EE

Simultaneously published in the USA and Canada
by Routledge
29 West 35th Street, New York, NY 10001

Routledge is an imprint of the Taylor & Francis Group

© 2004 Benjamin Zachariah

Typeset in Garamond and Scala by Keystroke, Jacaranda Lodge,
Wolverhampton
Printed and bound in Great Britain by TJ International Ltd, Padstow,
Cornwall

British Library Cataloguing in Publication Data
A catalogue record for this book is available from the British Library

Library of Congress Cataloging in Publication Data
Zachariah, Benjamin, 1972–
   Nehru / Benjamin Zachariah.
      p.   cm.– (Routledge historical biographies)
Includes bibliographical references.
1. Nehru, Jawaharlal, 1889–1964. 2. India–Politics and government
–20th century. 3. Prime ministers–India–Biography. I. Title.
II. Series.
   DS481.N35Z27 2004
   954.04′2′092–dc22

                                        2003022407

ISBN 0–415–25016–1 (hbk)
ISBN 0–415–25017–X (pbk)

CONTENTS

ILLUSTRATIONS

PLATES

(between pages 132 and 133)

CHRONOLOGY

	Personal	Political	General
1885		Founding of the Indian National Congress	
1886	Motilal Nehru moves to Allahabad		
1889	November 14: birth of Jawaharlal in Allahabad		
1899	Motilal's first trip to England Excommunication by his caste members for refusing to perform purification ceremony on his return		Boer War
1901–4	Jawaharlal privately educated by tutor Ferdinand Brooks		
1905–7	Jawaharlal's schooling at Harrow	1905–11: Swadeshi movement in Bengal. 1906: founding of the Muslim League	1905: Russo-Japanese War; vicarious victory for Indian nationalists
1907–10	Jawaharlal at Trinity College, Cambridge, studying for the Natural Sciences Tripos Graduates with Lower Second	Congress split at Surat. 'Extremists' expelled. Indian Councils Act: 'Morley–Minto reforms'. Separate electorates for Muslims introduced	
1910–12	Jawaharlal reads Law at the Inner Temple	All-India Hindu Sabha founded. Later becomes the Hindu Mahasabha	
1911		Annulment of the Partition	

	Personal	Political	General
		of Bengal. Capital of British India moved from Calcutta to Delhi. George V's 'Delhi Durbar'	
1912	Jawaharlal called to the Bar. August: returns to India		
1914–18		Indian soldiers sent in large numbers to fight on all fronts during the war	First World War
1915		Annie Besant begins campaign for Indian Home Rule through her newspapers. Return of Gandhi to India from South Africa December: Congress decides to allow Extremists back in	
1916	February 8: Jawaharlal marries Kamala Kaul, ten years his junior. Jawaharlal joins Annie Besant's Home Rule League. Winter: Jawaharlal first meets Gandhi	Home Rule leagues of Tilak and Annie Besant set up, in April and September, respectively. December: 'Lucknow Pact' between Congress and Muslim League on an agreed-upon set of constitutional demands to be placed before the government	April: Easter Rising in Ireland
1917	November 19: birth of Nehru's daughter, Indira	August 20: Secretary of State for India Sir Edwin Montagu's declaration on 'a progressive realisation of responsible government' in India	Russian revolution. Bolshevik declaration of peace on the principle of 'no annexations, no indemnities' and the right of all nations to self-determination

	Personal	Political	General
1919	Jawaharlal works closely with Gandhi in Punjab on the Congress enquiry team following the Punjab 'disturbances' and Jallianwalla Bagh	Government of India Act, 1919, passed. 'Dyarchy' and limited devolution of powers to the provinces introduced. Rowlatt Act passed extending wartime emergency provisions into peacetime. 'Rowlatt Satyagraha' Gandhi's first all-India campaign. Jallianwalla Bagh massacre	Versailles Treaty. Allegedly on the basis of Wilsonian 14 Points of January 1917 (which proclaimed right of nations to self-determination); but the peace settlement divides up the colonies of the defeated powers
1920	Nehru 'discovers' the peasants in his first rural political campaigns	Non-Cooperation-Khilafat movement begins	Treaty of Sevres with Turkey; abolition of the Khilafat
1921–2	December 6, 1921: Motilal and Jawaharlal arrested, 1921; their first imprisonment. Jawaharlal briefly released, then re-arrested on a new charge. Motilal released in 1922, Jawaharlal on January 31, 1923	February 5, 1922: 'Chauri Chaura incident'. February 12, 1922: Gandhi calls off the movement. Arrested on March 10	October 28, 1922: Mussolini's 'March on Rome': fascists seize power in Italy
1923–6	April 1923–1926: Jawaharlal chairman of the Allahabad Municipal Board	1924–26: 'Council entry' by the Swarajists led by Motilal Nehru and CR Das	
1926–7	March 1926–end 1927: sojourn in Europe during Kamala Nehru's treatment for tuberculosis in Switzerland. February 1927: Nehru attends Congress of	Workers and Peasants' Parties founded in Bengal, Punjab, Bombay and the United Provinces: Communist Party front organisations	1927 onwards: slowdown in world agrarian prices

	Personal	Political	General
	Oppressed Peoples in Brussels. November 1927: Motilal and Jawaharlal visit the Soviet Union. End 1927: return to India		
1928	Jawaharlal disagrees with his father's Report which accepts dominion status instead of complete independence	Simon Commission; (Motilal) Nehru Report	
1929	Jawaharlal elected Congress president for the first time. Also elected president of the All-India trade Union Congress	December 31, Purna Swaraj resolution: 'Complete Independence' demanded by Congress	Labour government elected in Britain. Wall Street Crash. Beginning of the Great Depression
1930	April 14, 1930 to October 11, 1930, and October 19, 1930 to January 1931: Jawaharlal in jail	March 12–April 6: Salt March. Inaugurates Civil Disobedience Movement 1930–1. First Round Table Conference in London on new constitution for India, boycotted by Congress	
1931	February 6: death of Motilal Nehru. December 26, 1931– August 30, 1933 Jawaharlal in jail	March 5: Gandhi calls off civil disobedience; Gandhi–Irwin Pact. March: Karachi Congress; Congress's first 'socialist' resolutions. Winter 1931–2: Second Round Table Conference. Gandhi attends as the sole Congress representative	Ramsay MacDonald's Labour government collapses in Britain. Replaced by 'National' government; MacDonald remains prime minister

	Personal	*Political*	*General*
1932–4	Jawaharlal Nehru emerges as focal point of the Congress left, but decides to remain outside formal groups. February 12, 1934– September 1935: Jawaharlal in jail (released for 11 days in August 1934)	1932–4: revival of Civil Disobedience; a failure. Rise of the Congress left. Banning of the Communist Party of India (CPI). May 1934: founding of the Congress Socialist Party (CSP). Appeals for left unity	January 30, 1933: Adolf Hitler becomes Chancellor of Germany
1935	September: Nehru leaves for Europe to join Kamala (she was undergoing treatment for tuberculosis)	Government of India Act, 1935, passed by British Parliament. 1935–9 CPI accepts Comintern's 'popular front' line against imperialism instead of fascism. Operates through Congress left	'Popular Front' policy inaugurated by Comintern to combat fascism
1936	February 28: death of Kamala Nehru. Nehru elected Congress president. Leads call to boycott the new Constitution. Opposes forming ministries	Elections from late 1936 to Provincial Assemblies under new Government of India Act	July: Spanish Civil War begins
1937–39	1937: Indira Nehru admitted to Somerville College, Oxford. Nehru backs and participates in the Congress 'mass contact' programme to gain support from marginal groups, in particular lower castes and Muslims, for the Congress	Ministry period. Congress in government in several provinces of British India	

	Personal	Political	General
1938	Nehru appointed chairman of the National Planning Committee. Nehru works as editorial writer and foreign correspondent for his own paper, the *National Herald*	Subhas Bose elected Congress president. Appoints a National Planning Committee	September: Munich Pact effectively gives Czechoslovakia to Hitler
1939	August–September: Nehru's first visit to China; meets Chiang Kai-Shek (Jiang Jieshi) and his wife. September: Nehru returns from China on outbreak of war to discuss Congress response	January: Bose re-elected with left's support against opposition from Gandhi and the Congress right. March–April: 'Tripuri crisis': Gandhi engineers Bose's isolation. Nehru hedges his bets. Bose resigns and forms the Forward bloc. October 29–30: resignation of Congress ministries in protest against Viceroy's declaration of war on India's behalf without consulting Indian political representatives	March: fall of the Spanish Republic. August 23: Nazi–Soviet Pact. September 3: outbreak of Second World War: Britain and France declare war on Germany following German invasion of Poland
1940	October 31, 1940: Nehru arrested. November 1940– December 1941: Nehru in jail	'Individual satyagraha' campaign begun by Gandhi to oppose censorship regulations. 23 March: Muslim League's 'Lahore Resolution', retrospectively called the 'Pakistan Resolution'. August: Viceroy's 'August offer'	'Battle of Britain'. May 10: coalition government under Winston Churchill takes over in Britain
1941		April 1941: Subhas	June 22, 1941:

	Personal	Political	General
		Chandra Bose arrives in Berlin	'Operation Barbarossa' begins; Germany attacks the USSR. August 1941: Atlantic Charter declared. September: Churchill claims it does not apply to the colonies. December 1941: Japan attacks the USA at Pearl Harbour; Germany declares war on the USA
1942	March 26, 1942: Indira Nehru marries Feroz Gandhi. August 1942–June 1945: Nehru in jail	March–April 1942: Cripps Mission in India. August–September 1942: Quit India Movement. Sporadic pockets of resistance remain	February 15: fall of Singapore to the Japanese. Japanese advance up to Burma. March 8: fall of Rangoon; April 29: evacuation of Mandalay. September–December: tide of European war turned by the USSR at Stalingrad
1943		February 8: Subhas Bose leaves Germany by submarine, arriving in Japan on April 24. From 10 February: Gandhi's 21-day fast; panic in the British imperial establishment. 1943–4: Bengal Famine	
1944	April to September: Nehru writes *Discovery of India* in jail	May: Gandhi released from prison. July: abortive Gandhi–Jinnah talks	June 6: Allied landing in Normandy: 'Second Front' finally opened. October: Churchill and Stalin meet in Moscow to decide on the future map of Europe

	Personal	Political	General
1945	June 14: release of Congress Working Committee members including Nehru, in anticipation of Simla Conference. Nehru comes out of retirement as a barrister to defend the INA prisoners	Simla Conference (June 25–July 14) called by Viceroy Wavell to try and secure agreement on the 'communal question'. November 1945–February 1946: INA trials. Winter 1945–6: elections; major gains for the Muslim League	May 7: Germany surrenders; May 8 V-E (Victory in Europe) Day. July: Labour comes to power in Britain. August: elections announced for following winter in India. August 6 and 9: atomic bombs dropped on Hiroshima and Nagasaki: last act of the Second World War and first act of the Cold War
1946	September 2: Provisional Government sworn in with Nehru as Prime Minister. Nehru declares intention to avoid aligning with 'blocs'	February: Royal Indian Navy mutiny. April–June: Cabinet Mission. August 16: Muslim League's 'Direct Action Day'. August 16–18: Great Calcutta Killings, beginning of chain of sectarian violence spreading across the country	February: Churchill's 'Iron Curtain' speech at Fulton, Missouri
1947	Nehru campaigns against communal violence and against communalism in his own party	August 15: Independence Day. Infiltration of 'tribals' into Kashmir from Pakistan. Accession of Kashmir to India	July: sterling made convertible with the dollar; massive flight from the pound. August: convertibility suspended
1948		January 30: assassination of Gandhi. September 13: 'police action' in Hyderabad state	
1949	October: Nehru's first visit to the USA	New Year's Day: Kashmir ceasefire	Truman Doctrine declared

	Personal	Political	General
		November 26: adoption of the Constitution by the Indian Constituent Assembly	Victory of the Chinese revolution. October: India recognises the People's Republic of China. India decides to remain in the Commonwealth
1950	Nehru's international diplomacy: advice to the Americans fails to prevent escalation of Korean War	January 26: inauguration of the Republic of India. April: creation of the Planning Commission. PD Tandon from the right-wing of the Congress elected Party president. December: death of Patel	China takes control of Tibet – previously under British Indian control, though nominally under Chinese sovereignty. June: Korean War begins
1951–2	Nehru gains control of the Congress Party after resignation of PD Tandon. Nehru central campaigner for Congress in the general elections	Acharya Vinoba Bhave's *Bhoodan* movement begins. 1951–2: first general election on universal adult franchise. States' governments also elected. 1951–6: First Five-Year Plan. 'Community development' schemes inaugurated	
1953	1950–3: Korean War. Nehru and Krishna Menon the main negotiators and intermediaries in peace negotiations; but excluded from final peace settlement talks	Land Ceilings Act. 1953–6: reorganisation of states on linguistic lines begins	March: death of Stalin. End of Korean War. India excluded from peace settlement talks at the insistence of South Korean dictator Syngman Rhee
1954	Nehru's enunciation of the *Panch Sheel*, five principles of peaceful	Indo-Chinese trade agreement concerning Tibet	July: Geneva Conference on Indo-China. April: Colombo

	Personal	*Political*	*General*
	co-existence. June: Zhou Enlai visits Delhi. Nehru visits China in October. Personal rapport established	French voluntarily relinquish their remaining colonial possessions in India	Conference; December: Bogor Conference; prime ministers of Pakistan, India, Burma, Ceylon and Indonesia – preparatory conferences to the Bandung Conference
1955	June 1955: Nehru visits USSR	1955: Avadi resolution of Congress: 'Socialist pattern' of society. Had been adopted earlier by Parliament, in late 1954	April–May: Bandung Conference. December: Bulganin and Khrushchev visit India
1956	Nehru denounces imperialist aggression in Egypt during the Suez Crisis; late to condemn Soviet actions in Hungary	Naga tribal rebellion. Troops built up in the North-East. 1956–61: Second Five-Year Plan; 'Mahalanobis Model'	20th Party Congress of the CPSU: Khrushchev's 'DeStalinisation' speech. Suez crisis. USSR's invasion of Hungary
1957	Nehru once again main campaigner for the Congress	Second general election. First elected Communist government in the state of Kerala	
1958–60	1959: Nehru dismisses Kerala government – surrendering to pressure from within the Congress, especially from the new Congress Party president, his daughter Indira	1958–9: beginnings of 'Panchayati Raj' – autonomous local self-government. 1959: Nagpur Resolution: cooperative joint farming declared a goal. Denounced by opposition as 'creeping collectivisation'	1959: Dalai Lama flees Tibet. Political asylum in India. Beginning of friction between India and China on the border question. Beginning of CIA activity among Tibetan political exiles in Kalimpong
1961		December: Goa 'police action': Portuguese Goa	Belgrade summit – 'non-aligned

	Personal	Political	General
		invaded and incorporated into the Indian Union. 1961–6: Third Five-Year Plan	movement' formally comes into being
1962	Nehru weakened in parliament; under pressure to align with the Western bloc	January: third general elections. October–November: China 'war'	October: Cuban Missile Crisis
1963	No confidence motion against Nehru's economic policy in Parliament defeated	'Kamaraj Plan' for the regeneration of the Congress Party. Nagaland separated from Assam (decision taken 1960). Resistance of Mizo people begins	
1964	January 6: Nehru has a stroke. May 27: death of Nehru		

PREFACE

Jawaharlal Nehru (1889–1964) is remembered as a major leader of the Indian nationalist movement and the first prime minister of independent India (1947–64). As a left-leaning leader of an anti-colonialist nationalist movement and an internationalist, he became well-known outside India in the 1920s and 1930s, speaking out against imperialism in other countries and expressing solidarity with anti-fascism and the republican cause in the Spanish Civil War. By the time of Indian independence in 1947, he was already a world leader of some stature. His importance grew, particularly in the context of the aspirations of other emergent nationalisms in the colonial and former colonial world, who looked to India as an example, and of the Cold War, which made the superpowers' desire to have India, strategically placed both geographically and ideologically, on their side. Within India, his reputation as one of the giants of the Indian nationalist movement and his credentials as Mahatma Gandhi's acknowledged political heir made him a dominant figure in Indian politics before and after independence.

It would not be untrue to say that educated Indians have a love-hate relationship with the figure of Jawaharlal Nehru. Much has been said, all with much emotion and involvement, about his legacy, his career, his mistakes, his failure to understand India, and so on. It is an extremely involved relationship, of filial homage or symbolic parricide in a deeply patriarchal society. He was in so many ways a positive figure: if not someone you actually admired, someone you might so easily have admired. He was the public face of India to the world for so many years – so many crucial years for our self-respect, our sense of independence, of being free. We might have wanted him to be someone else – very often: firmer, more self-assertive in his dealings with the lesser mortals, the self-interested mediocrities of his party; more radical in carrying out his various progressive pronouncements; readier to move with the left than to sit with the right; more far-sighted on Kashmir – everyone has his or her list. Few have allowed themselves to doubt his good intentions. His political opponents must bear much of the responsibility for disarming themselves in his presence: they were half in love with him themselves. 'He was our beautiful but ineffectual angel,' wrote the communist, Hiren Mukerjee, 'beating his luminous wings largely in vain.'[1] 'Our beautiful but ineffectual angel', because we all assumed he wanted to do what we wanted to do. He failed; but he could have succeeded – he so nearly did.

There was always in India an alternative icon: the Mahatma. He was, indeed, Nehru's own father figure; yet he was more remote, less intimate, less, in short, someone we would like to be. His moral authority was necessary, it worked well, but it wasn't altogether us. Who would want to *be* a Gandhi? At best a follower, a disciple –still difficult – but not actually the man himself. Nehru, on the other hand, would be nice to be. Powerful, but not obsessed with power. Vain, but not unreasonably so. Wealthy in his own right, but never crass. Upper-caste, but not caste-ist. Modern, urbane, well-read, well-regarded even by his – and our (at least until not long ago) British overlords, capable of beating them at their own games. With a gift for the right phrase in the right place – in English. And yet truly multicultural.

And he did embody an era, a whole period of India's history. Writing about Nehru today necessarily means abandoning some dearly held myths – some, indeed, that Nehru himself appears to have held on to tenaciously. But how much more important this process – of measured iconoclasm, hopefully, rather than troubled rejection or nostalgic idealisation – at a time when disputes surrounding collective identities in India are all funnelled through various understandings of the man and the era to which he lent his name.

The cause of biography has been both helped and hindered by the pleas of autobiography. Nehru was a most self-reflexive person, prone to conducting his periodic self-analyses in public, in his various autobiographical writings and in his letters, many of which were published at his own instigation. He is at his most persuasive when he presents himself as most vulnerable, with the result that the possible shortcomings of his self-analyses seldom become the object of scrutiny.

With time, a carefully cultivated image of Nehru began to take precedence over any actual engagement with his politics or his leadership. At the time of the official celebrations of Jawaharlal Nehru's birth centenary, in 1989, the advertising agency in charge of dressing up the proceedings in appropriate form selected an image to represent Nehru: a single red rose. The iconography of the red rose was not unambiguous. Nehru's own propensity for aestheticism might have been presented there, in the form of the daily rose he selected from his gardens at his home, Teen

Murti Bhavan, to wear in his buttonhole. The red rose may have been a symbol of love, intended to stand either for Nehru's love for India, or the sometimes perplexing love many Indians had for the man who came to be called 'Panditji' – an honorific connected with religion and caste that he himself hated. Or it might merely be the fate of a political leader to be reduced to an icon: Winston Churchill to his cigar; Gandhi to his larger-than-life silhouette with his still-larger staff in the artist Nandalal Bose's depiction of the 1931 Salt satyagraha; and Nehru, rather less satisfactorily, to his rose.

It would be disturbing if a single appropriate icon could be found to characterise Nehru. But this illustrates a wider problem of Indian politics: it is a politics of iconography, in which Nehru, along with Gandhi, appear as the twin legitimating icons. Icons can also be caricatures; and an iconic presentation of an icon is a caricature at second remove: thus the rose distils, from the icon that is Nehru, merely another icon. All this clouds a proper understanding of social and political currents in which these political actors were involved, of which they were only partially in control.

One of the major tasks of this book is to rescue Nehru from the mythologies that his supporters, his detractors, and he himself, did so much to create; mythologies that have been influential in academic and non-academic circles both within and outside India. In particular, this book will argue that the picture usually painted of a radical socialist gradually tamed by a combination of force of circumstance and the wisdom of age needs to be qualified. But it must do more than that. It must also ask a vital question: what were the social forces that made it possible for Nehru to rise to and to sustain his leadership in the Indian national movement? Or, to phrase the question somewhat differently, what was it that made possible the achievements – and the failures – that are credited to the leadership of Jawaharlal Nehru?

This historical biography is an interpretative essay that seeks answers to that question. It attempts an understanding of Nehru and his times; it tends at times to decentre its central figure, which in some ways makes it a curious kind of biography. There is not a great deal of discussion of Nehru's personal life. This does not mean that his personal life – or such of it that is accessible to researchers – was uninteresting; but in keeping with the central concerns of this book, and due to considerations of space, such discussion appears mostly where it has a clear connection to aspects of his public life. Two quiet claims to some originality can be made here. I think it is imperative to reconnect the domestic and international aspects of Jawaharlal Nehru's political life and vision; to deal with them separately is to lose track of their mutual interaction, and in consequence to decontextualise both. Secondly, in attempting to provide an opening out of critical discussion on Nehru, his times, his politics and his legacy, I have partially decentred the central theme that dominated contemporary debates: that of nationalism. It is possible to argue that to some extent Nehru sought to do this himself; his was a sceptical and provisional nationalism, tempered by the perspectives of internationalism and an understanding of the dangers of national chauvinism.

Some of this book is based on original research; much of it attempts to synthesise what has already been written. It is intended to be accessible to a general readership of informed laypersons and students as well as to specialists. Specialists will no doubt be impatient with the narrative that a book of this kind must provide, annoyed by my choice of emphases; non-specialists may wish for more of the very details that would irritate the specialist. But the main duty of this book is to the non-specialist. Suggestions for further reading are provided at the end – mostly work I have found useful or have engaged with – in lieu of the more conventional paraphernalia of academic footnotes that this book avoids. The specialist should be able to spot my sources, and perhaps my politics, from this discussion of sources.

The structure of the book needs some comment. The Introduction and Interlude deal with central themes that run through the narrative. There are two possible routes through the Introduction: the first, to read it straight through, and the second, to return to the more abstract themes in the latter sections having read the rest of the book. These latter sections allude to events and problems with which the lay reader may not be familiar. The rest of the chapters are more or less chronologically arranged, although the later chapters depart from a rigidly chronological narrative in favour of thematic coherence. The Conclusion returns to the central themes. The chronological table at the beginning might be useful for a reader wishing to keep a close eye on the sequence of events. Words in Indian languages are translated where they first appear, either in the text or in an endnote. I have tried not to stick to literal translations, preferring to provide a sense of the wider meanings the terms might have evoked to contemporaries. Chinese names are rendered in the Pinyin system of transliteration, except where the Wade-Giles is more familiar, e.g. Chiang Kai-Shek instead of Jiang Jieshi.

As with all academic ventures, and particularly in a book such as this, it is important not to suffer from the delusion of authorship. I should like in particular to thank those with whom I have had the privilege of discussing this book and the themes surrounding it, in some cases resorting to the Ancient Mariner's technique: the editors, Robert Pearce and Victoria Peters; the (anonymous) referees; Pertti Ahonen, Jill Alpes, Robert Anderson, Ganesh Bagchi, Chris Bayly, Crispin Bates, Debraj Bhattacharya, Bhaskar Chakrabarty, Subhas Ranjan Chakraborti, Rajarshi Dasgupta, Ari Ercole, Margret Frenz, Anna Gust, Annemarie Hafner, Joachim Heidrich, Petra Heidrich, Aparna Jack, MK Karna, Sudipta Kaviraj, Ian Kershaw, Aparajita Koch, Avinash Kumar, Kerstin Lehr, Jon Mclure, Hiren Mukerjee, Rakesh Pandey, Rajat Kanta Ray, Rathin Roy, Sulagna Roy, Subir Sinha, Hari Vasudevan, Jeff Vernon, Hugh Wilford, Ian Zachariah . . . They should not, I imagine, like to share the blame for what I have written. To that extent, at least, I should like to identify myself as the author.

The last chapters of this book were written during and in the aftermath of the American and British invasion of Iraq. As historians of imperialism, we might entertain the hope or fear that the theme is irrelevant to the contemporary world. Fortunately or unfortunately, this is not the case; yet the silencing of debates around the theme of imperialism has been a feature of public historical memory in the developed world since formal decolonisation was achieved. This deafening silence needs to be addressed, and I hope that in a small way this book might help in doing so.

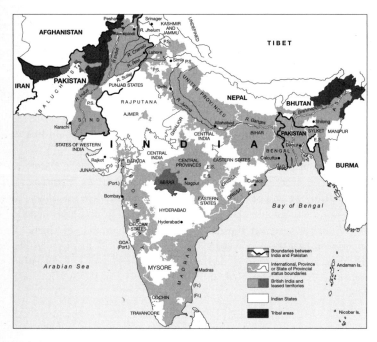

The Indian sub-continent at the transfer of power, 1947

Political cartoon by Shankar Pillai, November 10, 1963
© The Children's Book Trust, Delhi

INTRODUCTION

If a person had the luxury of choosing the moment in historical time in which to be remembered, Jawaharlal Nehru ought to have chosen the year 1955. The newly-independent Indian state, of which he was now prime minister, was a greatly-admired model for colonial nations struggling for independence, and Nehru himself was an appealing national leader: urbane, sophisticated and intellectual, committed to social justice, democratic, not sectarian. India had begun to recover from the traumas of a partition conducted on the basis of religious community, which had led to the formation of the Muslim state of Pakistan. Under Nehru's leadership, India had successfully resisted internal pressures to define itself as 'Hindu', which would have meant consigning its substantial minority of Muslims to the implicit status of foreigners, and leaving other minorities in an ambiguous position. Under his leadership, India's hopes of rapid economic development and an eventual emergence from poverty were generally considered to be bright; the rest of the world was beginning to look to India as a model for planned development in the non-communist underdeveloped world. Nehru's form of socialism seemed to avoid the authoritarian tendencies of the Soviet model; his credentials as a democrat who was not a puppet of the Western bloc were greatly enhanced by his being among the leaders of an emerging group of non-aligned states and by his opposition to the Korean War.

But of course Nehru could not choose his moment of remembrance; and this rather positive picture has been somewhat modified over the years.

It nevertheless does represent a good many of the positive achievements of India in the Nehruvian years. For some years after his death in 1964, Nehru was put forward as the personification of all that was positive and enduring in the Indian nation, or the nation-state – not only by his old party or its succeeding splinter groups, but by many of his old adversaries. These positive and enduring things – most importantly, secularism and state-led developmentalism, 'Nehruvian socialism' – then came under attack: their opponents blamed Nehru for constructing, or presiding over the construction of, an unviable and unrealistic model of India and of Indian nationalism; their defenders urged a return to the Nehruvian vision. Political groups to the left of the awkward sharing of power that had made up Indian mainstream politics now stood forth as defenders of the achievements of the 'Nehruvian period', and the 'Nehruvian consensus', which they felt were certainly worth defending against the onslaught of Hindu fundamentalists and economic liberalisers.

It is within the context of these debates that any piece of writing on Nehru written today will be assessed. And yet there are a series of questions that need to be asked before the debate becomes meaningful, before it acquires political or historical relevance. Why and how did Nehru come to be identified so closely with a period, a style of politics, an image of India? How did he come to epitomise desirable leadership for the emergent 'Third World'; or amplify the superpowers' Cold War anxieties with non-alignment? Perhaps these questions can only be built upon the answer to a prior and more fundamental one: how was it possible for a man such as Nehru to emerge as leader of so complex a set of forces as those in the Indian nationalist movement – with which he was often out of step ideologically and practically – and how did he manage to sustain his leadership in independent India?

This short historical biography sets out to try and answer these questions – or at least to suggest possible routes to answers. It is useful, at this point, to set out some of the recurrent themes that the book deals with; if they seem somewhat abstract at this stage, their relevance will become apparent as the narrative progresses. This introduction, then, is thematic; the narrative is taken up in the first chapter.

THE IMPORTANCE OF BEING JAWAHARLAL

A combination of factors brought Jawaharlal Nehru into political prominence. He belonged to a well-connected, affluent and important political family, high in the ranks of the emerging Indian middle class. Through his father, Motilal Nehru, a successful lawyer and moderate nationalist, he had connections with the Indian National Congress even before he had articulated any of his own political ideas. When he entered the political scene in the late 1910s, and through his personal battles with his father, he found a mentor and an alternative father figure in Mohandas Karamchand Gandhi, who not only nurtured the young Jawaharlal politically, but encouraged him to assert his independence against his father. Jawaharlal, therefore, by virtue of his class and his family tradition as much as by virtue of political conviction, had been inducted into politics at a reasonably high level.

Later on, Jawaharlal's professed left-wing ideas made him the focal point of various groups within the Congress searching for an alternative model of leadership to the Gandhian, which many believed limited and controlled political struggle, fed into the legitimising of Indian capitalists (Gandhi believed that the wealthy held property as 'trustees' for the community and the nation), and failed to serve the interests of the masses. Nehru was, they thought, ideally suited to this role because he was already an important member of the Congress. Those on the left who believed that the anti-imperialist struggle ought not to be split prematurely into a left and a right wing, and therefore ought to be carried out through the Congress as a single unified organisation, felt that Nehru was ideally suited to be their spokesman. But he consistently let them down; and soon the right wing of the Congress came to recognise that they could live with Nehru. Gandhi himself assured the right and the business interests that supported it that Nehru's socialist bark was worse than his bite, setting the stage for peaceful, or semi-peaceful, co-existence broken by periods of disagreement that often had more of a rhetorical impact than a real one.

Nehru owed his emergence to pre-eminence in Indian politics as much to his political allies as to his acceptability to political opponents. Much of British political opinion, certainly from the 1930s onwards, regarded Nehru as a desirable leader for an eventual post-independence India. In what was to them a turbulent and increasingly incomprehensible political scene, Nehru seemed to provide stability and reason; with him they could do business. Logically enough, sections of the British left – H.N. Brailsford, Harold Laski, Fenner Brockway; the Fabians, the Independent Labour Party – backed Nehru, who seemed clearly to be a political and ideological ally. In 1936, Brailsford wrote to Nehru, 'India has great need of you – especially, personally, of you. For I think I know, more or less, the other possible leaders. No one has your courage, your mental power, and above all, your vision of a humane, classless society. Try to draw strength from the belief that history has named you to lead.'[1] Nehru was of additional importance because, despite having some left-wing views, he was not a communist. And long might that remain so: Fenner Brockway, in 1938, warned Nehru against 'the clear intrigue which is going on to capture you for the Communist Party', and hoped that such a situation would not arise.[2] Stafford Cripps and Nehru were to become personal friends; already in the 1930s, it was with Jawaharlal Nehru that the Labour Party began to discuss Indo-British trade and commercial relations in a future independent India. But further to the right of British politics, Nehru was also widely regarded as leader-in-waiting. The argument was that if indeed Britain had to reckon with an independent India, future British interests could best be negotiated with Nehru: a Harrow and Cambridge man, perhaps hostile to British imperialism, but not to Britons *per se*.

A good deal of the British preoccupation with Nehru can perhaps be explained by his already important status within the Congress. But by selecting Nehru from among other potential candidates, British politicians also strengthened Nehru within the Congress. The fact, moreover, that large sections of the British left were willing to endorse him added to the tendency of the Congress left to work with and through him, both for practical reasons and in accordance with principles of inter-nationalism. Domestic and overseas support thus interacted to reinforce Nehru's claims to leadership in India.

THE NATURE OF LEADERSHIP UNDER COLONIAL RULE

What, then, of popular support? It is not intended here to suggest that mass support was a totally insignificant factor in Nehru's rise to promi-nence in the Congress. Indeed, one of the reasons Nehru was accepted by the Congress' right wing as the public face of the Congress was that Nehru was a popular leader. His involvement with trade union activities, especially in the 1920s and 1930s, gave him credibility in the labour movement, and his activities among the peasants, as a Gandhian in the 1920s and as a socialist in the 1930s, increased his reputation as a man of the people. To a large extent, however, this was as far as it went: Nehru allowed himself to be appropriated by the right as an election campaigner.

The importance of 'mass support' in a colony is of course not directly in electoral terms. *'Representation'* was not meant to be *representative*. In most cases, a number of hand-picked native notables were invited by the colonial government to represent various pre-defined 'interest groups' or 'communities'. These pre-defined entities were entities often imagined into being, and given their apparent rigidity, by the processes of imperial administration. The activities of officials keen to discover the essence of 'Hindu' or 'Muslim law' and write them down for the sake of convenient governance, or census-takers intent on cataloguing the complexity of the social fabric into manageable categories, created a spurious neatness to categories of religious community or prescriptive codes of social interaction, and cut them off from the ebb and flow of socio-political power in which they had once been embedded. These entities then became the basis of effective politics. Once written down in administrative documents, and consequently, as political activity came to be based on these imagined categories, the categories acquired reality, retrospectively justifying the administrative imaginings. Colonial 'reality' was therefore to a large extent a creation of the coloniser.

With time, elections – those crucial legitimising displays of 'mass participation' – to various administrative and legislative bodies did come into existence. They were not based on universal adult franchise (nor were they in the metropolitan country until the 1920s – in Britain, women were only granted full voting rights in 1928). The legislatures elected on the basis of narrow property franchises, and electorates divided into 'communities' (deriving their neatness, if not their justification, from the administrative imagination), had severely constrained powers of legislation. This caricature of parliamentarianism was the highest form of institutional politics in colonial India: even in the last stages of so-called 'training for self-government', at the end of the 1930s, a legislature's decisions could be overridden by the governor of a province or the viceroy of India.

What, then, *was* the importance of the 'masses' in colonial Indian politics? Since the vast majority didn't qualify for the vote, it could not have been in electoral terms. Radical groups sought to organise them outside the constraints of communal electorates and elections – although various kinds of legitimacy were habitually claimed by winners of elections, in the 1937 and 1946–7 elections, whose results were widely regarded as critical to the eventual partition of India, about 16 and 30%, respectively, of the adult population were eligible to vote, and many did not even register to do so.[3] But more moderate groups wishing to show strength of numbers also sought mass support outside the boundaries of electoral politics. The importance of making up numbers from among the 'masses' becomes clearer when seen in terms of the political equations of late colonial rule. The colonial rulers, as far as possible, refused to recognise hostile nationalists as legitimate – although at times more acceptable forms of nationalism, willing to co-exist with imperial control, might be encouraged. This is where the 'masses' came in. In order to force colonial rulers to recognise them, and therefore to negotiate with them rather than with the ruler's own loyalist notables, anti-colonial nationalists had to demonstrate mass support – this was a prerequisite for effective bargaining with the government. By demonstrating mass support, a group could demand recognition by the rulers, posing as interpreter of the popular will, as intermediary between the 'masses' and the government, and in effect offer to act as a buffer zone between potential popular unrest and the colonial rulers. Once a group was so recognised, it also gained a relative monopoly over voicing the demands of the masses it *claimed* to represent. Whether it actually did so or not is a different matter.

There was, therefore, always the danger of the 'masses' turning into a somewhat abstract concept – which is not to say that all political groups invoked the 'masses' in an instrumental manner. Mass support was far from an insignificant factor both in the claiming of legitimacy by a political group and in the running of a successful movement. But many of the claims made by elite groups to understanding what 'the people' really wanted must be treated with some scepticism. 'They cannot represent themselves; they must be represented' was a phrase which would have accurately summed up most organised political groups' opinion of the masses.

In some respects, of course, this was not peculiar to nationalism in a colony. If nationalism is the intellectual and ideological sleight-of-hand that convinces all classes to back the agenda of the national bourgeoisie, because that agenda is allegedly in the interest of the entire 'nation', Indian nationalism was no different. But the imperatives to mass participation – and to mass control – were different. The bourgeois nationalists had to be able to demonstrate mass support, to call upon it in order to make a show of strength effectively before the colonial government, and perhaps also British public opinion, and then it had to be able to control the masses, in effect to put them back in their box until they were needed again. This was, of course, not always successful: people, once mobilised for a great cause, could be reluctant simply to be instrumentally used to achieve others' agendas.

Where did Nehru fit into this picture? His sympathies lay for the greater part of his political career with a broadly defined left position; he himself was responsible for many of the left-wing pronouncements of the Congress. But as a loyal party man, he could usually be relied upon to follow a line even when it went against his own beliefs. As mobiliser he raised expectations, only to himself be instrumentally appropriated later by forces to the right of him. He was often conscious of this happening but unable or unwilling to prevent it. When he did make the attempt, as in his occasional threats to resign as prime minister if his path was not followed, he was thrown back on staking his personal prestige against that of his party – which might either be considered undemocratic from an internal party perspective, or an appeal to direct democracy, because both Nehru and the Congress knew that Nehru's reputation was what the Congress was most dependent on before an electorate. (It might also be noted in passing that this was more than a little reminiscent of Gandhian tactics; but where Gandhi's preferred form of moral blackmail was the fast, Nehru's was the threat of resignation.)

Beset by moral and political doubts, many of which did him great credit as an intellectual, Nehru's actions were often well short of politically effective in terms of the goals he proclaimed. He often felt an outsider, at odds with the political climate he was forced to work in, a somewhat inauthentic interloper who had had to do much hard work to *discover* India, but was nonetheless unsure of having made the right discovery, or if so, whether his discovery was to his own taste. Nehru is said to have remarked that he was the last Englishman to rule India – the ambiguity of this statement describes a long and continuing debate that was very much a part of anti-colonial nationalist struggles: the authenticity, or lack thereof, of the colonial intellectual, and following from that, the problem of colonial nationalist intellectuals 'indigenising' themselves.

THE PROBLEMS OF AUTHENTICITY AND MODERNITY

Phrased in various ways, and part of the internal polemics of anti-colonial nationalism, the problem ultimately boiled down to this: how representative were the nationalists of the people they sought to represent – the 'masses'? Were they not spokesmen for 'foreign' values, beliefs and institutions that had been forced into being by an alien power, and ought to have no place in an authentic, indigenous political framework? This was a polemic that came to be extremely useful in discrediting communists as agents of a foreign power; but it was also, for some, a more genuine problem.

Once again, the problem can be seen to have been dictated by the nature of the struggle: allegedly, for a colony to legitimately claim the right to independence, it had to 'qualify' in the eyes of its metropolitan rulers. And the qualification then recognised was a properly developed national consciousness. It was not adequate to question the criteria of such qualification, or indeed the metropolitan rulers' right to decide what the criteria were, or when they had been achieved: practically speaking, short of open opposition or anti-colonial war, nationalists had to put forward the claim that such qualification had been attained – even if subsidiary points in their argument might include a challenge to the ruler's right to decide the *criteria*, not to mention the *timing*.

On the imperialist side, the 'right of nations to self-determination' (proclaimed by Woodrow Wilson as the principle behind a post-First World War settlement, after the triumphant Russian Revolution had made it one of its own central principles) was interpreted as meaning 'in the fullness of time', when the colonies had learnt enough about the institutions given to them to 'qualify' for self-government. In the mean time, a principle of 'trusteeship' would operate: the imperialist powers would administer a country or a people not yet capable of having its own nation-state. Nationalists in these states, according to the 'trusteeship' argument, although they might exist, could be discounted as an inauthentic minority cut off from the people they claimed to represent by the elite education they had received under colonial rule itself. The rule of a (benevolent) outside power was therefore, according to the imperialist argument, better than that of an inauthentic minority that would exploit its own ignorant people (which, naturally, the imperialist power would be too civilised to do).

While attempting to refute these arguments, nationalists themselves took the charge of inauthenticity more than a little seriously; and India was no exception. Acutely aware of being incorporated into a world view that saw progress as a product, or at least a by-product, of imperialism, they sought to assess what aspects of so-called 'Western' progress they might profitably appropriate without losing the 'authentic genius' of India. It was upon such authenticity, as they knew, that criteria of nation-ness had to be based. As a result, there was a certain touchiness about the question of authenticity that dogged many a debate in which it ought to have been irrelevant. Matters were not made any clearer by the fact that many of the aspects of Indian 'tradition' hailed as properly indigenous could be shown, on closer scrutiny, to have been invented in the recent past. There was also the related danger of rendering an 'authentic' Indian tradition as a 'Hindu' one: ancient Indian achievements, glorified by Orientalists from Britain and Europe (and, not coincidentally, seen as 'Aryan' achievements), were situated in a so-called 'Hindu' period of Indian history. This glorious civilisation had been destroyed, according to British accounts of that history, by 'Muslim invasion'. The British version cast the British themselves as rescuers of India from this fate; many Indian nationalists' versions simply added the British to the list of invaders and destroyers of ancient glory, leaving the role of recovery to themselves as nationalists. But such nationalism, even when only inadvertently exclusionary, was unlikely to have any takers among Indian Muslims, cast as outsiders, invaders and barbarians in their own country's national mythology.

It was in this political environment that Jawaharlal Nehru found himself an unlikely leader. As a self-confessed adherent of 'modern' values, he was aware that the 'modern' had to be carefully separated from the 'Western'. This 'modernity' could then be considered universal, rather than 'Western', thereby avoiding being disqualified as not properly 'indigenous'. Nehru could not honestly claim the authenticity of an 'indigenous' culture, not merely due to his largely British educational background (this would have been shared by a number of members of the new Indian middle classes that grew up under colonial rule, who nonetheless sought to claim that authenticity in various ways). He was unconcerned with caste, religion and the forms of religious nationalism that were on offer in his time; and he was often rather impatient with the debates that stressed such forms of authenticity or mobilisation. The concern with 'indigenism' was to Nehru often too closely associated with reactionary and obscurantist politics, and with 'backwardness'.

However, if Nehru saw himself as a moderniser; so did most others in the Indian political arena. Those among the 'indigenists' who were sometimes described as anti-modern in the course of political debate, such as Gandhi, questioned the *criteria* of modernity, but were nonetheless publicly committed to achieving modernity – that commitment was a normative necessity, even if the descriptive content of modernity was not agreed upon. Instead of a universal modernity, they sought instead a particularly Indian version of modernity.

Throughout his career, Nehru was forced to grapple with these central questions of Indian nationalist debate in an attempt to find a legitimate idiom of nationalism that, though fitting the criteria of being authentically Indian, was not narrow or sectarian. Once again, these are problems central to the construction of any national consciousness: nationalism, according to its own somewhat circular logic, is something that every 'nation' automatically possesses. It is therefore both ubiquitous (everybody has one) and unique (nations must differ from each other in a distinctive way). It has been impossible for any 'nation' to find the perfect formula. To some extent, Nehru's way of dealing with this was not to attempt to resolve it. The Nehruvian period saw an emphasis on secularism, democracy and state-led developmentalism; a containment of religious nationalism and obscurantism; and an obligatory rhetoric of social justice which, although called 'socialism', was unable to deliver social justice. All these things took the 'nation' for granted instead of defining it; and it was this open-endedness that might be seen as its strength.

But this was in many ways a later, and perhaps separate, problem for Nehru; and the inadvertent coalition of forces that supported him, as we have seen, overrode these considerations. Some are born leaders; some achieve leadership; some have leadership thrust upon them. It is evident that Jawaharlal Nehru's rise to leadership contained elements of all three routes.

1

THE MAKING OF A COLONIAL INTELLECTUAL

Jawaharlal Nehru was born in Allahabad on November 14, 1889, the son of the lawyer Motilal Nehru and his wife Swarup Rani. By birth a Kashmiri Brahmin, Jawaharlal was born into a family whose traditions had more of the North Indian Persianised elite of the late Mughal Empire than the Brahminical in it. The Nehru family had moved to Delhi from Kashmir in the service of the Emperor Farrukhsiyyar, the same emperor whose grant to the East India Company of the *zamindari* of Calcutta[1] and the right to duty-free trade in Bengal had paved the way for British power in India. The family had then lost its position and fortune in the aftermath of the great Revolt of 1857, which saw the destruction of the last vestiges of the Mughal Empire, and had had to flee Delhi for Agra.

Jawaharlal's father, Motilal, was born in 1861 at a low point in the family's history. He was his father Gangadhar Nehru's third and post-humous son; the family had been supported by his two elder brothers, Bansidhar and Nandlal. Motilal was largely responsible for refounding the family fortune, rising to the highest ranks of the legal profession in Allahabad, where the family had moved in 1886, and where Nandlal also worked as a lawyer. Motilal's not inconsiderable wealth, therefore, was not so much inherited as re-earned, in the practice of a profession that had acquired great importance in British India, and one that had contributed greatly to the emergence of a new Indian middle class.

Motilal owed his wealth largely to his work for the old landed aristocracy, the *talukdars* of Awadh, whose property disputes and litigation over succession kept his practice busy. To these large landlords the British had promised security of status and landholding after the Revolt to ensure that they did not side with future revolts. It was the Conservative prime minister, Benjamin Disraeli's, idea that British rule should side with, and not against, the 'natural leaders' of Indian society, the landed aristocracy and the princes, to ensure stability of British rule in India. As far as his government was concerned, the causes of the great Revolt of 1857 lay in the British attempt to raise new classes to power at the expense of the old. Although these new classes had remained loyal to the British at a time when most of the country had risen in revolt, the new classes were a minority who by virtue of their newness could not provide the British with a necessary base of indigenous collaborators. The British link with 'natural leaders' was considered the key to the longevity, and assumed permanence, of British rule in India. This was a link that the Communist International, in one of its more felicitous phrases, was later to characterise as the 'feudal–imperial alliance' – where an old feudal aristocracy was kept alive by virtue of its support from the imperialists, instead of being destroyed by the new forces of capitalism unleashed on a colony by the metropolis.

Perhaps, however, the line between the old and the new India can be too sharply drawn as far as the 'new middle classes' are concerned. Motilal Nehru is an interesting, and perhaps not atypical, transitional figure among the professional classes in India. Both Motilal and his forefathers were service gentry: the latter had served the bureaucracy of the Mughal state, unfortunately in its time of decline; and Motilal served the legal system of the new British rulers. The clerical professions of the old regime sought employment in the clerical professions of the new. It was a logical shift for Motilal from a highly Persianised literary, bureaucratic and cultural world in which he grew up, and in which he continued to be comfortable, to the Anglicised world of the new political power. He wholeheartedly took to the task of mastering the conventions of the new milieu, wielding an elegant and acid pen in the English language, adopting European dress and European table manners. This was for him perfectly reasonable: adopting the cultural norms of the dominant political power was the means of upward social mobility and the marker of social status. But it was not that this was a purely instrumentalist choice. Having learnt Persian (but not Sanskrit, considered by the British to be the classical language of the 'Hindus') during his early schooling, he had then acquired English and proceeded to the British-run Muir Central College in Allahabad, where he was taught to admire English values, English culture and English institutions, embodying, he was told, the principles of liberty and progress. Introduced to this highly idealised picture of the rulers' culture without the experiences to question it, Motilal took time to achieve disillusionment.

His son Jawaharlal, one generation further into British rule, was educated into European cultural norms, and was quite comfortable in them. He was consequently not quite as comfortable in the North Indian elite tradition, though he could read and write Urdu (the Persianised and more literary version of the North Indian *lingua franca*, Hindustani, written in the Arabic script) as well as Hindi (the more Sanskritised version, written in the Devanagari script). The best and most useful education, according to Motilal, was one that would empower his son to conduct his affairs efficiently in the language of power: English. Accordingly, a few Sanskrit lessons from a *pandit*[2] gave way to two English governesses in succession, to teach him English and basic arithmetic, and then an Irish-French private tutor to teach English literature and the sciences, whose Theosophical leanings – of which more shall be said – briefly influenced the young Jawaharlal before his sceptical sense reasserted itself.

Jawaharlal's contact with the older cultural traditions of his family came mainly through its women, who were not expected to adopt the new values: the English-dominated world was the public domain of men. As a child, he heard mythological tales and stories from the Ramayana and Mahabharata from his mother and aunts. But the women of the time were not particularly well-educated; therefore Jawaharlal's literary and intellectual upbringing could not altogether draw upon elements that were undervalued by the old as well as the new society. Women were assigned definite roles in the old society and the new; folk tales and religious myths, for a self-consciously rationalist elite, were old wives' tales, pleasant, but not to be taken too seriously: religion was 'a women's affair'.[3] His other contact with the society that his generation would come to call 'traditional' came through the family's old servant, Mubarak Ali. From him, Jawaharlal heard stories of the great Revolt of 1857, the events of which had significantly affected both his own and Mubarak Ali's families. Later in his life, he was to return to these themes and to try to make sense of them.

The young Jawaharlal's private tutor, Ferdinand Brooks, had been recommended to Motilal for the job by Annie Besant, Fabian socialist, Irish nationalist and now a member of the mystic-religious Theosophical Society as well as of the Indian National Congress. Mrs Besant had come to India in 1893 as a devotee of the new faith of Theosophy, propounded by Madame Blavatsky, a Russian noblewoman, and H.S. Olcott, an American lawyer and journalist. An Irish Home Ruler herself, she was sympathetic to Indian demands for a greater share in government, and was close to the social circles that frequented the annual Congress sessions. Motilal, as befitted a member of these social circles, had attended the first few sessions of the Congress. Founded in 1885 by liberal Englishmen and Indian notables and with a view to voicing Indian opinion as did 'Her Majesty's loyal opposition' in Britain, it had a preponderance of members from the new Indian middle classes – doctors, lawyers, teachers and newspapermen. It was as yet far from the organised mass party of independence it was later to become; its annual sessions met for three days a year in the pleasant weather of the winter months, passed a few resolutions, and awaited the next session. Later, more radical nationalists would refer to its members as 'mendicants', begging favours from the British government and relying on the latter's non-existent goodwill for political change. Yet these radicals did inherit the main achievement of the moderate years – a strong (and also academically respectable) economic nationalism that attributed to British rule the economic decline of India and the lack of industrialisation in India.

The influence of Mrs Besant and the almost-influence of Theosophy on the Nehru family are worth dwelling upon. Theosophy claimed to be a universal religion; it borrowed much from what it understood to be Hinduism and Buddhism, and believed that a noble Aryan-ness could be found at the root of these ancient world religions. Theosophy became a movement capable of generating multiple meanings. Some who engaged with its ideas later became connected with Aryan supremacist or fascist organisations in Europe and elsewhere. Others remained content to maintain a mystical connection with it.

The influence of Theosophy on many Indians was more significant. In a social environment in which the culture and civilisation of India had been denigrated, continuously undervalued or considered inferior by the dominant values imposed by the colonising power, the suggestion that an Indian religion was actually considered noble by Europeans was an empowering one. Theosophy became the route for many English-educated Indians to return to 'Hinduism', playing a central role in the so-called Hindu revivalist movements that became endemic from the late nineteenth century, including the often explicitly anti-Muslim Arya Samaj, a social reform movement that stressed the noble purity (an approximate translation of the Sanskritic 'Arya') of an 'original' Hinduism that could allegedly be found in the Vedas. Indeed, even so apparently 'indigenous' a figure as Mahatma Gandhi had his faith in the validity of his own civilisation restored to him by reading the *Bhagavad Gita* in the Theosophist Sir Edwin Arnold's translation: *The Song Celestial*.[4] 'Hindu' thus came to mean, at least in part through Theosophy, a 'religion', a 'nation' or a 'nationality', and also a 'race'. The exclusion of non-Hindus from a concept of Indian nationhood in such formulations can be clearly seen; but in many of these formulations this exclusion was neither clearly articulated nor necessarily deliberate or self-conscious.

The Nehrus were not among the victims of Theosophy. Motilal was not inclined to take Theosophy too seriously, although he greatly respected Mrs Besant. A sceptic in religious matters, he also did not observe caste practices. He had, after his first trip to England in 1899, refused to perform the rites of purification for travelling across the seas required of him by his caste. He did perform certain ceremonies at home on appropriate occasions, but more as social duty than out of a sense of religious belief (his wife, on the other hand, practised her religion more actively). Theosophy, accordingly, had not much of an impact upon him; he was for a short while a member of the Society, but soon dropped out. Jawaharlal was also briefly attracted by the brand of Theosophy that his tutor placed before him, and joined the Theosophical Society at the age of 13. 'The Hindu religion especially went up in my estimation,' he wrote later[5] – reflecting the need of many Indians of his background in a European and Europeanising education to return to a positive under-standing of 'their' tradition. However, this was a passing phase, and when Motilal dismissed Brooks in circumstances not altogether clear to his son (Brooks later committed suicide), the main influence that remained was Jawaharlal's love for English poetry. Annie Besant herself remained for Motilal an important political ally, as well as the butt end of some gentle humour on his part for her attempts to find 'proofs of a "super-physical existence"'.[6]

Politics was not always a central concern for Motilal Nehru. The young Jawaharlal's childhood coincided with the years of success for Motilal's practice, and with success, he upgraded his lifestyle. He moved first to a bungalow in the Civil Lines, which in the functional segregation of the colonial Indian town was a gesture of defiant confidence on the part of an upwardly-mobile Indian; then, in 1900, to a palatial residence near the confluence of the rivers Ganga and Yamuna, named Anand Bhavan – the Abode of Joy. In doing so, Motilal added to the North Indian elite culture many of the trappings of an English upper-class life – appearing as the Edwardian gentleman complete with motor car (Motilal was among the first in India to own one), entertaining European and Indian society in grand style. This Anglicised life did not, of course, include the Nehru family's women, who as assumed upholders of 'tradition' remained outside the lifestyle adopted by the men. Male children, inhabiting the liminal zone between the women's inner world and the public world of the men, were, for all their exposure to the latter, still subject to some surprises. It was in Anand Bhavan, at one of his father's many dinner parties, that a very young Jawaharlal noticed with horror that the guests were drinking blood. It turned out this was merely an error of perception: he was used to the colour of whisky, but had never before encountered red wine.[7]

Motilal's visits to England in 1899 and 1900 did nothing to diminish his admiration for things British and, in 1905, he took with him his pregnant wife, his son and his young daughter, Vijayalakshmi, with a view to placing Jawaharlal in a suitable public school. Having found him a place in Harrow, Motilal and family spent the summer travelling to the health resorts of Europe, leaving Jawaharlal to find his feet in England. In September 1905, having left Jawaharlal at Harrow, they returned to India. Harrow was necessary, Motilal explained to Jawaharlal, for 'making a real man out of you'.[8] But it was a big step for a privileged son of a rich man, educated at home and living in the bosom of the family. 'Harrow agrees with me quite well,' Jawaharlal wrote to his father in the first weeks of his new public school life, 'and I would get on swimmingly with it, but for your not being here. This puts a jarring note into my every work and enjoyment.'[9]

On November 14, 1905, shortly after her return to India, Jawaharlal's mother gave birth to a baby boy who shared his birthday. Informed of this by letter by his father, and requested to choose a name for the infant, Jawaharlal protested: 'My vocabulary of Indian names is very limited and

I can't think of any appropriate one.'[10] The need for his intervention passed with the death of the infant just over two weeks after its birth, the second child lost by his mother – a son had been born before Jawaharlal but had also not survived.

HARROW AND TRINITY, AND THE BEGINNINGS OF A POLITICAL ORIENTATION

Harrow did indeed agree with 'Joe', as he came to be called there. He was a dutiful and competent student; he did well in French and mathematics, reasonably well in Latin, and studied German, though not with quite as much success. At sports, participation was obligatory, and his father insisted he participate, wishing his son to attain the full range of skills required of a gentleman in the making – although he regretfully noted that his son was 'backward in games'.[11] Joe had had tennis lessons at home in Allahabad; now he was to play football and cricket, for which he had no particular talent (in later years, when the two houses of Parliament, the Lok Sabha and Rajya Sabha, played their annual cricket match against each other, the prime minister was nonetheless to be a desired member of the Lok Sabha team). His father was particularly keen on cricket and football – team sports built character, he felt – and also shooting. As a member of the Boy Scouts, that imperial character-building organisation, Joe got a certain amount of training in shooting. His father advised him never to ride a bicycle, but gave him permission to buy a horse instead (he did not buy one). More to his own taste, he went skating and swimming, and enjoyed running. He was not, however, a particularly sociable student, and acquired a reputation for studious detachment among his schoolmasters, reading a great deal, but not sharing his opinions freely. Although he made some connections with other students at Harrow, his social and intellectual contacts, holidays allowing, were mainly with his older cousins, Brijlal, son of his uncle Nandlal, studying at Oxford, and Shridhar, son of his uncle Bansidhar, studying at Cambridge. One of the books he notes as having influenced his thinking in this period was the historian George Macaulay Trevelyan's book on Garibaldi. Having read it, he began to think about nationalism in general and about Italian and Indian nationalism in particular (a generation earlier, Indians had read and been influenced by Giuseppe Mazzini's writings on nationalism – Gandhi being among these readers).

Jawaharlal later noted that there had been a good deal of anti-Semitism at Harrow. He made no mention of anti-Indian sentiment; he seems to have taken its existence for granted. A few years later, his letters home from Cambridge provided plenty of examples of discriminatory practices against Indians, but they were so commonplace as not to invite particular comment.

Jawaharlal was a dutiful son, writing home to his parents regularly – in elegant and increasingly self-confident English to his father, in Hindi to his mother, exchanging news on politics (with his father), public school – and later, university – life, and on the progress of his two younger sisters – the older, Vijayalakshmi, or Nan, about five years old when Joe started at Harrow, and a second sister, Krishna Kumari, born in 1907, called Betty by one of her first English governesses. Motilal seemed to take a strong vicarious pleasure in Jawaharlal's experiences of English public school and university life, and managed to acquire a remarkable command of public school jargon.

Motilal had made clear plans for his son: he was to finish school, proceed to Cambridge, complete his degree with a First, and then pass the examinations for the Indian Civil Service (ICS). The importance of the ICS was self-evident to the Indian middle classes. An elite administrative corps recruited mostly from among public school-educated Oxbridge men, and to which few Indians had been appointed by virtue of the inaccessibility to them of this desirable route of qualification, the ICS was nonetheless a possible route through which Indians could stake their claim to participation in the administration of their own country. The age limit for the examination was set particularly low, and few Indians had completed their education early enough to qualify even to appear for the examination, heavily weighted towards the public-school-and-Oxbridge experience. It was considered a great achievement for an Indian to qualify for the ICS, in large measure because of the difficulties it involved. But it also reflected the limited goals of nationalists at the time: greater participation in government. There was a strong dichotomy between the urge for participation and the urge to dissent: did one participate in the running of the imperialist system, or did one oppose it? The answer seems to have been that one did both. Every Indian entering the ICS struck a blow against the carefully-cultivated imperialist myth of the incompetence of Indians. Dissent was to a certain extent enabled by this participation; and if dissent was to be confined to a reasoned economic nationalism and a demand for further participation in government, Indians' membership of the ICS might well be seen as a step in the right direction. In the mean time, the ICS was a good career.

In July 1907, Joe left Harrow, bound for Trinity College, Cambridge in October, having passed the necessary entrance examinations. He spent the summer between school and university travelling through Britain and Europe. His father, meanwhile, already had a list of instructions for him for Cambridge – a world he knew of only second-hand, but he knew the things that would be important: join the Union Society; row – Jawaharlal said he was too light to be anything but cox, which he didn't fancy (he was, eventually, cox of one of the Trinity boats); and buy a horse – Jawaharlal said it would be too expensive.

Meanwhile, Jawaharlal was, from a long-distance perspective, begin-ning to encounter Indian politics. The political scene was beginning to warm up in the year he began school at Harrow. The *Swadeshi* – which translates roughly as 'of our own country' – movement had its immediate cause in the partition of the province of Bengal, seen by the British as an uncomfortable seat of rising nationalism. Bengal had been the first region of India to be brought under effective colonial control, and also the first to develop a coherent anti-colonial movement centred on the city of Calcutta, then the administrative capital of British India. The division of the province, ostensibly an administrative measure, was widely felt to be an attempt to reduce the importance of Calcutta as a political centre, and to create a counter-balance to the organised power of the Calcutta *bhadralok*, the middle-class 'respectable people'. To this end, the govern-ment created a new administrative and political centre in eastern Bengal in Dacca (Dhaka) and encouraged the founding of a new political group, the Muslim League (historically to become very important), under the patronage and leadership of the Nawab of Dacca, an important Muslim *zamindar*.[12] This was to encourage Muslims to organise separately from the Hindu-dominated, and allegedly anti-Muslim, mainstream of a rising nationalist movement.

The resultant anti-partition agitation was the most widespread and effective anti-government movement that British India had hitherto seen. The Calcutta-based *bhadralok* agitators stressed the brotherhood of Hindus and Muslims, and accused the government of deliberately pursuing a policy of divide and rule. The movement foreshadowed the later more effective boycott and burning of British-made goods under Gandhi's leadership – indeed, Gandhi, then a young lawyer and political activist in South Africa, followed the movement with interest; his manifesto, *Hind Swaraj*, written in 1910, was largely a commentary upon the issues raised by the movement. *Swadeshi* also stressed the importance of indigenous manufactures, and self-strengthening education, particularly in scientific and technological subjects – incorporating earlier nationalist debates about the need for national self-sufficiency and the nature of valid borrowings from the 'West', also to be major planks of Gandhian politics later.

The movement spread quickly outside Bengal, with middle-class radicals organising boycotts and *swadeshi* demonstrations across the country. This was the moment of division between the old moderate 'mendicant' leadership of the Congress and the emergent 'extremist' leadership, men like the Marathi Brahmin, Bal Gangadhar Tilak, less squeamish about staying on the right side of the law. The extremists were acutely conscious of the need to take nationalism out of the confines of the debating chamber and into the realms of mass politics. To this end, they needed to employ a more popular idiom than the pedantic and formal English of an imagined British liberalism.

But in the search for such a popular idiom, the extremists drew strongly on Hindu – and often upper-caste – symbolism. This could obscure the genuine attempt on the part of the Bengal *swadeshi* agitators to reach out across those limitations. Nevertheless, an undoubted legacy of the rise of extremist politics was a rise in Hindu rhetoric in nationalist politics: the attempt to glorify historical figures who had fought against Mughal rule, now cast as alien and foreign; the worship of Mother India as a Hindu goddess; and more explicitly a reference to a glorious and untarnished ancient Indian past, identified with 'Hinduism'. The possibility of counter-mobilisation on the basis of Islam had showed itself early on, especially as some of the more enthusiastic of the *swadeshi* volunteers used coercive measures to attempt to stop poor peasants in rural eastern Bengal (most of whom were Muslims) from buying British-made goods. In the absence of cheap *swadeshi* alternatives, this was hardly practical – it could only be a sacrifice made by the more affluent – and the result was sectarian tension and occasional violence as religious leaders, encouraged by government officials, told Muslims that their interests and those of the 'Hindu' agitators were opposed.

Jawaharlal's sympathies, as he read about these events, were with the extremists; his father's moderacy began to embarrass him. Motilal was sympathetic to the campaign for indigenous manufactures and educational institutions, but could not see the point of boycotting political and educational institutions. Indians, he felt, still had much to learn from British practices and institutions. Moreover, he did not believe in extra-legal forms of agitation. A certain internalisation of British prejudices against the 'oily *babu*', as he called the Bengalis,[13] went alongside a grudging admiration for their ability to get a large movement going; but Motilal was convinced of the ultimate goodwill of the British government, and put his faith in its liberal impulses.

Following events from the point of view of the British press, Jawaharlal had been less able to maintain the illusion of British good intentions. Jawaharlal sought to argue with and to educate his father. He reported to his father that an evening paper had described Indians as 'invertebrates', who could not evolve towards self-government before a few aeons of geological time.[14] His travels in the summer of 1907, before he went up to university, had included a stay in Dublin with his cousin Brijlal, where he followed the Irish nationalist movement with some interest. Writing to his father from Cambridge, he recommended to him the model of struggle of the Sinn Fein – 'ourselves alone': 'Have you heard of the Sinn Fein in Ireland? It is a most interesting movement and resembles very closely the so-called extremist movement in India. Their policy is not to beg for favours but to wrest them.'[15] The moderates, Jawaharlal believed, were becoming irrelevant and would soon cease to exist. Motilal was unconvinced; politics apart, he was also unwilling to sacrifice his lifestyle for the ideal of *swadeshi* – in 1907, at the height of the movement, he bought himself a motor car. The *swadeshi* press promptly labelled him a *bideshi* (foreigner); Motilal, annoyed, could not see the point. 'Would you advise me to wait till motor cars are manufactured in India[?],'[16] he wrote to his son. (He later sold the car on to the Raja of Amethi as it was too expensive to run; but he bought himself a cheaper one later, arguing that once he was used to motoring, he could hardly be expected to stop.) Impatient and embarrassed by his father, Jawaharlal tried to provoke him into a more self-respecting attitude. Political criticism turned to taunts: 'I wonder if the insulting offer of a Rai Bahadurship or something equivalent to it would make you less of a moderate than you are.'[17] This one struck home – the government only offered such titles to Indians whose loyalist credentials were unquestionable. Motilal, suitably wounded, sulked until his wife intervened and restored communication between father and son.

The Indian National Congress split in 1907 at an acrimonious session in Surat, one of whose highlights was a slipper, thrown in anger, that struck the Moderate, Sir Pherozshah Mehta. The Congress was now in the hands of the Moderates, who, Motilal included, placed their hopes for a better share in government in the promised reforms piloted in Britain by the Liberal Secretary of State for India, 'Honest John' Morley. Lord Morley's reforms, as expressed in the 1909 Indian Councils Act, were a bitter disappointment to the Moderates. The majority of the Council that discussed legislation in British India was to be constituted by officials of the government and Indian notables, handpicked for their support for the government. The elected component was to be elected on the basis of a very narrow property franchise of about 9% of the adult population, and constituencies and electorates were to be separated in terms of religious affiliation: in some constituencies, Hindus would vote for Hindu candidates, Muslims for Muslim candidates. This measure, ostensibly to protect minorities from the domination of the majority, effectively ensured that politics was forced into sectarian boxes. How was a candidate to appeal to Muslims as a Muslim candidate in a separate Muslim constituency on the basis of a programme that argued that being Muslim wasn't the central point of political representation? And conversely, a 'general' constituency might end up as being considered a 'Hindu' one by default. The sectarian conflicts – or 'communalisation' of politics – that would be the inevitable result of such a division were noted by secular nationalists. But this was to have less of an impact at this point in time, with a very narrow property franchise in operation, than it had later under the widened franchise of the 1930s.

Then, in 1911, the government announced the annulment of the Partition of Bengal; but the capital of British India was moved from Calcutta to Delhi, where the new King, George V, was to hold a large Durbar to meet and to be paid homage by his Indian subjects. Meanwhile, the Indian National Congress had met to try and work out what was to be done, electing as President Sir William Wedderburn, a British former ICS officer who had been among the first organisers and sympathisers of the Congress in its early years. This Congress set up a Hindu–Mohammedan Conference to re-emphasise Hindu–Muslim unity. The delegates 'called each other "brothers", "cousins" and so on,' Motilal wrote to his son. 'It is certain that this Committee will either never meet or come to no conclusion whatever.' The same session of the Congress gave birth to an All-India Hindu Sabha (later the Hindu Mahasabha), against the opposition of Motilal, who refused to join it. Even unity, it seemed, had now to be established by separate organisations of elite Hindus and Muslims, speaking for their respective peoples – whether or not these peoples wished to be so represented, or were even aware that they had mysteriously acquired representatives. In nationalist organisations, as in imperialist ones, *representation* was not *representative*.

Despite their differences, father and son were both clear that the mystification of politics through the introduction of religious symbolism was a retrograde step. The *content* of extremist nationalism was for both rather questionable, as were the public pronouncements of its major proponents. At the Cambridge Indian Majlis (the 'native club', Motilal called it, until Jawaharlal pointed out to him that the 'native club' was not the Majlis, but a club for eating natives, which were a kind of oyster), Jawaharlal heard the Extremist leader and Arya Samajist, Lajpat Rai, speak on Indian politics. Although impressed by him, Jawaharlal was annoyed at his derogatory attitude towards Muslims, and his 'repeated references to the spiritual mission of India. India, he [Rai] said, was "God's chosen country" and the Indians the "chosen race" – a phrase which reminded me of Israel.'[18] Motilal was 'disgusted' by Madan Mohan Malaviya's objection to a song based on Vedic verses being sung at the 1910 Congress session on the alleged grounds that the Vedas ought not to be sung in the presence of non-Hindus – apparently the *Shastras*, the sacred books of the Hindus, said so.[19] The Nehrus were to spend much of their political lives opposing obscurantism of various kinds in Indian politics.

Motilal's main objection to the Morley reforms was on the grounds that they aimed 'to destroy the influence of the educated classes'. This would not succeed, he believed, because 'the law of the survival of the fittest is too strong even for Morley'.[20] Motilal's less than egalitarian appropriation of the right to be described as 'the fittest' was questionable, but his attribution of motive was not unfounded: British government circles had come to believe that it was the educated middle classes – inauthentic usurpers, unrepresentative of the 'real' India – who were at the root of nationalist agitation. The problem, from the British point of view, was that they were increasingly articulate, able to use principles already accepted in Britain to criticise British rule. Steps were to be taken, therefore, to disarm this educated class – education being, naturally, more dangerous if it was a recognisably British form of education. In March 1909, Jawaharlal reported to his father that Morley had been to Cambridge to discuss and set quotas for the number of Indians who could be admitted to Cambridge. The quota was set at three Indians per college, for 18 Colleges, which made 54 Indians the legal limit (there were about 90 at Cambridge at the time, over 30 of them at Downing College). Indians would also have to sign a certificate of loyalty to the Empire. The Masters of the Colleges generally concurred with the scheme. Christ's protested mildly; the Master of Downing refused to have anything to do with it, whereupon the other colleges retaliated by agreeing to take even fewer Indians if Downing took more than three, so that the number would not exceed 54. Jawaharlal thought that this was not particularly tragic; Indian students would simply go to the Continent or to other countries. 'They will then,' he wrote, 'be more fit for doing something than if they had been to Oxford or Cambridge.'[21]

Jawaharlal's account of his own intellectual development at Cambridge suggests that it was not particularly exhilarating. This was, perhaps, because it was difficult for an Indian to participate fully in the life of the university. Of the more interesting intellectual activities at Cambridge, Jawaharlal recorded in his autobiography the discussions on sex and morality that he participated in; none of those discussing these matters had much experience of them, but the discussions were nonetheless stimulating. Nietzsche, he recalled later, was 'all the rage' at Cambridge. In addition, his circles were wont to refer casually to Havelock Ellis and Kraft-Ebbing on sex and sexuality, and he himself had a weakness for Oscar Wilde and Walter Pater. The aesthetic ideal, he noted by way of retrospective self-criticism, took the place of religion for him and his colleagues.

Later writers on Jawaharlal's intellectual life stress the influence of Fabian socialism on the Cambridge of his time, and therefore on him. But these influences seem not to have been too direct; and if they had been, he might just as well have encountered them through Mrs Besant at home in Allahabad, for she had been a prominent member of the Fabians herself. In his first year at Cambridge, Jawaharlal went to a lecture by George Bernard Shaw on 'Socialism and the University Man'. 'I was more interested in the man than in the subject of the lecture,' he wrote to his father – though perhaps this was more to assuage his father's fears than the truth. He was fond of reading Shaw's prefaces to his plays – very much in keeping with the aesthetic ideal, and with his admiration for the well-placed word, although Shaw's usually quite explicitly political prefaces would definitely have given the young reader some food for thought. Jawaharlal's own account of the period records that he had been 'vaguely attracted to the Fabians and socialistic ideas'.[22] A later engagement with a gradualist and top-down socialism on his part – as prime minister of India – could perhaps be attributed to a belated engagement with familiar ideas – but this might be attributing too much of a reasoned choice and too little *Realpolitik* to the phenomena of Nehruvian governance, and too much freedom of choice to Nehru himself. But there were other, more radical contacts that Jawaharlal made in Cambridge. The Cambridge Indian Majlis used to meet at the home of the Dutt family. Upendra Krishna Dutt was a Bengali doctor who had set up his practice in the poorer part of Cambridge. His wife, Anne Palme, was a Swedish writer (and aunt of the future Swedish prime minister Olaf Palme); their three children, Rajani, Clemens and Ellie, were all future Communists. Rajani, six years Jawaharlal's junior, was later to be the Communist Party of Great Britain's leading authority on colonial questions.

Both Jawaharlal and his father were wary of the formation of cliques of Indians abroad, to which end they agreed that Indians were best avoided. For Motilal, perhaps, it was also a principle of his educational desires for his son that he learn the ways of the Western world first-hand; besides which, one could not choose the sort of Indians one was likely to meet accidentally in Britain the way one could choose the appropriate social circles in India. And yet his son's British and European experiences seem to have made him more conscious of his Indian-ness than his life in Allahabad had done. Jawaharlal encountered racial discrimination in Britain from which his elite status in India would largely have protected him. His skills as a horseman and with a rifle encouraged him to apply to join the Officers' Training Corps in Cambridge; he was told that this was closed to Indians. He made his observations on such experiences without explicit complaint, noting that it was part of the general environment. Once, returning from holiday in India in 1908, to an England he had now lived in for more than three years, he allowed himself a comment: 'When I arrived in England I had a feeling almost akin to that of a homecoming. The familiar sights and sounds had quite an exhilarating effect on me . . .

It is strange but in spite of the homelike feeling I am constantly reminded of the fact that I am a foreigner, an intruder here.'[23] Most of his Cambridge connections melted away in his later life; but despite (or perhaps because of) the desire to avoid Indian cliques, he made a number of lasting connections in Cambridge with fellow Indian students. Among these were J.M. Sengupta, later to be an important figure in Congress politics in Bengal, Saifuddin Kitchlew, later to be an important leader in Punjab politics, and Syed Mahmud, later to be a close comrade on the left wing of the Congress and a prominent political leader in Bihar. (Several years later, Mahmud confided to Jawaharlal that he had never met a Hindu he truly liked before he met Jawaharlal; Mahmud even named his son Jawaharlal after his friend, inviting the wrath of the traditionalist Muslims in his community.) Another among his circle at Cambridge, Dr Khan Saheb, was the brother of Khan Abdul Ghaffar Khan of the Khudai Khidmatgar, a party allied to the Congress, and was in 1937 to become premier of the North-West Frontier Province.

Meanwhile, Jawaharlal was clearly out of his depth with his academic work for the Natural Science tripos. He had not spent enough time and energy on academic matters; he had to admit his ignorance of many of his chosen subjects. He was disarmingly honest about this in letters to his father, preparing him for the worst. Motilal, as a result, abandoned his desire that his son enter the ICS, replacing that hope with the more realistic desire that he be called to the Bar and continue his father's profession. Others, Motilal rationalised the problem, were more suited to academic work – for instance, Jawaharlal's cousin Sridhar, who had also been at Cambridge, completed a PhD at Heidelberg and did pass the ICS examination. Jawaharlal eventually passed his Tripos in 1910 with a Lower Second – he had been to see the results, looked through the list of Thirds and, not finding his name, assumed he had failed, before finding his name in the list of Seconds. 'I would,' he wrote to his father, 'have been very content with a third.'[24]

THE LEGAL PROFESSION AND THE INEVITABILITY OF MARRIAGE

After Cambridge, Jawaharlal contemplated studying law at Oxford before abandoning this idea for the anticipated joys of London life. He then toyed with the idea of studying Economics at the London School of Economics at the same time as he studied for his barrister's examinations, but then settled for the easier option of doing just the one thing. In the mean time, he enjoyed a lifestyle of leisure and travel – and, inevitably, of extravagant spending, always running out of money and asking his father for more. His father usually concurred, though he once asked Jawaharlal for details of his spending – an indignant Jawaharlal offered to provide accounts of his expenses, but made it clear that he felt this to be an unwarranted interference with his lifestyle. After all, it had been his father who had suggested that he live a good life, and who continued to live one himself, ordering his stationery from London and asking his son to buy him gramophone records: the 'Chocolate Soldier' waltz and the 'Quaker Girl' waltz.

This was Jawaharlal's most extravagant time, fuelled perhaps by the knowledge that it was the last flush of freedom, and the last opportunity to live the life of leisure that had always been within his family's financial capabilities. The law was, fortunately, rather less demanding than the Natural Sciences tripos. 'I got through the Bar examinations,' he wrote, 'with neither glory nor ignominy. For the rest I simply drifted.'[25] In the summer of 1912, Jawaharlal was called to the Bar at the Inner Temple. After seven years in England, he was now to return to India to the somewhat tedious prospect of legal practice, in the shadow of his father, and the attendant family duties – inevitably, marriage.

While Jawaharlal was still at Harrow, his father had begun negotiations to find him a suitable wife. Motilal himself had been married in his teens, to a suitable Kashmiri Brahmin girl from Lahore, and his apparent Anglicisation did not extend to deviation from 'tradition' as far as choosing a bride from a suitable family for his son was concerned. This was a matter of social standing as much as – or perhaps more than – caste practices, which Motilal himself did not properly observe.

Jawaharlal, for his part, was not quite so enamoured of 'that wretched marriage business'.[26] He phrased his opposition first in terms of a defence of romantic love and of the rights of individuals. Was it right to expect people to take such an important step without knowing each other? Aware of losing the battle against having his marriage arranged, he attempted to open a second front. 'In my opinion,' he wrote to his mother in 1909, 'it is not essential for me that I should marry a Kashmiri . . . In my opinion, everyone in India should marry outside his or her community. Then why should not I act according to my beliefs?'[27] But it was not for him to act.

By 1911, Motilal had selected a suitable Kashmiri Brahmin girl for him to marry. The girl was to be trained in the social skills required of her in the Nehru family, including the English language and the use of the correct cutlery at the dining table. She had time; she was not yet thirteen and they would not be married for some years. Jawaharlal protested: he did not know the girl and would at least wish for his father to put off the engagement until he had seen the girl. 'My only fault is that I do not wish to marry a total stranger,' he wrote to his mother. 'Would you like me to marry a girl who I may not like for the rest of my life?'[28] But his betrothal was by now a *fait accompli*; her premarital training complete, he finally married Kamala Kaul, ten years his junior, on February 8, 1916. He regarded the marriage as a personal defeat, although he did his duty by his wife. Late in her life, towards the time of her very early death, he seems to have acquired a genuine affection for her, and this late love was greatly mixed with guilt when she died in 1936. His autobiography, published shortly afterwards, was dedicated 'to Kamala, who is no more'.

In the autumn of 1912, Jawaharlal returned home, after seven years in England. He was 22 years old, already losing his hair, as he noted ruefully, and destined to join his father's practice. Law interested him to a certain extent; it was not exactly fascinating. He was too accustomed to being a self-sufficient individual agent (taking financial comfort for granted, of course) to enjoy working under someone, least of all his father.

Jawaharlal was later to want to draw a line under the early phase of his life: he had been, he wrote, 'a bit of a prig, with little to commend me'.[29] Perhaps this was being a trifle unfair to himself. He was beginning to find his own political understanding; and for a man of his class position, at the pinnacle of the British Indian social hierarchy, he could have afforded the luxury of political disengagement. He had the added benefit of a metropolitan education, of immense importance in colonial India. Doors would inevitably open for him; but he had to decide which doors these were to be.

2

THE YOUNG GANDHIAN

Politics was relatively quiet in India at the time of Jawaharlal's return. The leaders of the Swadeshi movement were in jail, and the government's apparent concession of the annulment of the partition of Bengal had been balanced by the transfer of capital from Calcutta to Delhi, celebrated by the pomposity of the King and Queen's Delhi Durbar in 1911. The Durbar, a British appropriation and reconfiguration of Mughal courtly ceremony as a display of imperial power, was intended as a restatement of imperial authority over India. 'This silly show,' Motilal had called it, and quoted with approval the remarks to him of Sayajirao Gaekwad, the ruler of the princely state of Baroda, 'that it would have been all right if we had not to act in it like animals in a circus.'[1] Motilal had nonetheless dutifully attended the Durbar, and Jawaharlal, in England, had ordered proper dress clothes for his father for the occasion. (The Gaekwad had later been forced to apologise for a breach of etiquette – apparently he had shown insufficient deference to the King and Queen at the Durbar, merely bowing slightly to them and then walking away twirling his stick – and Motilal felt that it would have been better for him to have behaved himself than have had to make so 'abject' an apology.[2])

The *Geist* of the Delhi Durbar – reluctant acquiescence in or quiet acceptance of British hegemony – seemed still to haunt politics in India in 1912, apart from the move towards secret societies engaging in individual acts of terrorism against British rule. More mainstream political groups were less adventurous. Some turned to quiet, self-strengthening programmes of social service; others got on with their lives. Jawaharlal attended the annual Congress session that year – but not much happened. Some Moderates used the space to welcome the Morley-Minto reforms; with their central figure, Tilak, still in jail, the Extremists were without leadership.

Meanwhile, in Allahabad, Jawaharlal began his career as a lawyer, desultorily working in his father's practice, joining the Freemasons, and generally taking on his socially allocated role, very much in the shadow of his father – neither father nor son was in much doubt that some, at least, of Jawaharlal's success as a young lawyer could be attributed to Motilal. Motilal, who took it for granted that this was the desired state of affairs, was somewhat insensitive to the fact that his son might not see it the same way. Jawaharlal was not a very good public speaker – he was always clear, logical and cogent in his arguments, but without significant demagogic skills. This was obviously a disadvantage to a practising lawyer. It was also something that stayed with him through his political career, but he did his best to overcome it – meticulously crafted and rhetorically magnificent speeches were often delivered by him with somewhat less of an impact than they might have had in another's mouth – though the significance of many of the occasions on which he was called upon to speak lent his words the gravity that his voice alone could not have given them.

THE GREAT WAR

The outbreak of the First World War in 1914 interrupted the boredom of Indian public life. The hope of Turkish and German help for Indian nationalists spurred diverse groups to action. Militant pan-Islamists began to organise Indian Muslims against the British on the grounds that Britain was at war with Turkey, the seat of the *Khalifa*, which claimed spiritual leadership over all Muslims. Terrorist organisations attempted to organise arms supplies and plan sabotage and military action, achieving some successes in Bengal and the Punjab. Groups of revolutionaries began to gather in Berlin, where the Indian Independence Committee was set up in 1915 (many of its members were later to form the core of the early Communist Party of India), a 'Provisional Government of Free India' was set up in Kabul, and the *Ghadr* ('Revolution') party, a group active mainly in the Punjab with its leadership in exile, made attempts to organise rebellion among the army and the peasantry. Large sections of the Indian people wished for a victory for the Central Powers. Many Muslims sympathised with the Ottomans; tribal rebels' millenarian uprisings against British administrators drew support from rumours that 'Kaiser *baba*' was on their side and would make British bullets harmless; and rioting crowds were heard to shout 'German *ki jai*' (victory to the Germans). Jawaharlal would later characterise the spirit of the time as that of 'vicarious revenge': even among the middle classes, despite declarations of loyalty, there was little enthusiasm for the British cause.[3]

The British response was, not unexpectedly, cruel, with executions and deportations the order of the day. The Defence of India Act, passed in March 1915, empowered the government to suppress the rudimentary civil liberties available in India, setting up special courts to authorise executions, hand out life sentences and imprison suspects indefinitely without trial. Particular targets were Bengali terrorists, Punjab *Ghadr*-ites and pan-Islamic activists – the latter two had significant popular support, and the *Ghadr* was considered particularly dangerous due to its ability to reach out to the ordinary soldier and peasant.

Much of this was not particularly significant to groups around the Congress. Moderates and Extremists had begun to come together after Tilak's release from exile in Mandalay in June 1914, and by December 1915, the Tilak group had re-entered the Congress. The war, it was believed, provided an opportunity to demand 'Home Rule' on the Irish model for India. To this end, Annie Besant and Tilak set up Home Rule Leagues in 1916. The British war effort, however, was not to be opposed but supported; in exchange, the argument ran, Indians would be in a better position to bargain for self-government after the war.

The dominant faction in the Muslim League – a party founded during the Swadeshi movement, encouraged by British officials as a counterweight to the agitation in the hope that it would form the basis of Muslim collaboration and loyalty to the government – also accepted this argument. In December 1916, at Lucknow, the Congress and the Muslim League agreed on a set of constitutional demands to be placed before the British Government of India, and struck a bargain (the 'Lucknow Pact') in which the Congress accepted separate electorates (established by the Morley-Minto reforms) and the League accepted under-representation for Muslims in Muslim-majority areas in return for over-representation in Muslim-minority areas. This was a bargain that accurately reflected the

League's composition as a party now dominated by Muslim *zamindars* whose main strength lay in the United Provinces (Muslims were a minority there) and was resented by Muslims in Bengal, where they were a majority, although a majority comprising mostly poor peasants. The assumption behind the Lucknow Pact was, of course, that elite groups would agree among themselves on what to demand from the government, unproblematically arrogating to themselves the right to represent ordinary people.

The Nehrus supported both Home Rule Leagues, though for reasons of personal connections were closer to Annie Besant's league. Tilak's rival league was more radical, demanding that a concrete date be named for the granting of self-rule (still defined as self-rule within the Empire). Besant's league utilised the organisational network of the Theosophical Society both for agitational purposes and in order to draw in the intelligentsia. Motilal Nehru joined Besant's league as a response to the repression of the movement by the government (Besant herself was interned in June 1917) and – in accordance with his status – became president of its Allahabad branch, even as many of his fellow Moderates dropped out of the movement. Jawaharlal campaigned for Besant's Home Rule League, but was more sympathetic politically to the Tilak league. This was a time of emotive nationalism. 'My vague socialist ideas of college days,' Nehru wrote, '[had] sunk into the background': the inspirational moments he remembered from the war years were the Easter Rising in Ireland, with Roger Casement's speech at his trial in June 1916 seemingly describing 'exactly how a member of a subject nation should feel'.[4]

Life for the Nehrus was however not substantially disrupted by this burst of political activity. In February 1916, Jawaharlal's long-awaited marriage took place, an event to which he had a traumatic relationship – several years later he could still only refer to it in a somewhat abrupt, awkward and embarrassed way, giving the event just two lines in his autobiography.[5]

Meanwhile, in 1915, some interest was aroused in India at the return to India of a man called Gandhi, fresh from his political victory over General Smuts on the matter of better treatment of Indians in South Africa. Gandhi knew Gopal Krishna Gokhale, one of the leading intellects of the Moderate group and of the Indian nationalist movement, and had stayed with him in the winter of 1901–2 in Calcutta. On his return to India, in 1915, Gandhi clearly had intentions of joining politics in India, but took Gokhale's advice to feel his way into it rather than jump in at the deep end. He spent a year touring India, during which his mentor Gokhale died. Setting up an *ashram* for himself near Ahmedabad, on the model of his *ashram* in South Africa, he began to explore the possibilities of using his political strategy of *satyagraha* or 'truth force' – his version of civil disobedience – in Indian politics.

Jawaharlal first met Gandhi in the winter of 1916, at the Lucknow Congress, but was unable at the time to relate to his style. The reasons would not have been hard to find. Gandhi's politics seemed particularly elusive, and often contradictory. Despite being a protagonist of non-violence, which he publicly claimed was the essence of 'Hinduism', Gandhi supported the British war effort, on the grounds that Indians, as subjects of the Empire, had certain duties if they expected rights. At the same time, he appealed for the British to release the Ali brothers, interned for their support of the Ottoman cause, and later to be Gandhi's allies in the Khilafat Movement, putting before the government the possibility of greater harmony between government and Muslims if they should do this. Gandhi's recruitment speeches stressed the return of Indian 'manhood' through participation in the war, through learning to use arms, and therefore being able to protect their women. Such patriarchal, military rhetoric might have seemed unbecoming of a man of non-violence – but no one was to accuse Gandhi of consistency, especially as they got to know him better. He was a bit of an enigma for the elite group of politicians with whom he now began to work. His dramatic use of clothing, imitating peasant dress, his spinning wheel, his asceticism, his self-conscious anti-intellectualism and his Hindu rhetoric, even as he talked of Hindu–Muslim unity, were anathema to many who thought of themselves as modern, secular intellectuals – the Nehrus, for instance – as well as to many elite Hindu revivalists, who certainly had not intended to make peasants of themselves. (Nor did Gandhi, for that matter; but they did not know this at the time.) And yet Gandhi had successes to show for this strange style of politics, in South Africa, and then in local conflicts in India in 1917 and 1918, where he was able to engineer a number of compromises: in Champaran, Bihar, where he took up the cause of the peasants against European indigo planters, in Ahmedabad, where he negotiated a pay rise for the workforce in the cotton mills, and in Kheda, Gujarat, where he intervened on behalf of poor cultivators. He began to command some respect.

As the war drew to a close, Indian political leaders braced themselves for the anticipated political changes. The war had had far more than an indirect impact on India. Indian support had not been insignificant: about 1.5 million Indian soldiers had fought, and not a few had died (about 60,000), in the service of Britain. India had effectively supplied a free army, paid for predominantly from Indian revenues, as had been the case several times before; but this time, in addition, the (British) government of India had voted to provide a 'gift' on behalf of the 'Indian people' of £100 million for the war effort. Some changes had not altogether been anticipated. India became a centre of war production: of munitions, but also of uniforms and jute sandbags, leading to the development of Indian industry. Wartime disruption of trade inadvertently created an import-substitution effect, as regular British exports to India were slowed down. The Indian Munitions Board explored the possibility of industrialising India quickly for greater efficiency as a centre of war, something earlier viceroys with an understanding of military imperatives, such as Lord Curzon, had believed to be desirable. An explicit policy of industrialisation by the government had long been one of the main demands of Indian economic nationalists, taking their argument from the German model propounded by Friedrich List: every nation had to have its own industry to be strong, and a government's duty was to protect infant industries until they were strong enough to stand on their own feet and compete in the world market. The government appeared at last to be conceding this; but after the end of the war these plans were quietly dropped.

AFTER THE WAR: CHANGING THE CONSTITUTION

Then, in August 1917, a statement was read in Parliament to the effect that the goal of British rule in India was 'the increasing association of Indians in every branch of the administration' and 'a progressive realisation of responsible government in India'.[6] This, perhaps, was the expected reward for Indian support during the war. The Secretary of State for India, Sir Edwin Montagu, visited India at the end of 1917, making the customary cold-weather tour of the British administrator, and produced a set of proposals and a time-frame of 'training' in self-government for Indians, the results of this training to be examined in ten years' time. The provinces of British India would be provided with a degree of autonomy from the central government, and provided with their own legislatures; elections were to be held on the basis of a very narrow property franchise, and separate electorates and reserved communal seats were retained.

Central to these proposals was the principle of 'dyarchy': legislation would be divided into legislation on 'transferred' subjects that could be introduced by elected ministers, and voted on by elected members of provincial legislatures, and legislation on 'reserved' subjects, introduced by the governor as imperial proconsul, that could be discussed but not voted on by elected members. The 'transferred' legislation was still subject to the governor's veto; and even as British administrators grandiosely referred to the new legislative spaces available to Indians as the 'nation-building departments', a reorganisation of government finances appropriated all flexible sources of finance to the centre, leaving to the provinces the inflexible and non-lucrative sources such as land revenue. In this scheme of provincialised politics, Indians could be given a safe play-pen in which, if they could harm anyone at all, they could only harm each other.

British tactics to pacify Indian opinion also included promises of economic change. The principle of 'fiscal autonomy' was to be a central tenet of the new order: henceforth, it was stated, decisions affecting the economic and financial life of India would not be made in London but in Delhi. Given that the government of India was as British as the one in London, this hardly mattered, as many subsequent episodes were to show. But if combined with the principle of 'Indianisation', these changes appeared to bode well for the future – even if, for the present, it meant packing committees and commissions of enquiry with a few pliant Indians who would back the opinions of the official bloc to come up with the report that the government desired, leaving Indians outside the official consensus to write long notes of dissent for the nationalist press to quote.

From the moment of the August 1917 declaration, the public rhetoric of British rule was that the British were willing to leave India – but always tomorrow. The rhetoric of the need for qualification in self-government before the departure of the British was renewed and intensified, alongside a longer-running theme: India was composed of mutually antagonistic 'communities' who would only fight each other if the British did not remain to referee conflict. Nonetheless, once the declaration of impending departure had been made by the British, the declaration became the catalyst for wide-ranging discussions on the nature of a future, possible independent India – even among those who believed the rhetoric of departure was false, and knew the struggle was still to be a long, hard one.

Sections of moderate opinion decided to accept the new Montagu–Chelmsford reforms, as they came to be called. The British tactics of winning over the moderate sections of Indian opinion by apparent concessions, and isolating more radical voices by making them seem unreasonable, appeared to be working, claiming among its more notable victims Mrs Annie Besant. This was the parting of ways between two old allies: Motilal Nehru rejected the new reforms. This left him in a situation of relative political isolation, as he was now distanced from many Moderates, and still far from inclined to throw in his lot with the Extremists (his attempt to run a newspaper called *The Independent* – a name that underlined his isolation at the time of its founding – came to grief in a few years, despite energetic help from his son, Jawaharlal, due in large measure to bad management).

Promises of benevolent supervision of a transition to self-government were not all there was to British rule after the war. There was a stick to go with the carrot, as a reminder to those who were tempted to imagine that British rule would now be a gentler beast. It had been assumed that emergency repressive legislation put in place during the war would now be removed, especially with the rhetoric focused on friendship and eventual independence. This was not to be. In 1919, the Anarchical and Revolutionary Crimes Act (the Rowlatt Act) was passed, allowing wartime provisions for arbitrary arrests and imprisonment to continue after the war.

This was the opportunity for Gandhi's first campaign on a national stage. Gandhi called for an all-India Satyagraha to resist the Act: deliberate civil disobedience of the Rowlatt Act, including allowing the government to arrest the Satyagrahis, 'courting arrest', as it came to be called in Indian political life. Working with some existing organisations, Gandhi also set up a Satyagraha Sabha, a 'truth force committee', to coordinate the campaign. Gandhi held meetings with Motilal Nehru in Allahabad regarding a political strategy to campaign against the Act, but there was no meeting of minds. Jawaharlal, on the other hand, was greatly attracted by the Satyagraha Sabha, which seemed at last to provide an opportunity for meaningful political activity. His father was not so certain: politically, he was sceptical that going to jail would put any pressure on the government; and personally, he was not at all keen on his son going to jail. The issue became the subject of discord between father and son – a continuance of earlier disagreements on political matters, but also the beginning of a greater divergence than had manifested itself in theoretical disagreements. (The personal angle was not openly put forward in their discussions with each other; Jawaharlal discovered later that his father had tried sleeping on the floor to find out what it was like, deciding that this would no doubt be Jawaharlal's lot in prison.) But the political differences between Jawaharlal and Motilal were still rooted in their earlier disagreements: defying of laws appealed to Jawaharlal, but not to Motilal, who, even if no longer a Moderate, was still a constitutional politician and a lawyer at heart. Motilal's form of political involvement was to appeal to the Secretary of State for India, Edwin Montagu, for permission to provide legal assistance to the victims of the Act; Jawaharlal, for his part, joined the Allahabad Satyagraha Sabha.

The Rowlatt Satyagraha was, in retrospect, a small-scale movement, and one in which Gandhi's control over his following gave early indications of imperfection: despite his exhortations to non-violence, there was some amount of violence, causing Gandhi to call off the movement – in effect, to disown it, because it was far from clear that all the unrest that followed his call for satyagraha could be attributed to the call. The highlight of the Rowlatt Satyagraha was an all-India *hartal* or general stoppage of work and closure of all shops on April 6, 1919 – postponed from March 30. April 6 was a Sunday, as March 30 had been – Gandhi even asked employees who had to work on Sundays to get their employers' permission to stay away from work. The Rowlatt Act, ironically, was never used against anyone (the Act itself was repealed in 1922). Both the Act and the Satyagraha against it were quickly overtaken by an event that made the Act seem irrelevant, and its author, Sir Sidney Rowlatt, seem like a gentle libertarian: the Jallianwalla Bagh massacre in Amritsar, Punjab, on April 13, 1919.

JALLIANWALLA BAGH

On April 13, with the Punjab under martial law, an army unit led by General Dyer marched through the narrow streets of Amritsar into Jallianwalla Bagh. There was a large crowd of people in the square, including village people who had come into the town for the *Baisakhi* festival – but this was, indeed, an illegal public demonstration in defiance of the ban on public meetings. Dyer's battalion got into firing positions and fired 1,650 rounds into the surrounded crowd, without warning, and without providing the opportunity to disperse. There was only one exit, which was blocked by the army, and the only other shelter was a well at the centre of the *bagh*, into which several men, women and children dived in the hope of avoiding the hail of bullets; many died in the well. Dyer's men kept on firing until their ammunition was nearly exhausted (leaving only enough to defend themselves should the need arise); and then they left, leaving the wounded where they were. The official estimate of the dead was 379, and of the injured 1,200, although it was widely agreed that the actual figure was much higher. An armoured car with a mounted machine gun had been left outside the *bagh*, because the passage had been too narrow to drive it through. Both these last details became known before the official commission of enquiry set up after the incident, the Hunter Commission – the source was General Dyer himself, who believed Indians had to be taught a lesson, and the firing had been undertaken in order to 'produce a moral effect'.

It did produce a moral effect, but not the one that Dyer had anticipated or desired. The sense of outrage and revulsion against British rule that followed the massacre effectively killed moderate opinion in India. Two days after the publication of the Hunter Commission's Report, on May 30, 1919, the poet Rabindranath Tagore, who had effectively renounced direct political action following the Swadeshi movement, renounced his knighthood in protest – it had been awarded to him in 1915, largely on account of his having won the Nobel Prize for Literature in 1913. Dyer was reprimanded by the Hunter Commission and returned to England, but it was widely felt in India that the Committee had not gone far enough: Gandhi described its report as 'page after page of thinly disguised official whitewash'.[7] In England, the *Morning Post* raised £26,000 by public subscription for Dyer, a huge sum of money by any standards, to ensure that he lived a comfortable life thereafter. General Sir Michael O'Dwyer, who had been Lieutenant-Governor of the Punjab in 1919, had initiated several repressive measures during the Punjab 'disturbances' and had publicly backed Dyer after the massacre, was exonerated of responsibility, and the House of Lords rejected the censure passed on Dyer by the Hunter Commission. When, in March 1940, Udham Singh, a Sikh orphan who had as a young boy survived Jallianwalla Bagh protected from the hail of bullets by the bodies of the dead and wounded under which he had found shelter, shot and killed O'Dwyer in London, his act satisfied a widespread desire for revenge that had not altogether died down over twenty years later.

The Congress began to organise relief work in the Punjab, and set up its own enquiry committee to provide a second opinion to that of the Hunter Commission. Jawaharlal, sent to the Punjab as part of the Congress investigation team, clinically reported his findings in his notebooks, allowing himself a moment of hope as he recorded the tale of an infant who had been in open firing range throughout the massacre at Jallianwalla Bagh but had miraculously survived unhurt. Details that emerged of the Punjab under martial rule were not particularly palatable to Indian opinion: torture, public floggings of Indians, the enforcing of an order insisting that all 'natives' *salaam* all *sahibs* (a form of salute specifically implying inferiority), and making all Indians crawl down a lane where a white woman had been insulted (or assaulted, depending on the version of the story). Jawaharlal's notebook recorded dryly that the 'crawling order' did not require Indians to pass through the lane on their hands and knees, as most people outside the Punjab had assumed, but to crawl along it on their bellies.

During the enquiry, Jawaharlal had the opportunity to see much of Gandhi. Gandhi's conducting of the Congress enquiry, and his inter-actions with the Hunter Committee, greatly impressed the young Jawaharlal. Jawaharlal also sent his father summaries of the Hunter Report. Motilal was shocked – he was unable to recognise any British good intentions now. 'My blood is boiling,' he wrote to his son.[8] At the end of 1919, Jawaharlal found himself in a railway compartment with a group of military men travelling from Amritsar to Delhi. The group turned out to be General Dyer and his fellow officers. Dyer regaled the gathering, including the inadvertent listener on the upper berth, with tales of martial law and of Jallianwalla Bagh, and boasted that he had had the whole town at his mercy and had thought of reducing it to ashes, but then took pity on it.

On December 27, 1919, at the Amritsar Congress session, Motilal's presidential address was very critical of Lieutenant-Governor O'Dwyer. The 'Punjab wrongs', as Gandhi was to describe the situation, had created a new solidarity within the Congress. Jawaharlal was to describe Amritsar as 'the first Gandhi Congress'.[9] The Ali brothers, recently released from jail, joined the Congress at Amritsar; their ability to command support from ordinary Muslims seemed to address the Congress's long-standing concern with limited Muslim participation in the Congress's activities. The momentum gained in Punjab was carried forward into the Non-Cooperation-Khilafat Movement.

THE NON-COOPERATION-KHILAFAT MOVEMENT: JAWAHARLAL AS GANDHIAN

Among Indian Muslims, the danger to the *khalifa* remained an emotive issue with immense mobilisational potential, especially after the defeat of Turkey in the war and the harsh terms of the Treaty of Sevres, signed on May 14, 1920. In June 1920, Gandhi proposed an alliance: if the Khilafat movement accepted non-violence as its guiding principle, he, Gandhi, was theirs to command. The Ali brothers reacted positively; some Muslim League members and many *Maulvis* were unhappy with this. Gandhi, at a meeting of Muslim leaders in Allahabad, set out the problems before such a movement. 'He spoke well in his best dictatorial vein,' Jawaharlal, who was present, later wrote.[10] They were, Gandhi said, fighting a powerful enemy. They should therefore subject themselves to Gandhi's dictatorship and discipline – always subject to their goodwill and acceptance. They could throw him out, but as long as he was the leader he was the dictator – Gandhi used the analogy of martial law. The meeting accepted Gandhi's proposals, with the Khilafat Committee of 1920, and not the Muslim League, taking the lead (most Leaguers stayed out of the ensuing struggle). At this time, Congress had not yet accepted Gandhi's proposals. Later, in September, at a special session of the Indian National Congress in Calcutta, the Congress endorsed Gandhi's position by a narrow majority of 144 to 132 in the Subjects Committee (and a wider 1,855 to 873 margin at the open session);[11] the details were worked out at the regular Nagpur session over the Christmas period.

Motilal was one of the few established leaders of Congress who voted for Non-Cooperation at Calcutta. The movement that followed saw a complete transformation of Motilal, politically as well as sartorially. His house, Anand Bhavan, became the virtual headquarters of the Non-Cooperation Movement in the United Provinces. He swapped his suits tailored in London for hand-spun *khadi* clothes. The politics of dress was central to Gandhian politics and for new entrants, a renunciation of

'Western' dress and an adoption of *khadi* was part of a symbolic transition to the new politics. But Motilal never endorsed the entire range of Gandhian ideas, certainly not those contained in Gandhi's manifesto, *Hind Swaraj*, which claimed that any form of machine-based civilisation, or any acceptance of the 'Western' professions introduced by the British to India, would amount to a betrayal of *swaraj*, for with them all India could hope to have was 'English rule without the Englishman'.[12]

Chittaranjan (C.R.) Das, who had opposed Non-Cooperation at Calcutta, eventually moved the central resolution of Non-Cooperation at the Nagpur session, providing for agitational activities ranging from renunciation of voluntary association with the government to the refusal to pay taxes – the Congress leadership would decide when and where these measures were to be applied. Das's acceptance of non-violence can only be seen as strategic; he was known to be sympathetic to the Bengal terrorist movement, and had been the successful defence lawyer in the famous Alipore Bomb Case in 1908; among the accused was the terrorist-turned-mystic Aurobindo Ghosh. The terrorists had pledged their support for complete independence from British rule – a demand taken up by the Congress as late as the end of 1929. For now, Gandhi's deliberately ill-defined '*swaraj*' was the goal: to be attained, in the language of the resolution, 'by all legitimate and peaceful means'. The 'Punjab wrongs', the 'Khilafat wrongs' and '*Swaraj*' were the three central issues selected. Gandhi's programme involved spinning on the *charkha*, boycott of foreign cloth, and of course *ahimsa* (non-violence).

Meanwhile, Gandhi took it upon himself to further young Jawaharlal's political education. After the Calcutta session in September 1920, Gandhi, taking Jawaharlal with him, went to Shantiniketan, where the poet Rabindranath Tagore had, in 1901, set up his radical experimental university, Vishwa Bharati. Here, Jawaharlal also met the Reverend C.F. Andrews, later active in the anti-indentured labour movement, and an old associate of Gandhi from his South Africa days. Andrews gave him some books to read on imperialism in Africa, including E.D. Morell's *Black Man's Burden*. This was the beginning of a long-term and productive dialogue between Jawaharlal and 'Charlie'. Jawaharlal regarded Andrews as one of the few foreigners who had been able to understand the daily feelings of humiliation suffered by Indians under imperialism.

The November 1920 election boycott, soon after the call for a movement, was a vital test of popular support. The Congress considered it a great success. A great majority of voters abstained from voting (even though there were strong regional variations: in Madras presidency, for instance, there was a turnout of over 50% in some districts). But if there were no voters, there were candidates, even if not Congress ones; some candidates were elected unopposed, and some polling booths did not see a single voter, but even a handful of voters could elect a candidate. Jawaharlal and some younger members of Congress had favoured a style of council boycott modelled on that of Sinn Fein – who had been elected to Commons seats but then refused to enter the Commons. Accordingly, the Congress should win seats, showing strength of popular support, and then refuse to enter the Councils. Muhammad Ali also supported this form of boycott, but he had been away in Europe on a Khilafat delegation and had been unable to voice his opinion in time. Gandhi had his way, arguing that the message of total boycott was easier for the masses to understand. This was more consistent, of course, with Gandhi's proclaimed position – educational institutions, the professions, and all things imposed by the British, should be boycotted, otherwise *Swaraj* would just mean English rule without the English. Gandhi's desire to be a dictator on the Roman model for the duration of the struggle also obviated the use of tactics that he did not approve of. But one of Gandhi's arguments made at the time was to prove prophetic more than once: he reasoned that once people were elected to the councils they would be drawn in by the logic of their operation, and would be unable to resist participation.

The movement was a total transformation of formal Indian politics. From erudite and complex constitutional and legal questions debated in *ersatz* legislatures and quasi-councils to an alliance of radical pan-Islamic and Hindu opinion was a big jump indeed. This was an immensely successful popular movement – the British government, unable to understand its success or its driving forces, drew on official paranoia to call it a 'Bolshevik' movement, and Gandhi a 'Bolshevik'. This was a complete misunderstanding. Many Indians were indeed influenced by the Bolshevik Revolution after 1917 – mainly the declaration of the right of self-determination and of equality of all peoples – but they had not even tentatively engaged with it yet. The early responses were diverse. Hindu nationalists like Lala Lajpat Rai hailed the Russian Revolution as a great moment in human history, while distancing themselves from its egalitarian goals and managing to remain fundamentally Hindu obscurantists.

There were reports that the ruler of a small princely state in Mewar had been threatened by his peasants that he would meet the fate of the tsar, but since the source of such reports were British officials, how far this can be attributed simply to imperialist panic is difficult to ascertain. One thing was clear: the Bolshevik Revolution promised liberation – the Soviet insistence on the right of self-determination and independence for all peoples, and the genuinely non-racist fraternal declarations emanating from the USSR clearly impressed many in India, and to that extent Indians were very interested in events in Russia. But this fell short of a clear engagement with all socialist principles. Only a few intellectuals had read any Marx, far less Lenin. Some Indian political agitators in exile, men like M.N. Roy, Abani Mukherji and Virendranath Chattopadhyay, were moving towards communist politics (Roy actually attended the Second Comintern Congress in 1920 as a delegate from Mexico). In 1920, S.A. Dange, a prominent trade unionist from Bombay, wrote a book in which he debated the relative merits of a Gandhian, non-violent, and a Leninist, insurrectionary, movement largely in terms of appropriate tactics against the British colonial state, even as he insisted that without participation of peasants and workers, no movement could succeed in India.[13] This could be read as an attempt to ride the tide rather than swim against it, for by 1921 Dange described himself as a Leninist; the relative newness of the Leninist position in India would have required him to present the ideas somewhat gently to a new audience. Not many knew of M.N. Roy's debate with Lenin over the latter's view of Gandhian leadership as 'progressive'; nor had many people heard of Roy.

One line of criticism of the Non-Cooperation-Khilafat Movement by sceptics and opponents within the nationalist movement was that linking up with pan-Islamic tendencies through the claim to the brotherhood of Hindus and Muslims centrally brought religion into politics. The Muslim Leaguer and Congressman (it was, until the 1940s, possible to belong to other groups and still be a member of the Congress and it was only in 1938 that members of 'communal organisations' were excluded from it) Muhammad Ali Jinnah, who detested the obscurantist religious sentiments invoked on both the Hindu and Muslim sides by such anti-rational politics, was one such critic. (He was to learn the lessons well, when he decided to use similar tactics himself in the 1940s – with fewer qualms about potentially violent consequences.) Many critics were not taken seriously because they had dubious credentials in the eyes of the enthusiasts for the movement: they were too moderate, too timid, they feared the irrational masses and preferred the safe environment of the debating chamber (indeed, the government hoped that Gandhi's appeal to the uneducated masses would alienate the educated classes and push them closer to the government). But the criticism raised a question that had emerged before. Religion as a mobilisational tool in Indian nationalist politics was not new. The great Maharashtrian nationalist, Bal Gangadhar Tilak (who coincidentally died just as Non-Cooperation was launched) had already turned the Maratha king Shivaji into a proto-nationalist who fought the 'foreign' Mughals for the sake of a 'Hindu' nation, and the festival of the elephant-god Ganapati into a tool of political mobilisation. The newness lay in the use of religion not as a sectarian but as a unifying force.

Jawaharlal was somewhat troubled by the over-use of religious rhetoric during the movement, both on the Hindu and Muslim sides. But he suppressed these doubts, in part at least for instrumental reasons – Gandhi had an amazing ability to reach out to 'the masses' and this rhetoric seemed to be working very well – and then again, Gandhi was the movement's dictator: 'having put our faith in him we gave him an almost blank cheque, for the time being at least.'[14] In common with others, Jawaharlal decided that something that worked so well was not to be questioned. Gandhi had his peculiarities; his description of impending *Swaraj* as *Ramarajya*, a utopian state of political and spiritual harmony stemming from the restoration of the mythical king Rama, was vague and fraught with religious connotations; no one was any the wiser about what either term ought to mean in practical terms and many were not altogether convinced of non-violence as a creed for all time. And yet Jawaharlal admired the moral and ethical side of *satyagraha*; the spiritualisation of politics was morally uplifting as long as it was not meant in a narrow, religious sense, and he noted that he had not felt so almost-religious since his early boyhood and his infatuation with Theosophy. Despite misgivings, very few saw or wished to acknowledge at the time that the movement was often no more than a coalition of sectarianisms – in his socialist avatar, Jawaharlal was to look back at the Khilafat movement as a 'strange mixture of nationalism and politics and religion and mysticism and fanaticism', with the nationalism itself being a mixture of a Hindu nationalism, a Muslim nationalism and a broader Indian nationalism – all held together by Gandhi.[15]

What was not clear at the time, and was not commented upon, was the almost colonial assumption among many Non-Cooperators who thought of themselves as secular intellectuals that the 'masses' wanted religion and would not be moved by anything else. (The secular intellectual's misgivings were not Gandhi's misgivings: he said repeatedly that he thought a politics separated from religion would be devoid of morality and would be alien to Indian tradition.) And so it came to pass that a quasi-mystical religious style of politics was often promoted by non-believers. This second-guessing of the 'masses' was typical of Indian politics: claims had to be made in their name, but their agendas were not central to the politics of the leaders they had somehow acquired without necessarily wanting. And if the sceptics had looked more closely, they might have been less worried about outcomes: religion, or a quasi-religious morality, depending on how one looks at it, was offered to the 'masses', but in a form that could place the Congress leadership in control. It was Gandhi who retained the right to interpret what correct behaviour was, and it was he and his deputies who castigated the 'masses' for not living up to the standards set for them.

Be that as it may, the success of the movement caught its organisers by surprise. One of the indices of the movement's success, as far as the government of India was concerned, was the visit of the Prince of Wales – the future King Edward VIII – to India in 1921. The government particularly wanted this to be a success, with happy crowds waving to His Royal Highness, so that whatever happened elsewhere, the appearance of order and stability could be maintained – but empty streets and *hartals* greeted him wherever he went.

It was elsewhere, however, that Non-Cooperation and Khilafat had the furthest-reaching consequences. Peasant interpretations of Gandhi's moral codes of *ahimsa* and *satyagraha* always threatened to transgress Gandhi's careful strictures. It is often easy to see why this should be so. If burning foreign cloth was not associated with violence, by extension, burning the property of the oppressor – a landlord, moneylender or a government official – was not associated with violence. Again, if Gandhi set himself up as a holy man or a quasi-divine figure, he threw himself open to multiple appropriations. Many campaigns were undertaken in Gandhi's name; so much confidence was vested in him that in some areas the receipts for the four annas' Congress membership fee that had been central to the conversion of the Congress to a mass party were circulating as currency, referred to as 'Gandhi notes'. The Congress and Gandhi were shocked at the lack of authorial control over their utterances, disturbed at the appropriations of a movement designed by them, by signs of autonomy on the part of the 'ignorant' peasantry. Their issues were not necessarily relevant to the peasants. It was found that in some areas, 'Khilafat' was interpreted as originating from the Urdu word *khilaf* – 'to go against', rather than from *Khalifa*, which in addition to not being relevant to non-Muslims was not necessarily relevant even to Muslims, not all of whom were religiously inclined, or at least inclined to defer to a supreme spiritual leader. Gandhi's style also lent itself to his being interpreted within the parameters of popular Hinduism, with the 'darshan' or sighting of a holy man as auspicious. Gandhi's use of rhetoric and imagery from Tulsidas's Hindustani version of the Ramayana, well-known in oral form to his North Indian audience, and the theatrics of his style of dress, all added to this tendency.

It is possible to say, therefore, that the success of Non-Cooperation had little to do with its proclaimed goals, and more to do with the (sincere or strategic) appropriation of Gandhi for different agendas. Gandhi became a polyvalent symbol available for multiple causes: people could make of him or his message what they would. The need among the peasantry for a popular, possibly even quasi-mythological figure to rally round has been commented upon at some length; counter-arguments have pointed out that this view could make the mistake of attributing passivity to the peasants, lumped together as a sack of potatoes devoid of political consciousness and of agency. Empirically, however, it can be shown that the implied solidarity of a wide movement, together with the millenarian hopes of a peasantry, or more generally an oppressed group, can be a powerful impetus to action – even if that action bears no resemblance to the proclaimed aims of the movement that sparks off the action. So perhaps it was not illogical that the widespread dissatisfaction among the peasantry in India, largely against their immediate oppressors, the land-lords, was given an impetus by Gandhi's call to action. Gandhi could, as it were, replace 'Kaiser *baba*' as a resource of hope and support, with victories being attributed to him even when they were achieved by peasants themselves or their local leadership.

Urban labour unrest, by contrast, was not associated with the Non-Cooperation-Khilafat Movement, neither appropriating nor being appropriated by Gandhi. From 1919 to early 1920, there had been a wave of strikes in factories throughout India, particularly in the main industrial centres; and again, throughout 1921, strikes were widespread. The wartime boom in industries such as jute had ended, and the subsequent recession had resulted in production cuts, reduction of the working week, and attempts to keep wages down. Union leadership at the time was still predominantly in the philanthropist rather than in the radical tradition, and the middle-class leadership at the inaugural session of the All-India Trade Union Congress in Bombay in 1920 appealed for 'partnership' between workers and capitalists. (This was to change by the end of the 1920s.) In some regions, local Congress leaders helped organise strikes – but Gandhi specifically rejected the idea that strikes could be part of the movement. 'We want to harness capital to our side,' he wrote in his paper, *Young India*. To this end the Congress 'must gain control over all the unruly and disturbing elements'.[16]

Indian capitalists, meanwhile, had to be told not to panic in response to Gandhi's emphasis on hand-woven cloth, made from yarn hand-spun on the *charkha*, and his proclaimed hostility to machines: all he intended, at least for the present, was to 'supplement' mill-production of cloth.[17] Indian capitalists naturally wished to take advantage of the boycott of Manchester goods. But Gandhi's assurances notwithstanding, what was to be considered *swadeshi* cloth? This was in part a problem of definition – mill-made cloth could be endorsed as *swadeshi*, although strictly Gandhian principles appeared to rule this out. Some mills, however, used yarn made in Manchester. This was not considered acceptable and the Congress was drawn into bargaining with businessmen to ensure that *swadeshi* cloth was not made with foreign yarn that was merely woven in Indian mills. Eventually, a deal was made between some capitalists and the Congress, which set a maximum permissible percentage of foreign yarn in Congress-endorsed '*swadeshi*' cloth. But mill owners had also to be rebuked for weaving coarse cloth on their machines and passing it off as hand-woven *khadi* – the latter was still a few rungs higher up the moral ladder in the Gandhian scheme of things.

DISCOVERING THE PEASANTRY

For Jawaharlal, this was a period of emergence from the narrow limits of his social spaces. In 1920, he was totally ignorant of working conditions in factories, and had only second-hand knowledge of the conditions in which the peasantry lived, both of which were later to be central among his public concerns. In June 1920, before the call for Non-Cooperation had been made by the Congress, he was invited to return with them to the countryside by a group of about 200 *kisans* (peasants) who had marched on Allahabad to draw attention to their grievances: oppressive and inhuman treatment, extortionate taxation and insecurity of tenancy. Their immediate oppressors were not the British government, but the Awadh *taluqdars*, the 'natural leaders' of the countryside whom Disraeli had seen as so important to the continuance of imperial rule after 1857 – and whose custom had been the basis of Motilal Nehru's wealth. Jawaharlal spent three days in the countryside in Partabgarh, and saw the conditions in which the peasants lived for the first time. Further excursions into the countryside and further wanderings among the peasants added up to useful educational experiences. Previously, he had taken peasants for granted – they existed, he knew, but their lives did not impinge upon his own. He discovered, among other things, that police were able and willing almost routinely to shoot upon peasant gatherings and had few qualms about the numbers they killed. What surprised him was that the cities had no idea of the agrarian movement that had started up only a few miles away – no newspaper, not even the nationalist press, had reported it. As he now discovered, the agrarian movement was entirely separate from the Congress. Leadership in Partabgarh was provided by one Baba Ramchandra, from Maharashtra in Western India, who had been to Fiji as an indentured labourer and had little formal education. Other regions had thrown up local leaders as the situation demanded; but those who were unable to attract and amplify attention at the formal institutional level of colonial politics were imprisoned in local contexts with little outside support, fighting the combined and organised forces of their landlords and the colonial authorities that backed them.

When the Non-Cooperation Movement began, peasants were able to link up with it and claim the authority of Gandhi for their own agendas. This was not to the liking of the Congress leadership; but it was at least in part this leadership who offered Gandhi's authority to the peasants to appropriate. Ironically, it was Jawaharlal who found himself taking the Congress's message to the *kisans* in the United Provinces countryside. In his early days of speaking at public meetings he could sometimes be at a loss for what to say. But he felt less awkward about speaking in public before the peasantry, 'these poor unsophisticated people', than before other audiences – he was unembarrassed about his lack of oratory skills and found he could address them in Hindustani in a conversational style rather than a declamatory one – although he feared that his language or his thoughts might not have been 'simple enough for them'.[18] Having discovered the peasantry, his job was to enforce the Gandhian line. To do this, he had to run down the alternative leadership; in effect, to wean the peasants from men like Ramchandra – in his speeches he insisted that Gandhi was the true holy man, and all others, including Ramchandra, were fakes.[19]

This phase of his political career should have been embarrassing for Jawaharlal's later socialist self. Gandhi was clearly the less radical of the holy men, it had to be said, as Ramchandra was willing to back far more effective and relevant measures for the *kisans* than Gandhi was – Gandhi notably refused to back the non-payment of rent to landlords as legitimate protest. But at the time, Jawaharlal faithfully put forward the party line. At one meeting, in Faizabad district, he denounced the looting of a *taluqdar*'s property, and called upon the guilty persons to confess their misdeeds by raising their hands. Several did so, in the presence of police, and Jawaharlal later suffered some guilt at 'having exposed these foolish and simple folk to long terms of imprisonment' and having inadvertently contributed to the government's repression of the movement – attributing his actions to his allegiance to 'what I conceived to be the spirit of Gandhiji's *satyagraha*'.[20] The language of his discovery of the peasantry was extraordinarily patronising: 'simple', 'ignorant' peasants who had to be told what to do. Jawaharlal continued to be surprised at the *kisans'* capacity for autonomous action, but this was not enough for him to rethink his paternalist attitude.

These were exhilarating times for the Nehrus, father and son, providing them with an excitement far in excess of anything they had experienced before. It had to end. On December 6, 1921, Motilal and Jawaharlal were arrested at Anand Bhavan by a rather nervous police officer, who was obviously aware of the importance of the people he had been sent to take into custody. The next day they were sentenced to six months in jail each. They had been in jail for about three months when they heard that Gandhi had called off the movement at the peak of its success, on February 12, 1922. They were aghast – this was a movement that should have culminated in *swaraj*. Gandhi was then, on March 10, himself arrested – a good move by the government, who had feared aggravating civil unrest had they arrested him at the height of Non-Cooperation.

Gandhi had had his reasons for his unilateral declaration of retreat. On February 5, at Chauri Chaura in the United Provinces, a crowd of people, infuriated at being beaten up by a group of policemen who they greatly outnumbered, and tired of refraining from retaliation as required of *satyagrahis*, had ceased to be non-violent and had chased the policemen back into their police station. When the police barricaded themselves in, the crowd set fire to the building and the policemen were burnt alive. Gandhi was greatly troubled by the 'Chauri Chaura incident', and concluded that the people were not yet morally developed enough to practise non-violence. There had, he explained, been a few earlier incidents of violence that had concerned him, but this was the last straw. If *swaraj* were to be achieved by violence, then that *swaraj*, according to Gandhi, was not worth having, for the people would not be worthy of it.

Amazingly, the movement died down quickly, perhaps demonstrating that for all the autonomy of meanings Gandhi's call to action might have had, it was Gandhi who had to a large extent been the legitimating authority behind its spread: once he explicitly withdrew support, popular initiative seemed to lose its legitimacy. At the end of the movement, then, a number of larger questions had emerged. Was there to be a set of emergency brakes that the Congress leadership had to hold in reserve against the tendency towards autonomous action among its followers? Could the agenda for national struggle only be set by representatives of the national elite – an intelligentsia, a rising national bourgeoisie or a class of professional political activists? Why did so many people join a movement called by a self-appointed elite? Could the strength of numbers have been the result of a conjuncture of diverse desires that the leadership was unable to comprehend or appreciate? These questions remained unanswered.

Imprisonment was the beginning of a pattern that would be recurrent for Jawaharlal for the rest of his political career under British rule: being in and out of jail at His Majesty's pleasure. So would it be for his father, whose early life and later physical condition did not equip him as well for the experience as his son. These imprisonments could do much to damage the elite lawyer's faith in the due process of law, as the legal grounds for the imprisonments could be quite dubious. Motilal, Jawaharlal averred, had been jailed on a perjurer's evidence – he was tried as a member of an illegal organisation, the Congress Volunteers, to prove his membership of which a form with his signature on it in Hindi was produced. But since he seldom signed his name in Hindi, very few persons could have attested to it being his signature. Finally a man was found who did the needful and swore to it being Motilal's; he was illiterate, and held the signature upside down as he examined it.

Jawaharlal himself was released after three months in prison when someone in authority came to the conclusion he had been wrongly sentenced: distributing notices for a *hartal*, the official charge, was not – then – an offence (it was later to become one). Once released, Jawaharlal had the privilege of attending Gandhi's trial – an inspirational moment of anti-colonial nationalism staged in a courtroom, ranking alongside Roger Casement's performance that Nehru had been so inspired by. Gandhi's speech reversed roles and put British imperialism itself on trial, outlining its record in India and tracing his own transition from loyal subject to seditious outlaw as a moral duty to resist injustice. 'I am here, therefore', he concluded, 'to invite and submit cheerfully to the highest penalty that can be inflicted upon me for what in law is a deliberate crime, and what appears to me to be the highest duty of a citizen.'[21]

Jawaharlal then went back to political work in Allahabad, picketing cloth merchants who had broken their pledge not to deal in foreign cloth. (Cloth merchants and businessmen had remained a problem for the Congress throughout the Non-Cooperation Movement; many cloth merchants had joined in the boycott due to the conjunctural factor of the rupee-sterling exchange rate changing from a 2s 4d rupee in December 1919 to a 1s 3d rupee in 1920–1, making their projected purchases far more expensive and therefore making the boycott a convenient excuse not to honour their contracts; now, with prices having settled down, this was no longer the case.) Soon afterwards, he was arrested and charged with criminal intimidation and extortion, with sedition thrown in for good measure. He was sentenced to a year and nine months in prison; he had been out of jail for six weeks. Jawaharlal remained in Lucknow district gaol until the last day of January 1923, when he was released on a surprise amnesty. He suspected this was because the Congress was so busy engaged in mutual squabbles that they were not considered a threat – it seemed, therefore, that the government thought it might be a good gesture to make. Gandhi remained in jail until early 1924, when he was released due to ill health. (It should not seem from this that nationalist prisoners were able to treat prison as a sort of rest cure in between movements. Some prisoners were indeed treated well in jail, especially those who were considered moderate enough to do business with later. Those considered terrorists were not so well treated, with their rate of death in custody, often on the far-off penal colony of the Andaman Islands, extremely alarming to those who cared to glance in that direction.)

DISAPPOINTMENT

In 1922, Motilal Nehru had emerged from jail to find the Congress and the 'national movement' in fragments. He had accepted Gandhi's call for a boycott of government and all its institutions more for strategic than ideological reasons. Now that Gandhi had so unceremoniously betrayed the movement, and retreated to his *ashram*, something ought to be done. Intra-Congress debates threw up two broad groups, the 'no-changers' and the 'pro-changers'. A new strategy was required – so argued the pro-changers, C.R. Das and Motilal Nehru. Both had not felt that the Non-Cooperation Movement necessitated abstention from other arenas of struggle. Now that the Movement was no more, the earlier rules ought not to apply anyway. Struggle was to be continued through the reformed Legislative Councils, which if nothing else could be arenas for agitation and publicity. A new party was created for that purpose, the Congress Khilafat Swaraj Party – the Swaraj Party for short. Motilal and C.R. Das developed a close understanding that broadened into friendship, cut short by Das's death in 1925.

The new party turned in very good electoral performances and was able to regularly outdebate the official bloc within the legislature. The Swarajists formed a loose alliance with Muslim and moderate members of the Central Legislative Councils, which was also able to outvote the official bloc in terms of numbers, and repeatedly did so throughout 1924. But the 1919 Constitution gave the viceroy powers to veto decisions of the Legislature, so nothing concrete came of it. Nonetheless, it was good propaganda. In December 1924, under Gandhi's presidency, the Indian National Congress came to agree with the Swarajists' position, retrospectively endorsing their decision. But by this time the Swarajist leaders were themselves not so sure that they agreed with their own position. What had begun as participation in the Councils in order to obstruct the working of an imposed Constitution became for many an opportunity for 'dialogue', as many British administrators had hoped. Some members of the Swarajist were weaned away to join the official bloc by offers of influential or lucrative posts. Jawaharlal was perhaps merely reading the message of these years when in the 1930s he was deeply opposed to participating in the Constitutional machinery for fear of being a party to imperialist exploitation. Motilal also realised that this was beginning to happen. The propaganda value of continuously being able to defeat the government and then being unable to make any difference to laws being passed or not was by now wearing a bit thin. The point that had to be made had been made. In 1926, Motilal led the Swaraj party out of the Central Legislative Assembly.

Meanwhile Jawaharlal had also returned to the desultory politics of the locality that had been left for Indians to play in. Jawaharlal had opposed council entry – it would, he had argued, inevitably lead to compromise and dilution of objectives. But, in April 1923, he reluctantly allowed himself to be pushed forward as the consensus candidate for chairmanship of the Allahabad Municipal Board. (He was not alone in this: leading Congressmen were indeed becoming presidents of municipalities and corporations in the 1920s – the natives could discuss their own 'schools and drains' without subverting the British Empire, as one administrator had put it some four decades earlier.[22]) C.R. Das became the first mayor of Calcutta, Vithalbhai Patel the president of the Bombay Municipality, and Vallabhbhai Patel, his brother, of Ahmedabad. Municipal politics gave Indians – Congressmen not excluded, despite the new moral connotations of Congress membership – plenty of scope for petty factionalism.

As chairman of the Municipal Board, Jawaharlal dealt mainly with practical issues of administration – among them regulating prostitutes rather than banning them (he cited some European examples);[23] organisational matters for the Kumbh Mela, the great festival held at the confluence of the sacred rivers of the Ganga and Yamuna at Allahabad; finances; and of course hygiene. During his tenure, the Education Committee of the Allahabad Municipal Board introduced the Boy Scout movement and the singing of Muhammad Iqbal's (1876–1938) patriotic song 'Hindustan Hamara' ('Our Hindustan') into their schools. Jawaharlal congratulated them on the latter – a small gesture towards the national movement at a time of general disillusionment. Iqbal later came to be considered the national poet of Pakistan; 'Hindustan Hamara' claims that 'Hindustan' is the greatest land in the world, and has the refrain 'Hindi hai hum' ('We are Hindi') – a term denoting geographical rather than religious loyalty, as opposed to 'Hindu', which by now had religious connotations. Iqbal, a poet who wrote in Persian and Urdu (or Persianised Hindustani), was following established usage – the term 'Hindi' referred to the inhabitants of 'Hindistan' or 'Hindustan' – the land beyond the river Indus, Sindu, or with the consonant appropriately shifted, 'Hindu'. The Greeks called it the Indus, hence the land 'Indoi' (the Greeks do not pronounce the 'H').

These patriotic moments of solidarity, sung and unsung, were poor consolation for the loss of the unsectarian solidarity of the Khilafat years; from 1922 onwards, sectarian groups resumed their propaganda and Hindu–Muslim violence became endemic around the issues of cow protection and the playing of music before mosques.

PERSONAL AND POLITICAL DEVELOPMENT

At a personal level, a number of Jawaharlal's problems remained unresolved. He was still financially dependent on his father, along with a family that comprised himself, his wife Kamala and his four-year-old daughter, Indira – a family that he now allowed himself the time to discover. Although, as he recounts, the relatively asceticised life of the Nehrus after Gandhi's moral intervention in their lives meant that his family was far less of a burden on his father than it would have been in earlier times, this dependence was nonetheless galling. Gandhi offered his advice: Jawaharlal should find a job and break out of his cycle of dependence. But the larger, more troubling problem that he had not yet been able properly to articulate remained: he had as yet found no proper intellectual moorings, no *raison d'être*, through his political engagement, even as he acquired great respect and love for his political mentor himself.

At a political level, at least, Jawaharlal's discontent was a shared discontent. The aftermath of the Non-Cooperation Movement was a frustrating time. The period of council entry and the greater use of the legislatures had plenty of defeats of the official bloc to show for itself, plenty of debating points scored. However, without the power to influence legislation this was mock heroics. If it was hoped that these would raise awareness of political issues outside the legislatures, this was probably too hopeful. Obscure issues debated in obscure and pedantic English, without a party wing capable of bringing the issues to ordinary people in meaningful forms, was hardly popular politics. And 'popular' politics, too, had been shown to have its limitations. The 'masses' were not altogether amenable to the control of their social superiors, and not all their social superiors agreed as to whether, or to what extent, they ought to be controlled, and to what ends – although very few at the time were willing to let them set their own agenda.

Gandhi, who had done so much to turn the Congress into a mass party, had at a vital juncture retreated into the background to think, pray and meditate. Many who had supported him on the grounds that his effectiveness as a mass mobiliser should override their own misgivings about the style and content of his politics – he was somewhat mystical, in the style of the Hindu holy man, an ascetic – were slightly wary of him and his leadership thereafter. Nevertheless, his tremendous personal conviction could at least for a time rub off onto people around him. Gandhi himself had gained much respect from his colleagues and even if they disagreed with him, few could bring themselves to doubt his sincerity.

This was not the case with all of Gandhi's followers. It was not just the 'masses' that he had brought into nationalist politics. A number of Indian businessmen were increasingly keen to participate in nationalist activity. They were a curious conglomeration of people, with trade and business often organised on the basis of clan and ethnic networks – notably the Marwaris, moneylenders and traders from Rajasthan with links across India, and now making their mark in emerging industry. In Gandhism they found a space: suffering from discriminatory legislation and business practices that favoured their British competitors, they welcomed nationalist pressure on the government, as long as it did not go so far as to empower their employees or disrupt commerce. And Gandhi, with his claim that the wealthy held their wealth in trust for the 'nation', could legitimate their position in the eyes of a wider public, accustomed to thinking of them as grasping moneylenders or devious capitalists. Other business groups were more circumspect: relying on good relations and possibly contracts with the government to operate, they could not afford to identify themselves with people and movements the government was still describing as 'Bolshevik'. The difference between Gandhism and 'Bolshevism' was soon to become clearer.

Between 1922 and 1926, another division became evident: there was a sharp distance between different generations of nationalists. Younger nationalists like Jawaharlal were beginning to think beyond purely political questions – there was an economic side to consider as well. This was in part a consequence of young urban intellectuals, schooled in non-hierarchical principles, being forced to discover and confront the nakedness of exploitation and poverty in India. The older generation's unquestioning acceptance of the Indian's right to exploit the Indian even as they questioned the British right to do the same was at the very least anomalous. Many of Jawaharlal's generation later rendered this difference in terms of a backward 'feudal' polity and a corresponding attitude bolstered by the British protection of their Indian collaborators and intermediaries, and therefore of the preservation of an old feudal order that would have vanished without British support and without British obstruction of Indian capitalist development. But they did not yet have the intellectual tools to put it in such precise terms.

There was, however, a wider politics emerging. The aftermath of the Russian Revolution had a strong impact on India, which came to be manifested in the growth of left-wing parties, Workers' and Peasants' Parties (which were initially a front for the Communist Party) founded between 1926 and 1928, and eventually, more openly, the Communist Party of India. There was an increase in trade unionism, trade union organised workers' agitations and great strikes in the late 1920s, all leading to fear on the part of the government as well as of Indian capitalists. For a while a sense of shared interest in suppressing workers' movements made the government more inclined to compromise with Indian capitalists, who for their part argued that without better conditions for business they had no choice but to further exploit workers and inevitably stoke the fires of discontent; therefore it was the government's job to help Indian business. This was reflected in the bargaining surrounding the imposition of tariffs in India. Hitherto, India had been one of the most open markets in the world, with the British assuming that a combination of political control and international competitiveness would enable them to dominate Indian markets. Now, with strong competition from Belgian and German steel, and from Japanese textiles, as well as with the need to use tariffs as a source of government income, these assumptions had to change. The problem was to set the tariffs at a level that excluded foreign competition but not British goods, and to accommodate some of the Indian capitalists' demands at the same time. This was a delicate balancing act, not always smoothly achieved. What was clear was that the government and the Indian capitalist class would come together in cooperation against workers' militancy. Events in business bargaining and factory politics began to convince more and more people who were inclined to take the side of the downtrodden that Indian capitalists were at best ambiguously anti-imperialist and at worst collaborators.

Meanwhile, and perhaps paradoxically given the rise of class-based politics in various other contexts, increased tension between Hindu and Muslim groups became more evident. The temporary unity during the Non-Cooperation-Khilafat Movement was now receding, with older Hindu agitations for cow protection once again coming to the fore. Gandhi had appealed to Muslims as brothers not to kill cows and pointed to the Hindus' own cruelty to animals, in the spirit of 'he who has not sinned, cast the first stone'. But he was not able or willing to deflect debate away from cow protection as an issue altogether. This was part of a larger problem. The Congress was uncomfortable with, and not altogether willing to confront, the issue of such sectarian tendencies, pointing instead to the government's strategy of 'divide and rule' as the root cause, which for its part the government strenuously denied ever having practised. And although the government was certainly guilty of stirring up Hindu–Muslim tensions whenever it could or whenever it might be useful, this was an insufficient explanation for the periodic tensions or violence that emerged between religiously defined communities. A better approach was available according to the poet Rabindranath Tagore's famous dictum: we accept that the British divide and rule. But there must be a flaw in our character that enables them to do this.

More questions than answers had been brought to the fore by the period of intense activity and the lull that followed it. After the anticlimax of the end of Non-Cooperation and the futility of participation in councils and municipalities, Jawaharlal was susceptible to – and in search of – a new political orientation. To the right of Gandhi was a group of conservative Congressmen, gathering under the broad banner of the increasingly vague term 'Gandhian', and often drawing on conceptions of Hinduism that Jawaharlal rejected; and the growing alliance of the so-called 'Gandhian' wing of Congress with the interests of Indian big business was not particularly attractive to him. Leftwards was the only logical way for him to go.

3

'INEFFECTUAL ANGEL', 1927–39

The way out of the impasse that was Indian politics in the mid-1920s seemed to be provided by socialism; and it was to socialism that Jawaharlal now turned to make sense of the world. Once again, Jawaharlal's political education was to be continued outside India. In March 1926, he, his wife and daughter set sail for Europe: Kamala was ill, with a variant of tuberculosis, and a Swiss sanatorium beckoned. The family managed to intersperse bouts of treatment for Kamala with skiing trips and tours of the major cultural sites of Europe, while Jawaharlal read widely and tried to teach himself French (although he had studied the language at Harrow, he did not feel that that training had equipped him to use it).

In February 1927, Jawaharlal attended the International Congress against Colonial Oppression and Imperialism at Brussels as the representative of the Indian National Congress. Among the organisers of the Brussels Congress were the Dutts, Rajani and Clemens, connections from his Cambridge days; the main initiative for the Congress is said to have come from the German communist Willi Münzenberg. The Brussels Congress set up the League against Imperialism and for National Independence, which was to be one of the front organisations of the international communist movement, involving itself in coalitional politics in order to build up power and influence. Others were also involved, notably the Independent Labour Party (ILP), at this point a breakaway group of the British Labour Party, with Fenner Brockway and James Maxton being its dominant voices. Maxton and Brockway had committed Labour in 1926 to supporting India's demand for complete independence, and Brockway believed that the ILP's participation in the League against Imperialism (LAI) would help convince Indians of the seriousness of the British left's commitment to anti-imperialism. The ILP kept up its LAI links until 1929.

At Brussels, invited members of various incipient or developed national liberation movements, and various communist parties, joined together to discuss common problems; sympathetic anti-imperialists from the metropolitan countries and prominent intellectuals, among them Romain Rolland and Albert Einstein, lent their weight to the proceedings. Sun Yat-Sen's widow, Song Qingling, brought to the Congress the legitimacy of a nationalist movement struggling against the informal empire of the Western powers in China, ironically a mere two months before the Guomindang–Communist Party alliance collapsed in violence in Shanghai, initiated by her sister's husband, Chiang Kai-Shek. (Nehru invited Song Qingling to the next session of the Indian National Congress, but the British government refused her a visa.)

It was at Brussels that Jawaharlal's career as an internationalist really began to take off. He played a large part in the proceedings of the Congress, drafting a number of resolutions and making several of the major public statements. Jawaharlal's understanding of imperialism as an economic and political system rather than as a form of local oppression owed a lot to these discussions: his understanding of the need for capitalist countries to continually seek outlets for goods and capital, therefore the need for colonies as captive sources of cheap raw material and outlets for the profitable investment of surplus capital, was sharpened here. The exhilarating sense of not being alone, of the solidarity born of injustice and oppression and the recognition that the urge to change was shared across the world was also uplifting. He acquitted himself well in his speeches to the Brussels Congress, his first performance on a world stage. Jawaharlal noted in one of his speeches that in the years to come, it would be American imperialism that would be the major threat to the world, judging by developments in Latin America, and that it would either replace British imperialism as the major threat, or lead to the formation of 'a powerful Anglo-Saxon bloc to dominate the world'.[1] Jawaharlal took the liberty, endorsed by his father, of interpreting the Indian National Congress's vague formulation of its goal, '*swaraj*', as 'independence'. At the same time he argued that mere political independence without economic freedom for workers and peasants would not be true freedom. (This was to be a statement echoed in the Communist Party of India's post-1947 slogan, '*Yeh Azadi Jhuta Hai*' – 'This Independence is a Lie' – withdrawn in 1956 after the Soviet leader Nikita Khrushchev's visit to India in December 1955 and his warm endorsement of the Nehru regime.)

One could not, however, accuse Jawaharlal of being unduly optimistic regarding the prospects of international solidarity. In his report written for the Indian National Congress in 1928, he commented that one of the themes at Brussels had been solidarity between oppressed peoples and the working class in the oppressor country. Jawaharlal observed that such cooperation would be difficult to achieve; it would be easier to create cooperation among the different oppressed peoples themselves. But if such cooperation had to be achieved, nationalist movements of oppressed peoples would need to stand clearly for 'the economic liberty of the masses'.[2]

Jawaharlal's European sojourn was the beginning of his close relationship with the international left. In Berlin in 1926 – Berlin fascinated him, as the centre of all that was exciting in political and intellectual life, the city of radicals and exiles – he had met the communist, Virendranath Chattopadhyay, brother of the poet and sometime Gandhian, Sarojini Naidu. 'Chatto', as he was known, was an important member of the Indian exiles' group in Berlin, as well as one of the organisers of the Brussels Congress. This was the beginning of a friendship, carried out mostly by correspondence, that was as warm as it was fiercely critical, with Chatto repeatedly castigating Jawaharlal for his weakness and vacillation in political situations. Chatto was at the time living with Agnes Smedley, an American involved with the Indian nationalist movement in exile, first in New York and then in Berlin, later to be closely involved with the Chinese Communist Party. Jawaharlal was to continue a long correspondence with her that sustained for him a lasting fascination with China.

In November 1927, Jawaharlal and his father, who had arrived in Europe that autumn, were invited by the Soviet Ambassador in Berlin to visit the Soviet Union on the occasion of the tenth anniversary of the revolution. They arrived on November 8, the day after the main celebrations, and the Nehrus, Motilal in particular, were carefully non-committal about their support for the USSR. However, writing on his experience of a not yet completely Stalinised Soviet Union for the *Hindu*, a newspaper in India, the younger Nehru was enthusiastic: here, potentially, was a country that could solve the problems that afflicted the world.[3]

BACK IN INDIA

On their return to India, the Nehrus were able to enter a political arena recovering from the *ennui* of the mid-1920s, revitalised for them by the British government. The next wave of constitutional 'reforms' was due to be enacted by the British Parliament for India, and an Indian Statutory Commission under Sir John Simon had been appointed on November 8, 1927, to review India's progress towards a higher stage of political development and therefore its fitness for self-government, as required by the 1919 Government of India Act. All its members were white; this was considered insulting even by those who had reluctantly accepted the British claim of the right to adjudicate on fitness for self-government. Here was a Commission with not even the odd loyalist Indian to provide the fig leaf of Indian representation.

An organised response became necessary. The Simon Commission was to be boycotted and an All-Parties Conference organised, with the cooperation of the Congress, the Muslim League and other groups such as the Liberals, the inheritors of the old Moderate tradition. Secretary of State Lord Birkenhead's taunt that Indians were incapable of agreeing on anything was to be met with a proper constitutional framework devised by Indian groups working together. The committee that was to draw up this constitutional framework was chaired by Motilal Nehru.

Jawaharlal was not a member; in terms of constitutional goals, he was at odds with the committee and the eventual Nehru Report, named after his father, that emerged from the deliberations. At the Madras session of Congress in December 1927, he had piloted a resolution that declared complete independence from the British rather than dominion status under the British crown (with a British-appointed governor-general the constitutional head of state) as the ultimate goal for Congress. The resolution had been passed, only to be diluted and disarmed by amendments proposed by the Gandhians, and publicly attacked by Gandhi himself; the Congress Constitution continued to define its goal as *swaraj*. The Nehru Report rejected the Gandhian model of a collection of autonomous villages as outlined in his manifesto, *Hind Swaraj*, in favour of a more conventional framework for a state; with this the younger Nehru was in agreement. However, the Report favoured dominion status as a compromise formula to bring as many people as possible on board, and concentrated instead on the 'communal problem'.

The Report recommended the abolition of separate electorates, advocating instead joint electorates with reserved seats for minorities. Jawaharlal's view, which had some support outside the committee, was that these seat reservations should then be abolished in ten years' time; this was not incorporated into the Report. The Muslim League, whose participation was coordinated by Muhammad Ali Jinnah, had done much of the preliminary spadework to get sections of Muslim opinion to accept the compromise of joint electorates with reserved seats. He expected one-third of the seats in an eventual Central Assembly to be reserved for Muslims, representation for Muslims in proportion to population in Punjab and Bengal (which were Muslim-majority provinces), and the creation of three new Muslim-majority provinces, Sindh, Baluchistan and the North-West Frontier Province. This was strongly opposed by the Hindu Mahasabha, who opposed the federal structure of the proposed constitution, reserved seats in the Muslim-majority provinces of Punjab and Bengal, and the creation of new Muslim-majority provinces. The Nehru Report, in trying to make concessions to the Mahasabha, lost the support of Jinnah's branch of the League: reserved seats were only accepted at the Centre and in Muslim-minority provinces; and the creation of Sindh as a separate province was deferred to an imagined period after the attainment of dominion status. Jinnah, who had accepted a split in the League to take the risk of participation in the All-Parties Conference, made a further compromise attempt at the Calcutta session of the All-Parties Conference in December 1928, pleading desperately that without Hindu–Muslim unity the future of India could only be a bleak one. By March 1929, he withdrew from the negotiations. The Nehru Report was dead. Of some academic interest was its demand for universal adult suffrage for both men and women, and the attack by some of the delegates at Calcutta on the right to private property (which hardly put its sanctity at risk).

The Simon Commission had succeeded in re-igniting political activity; the anti-Simon Commission black flag demonstrations once again brought large numbers of people out onto the streets for a national cause. The year 1928 saw large-scale demonstrations following the tour of the

Commission through the country, and consequently the opportunity for the colonial state apparatus to be deployed with some vigour against the population. Jawaharlal, demonstrating against the Commission at Lucknow, had his share of being beaten up by the police, as had most Congressmen in the process of the peculiarly Gandhian activity of using moral force against physical violence. In a particularly brutal police *lathi*-charge (a *lathi* is a long wooden truncheon of considerable use as a weapon at close range, capable of causing serious injuries) on October 30 in Lahore, the Punjab Congressman, veteran Swadeshi activist, Arya Samajist, and Hindu Mahasabhite, Lala Lajpat Rai, was seriously injured; he died on November 17. (Two months later, the English police officer thought to be responsible for the attack was shot dead; not everyone believed violence ought to be met with non-violence. This act was undertaken by the 'Hindustan Socialist Republican Army', and thought to be the work of a terrorist-turned-communist called Bhagat Singh – but they killed the wrong policeman. For this act, Bhagat Singh was executed in 1931, on the basis of decidedly unsound evidence; what he had indeed done was to detonate two explosives in the Central Legislative Assembly in 1929, not to hurt anyone – the bombs were not designed to kill – but 'to make the deaf hear'.[4])

According to Motilal Nehru, Lajpat Rai's death also wrecked the Nehru Report. Rai was a key figure in the negotiations, and Motilal had urged Rai to get the Mahasabha to accept the demand for one-third Muslim representation in an eventual Central Assembly, *because it would make no difference to a Hindu majority in the House*. After some hesitation, Rai agreed – but said that it would be unwise to give in straight away as the Muslims were making other 'unreasonable' demands. 'Ultimately we agreed that the Hindu opposition to the Muslim demands was to continue and even be stiffened up by the time the Convention was held. The object was to reduce the Mohammedan demands to an irreducible minimum and then to accept it at the Convention. The death of Lalaji before the Convention was a great blow to Hindu–Muslim unity.'[5]

The details of these negotiations are in many ways not as important as the notable continuation of a trend: Indians were now imprisoned in the colonial numbers game, debating whether a seat here or there could be conceded, whether a proportion of the population was to be defined as 'Hindu' or 'Backward Caste' or 'Muslim', in order to play the game within a system defined by the British. Frustrated members of failed commissions or authors of compromise formulae pointed the finger outwards at British divide and rule tactics with some justification; but although they might have claimed deliberate conspiracy on the part of the government, there was no longer any need for a conspiracy: the structures were in place to amplify and direct politics towards sectarianism, and the only way out was to opt out of those structures altogether.

From 1928 to 1935, the long and tortuous process of discussing a new Government of India Act ground on. Jawaharlal was quick to spot a trend and to give it a description: the national movement, if there was to be one, should not get into the pattern of discussing the details of piecemeal or gradual constitutional reforms. It was essential that the right of a British government to decide on the future of India must not be conceded in any way, and to agree to discuss details would indeed be to concede that right. In this way, the government was still able to set the agenda to which Indians would be forced to respond. This would perpetuate a curious theatrical game played out before an actual or imagined imperial audience, of declaration and counter-declaration of the Indians' fitness to rule themselves.

Two processes were henceforth to be discerned in Indian politics. One was that of formal politics set up and manipulated by British governments in India and in Britain. The other sought to organise popular movements and speak for underprivileged groups in Indian society – with varying degrees of success. Jawaharlal, always a clearer thinker than a decisive actor, sympathised with the latter trend even as he continually found himself embroiled in the former; his clearest statements were accompanied by his most compromising and ineffectual political actions.

FINDING A VOICE

The Nehru Report had accepted dominion status on the basis that this should be granted within a year, failing which the Congress would raise the stakes and demand complete independence. That year passed without a clear response from the government; and in Lahore, at midnight on December 31, 1929, the Congress passed the *Purna Swaraj* Resolution – this was rendered in English as 'complete independence' and was, henceforth, to be the goal of the Congress as an organisation. This was Jawaharlal's resolution from two years before; now, as Congress president, he had his way. On January 26, 1930, 'Independence Day' was celebrated across India, with everyone called upon to take an Independence Pledge; the national flag (at the time, this was the flag of the Indian National Congress) was unfurled, and processions and public meetings were held.

Even this victory was only narrowly secured. In October 1929, the viceroy, Lord Irwin, had declared that dominion status was the logical goal for India, and promised that after the publication of the Simon Commission's report, there would be a round table conference, with various Indian interests represented, to discuss the proposals. Gandhi, convinced of Irwin's good intentions, decided that the Congress should join the Liberals and other moderates in responding positively, through the so-called 'Delhi Manifesto', setting out conditions for cooperation: among them a general amnesty for political prisoners, adequate representation for progressive political organisations at the conference, and an agenda that did not discuss *when* dominion status was to be established, but the details of a scheme for a dominion constitution. Even the Nehru Report had gone further than this.

In May 1929, Gandhi had pushed Jawaharlal upwards to the position of Congress president, from general secretary of the All-India Congress Committee. For Gandhi this was a means of controlling his young protégé. Gandhi was only too aware of his power over the younger man who called him *Bapu*. On the issue of the response to Irwin's statement, Jawaharlal had signed the 'Delhi Manifesto', and had been persuaded not to resign from his official positions in Congress on the grounds that the British would never accept the conditions. Gandhi knew, therefore, that Jawaharlal's revolutionary zeal could be curbed by the nature of the office to which he was appointed.

At Lahore, Jawaharlal's presidential speech acknowledged that he was not the Congress's favoured choice for the job. Nonetheless, he used the speech as a manifesto: he was a socialist and a republican, no believer in kings and princes either of the hereditary kind or of the new, capitalist kind. The problems of India could not be solved by a narrow nationalism, but by socialism. With this in mind, he advocated that the Indian National Congress and the All-India Trades Union Congress should work together. In 1929, Jawaharlal had also been elected the president of the AITUC, a platform he used, among other things, to criticise the anti-worker orientation of the second Labour government in Britain. But he sent out conflicting signals. The previous year he had attended the annual AITUC session at Jharia as a delegate and had piloted a resolution affiliating the AITUC to the League against Imperialism; he had spent the intervening year publicly denying that the LAI was a communist organisation, preferring instead to say that although there were communists in it, it was an organisation independent of the CP. Now, as a president with no trade union experience at all, he appeared as adjudicator between those who wished to affiliate the AITUC to the Second International and those who wished to affiliate the AITUC to the Third International. He advocated neither: the Second International was too concerned with being anti-communist, the Third had recently been proved wrong in China when the Guomindang had turned on its communist allies, and it would be dangerous to be bound by its methods even if one had (as he had) sympathy for the communist point of view.

Within the Indian National Congress, as far as practical politics was concerned, the initiative remained with the old guard. Jawaharlal was entrusted with building up Provincial Congress Committees, with implementing the Gandhian 'constructive programme' of spinning and weaving, and – along with Subhas Chandra Bose, the Bengali Congressman whose popularity had already given the government considerable cause for alarm – with organising the Congress Volunteer Corps to work in villages and among city labourers. (The 'Hindustani Seva Dal', as it was also known, had been set up in December 1923 to provide 'a well-disciplined all-India corps trained to do national work under the general guidance of the Congress';[6] at the time there had been some opposition to a militarised element in the Congress, but Jawaharlal was not among that opposition.) The last appealed slightly more to Jawaharlal, for this opened out the possibility for political propaganda among the masses, conducted by a dedicated band of young men and women. But the All-India Congress Committee resolution that authorised this had been passed more to fob off a troublemaker than as serious politics: after all, the Volunteer Corps were supposed to be loyal to the 'constructive programme'.

This was an important moment in the history of the Indian nationalist movement. Many were looking for a new orientation. The problem of the increasing influence of the vested interests of businessmen and large landowners within the Congress seemed troubling. An independent dissatisfaction with Congress politics and a separate mobilisation on the left could potentially come together. The intellectual coherence of a socialist position – certainly as opposed to a Gandhian one – also appealed to some of the younger members of Congress. On the other hand, there was a definite fear that Jawaharlal was leading Congress increasingly towards the position of the communists; this fear united capitalists and government. The increasing organisational success of the emerging Indian communist movement had begun to create British panic, leading to 'conspiracy' cases against communists. By this time the British tendency to attribute every form of unrest or anti-government activity to 'Bolsheviks' had subsided slightly in favour of a tactic that sought to distinguish communists from non-communists with a view to divide and rule; but the full weight of the state's repressive machinery was always available for use against communists.

From 1929 onwards, the infamous Meerut Conspiracy Case ran its course. This was the culmination of a general trawl of India to find political agitators who could be indicted, arrested and sentenced as communists; various such agitators were rounded up, including a number of British communists. The government had intended to prosecute Jawaharlal as a communist himself, but they could not find the requisite evidence, in part because the intercepted internal correspondence of communists themselves revealed that they did not take Jawaharlal's socialist statements very seriously. Jawaharlal was, however, on the defence committee, as was his father; but the defence committee did not last long, its demise attributed by Jawaharlal to a lack of coordination: 'There were different types of people among these, with different types of defences, and often there was an utter absence of harmony among them.'[7] The case eventually led, five years later, to the banning of the Communist Party of India.

THE CIVIL DISOBEDIENCE MOVEMENT

The Lahore Congress's full session had authorised the All-India Congress Committee to start a programme of civil disobedience at any point it deemed fit – in effect, leaving decisions of timing and aims to Gandhi, for civil disobedience was his own creation and most people agreed that such tactics required Gandhi himself at the head. Gandhi, however, seemed to be in no hurry to start a movement. Those sceptical of his intentions have pointed out that in the years 1928 and 1929, with strikes and labour militancy at its height, Gandhi's starting up of a movement would have led rapidly to a situation in which he could no longer control its directions – and he was particularly keen on keeping control.

In February 1930, Gandhi selected his moment, and his issue: salt. This was a non-divisive and emotive issue: the government had a monopoly on the manufacture of salt, and its tax on salt was paid by all Indians. It was also a symbolic issue (in 1931, the salt tax was actually increased and no one said very much about it). Earlier that month, Gandhi had placed a strange conglomeration of demands before the viceroy, suggesting that there would be no need for civil disobedience if these could be met, and that the Congress would cooperate in constitutional discussions. For Gandhi's allies in the Congress, including the Nehrus, his behaviour was getting more and more eccentric, and now things were beginning to border on the ridiculous. Far from upholding the principles of the Purna Swaraj resolution, here was Gandhi bargaining with the British government about lesser details: the salt tax should be abolished, total prohibition should be imposed on the sale of alcohol, the rupee should be devalued from 1s 6d to 1s 4d, there should be a protective tariff on foreign cloth and land revenue should be reduced. The more substantive of these smelt uncomfortably like a list of business conditions drawn up by Gandhi's businessmen friends, G.D. Birla and Sir Purshotamdas Thakurdas. A further demand, that political prisoners be released, was more radical; but Gandhi seemed far less interested in this. Once the movement began, demands directed at the government also merged with Gandhi's interest in the moral policing of the masses: the people should refrain from drinking alcohol and smoking *ganja* (marijuana) and generally behave in a disciplined and non-violent manner.

On March 12, the Salt March, with which Gandhi kick-started civil disobedience, began at his Sabarmati Ashram. Gandhi had asked that only those morally committed to *ahimsa* and not those who used it as an expedient tactic should accompany him on the march; 71 male followers from the ashram began the 240-mile march to the sea with him. On April 6, 1930, Gandhi walked into the sea at Dandi and collected salt, thereby breaking the government's monopoly. Civil disobedience in 1930 relied on two main planks: the salt campaign, involving illegal production of salt and *satyagraha* in front of government salt works (provoking violent retaliation against non-violent agitators), and boycott and burning of foreign textiles. Huge numbers of people responded to the call for civil disobedience, confirming to the Congress and to the outside world that faith in Gandhi as a mass mobiliser was not misplaced.

Civil disobedience was fuelled and given momentum by the conjunctural situation of depression-induced peasant poverty; India was by 1930 feeling the onset of the Great Depression. Agricultural prices had already begun to fall by 1927, devastating for an economy forcibly commercialised before self-sufficiency in food had been achieved, and in which the revenue and rent demands were set in cash. Cultivators were faced with an impossible task: their produce was not worth enough on the market to meet the cash demands, even if they deprived themselves of food to attempt to sell it to raise money. Moneylenders did not wish to lend on the security of land, which they felt was not worth enough because of low prices for agricultural products. Instead, they called in their loans – which they could only do because peasants were forced to make distress sales of hoarded gold, the traditional form of savings in countries with uncertain conditions.

Financial readjustments were of course required in such a situation. The government realistically recognised that to attempt to collect the full amount of tax due to them would be impossible and reduced taxation rates. Not all landlords were immediately willing to pass the relief down to their tenants, however, and landlord–tenant tensions also created the conditions for a landscape of political unrest in the countryside, in which *kisan sabhas* (peasant associations), *krishak samities* (peasant committees) and *praja samities* (tenant-farmers' committees) were organised and amalgamated into a vibrant movement. But Gandhi's principle of never pitting Indian against Indian ruled out no-rent campaigns except in the most exceptional circumstances; he preferred no-revenue campaigns that targeted the government as the enemy.

Once again, the visible successes of Gandhian tactics created great hopes. The trouble was, Muslims did not participate in large numbers – Gandhi's Hindu holy man imagery was not particularly conducive to appealing to a Muslim cultural milieu, even if a Muslim was not a religious Muslim. Nor did the urban working classes participate. On the other hand, women, teenagers and students joined in larger numbers than during the Non-Cooperation-Khilafat agitations of 1920–2. And once again, Gandhi's usefulness as a symbol around which to mobilise was visible. One of the most audacious acts of 1930 was in Chittagong in Bengal in April, where a group of terrorists led by one Surjya Sen seized the local armoury and issued a proclamation of independence in Gandhi's name, hardly an act of non-violence. Throughout the late 1920s and

1930s, the Bengal terrorist movement, mirrored by that in the Punjab, was far more disturbing to British officials than Gandhi's movements: many middle- and low-ranking British officials were killed. Gandhi later expressed his horror at the fact that there were several women terrorists – women were nurturing by nature, how could they possibly do something so unnatural as kill people? But during the movement, although there was enough violent resistance to far outweigh the violence of 1922, he made no effort to call off the movement on the grounds of its violence.

This time around, the British government did not wait as long as in 1922 before interning the Congress leaders. For Gandhi, they selected an obsolete law of 1827, under which no trial was necessary, thereby avoiding giving him another public forum from which to denounce British rule. The Nehrus were also, inevitably, imprisoned. This time, the Nehru family's participation in politics had been widened by Kamala Nehru's role in organising women to come forward in large numbers to participate in *satyagraha*; she was arrested on New Year's Day, 1931, and awarded the dignity of a jail sentence to go with her work. Jawaharlal found this curiously touching, and felt closer to his wife than he had ever been able to before. For her part, Kamala was proud, as she put it, to join her husband in his struggle and in jail – a curious route to the heart of a man to whom she had now been married for nearly fifteen years.

Jawaharlal's jail notebooks provide an overwhelming sense of the slowness of life in jail, but also an indication of why anti-colonial nationalists could afford the luxury of being intellectuals: they had much time for books. From April 14 to October 11, 1930, and again from October 19, 1930 to January, 1931, Jawaharlal was in prison. The tedium of life could be relieved to some extent by self-education. Jawaharlal read lots of Shakespeare, a number of books on China, a book on eugenics, Oswald Spengler's *Decline of the West*, Emil Ludwig's historical biographies. He read Gandhi's influences, Ruskin and Carlyle, also Bukharin's *Historical Materialism*, Kropotkin's *The Great French Revolution*, Trotsky, *My Life*, much Bernard Shaw, Ramakrishna's *Hindu View of Life*, a great deal of history, French literature (Voltaire, Rabelais, Balzac, Proust, Baudelaire), Sappho, James Joyce, William Morris, Henrik Ibsen, Nietzsche's *Beyond Good and Evil*, R.H. Tawney's *Religion and the Rise of Capitalism*. To educate his visual senses, he had books containing reproductions of the works of Auguste Rodin and Aubrey Beardsley.[8] Apart from this, there were endless rhythms at the spinning wheel. 'One

month of spinning in Naini Prison completed today [May 26, 1930].
Have spun 8,520 yards during this period.'[9]

Observing events as best he could from his cell, Jawaharlal was still
actively thinking on political issues. The civil disobedience movement,
he felt, must be carried on to the end – otherwise it would be a wasted
effort. He made notes on the constitutional proposals being discussed:
'Federation – social change far more difficult than ever now. Nothing
but a bloody revolution will then be able to bring it about.'[10] The
proposed federation was weighted in favour of 'stability' through the
princely states appointing their own representatives alongside the elected
representatives (though on a limited property franchise) of the British
Indian provinces.

This was to be Motilal's last campaign against British rule. Released
from prison on September 8, 1930, after ten weeks in prison due to
ill health (despite his protests that he would not accept special treatment),
he died not long afterwards. Jawaharlal was released on 26 January, 1931,
and was able to spend a few last days with his father. The Congress
Working Committee was meeting in Allahabad, at the Nehrus' house
that was now also the headquarters of the Congress; many Congressmen
came to see the old man who they knew they would not see again. 'There
he sat,' Jawaharlal recalled, 'like an old lion mortally wounded and with
his physical strength almost gone, but still very leonine and kingly.'
Motilal died at a Lucknow hospital on February 6, 1931. The loss of
Motilal affected Jawaharlal strongly; father and son had drawn closer than
ever before. 'I found it difficult to realise that he had gone,' Jawaharlal
noted; he believed that it was 'the wonderfully soothing and healing
presence of Gandhiji' that saw him and his family through those difficult
times.[11]

A few weeks later Gandhi – again – called off the movement. He
had agreed to discuss constitutional reforms with the viceroy in February,
and by March 5 he had unilaterally suspended civil disobedience.
Circumstantial evidence points clearly to the fact that he was under
pressure from businessmen: a deal at this stage might secure benefits,
whereas the disorder created by the movement was disrupting business
conditions. Jawaharlal recalled a sense of *déjà vu* at this second disappointment. 'This is the way the world ends,' he was to wryly observe,
quoting T.S. Eliot, 'not with a bang but with a whimper.'[12] Had his father
been alive, he was heard to say, such a situation would not have arisen

again – a suggestion that seemed to hurt Gandhi. It was not only Jawaharlal who was beginning to feel increasingly frustrated and annoyed that Gandhi's personal and moral experiments were to be projected onto the country at large, to be undertaken and withdrawn seemingly entirely upon his personal whims. To add insult to injury, Gandhi even seemed willing to abandon his own clause about political prisoners: despite his pleas, on March 23, 1931, the British government executed Bhagat Singh and two of his comrades.

But for all his anger and disappointment, Jawaharlal was unable and unwilling to become a focal point of anti-Gandhi tendencies in the Congress; when Gandhi astutely suggested that Jawaharlal move the resolution at the Karachi Congress in March that the Congress (again retrospectively) ratify the Gandhi–Irwin Pact, he did so, throwing his now slightly more substantial political weight behind the compromise that he opposed so strongly. Jawaharlal's personal and political feelings were now severely out of joint. Gandhi, after all, was the alternative father figure in whom Jawaharlal had sought solace after Motilal's death, and the Mahatma was able to rely on his emotional dependence.

Gandhi duly attended the Second Round Table Conference in London to discuss the new Constitution in the autumn of 1931. The First Round Table Conference had taken place without the Congress, as the Third was to do the following year. Gandhi achieved nothing by attending as the sole representative of the Congress; he had however, by going to London, given the proceedings greater legitimacy – this was Lord Irwin's victory. The Congress had to accept being treated as one among many Indian 'interests' at the conference, rather than as the party with the largest mass base in the country; Gandhi's lone voice could carry no weight even with the support of his Indian businessmen friends. Returning to India, Gandhi tried to re-start civil disobedience (which nominally ran on from 1932 to 1934), but the momentum had been lost. Congress leaders were re-arrested when it was thought necessary, and the Constitution-making process went ahead now more as an internal issue of British administrators who disagreed on how best to hold India to the Empire than as a problem that Indians ought to be allowed to be concerned with. British and Indian businessmen, for their part, became entangled in market-sharing negotiations, aimed at shutting other competitors such as the Japanese out of Indian markets. The negotiations failed.

The Round Table Conferences confirmed what they had been set up to confirm – that Indians could not agree amongst themselves. In 1932, a 'Communal Award' designed by British Prime Minister Ramsay Macdonald perpetuated separate electorates for Muslims and proposed to extend the logic of protecting minorities in this way to the 'Backward Castes', untouchables and low castes in the 'Hindu' social order. According to the logic of colonial representation, the Backward Castes had a spokes-man who would speak for those who could not speak for themselves: Dr B.R. Ambedkar, who had studied economics and had a PhD in public finance from Columbia University in New York; he was of low-caste origin and had managed to finance his higher education through the patronage of the ruler of the Princely State of Baroda. Ambedkar wished to utilise British state power to improve the position of backward castes, and accepted the British award of special status. But here Gandhi intervened in a way he had been unable within the rules of the Conferences themselves – he went on a 'fast unto death'.

Gandhi's claim was that if 'Backward Castes' were recognised as a separate community, it would be a failure of 'Hindus' to have a properly humane and inclusive religion. The fact that many of these castes had been so systematically excluded from mainstream 'Hindu' society as to never have properly belonged to the category 'Hindu' at all, or that the category 'Hindu' was itself to a large extent a neologism, was not considered. Gandhi had, of course, campaigned for the abolition of caste restrictions among Hindus. But the fact that this continued to be a long and hard task was itself evidence that the 'Backward Castes' were not about to be welcomed into 'Hindu' society overnight. Be that as it may, Ambedkar gave in and signed the 'Poona Pact': the Backward Castes would not be separately represented, and in effect they were to be Hindus. Perhaps unwittingly, Gandhi had greatly strengthened the position of Hindus in the colonial numbers game that was to be so important a feature of politics in the last stages of colonial rule. Ambedkar was extremely bitter about the fact that Gandhi had outmanoeuvred him: he did not want to be responsible for the great man's death and ever afterwards be considered a traitor to his country. A fact that seemed to once again escape unnoticed was how important the *selected* representatives of 'communities' were in deciding the fate of those 'communities'.

JAIL AGAIN, AND A EUROPEAN INTERLUDE: KAMALA'S DEATH

By the end of 1931, Jawaharlal was behind bars again, arrested on December 26 and sentenced to two years' imprisonment for organising and supporting agrarian agitation in the United Provinces. For him, jail was getting more and more familiar. Once again, he read books, and wrote letters to Indira, his daughter, in the form of essays on history (later published as *Glimpses of World History*). He was released on August 30, 1933, twelve days early – his mother was seriously ill (she eventually died, after a long illness, in January 1938).

Jawaharlal used his time outside jail to publicly denounce 'communal' groups, being particularly harsh on Hindu communalism as organised in the Hindu Mahasabha. He was also critical of Muslim communalism, but took the view that to some extent it was understandable because minority communities are afraid of the majority. This was to be a recurrent theme in his public pronouncements – the responsibility of the majority towards the minority.

In India and outside, impatience with Nehru was building up among the left. 'They feel that you are too weak,' Vithalbhai Patel had reported to Jawaharlal in 1931.[13] A few left-wing resolutions of no particular practical significance at annual Congress sessions were poor evidence of commitment. In October 1933, Jawaharlal's serialised thoughts on *Whither India?*, thereafter published in pamphlet form, sought to answer the vexing question of what was to come after independence: surely, socialism – the end of 'exploitation of nation by nation and class by class', and the beginning of a redistribution of wealth among the masses. The question that had hitherto been asked, of whether socialism ought to be brought about gradually or by violent revolution, was no longer all that relevant: the Depression had shown that the only viable social system would have to be one of socialism, as capitalism had been found wanting and was beginning to collapse of its own accord.[14] This statement of political intent earned him a reprieve of sorts in left-wing circles that had increasingly begun to doubt his intentions: 'I had decided,' one union leader wrote to him, ' . . . no more to burn incense to a leader whose feelings were so correct, but actions halting.'[15]

Government sources in this period still seemed to regard Jawaharlal as a communist, a Leninist who wished to be a Lenin. Examining his speeches for evidence that could help them put him back in prison they eventually found something useful. In his speech to the AITUC at Kanpur in December 1933, and again in January 1934 in Calcutta, he had denounced imperialism. For this he was arrested on February 12 in Allahabad, brought to Calcutta, tried for sedition, and sentenced on February 16 to two years' simple imprisonment. 'Individuals sometimes misbehave in this imperfect world of ours,' Jawaharlal noted in his statement to the court; 'so also officials and those in power. Crowds and mobs of people also lose control of themselves sometimes and misbehave. But it is a terrible thing when an organised Government begins to behave like an excited mob; when brutal and vengeful and uncivilised behaviour becomes the normal temper of a Government.'[16]

From prison, Jawaharlal attempted to fulfil his parental duties by getting Indira into Vishwa Bharati, Rabindranath Tagore's university at Shantiniketan. Her education had suffered, he wrote in his statement accompanying her application, due to political troubles that had in turn caused domestic upheavals. Her parents had tried to find out what her own inclinations were, but had been unable to do so. She should do something at university that 'would enable her to do some socially useful work in after life efficiently, and at the same time enable her to be economically independent. She is not likely to have an unearned income and it is not considered desirable by her parents that she should depend for her subsistence on a husband or others.'[17] At some point, it was envisaged that Indira should continue her education abroad in England or on the Continent. (Eventually, in 1937, through Harold Laski's good offices, Indira was able to go to Somerville College, Oxford, after failing the entrance examination. She did not take a degree.)

Jawaharlal was let out of prison for eleven days in August 1934, when his wife was seriously ill (she had had recurrent tuberculosis from 1920 onwards, and had never been completely healthy thereafter; it is recorded, in a society that judged women by their fertility, that in 1925 an infant son born to her had died, and in 1928 she had had a miscarriage). This time she made a recovery, and Jawaharlal was put back in jail. From June 1934 to February 1935, Jawaharlal used his time in jail to write an autobiography (it was published in 1936 under that simple title). This was a curious attempt at the genre: the private person does not altogether emerge, but personal stories are told to make political points. Admittedly, the Indian national movement, with which Jawaharlal's generation had

had their lives inextricably intertwined, and in which so many of their memories and personal experiences were deeply embedded, left little time for a personal life, all personal events being experienced through the political. From the 1920s, the Congress's Gandhian training required that the personal was theatrically proclaimed to the outside world as the political. Gandhi's exhibitionism of the soul required that he present his personal development as political progress; Jawaharlal's autobiography did not take this quite as far.

In September 1935, Jawaharlal found himself released from prison: Kamala was ill again and had been for some time in Europe for treatment. On 2 September, her doctor had informed Jawaharlal and the government of India that she would not live long. The government's generosity had been pushed strongly from behind the scenes by powerful forces. From November 1934, Labour Party Members of Parliament, including Clement Attlee, had interceded with the Secretary of State for India to allow Nehru to take his sick wife to Europe. But Nehru had refused special treatment that was denied to other, lesser, prisoners. The seriousness of Kamala's condition made him change his mind. What was indicated by these moves, however, was that some sections of British official opinion already saw in Nehru the future leader of independent India, and many of them were building bridges in order better to deal with him later. The Labour Party's famous 'weekend at Filkins' in 1938, at which they discussed with Nehru the terms on which a Labour government would be willing to transfer power to India, was the logical continuation of these early overtures.

Nehru (he could now, after his father's death, legitimately claim that name alone) took a plane to Germany to join Kamala in Badenweiler, in the Black Forest, on the understanding that he could not return to India before his sentence expired in February 1936. The Nehrus then moved to Lausanne in Switzerland. In Lausanne, coincidentally, Nehru met Rajani Palme Dutt, who was visiting a fellow CPGB member, Ben Bradley, at the same spa; they spent three days together discussing politics. Nehru also found time to visit Britain in November 1935, and again in January 1936, resuming old contacts and making new ones: he met, for instance, Paul Robeson through the good offices of Cedric Dover, an active member of the Congress Socialist Party then in London.[18] Dover encouraged Nehru to read more about Soviet policies towards the 'nationalities', and promised 'the creation of a Eurasian alliance in the anti-imperialist struggle' on his return to India (Dover himself was a Eurasian, or an 'Anglo-Indian' as the revised and more polite terminology of the new Government of India Act put it, although by this time the original 'Anglo-Indians' referred to themselves as 'Europeans').[19]

The Government of India Act of 1935 had finally been passed. It had had a stormy history, raising the bogey in Britain of the government giving away India at a time (during the Depression) when British industry most needed its Indian markets, and in India of a permanently-entrenched system of divide and rule that the British government had enshrined in the functioning of the constitution, enabling Britain to pose as perpetual referee of Indian conflicts and indefinitely defer meaningful self-government. The process that had begun with the Statutory Commission's multi-volume report, passed through three Round Table Conferences, a Parliamentary Select Committee and a White Paper, had outlived two governments (the Conservatives who had appointed the Simon Commission, and the Labour government of 1929–31) and almost a third (the coalitional National Government formed to deal with the Depression) in Britain before it was passed. In its final form, it set out a scheme of provincial autonomy, in which British Indian provinces were to be ruled by elected Indian ministries, but the governor would have reserve powers to take over the running of the province if he saw fit. Separate electorates were maintained; with the vastly raised stakes of the 1935 Act, providing as it did the right to control British Indian provinces with the mandate of an electorate set at about 16% on average, this could potentially lead to 'communal' discrimination in matters of employment, or worse, to violence condoned by one 'community' who controlled the government against another. There were, moreover, 'safeguards' for British business and financial interests, and British businessmen and the 'European community' were also granted reserved seats and over-representation in legislatures – as Indian 'minorities'. One such businessman, Sir Edward Benthall, who had been instrumental in campaigning at the Round Table Conferences for Europeans in India to be recognised as an Indian minority and thereby to qualify for safeguards as had the Backward Castes and the Muslims, had reassured his colleagues that as long as 'Europeans' controlled the Finance, Commerce and Home departments, Britain could rule India indefinitely even if all other posts and all the provinces were to be ruled by Indians. In the end, even this limited scenario did not arise: the princes were greatly suspicious of the federal provisions that placed them in a central chamber alongside democratically elected members and refused to accept them, so the Centre continued to be based on the old constitution.

Kamala Nehru died on February 28, 1936. Carrying her ashes, Nehru returned to India in March 1936 via Rome. Here again he saw evidence of his growing international importance. Signor Mussolini himself tried to meet him when he was in transit at Rome airport, but he managed to avoid the meeting. Earlier, the Italian Consul at Lausanne had visited Nehru to give him Mussolini's personal message of sympathy and condolence after Kamala's death. 'The Duce is evidently interested in me,' Nehru observed wryly to one of his communist friends.[20]

While Nehru was in Switzerland, a fellow exile from India was also in Europe: Subhas Chandra Bose was living in Vienna. Bose had, like Nehru, spent the past years in and out of British colonial jails – notably in Mandalay from 1924 to 1927, where he had been imprisoned without trial on suspicion of supporting the Bengal terrorist movement. Despite being in prison so often and for so long, he had managed to build up a formidable following and was seen as a particularly effective propagandist and organiser. Imprisoned again in 1930 during the Civil Disobedience Movement, he succeeded in being elected mayor of Calcutta even though he had to carry out his campaign from jail. In prison once again from 1932–3, he was released on grounds of ill health on condition that he go into exile in Europe – an offer he had refused in the 1920s – and he had briefly been allowed to return to India in 1934 for a few days when his father died, only to be externed again. Now he asked Nehru whether he ought not to return to India, knowing well that he would probably be arrested immediately upon his return. Nehru advised him to return; Bose agreed, adding that he would throw his weight behind Nehru for leadership of the national struggle and the Congress.

The two discussed Indian politics, and agreed that the two main tasks would be to prevent the Congress from accepting office under the new constitution, and to broaden the composition of the Congress's 'Cabinet', the Working Committee. Bose saw for Nehru a major role in this. '[Y]ou are the only one to whom we can look up to [sic] for leading the Congress in a progressive direction,' Bose wrote. He was particularly astute regarding the internal equations in the Congress: 'even Mahatma Gandhi will be more accommodating towards you than towards anybody else.

I earnestly hope that you will fully utilise the strength of your public position in making decisions. Please do not consider your position to be weaker than it really is. Gandhiji will never take a stand which will alienate you.'[21] Bose also returned to India in March 1936, and was promptly arrested and imprisoned again; he remained in prison until March 18, 1937.

CONGRESS EQUATIONS

Nehru returned to a very different political environment from that he had known before his interludes in jail and in Europe. Disappointment with Gandhi's leadership had inaugurated a new phase in Indian nationalist politics. Disagreements about the validity of Gandhi's political views had often been combined with a faith in Gandhian tactics, but Gandhi's tendency to unilaterally call off a movement, his compromises at the moments of the movements' greatest strengths, had disillusioned too many. They had already been looking at other forms of political movement and left-wing, or more specifically socialist, ideas, Marxian or other, were beginning to make an impact (as were, also, some more authoritarian trends drawn from European fascism — but which did not come to dominate Indian nationalism at the time).

From 1934, Gandhi withdrew from active Congress politics to the relative safety of his 'constructive programme'; the time was ripe for a move to explicitly establish a Congress left. In 1934, the Congress Socialist Party (CSP) was founded as a group within the Congress, and called for the formation of a United Front of all anti-imperialist forces, including the Communist Party of India. The Communists, who had just been banned, joined the CSP a year later, when the CPI adopted the Comintern's Popular Front policy (its earlier 'class against class' line had seen Nehru expelled from the League Against Imperialism in 1931 for being too involved with bourgeois nationalism; even Nehru admitted that the League had 'had ample provocation').[22] The CPI then interpreted the directive to unite with bourgeois democratic forces against fascism as a directive to unite against imperialism. The reasoning was simple: if fascism was capitalism in crisis in a developed country, and imperialism was capitalism abroad, in the absence of a serious fascist threat in the colonised country, it was logical that the popular front be formed against imperialism.

The CSP as it was constituted in 1934 already contained Marxist and non-Marxist, even anti-Marxist, socialists. Its most influential spokesman was Jayaprakash Narayan, who as a student in the 1920s at Madison, Wisconsin, had been a member of the Communist Party of the United States of America. Jayaprakash Narayan explicitly adopted a Marxist and a Leninist programme and framework of analysis, claiming that the CSP remained part of the Congress as a matter of strategy and sought to win over those of its members who were 'objectively anti-imperialist' – 'petty-bourgeois' elements and peasants. The only force capable of fighting imperialism was the masses 'because they are not dependent on it'; while the Indian bourgeoisie was 'not in a position to play a revolutionary role' due to its close ties with and dependence upon imperialism.[23] The CSP therefore sought to work together with the trade union movement and the growing *kisan* movement, now organised in *kisan sabhas* with an all-Indian leadership. (The *kisan* movement was perfectly happy to affiliate themselves to the CSP, but its leaders did not wish to be bound by the rules of the Congress organisation, because they felt this would curtail both their freedom of action and the *kisan* movement's radical content.)

At the same time, the first battle to be won was that against British imperialism, for national independence. The CSP's role was therefore to work within the Congress, the main anti-imperialist organisation in India, for the attainment of independence, while at the same time moving the Congress towards the left to prepare it for the later struggle for socialism that was to take place after the attainment of independence. The CSP was a relatively small group, but its members believed it was destined to grow, although, they acknowledged, it was unrealistic to expect a socialist group to dominate the Congress in the near future. The CSP appeared to take the possibility of fascism in India more seriously than the CPI. They sought to mobilise the petty-bourgeoisie in unison with the proletariat and the peasantry, arguing that the former were a disillusioned class due to large-scale unemployment; some sections of them suffered, like the working class, and were capable of being either on the side of fascism or of socialism, depending on the leadership offered to them.

Some of this new cluster of socialists had turned to the CSP largely through an admiration for the achievements of that other 'backward' country emerging from backwardness, the Soviet Union. News of Soviet miracles with the Five-Year Plan and collectivisation, and the good press the USSR was beginning to get even among the respectable left in the light of the USSR's immunity to the economic disasters the Depression had brought to the rest of the world, played a large role in this. Others were far more moderate, emerging from their student days in England with an affinity towards Fabian socialism or merely defecting from the Gandhians in the hope of something more radical and less compromising in every important situation. Indeed, some of them hoped to get Gandhi involved in the CSP by convincing him of their point of view: Gandhi remained to them a great and popular leader, unfortunately too reticent to take his own tactics to their logical conclusion. They were particularly frustrated by his insistence that industrialisation was inherently evil, and that India's future lay in reviving her village industries, using only very basic technology, and decentralising state power so that the relevant economic and political unit was the village.

For the CSP, it seemed self-evident that the person to work with in the higher ranks of the Congress was Jawaharlal Nehru. The CSP saw him as one of them, their strategy of raising the profile of the left crucially dependent on what they hoped Nehru would do for them. Consequently, Jawaharlal acted as a sounding board and a junction box for many of the ideas and programmes of the left; as one regarded as their spokesmen, he was often instrumental in the acceptance or rejection of these ideas as strategy or potential policy. He was involved in influencing the political ideas of a number of people. Conversely, it was also important for the CSP to continue to educate Jawaharlal so that he was in tune with their ideas and goals. This was especially important because for all their hopes and for all his expressions of sympathy, Jawaharlal never joined the CSP.

It was also in this period, however, that Nehru became the spokesman for, and the political focal point of, self-proclaimedly 'modern' trends in Indian politics, as opposed to the 'indigenist' trends. The former cut across conventional left–right boundaries, with industrialists, technocrats and socialists sharing a faith in 'modern' goals – in practice, that of an industrialised, independent and self-sufficient state – while Gandhians as well as a number of Hindu sectarians proclaimed faith in a society and polity compatible with 'indigenous' traditions, although they defined this differently and not always consistently, and certainly refused to concede the point that their goals were less 'modern'. This left Jawaharlal with two main roles to juggle, overlapping but often in contradiction: the simply 'modern', pro-industrialisation and pro-technology one, and the more politically committed 'socialist' one. Jawaharlal's juggling of the mutually entangled roles of 'modernist' and 'socialist' left much to be desired.

The nationalist movement had from the mid-nineteenth century consistently claimed the right to industrialise India; the business interests that now worked with the right wing of the Congress, pouring substantial funds into the Congress coffers, could legitimately claim to be heirs to this line of thinking. From their point of view, the government had to be pressurised to provide better conditions for the growth and development of industry in India. In as much as such demands were 'national' demands, they could expect support from the Congress as a whole. The left wing of the Congress often found itself in the position of backing capitalists' demands as 'national' ones while at the same time opposing capitalists' everyday activities of trying to bring down wages, keep flexible working hours and therefore a flexible workforce, and providing extremely poor working conditions. Businessmen sometimes used the infant-industry argument in an instrumental manner: better working conditions could only be provided at a later stage of development of industry, for the early industrialisers had had a free hand to exploit their labour force in the early days of the industrial revolution. The left's duty was to disaggregate what it considered business's legitimate national demands from what it regarded as illegitimate exploitation of labour in the name of national advancement – taking it back to the general argument that capitalists were only provisionally anti-imperialist, when they needed to extract further concessions from the government by working with the national movement. Paradoxically, the legitimacy of capitalists within the Congress was provided by Gandhi's 'trusteeship' theory – the rich held their wealth as 'trustees' of the nation – which also meant that the pro-capitalist right wing of the Congress referred to itself as the 'Gandhian' wing, even as capitalists distanced themselves from Gandhi's anti-industrialisation rhetoric.

Jawaharlal's contributions to the Congress left often remained characteristically intellectual: as a journalist and pamphleteer, and as organiser of the circulation of left-wing propaganda. Jawaharlal was on the board of editors, alongside several Congress Socialists, of the National Publications Society, whose aim was to publish literature 'for the enlightenment of the masses, and dealing with day-to-day problems that affect them'.[24] Jawaharlal's patronising attitude towards the people he sought to enlighten was largely unchanged from his Gandhian days. The Socialist

Book Club, one of his initiatives (modelled on the Left Book Club in Britain, of which he was a member), proposed to provide 'socialist classics' suitably 'abridged' for Indian readers.[25] (Nehru's membership of the Left Book Club was more notional than real; many of its books did not get to him due to Indian censorship regulations that empowered Customs to confiscate books that were deemed subversive: 'apparently Mr Gollancz's [the publisher's] name is not liked by the customs officials in India').[26]

In 1936, Jawaharlal, once again Congress president, made further radical statements of a socialist nature, alarming a number of right wing Congressmen and businessmen, who came out in the press against his preaching of 'class hatred'. Gandhi, who had once again been instrumental in elevating Jawaharlal to the presidency, calmed them down, thereby averting a major crisis in Congress unity, pointing out that the Working Committee was dominated by 'Gandhians', and that Nehru continued to be bound by the principles accepted by the Congress and by the office to which he had been elected. Gandhi was firmly of the belief that the best way to control Jawaharlal's radicalism was to imprison him within the Congress's higher ranks. This would confine his activities to words. Nor did Gandhi necessarily take his political commitment very seriously. 'I would,' he wrote to the Quaker, Agatha Harrison, one of the coordinators of the case for Indian independence in Britain, 'strain every nerve to prevent a class war. So would he, I expect. But he does not believe it to be possible to avoid it. I believe it to be perfectly possible if my method is accepted.'[27]

Whether or not Gandhi was correct in attributing to Nehru a fear of actual class war, he was correct in one respect. Jawaharlal had a remarkable capacity to sacrifice his own professed political convictions for the sake of consensus and compromise. The Congress Socialists' dependence on him to give them a voice with the so-called 'Congress High Command' was misplaced, as his commitment to party unity completely overrode his commitment to the left. The pivotal role in the Congress continued to be played by Gandhi, who had apparently retired from public life to concentrate on 'constructive work' in the villages. The right's great respect – and need – for Gandhi, the left's for Nehru, Nehru's unwillingness to take steps that might bring about an open conflict with Gandhi, and Gandhi's intermediary role became the basis of Congress's functional unity. Indian business interests, reassured by Gandhi, decided they could live with Nehru in a leadership position. Meanwhile, the British could always be relied upon to provide unifying issues of national significance.

But beneath this apparent unity, throughout the mid- to late 1930s, there continued a struggle for the heart of the Congress – a struggle that divided broadly into a left and a right. And the struggle within the Congress was also mirrored outside it. The fate of the Congress was seen as the fate of the Indian nationalist movement in microcosm. How was that nationalism to be defined – as a broad, inclusive and secular one in which all religions and regional groups could feel a sense of belonging, or a specifically upper-caste-Hindu-tinged nationalism, even when not explicitly stated in those terms? Outside the Congress, groups watched with interest and anticipation – if the right won, or seemed to be winning, the Congress would be an organisation of Hindu and upper-caste property owners, and minorities such as the Depressed Classes and Muslims could not work with or within it. Muslims who were more inclined towards social equality or radical social change than towards the Muslim *zamindar*-based social order that the Muslim League defended at the time were more comfortable with the left wing of Congress, even if they did not altogether see themselves as 'socialists'. Many of these smaller groups only contemplated working with the Congress for the same reason as the socialists had decided to work within it: the Congress was the pre-eminent nationalist body, it was an organisational platform, not a political party, and its immediate goal was a shared one of independence from British rule. But if the left won, other problems would emerge: what, in particular, would become of property owners? This question divided Muslims, Christians, Backward Castes and regional 'interest groups' amongst themselves as much as it divided 'Hindus'.

The right, for its part, was also an organised political group. One of its main organisers was the businessman G.D. Birla, the man who was widely acknowledged as having advised the Mahatma on what to say at the Round Table Conference in 1931. Birla, who had a deliberately ambiguous relationship with the Congress (he was not actually a member), had even been willing to use his contacts with British businessmen and politicians to explain to them that they had misread Gandhi. Despite appearances to the contrary, Birla argued (not in public, of course), Gandhi, far from being a radical opponent of British rule, was a friend: a moderate whose hand within the Congress ought to be strengthened against the Congress left, and against socialists and communists outside the Congress. Birla had powerful spokesmen within the Congress in men like Vallabhbhai Patel and Bhulabhai Desai, right-wingers who identified themselves as 'Gandhians', which enabled them to speak for large numbers of the rank and file who were still loyal to Gandhi.

In such equations, therefore, the British government also played a role in enabling business to have a strong political voice. Since most often for government to negotiate openly with Congress would be to concede the latter too much legitimacy, an intermediary group could be useful. This suited business well, enabling them to pose as a moderating influence (though not averse to sharing the benefits, if any, of Congress agitations) while attempting to secure smooth business conditions. The Congress's role, as business saw it, was to put pressure on the British government to extract further concessions for business; its role was not supposed to be to disrupt business conditions with support for labour agitation or wider unrest. This was of course realised by the Congress left, confirming the conviction that business was only provisionally anti-colonial. But it was not merely the Congress left that did not trust Indian businessmen. The British government also recognised the provisional and opportunist nature of Indian businessmen's support, and reserved the right to suspect the worst of them.

The Congress was thus by this time beginning to provide the acceptable face of political dissent. This has been attributed to capitalists and landlords occupying a pivotal role in Congress politics, a role enhanced by the narrow property franchise of the 1935 Government of India Act. While landlords were in a position to tilt the equation in provincial politics, big business had more of an all-India influence, being among the main financiers of the Congress organisation. And if the moderating hand of property and the responsibilities of office could make of the Congress the legitimating organisation of British imperialism, what could be better than that? For if the pre-eminent national organisation in India (whom the British were now willing to acknowledge represented the *majority* of the Indian people, even if not the minorities who the British had to stay on to protect) was a party in government, was it possible to claim any longer that Indians did not have self-rule?

THE STRUGGLE FOR THE CONGRESS: 'WRECKING' THE CONSTITUTION OR RUNNING THE EMPIRE?

One of the first tasks of the new left coalition in the Congress was to address the problem of the new Government of India Act of 1935. The CSP's line on the Act was to denounce the 'slave constitution' and refuse to have anything to do with it. But the Congress was under considerable pressure to work with the Constitution from business leaders and landlords. There was consequently considerable pressure from the right wing of the Congress to accept office under the terms of the 1935 Act. Power, they believed, was being offered to them and should be accepted.

The left's first proposal was to refuse to participate in the elections. Any participation was an acknowledgement of the validity of the constitution, which ought not to be legitimised in any way. They were defeated on this. It was then suggested that to win the elections and then refuse to fill the seats or form the government would destroy the constitutional machinery, demonstrating the Congress's popular support while exposing the fact that the constitution could not be accepted by the vast majority of people. (Nehru had, in the end, drafted the Congress's election manifesto, which *inter alia* rejected the 1935 Constitution without specifying how this could be done by contesting the elections.) In the end, neither happened; the elections, held in January and February of 1937, led to massive Congress victories. The Congress contested 1,161 out of a total of 1,585 seats and won 716 of them. Then, from April 1937, the Congress proceeded to run the governments of nine out of eleven of the provinces of British India, six of these on its own, and three in coalition.

Nehru had argued that office acceptance 'would inevitably mean our co-operation in some measure with the repressive apparatus of imperialism, and we would become partners in this repression and in the exploitation of our people.'[28] His prophecy came true (he had the remarkable capacity to identify the implications of a particular position and yet be completely unable to extricate either himself or the Congress from them). During the 'Ministry period', the Congress was at war with itself, its right–left divide clearly manifesting itself. Ministries tended to be drawn from the right; the left had a few representatives, but often found itself effectively in opposition – not in the House, where effective opposition was made extremely difficult, but outside it. Some Congress ministries actively worked with their British governors and the police to persecute and arrest socialists – Rajagopalachari's ministry in Madras was notable in this regard. The CSP-affiliated organisations like the *Kisan Sabhas* and the left wing of the trade union movement – now that the CPI was illegal it also operated through the CSP – were engaged in struggles against the Congress governments, who in effect were running the imperialist system. The Congress-run provinces were ruled as pro-landlord and pro-business; if landlord and business interests clashed, then and only then could the 'masses' get something by mistake. For the most part Congress governments enacted repressive legislation against workers and supported Indian business interests, failed to deliver on land reform pledges and stood with landlords against peasants. It could, of course, be argued that this accurately reflected their mandate; for with a property-related franchise that granted about 16% of the population a vote, it was those with property who elected governments to represent them.

LEADING THE DISSENTERS: MASS CONTACT AND SECTARIAN POLITICS

As the great hope for an organisation that was beginning to be seen by its own membership as demoralised and fragmented, Nehru was now the focal point for the left as well as for other discontented members of the Congress. In the light of fascist successes in Europe, and fascism's apparent ability to form disciplined national units and demonstrate a strong collective will behind a strong leader, not a few people began to think in terms of similar leadership that could take India to independence and strong nationhood. They began to cast Nehru as such a leader. 'I shall put it in Hegelian terms,' one correspondent wrote to him in 1936, 'Capitalism is the thesis, Socialism is the antithesis and Fascism is the synthesis.' He hoped that Nehru would be a Mussolini rather than a Hitler.[29] Nehru had furiously replied that he hated Fascism's 'crudity'.[30]

But the question was not about to go away. In November 1937, the *Modern Review*, a popular monthly journal with a significant national circulation among intellectuals, ran an article entitled 'The Rashtrapati' ('leader of the nation') by someone using the pen name 'Chanakya'. It warned readers of a growing tendency to see Nehru as a saviour of some sort, even a Führer, and suggested that it might even appeal to Jawaharlal's not inconsiderable vanity to see himself as a Napoleon or a Caesar, but made it clear that such thinking was detrimental to the democratic principles for which the national movement ought to stand. It was assumed that this piece had been written by an opponent of Nehru's in the Congress, or possibly by a communist; but Nehru had, in fact, written it himself.[31] It could justifiably be said, perhaps, that he wrote it partly as a warning to himself; for if Nehru was never in danger of becoming a fascist, he certainly had tendencies towards an impatient authoritarianism with people he regarded as his intellectual inferiors that he had the grace to recognise himself.

Nehru now had a role to play in the left's response to the victory in the elections and its defeat over office acceptance. An analysis of the elections brought with it some uncomfortable messages: the Congress had failed to win over large sections of the people, notably Muslims, who had voted against them. They had been unable even to find enough candidates for Muslim seats, contesting only 58 of the 482 Muslim seats (they won 26 of them). Quite apart from the question of whether the Congress accepted office or not, this had implications for its aspirations to be a mass party. (As Congress president, Nehru found himself publicly defending an anomalous situation: among the Muslims who were in the Congress were a number of *ulema*, Muslim clerics whose activities during the election campaigns and after tended towards the use of Muslim religious rhetoric. These were people, Nehru said, who had been associated with the Congress or the Khilafat movement and if it was true that some of them had 'threatened to excommunicate Muslim voters' for not voting for the Congress's candidates, this was 'highly improper'. Nevertheless, they were entitled to be in the Congress.[32])

It was not, however, that the Muslim vote had gone *en bloc* to any other party: the Muslim League, for instance, had been surprised by its dismal performance in the elections, particularly in the Muslim-majority provinces. The North-West Frontier Province had returned a coalition of the Congress and the Khudai Khidmatgar ('Servants of God'), a non-violent party largely of Pakhtoon ethnicity allied to the Gandhian wing of Congress. The Punjab had voted Unionist, a loyalist party with strong links with land ownership, dominated by Muslims, but with important Hindu leaders; Bengal had been won by the Krishak Praja Party (KPP), a pro-peasant party with a strongly Muslim membership (reflecting the composition of the peasantry of eastern Bengal) – it was only here that the Muslim League, still largely seen as a party of United Provinces landowning elites, had been granted a foothold, forming a government in coalition with the KPP. (In all, the League won only 109 of the 482 seats reserved for Muslims, did not contest all the seats and gained just 5% of the Muslim vote.)

Retrospective wisdom, both of historians and of politicians, has it that in the Congress-ruled provinces, some concessions to the Muslim League in 1937 with regard to sharing power might have prevented the demand for Pakistan and eventual partition. Nehru, as Congress president in 1936–7, has traditionally been blamed for not being willing to come to some such agreement. It is clear that he made some incautious and inappropriate remarks, declaring, for instance, that the elections had proved that there were only two political forces in India of significance: the Congress and the British government. But the Muslim League had been completely defeated in the 1937 elections, by whatever standards one chose to apply, and to share power with the League would have been to grant them the right to represent Muslims unearned. This could only have served to legitimise the League and to undermine the legitimacy of the Congress's own claim to represent Muslims, besides being a perpetuation of the anti-democratic politics of the British Empire in which a self-appointed or government-appointed organisation was granted the right to represent a group of people as a whole – without anyone asking by what right. There were, moreover, anomalies of electoral politics and party affiliation that made distinctions between the Congress and the Muslim League not altogether as strong as they became later: in the United Provinces, some of the campaigners and candidates for the League were close to the Congress or were even Congress members; others had no fixed attachments and had stood for office because they had been asked to do so. Nehru regarded many of them as reactionaries and opportunists.

Nehru was, in fact, a strong believer that 'communal' identities only survived in India because they were backed by strong vested interests and encouraged by the British. If, his argument went, the masses were able to find people to represent their true economic interests, and be allowed the means to recognise who these representatives were, they would find that their economic selves were far more important to them than their communal selves – a version of the 'false consciousness' argument of many socialists. For the left, religious sectarianism was an epiphenomenon, an irrational response to poverty and oppression. If made aware of their actual class interests, Hindu and Muslim peasants and workers would act together. This would defeat British divide and rule strategies as well as attempts by Indian vested interests to exploit the masses.

From 1937 to 1939, Nehru, from the higher ranks of the Congress's central organisation, sought a role as the conscience of the ministries. To Govind Ballabh Pant, premier of the United Provinces, he repeatedly complained of the 'reactionary' policies of his ministry. To B.G. Kher, premier of Bombay, he wrote in 1939 reprimanding him on his statements equating the communists' position on class struggle with communal organisations' preaching of religious hatred, and pointed out that this was not consistent with Congress policy (the CPI were still allies in a Popular Front). To the rest of the Congress, he spoke at length on the importance of not getting sidetracked by provincial government or the powers of patronage accompanying political office, and of keeping an eye on the main goal of independence. These interventions did little more than set out his frustrations at the turn of political events on paper.

One problem now had to be centrally addressed: the emergence of strong political forces outside the Congress, and the emergence of specifically Muslim politics. Waverers who in the early 1930s might have joined a Congress reoriented towards the left now saw the necessity to stay outside an organisation that tended towards the right. Internal groups within the Congress now included organisations like the Congress Nationalist Party, right wing, with strong tendencies towards Hindu sectarianism, run by Madan Mohan Malaviya and the Benares Hindu University group; many Congressmen were also members of the Hindu Mahasabha, which was a frankly sectarian organisation. Hindu groups, moreover, were becoming more and more influenced by fascist paramilitary organisations and had themselves built up such organisations, notably the Rashtriya Swayamsevak Sangh (RSS) – a national 'volunteer corps' that wore khaki shorts and paraded in Brown Shirt style. The Congress contained enough people with dual membership of or dual loyalties to such organisations. Without a leftward reorientation, minorities would be justified in having nothing to do with the Congress.

The Congress, clearly, had to work for more support from the masses, to politicise them and bring them in behind the Congress for the interim goal of independence and, from the left's point of view, the longer-term goal of socialism. So, in 1937, the Congress launched its 'Mass Contact Programme', with Nehru as one of its main protagonists, attempting to bring the Congress more closely in contact with those sections of the masses who were not yet Congress supporters. Muslim mass contact, in particular, was to be a central concern. This provoked a debate on the left: some opposed 'Muslim' mass contact on the grounds that it followed a sectarian logic itself. Would there then be a Muslim mass contact committee for Muslims, a Sikh mass contact committee for Sikhs, a Christian mass contact committee for Christians, a Harijan mass contact committee for Harijans, and so on? Was that not simply acknowledging that communities were separate entities rather than that classes were? But such debates were, by now, ideological luxuries, because the bald fact was that Muslims had to be convinced of the possibility of trusting the Congress.

This was next to impossible in the current circumstances. The case that cropped up most in these debates was that of Bengal. The CSP considered the Bengal Congress one of the most backward and right wing of the Provincial Congresses, dominated by cliques whose ostensible observance of the secular creed of the Congress could not hide the fact that they were anti-Muslim and often also members of the Hindu Mahasabha. The KPP's victory in the elections, on a mixture of peasant and Muslim rhetoric, reinforced the CSP's belief that an economic programme could potentially work best in Bengal, both to combat communalism and to actually deliver to the masses a government that would reflect their needs. The CSP also believed that the main obstacle to this was not so much the KPP as the Bengal Congress itself. The Bengal Congress represented the interests of the Bengali Hindu *bhadralok*, whose more influential sections held their wealth in *zamindari* lands granted by the Permanent Settlement of the Governor-General, Lord Cornwallis, in 1793, and who lived off this income often as absentee landlords in Calcutta, while their estates were run on their behalf by agents, sub-agents and sub-sub-agents, all of whom lived off the work of the primary producer. Even the slightly extended franchise of the 1930s meant that the Congress, as a *zamindar* party, could not win an election. There was no room for a left to function within the Bengal Congress. As a result, space was left to the KPP, a peasant-Muslim party that could easily, by a change of emphasis, become a Muslim-peasant party, especially while the KPP remained in alliance with the Muslim League. According to the Congress Socialists, the KPP was not unambiguously a party whose rationale was based on defending the economic and social needs of a poor peasantry – in an area where the Hindu–Muslim divide corresponded so closely with the *zamindar*–peasant divide, the

KPP, without clear principles, socialist or communist, and with a leadership drawn from the emergent Muslim lower middle class, could easily develop into a populist Muslim communal party. CSP members predicted this change correctly, but could do nothing about it; 'mass contact' failed to make major gains in Bengal.

Recent research suggests that the sharp distinctions between class identities and community identities that political parties on the left tried to draw were not altogether relevant to the people for whom they were trying to draw them. In Bengal, there existed *Kisan sabhas* and *krishak* and *praja samities*, with membership drawn from lower castes and Muslims, but with leadership drawn from higher strata of society. The Krishak Praja Party had emerged out of the organisation of the *praja samities* for political action. The Bengal *Kisan Sabha* was dominated by communists. But people working within the '*kisan* movement', as they often collectively described it, in the mid-1930s, did not see a major distinction; they were all working towards the uplift of the peasants. The immediate enemy was the *zamindari* system as a whole; there was widespread support when the abolition of the Permanent Settlement was discussed, but this was the mainstay of the incomes of a number of Calcutta Hindu *bhadralok* who dominated the Bengal Congress. In the United Provinces, things were different. When the abolition of *zamindari* came up for discussion there, many *zamindars* were UP Muslims, the main support base of the Muslim League; they could depict Congress government-led initiatives towards land reform as anti-Muslim and therefore 'communal'.

The Muslim League now charged the Congress with trying to confuse the Muslim masses, among other things with its 'mass contact programme'. Nehru, for the Congress, explained the programme: 'mass contact' was to increase the Congress's appeal to all sections of society, but it had been acknowledged by the Congress that it had not done as well with Muslims as it could have done. This was unproblematic to acknowledge at a time when the League could not possibly make a counter-claim to represent most Muslims itself. The Muslim League and its ally the KPP also accused the Congress governments of 'atrocities' against Muslims in the Congress-ruled provinces, providing fuel to a polemical set of exchanges. Nehru replied by offering to investigate these atrocities jointly with the accusers, but invited them first to substantiate their claims; his invitations were refused, with the League and the KPP continuing to make dark allegations.

Nehru was now placed in an awkward position: he knew quite clearly that some of the 'reactionary' policies he had been writing to provincial premiers about related to communal tendencies in the ministries, but he had to maintain public solidarity with the Congress. Nehru was willing publicly to acknowledge that there had been problems, but tried to separate the ministries' activities from those of small sections of underlings – this was a disingenuous argument, given that in private he could acknowledge just what was happening. The Muslim League and its allies were definitely opportunistically using the 'atrocities' stories. But to some extent they were true – even though he could hardly have been expected to take any action without evidence. He could, however, take refuge in the fact that the Muslim leadership seemed more interested in indicting the Congress than in addressing the grievances of those suffering: it was less the suffering that was important than its appropriation for political gain. He decided to publish his correspondence with League and KPP leaders – indicating that there was a willingness on the Congress's side to do something if the allegations could be substantiated.

On Nehru's part, at least, there was still a certain wilful blindness with regard to dealing with the communal problem. When, in late 1939, Nehru's old friend Syed Mahmud, a CSP member, suggested that the Congress ministry in Bihar (of which Mahmud was himself a member) should share power with minorities, Nehru reacted sharply, assuming Mahmud meant sharing power with the Muslim League, and accused him of a 'reactionary outlook'. In December, when the ministries no longer existed (having resigned in protest against the viceroy's unilateral declaration of war on India's behalf), Mahmud clarified: the Congress had severely misgoverned the province and had failed to win the confidence of minorities, not merely Muslims, but also lower castes and Christians. 'The Congress is full of provincialism, caste prejudices and [Hindu] revivalism,' he wrote.[33] If the Congress had offered to share power with *all* minorities, not just Muslims, and not with the Muslim League, this might have generated more confidence. Nehru repeated his charge that Mahmud's suggestions were 'reactionary': a 'progressive' government could not be formed on a communal basis – of Hindu or Muslim majorities or minorities. The communal problem was, in fact, 'a very minor problem. The real problem is a political problem – the conflict between an advanced organisation like the Congress and a politically reactionary organisation like the League' – which merely exploited religion to create communal conflict.[34] Given Nehru's own assessment of the record of the Congress ministries, it is difficult to take his statement on the Congress's 'progressive' credentials as more than the projection of an unfulfilled desire; his internal correspondence reveals that there was a great divergence between his statements made publicly on behalf of the Congress and internal criticism.

ESCAPES: JOURNALISM AND EUROPE

Faced with his own entanglement in the reactionary tendencies that controlled the Congress, in which he was unable to make an impact, Jawaharlal took refuge in journalism. In 1936, he began to consider running his own newspaper; on September 9, 1938, the inaugural issue of the *National Herald* appeared from Lucknow (the paper remained in more or less continuous financial difficulties). Nehru began to take on the role of the opposition to the United Provinces Government from its pages. The *National Herald* editorial desk seemed to become his spiritual and political refuge; this was a very active period of writing for Nehru, with his unsigned editorials presenting to a wider audience some of the principles he was quite unable to stand for in open public life. He also wrote the occasional signed article, the frequency of the latter increasing as he took on the job of foreign correspondent for his paper in the crucial year of Munich.

The international situation, paradoxically, was a space in which Nehru was able to make an impact as an internationalist and as a principled spokesman for liberty, even as he was reduced to ineffectiveness in domestic politics. In 1937, he visited Burma and Malaya and was warmly received in both countries. Leaving India in June 1938, he travelled to Barcelona, where he experienced the agonies of the Spanish Republic. On July 17, he was among the speakers at Trafalgar Square at a rally on the second anniversary of the outbreak of the Spanish Civil War, where he explained to the 5,000-strong crowd the similarities between fascism and imperialism. His anti-fascist and anti-appeasement editorials were unambiguous in their condemnation of British foreign policy, and predicted that war was inevitable. While in Europe he made several public appearances at which he spoke of the need for Europeans to support the demand for Indian independence, and the interconnectedness of struggles for freedom and against fascism and imperialist aggression across the world, particularly in Spain and China. He warned against a 'European complex' that could not relate to events in Asia, but assured his audience that these events had a strong bearing on the world situation. In many of his speeches he spoke of China as a 'sister nation'. He also dodged the attentions of Nazi officials eager to meet him to clear up 'misunderstandings', as they politely put it. Although British intelligence sources reported that Nehru's visit to Munich from August 6 to 8 had included a visit to the headquarters of the Nazi Party, where he had long deliberations with the officials there, the sources ruled out Nehru's responding to any overtures the Nazis might have made towards him because of his honourable anti-fascist credentials.[35] He was in Europe to report the Munich pact that condemned Czechoslovakia to Nazi dismemberment; he had been in Prague to record the responses of the capital to the negotiations that affected that country's future.

In June 1938, Nehru, in Britain, met with politicians of the Labour Party to discuss possible terms of a treaty for transfer of power to India when Labour came to office. Sir Stafford Cripps, Harold Laski and other Labour politicians, as well as Krishna Menon of the Independence for India League, a campaigning organisation based in London, had a 'weekend at Filkins', at Sir Stafford Cripps' country seat, together. After much hard bargaining, the terms included a constituent assembly to be elected on universal adult franchise, but with communal constituencies plus other reserved representation. Only those rulers of the Princely States who accepted this electoral system could send representatives to the constituent assembly, and the constitution that it brought into being would override existing British treaties with the princes. On economic issues, the terms were particularly precise. There would be a British–Indian treaty according to whose terms the Indian debt to Britain (considered by Indian opinion to be forced lending to obtain higher returns on investment than would have been possible elsewhere) would in part be cancelled. A part of that debt (represented by assets within India evaluated by an impartial tribunal) would be taken over by the government of independent India. India would agree to buy British manufactured goods over a period of years to an equivalent amount of the cancelled debt, protecting British exports to India for a while.[36] These were concrete proposals; they also contained an important concession to Britain. Indian debt was an extremely touchy issue, and in 1931 the Congress had repudiated it as properly belonging to Britain, not to India, as it required an independent government to run up debts on a country's behalf. It was not clear that Nehru was at the time properly empowered to deliver on his side of the promises, or had a mandate from the Congress to discuss these issues.

While he was in Europe, Nehru received a request from the new Congress president, Subhas Bose, to chair a proposed National Planning Committee. Bose had been elected president for that year on Gandhi's instigation; he now proceeded to take an active part in the Congress's reorganisation. The National Planning Committee was the first step towards a project that had long been dear to the hearts of the Congress left: it was to discuss economic and social planning for an eventual independent India. This was to be far more than mere details of production targets and locations of industries: the nation's aspirations were contained in the project. Subhas felt that Nehru was the logical chairman for such a committee, given that he had so often in the past decade publicly proclaimed his commitment to socialism, to a modern industrialised economy and to economic planning. Nehru accepted; but the fate of that Committee revealed in microcosm the fate of 'socialism' in India: dogged by compromises and by divergent agendas, it produced a fascinating series of documents that were of little use as plans, but said much about the debates that were coming to a boil about the future of India. Nehru sought to defuse political discord at a very early stage in its debates by declaring that apart from a few statements of a general nature, 'the Congress has not in any way accepted socialism'.[37] This was a telling statement from the chairman of a committee whose brief was to consider the acceptability of social and economic planning on a scale comparable only to the USSR, and whose central role model was the USSR. But the Soviet Union was admired not only by socialists; British imperial administrators and Indian capitalists alike had been impressed by Soviet achievements in the material sphere and sought to emulate them without bringing socialism on board.

Nehru had also, while in Europe, come into contact with individuals and organisations working to control and direct the flow of Jewish émigrés and refugees now moving across Europe away from Nazi persecution. It was suggested to him that some of these people might seek shelter in India. Nehru took the line that it would be impossible for a poor country to accept large numbers of refugees, but that some technically qualified persons might be of use to long-term economic planning measures. Nehru believed that Jews, as representatives of a technologically superior

Western civilization, were going to be useful to backward countries. (This was an assumption he had used before when discussing Jewish immigration into Palestine. Jews were 'exploited in Palestine' by British imperialism's divide and rule tactics: 'Palestine is and must continue to be essentially an Arab country. If that is admitted cooperation is easy and Jews will be welcomed in Palestine, as well as in Trans-Jordan, to help, as they are in a position to do, in the development of the country.'[38]) With this in mind, he wrote to Govind Ballabh Pant, prime minister of the United Provinces, and to Subhas Bose, Congress president. Pant was responsive, but not overly helpful; Bose was dismissive: the Jews were none of Nehru's or India's concern, because India had larger problems of her own. A few Jewish technicians and scientists did find their way to India in these years; their numbers were not significant.

THE 'TRIPURI CRISIS'

Crucially for long-term trends in Indian politics, Nehru was by now losing support at home among his natural allies: socialists were becoming increasingly disillusioned with his inaction and with his desertions at crucial moments. By 1938, even the most optimistic were beginning to be sceptical of Nehru's commitment to practical support for the left. '[I]t would be unfair of you, who are naturally used to doing things on a grand scale,' Jayaprakash Narayan wrote to Nehru, 'to noncooperate with the efforts of Socialists in India just because they are puny as compared with those of older and wider organisations. We are, I think, not unjustified in expecting that, if you will not fully identify yourself with us, you will, as a socialist, at least help us in doing well the little we may undertake to do.'[39] If the criticism was harsh, it was also a criticism born of hopes betrayed.

The activities of the Congress left, from its modest beginnings in 1934, were not quite as 'puny' as Jayaprakash thought. By 1938, the Congress presidency was held by a man supported by the left who was willing to back his rhetoric with action, and in 1939, it was the right that was willing to split the Congress to avoid a left-wing swing. The Congress's new president in 1938, Subhas Chandra Bose, was of course the other Congressman apart from Nehru with first-hand international experience. Externed from India by the government, he had spent the mid-1930s in Europe; arrested as he returned to India in March 1936, he had been released a year later, on March 18, 1937, and had been welcomed into the Congress left. Gandhi then asked him to accept the presidency of the Congress, and he had duly ascended to it in 1938. It seems likely that Gandhi sought to do with Bose what he had so successfully done with Nehru: kick him upstairs the better to control him.

Bose had always had the ability to inspire large numbers of people. He has sometimes been described as a fascist on the make – this was made easier retrospectively after his activities in the Second World War in trying to ally with Germany and Japan to liberate India from the British. But his relationship with fascism was more complex. He may well have retained some admiration for the successes of strong leaders; he had indeed once praised Mussolini's Fascists and called for 'a synthesis between Communism and Fascism' (in his book *The Indian Struggle*) – but later retracted this, claiming that he had not known enough about them at the time, and that fascism had therefore appeared to be 'merely an aggressive form of nationalism'.[40] Cleared of charges of fascism by none other than Rajani Palme Dutt – Dutt himself publicised his interviews with Bose to de-fascistise him – Bose was able to take command of the Congress with the support of the left under the Popular Front policy.

Bose nonetheless remains difficult to classify. It is true that he stressed physical discipline and military preparedness among volunteer groups in the national movement, but he had this in common with a great many groups, both inside and outside the mainstream of the nationalist movement – and, it might be added, worldwide. If they all had proto-fascist views, perhaps this is a call to reassess the history of worldwide fascism in terms of how far it was part of the spirit of the age – and not an aberration – rather than classify movements and groups as fascist on the basis of retrospective identification of characteristics of fascism that may have been common to more than merely fascist groups.

From 1938, the Congress Socialists, by now weary of waiting for Nehru to do something, began to work through Bose. Indeed, Bose's presidency of the Congress produced the initiative that became the hallmark of 'Nehruvian' politics and the Congress' post-independence vision – a planned economy with a quasi-socialist touch – represented in the work of the National Planning Committee. A brief wave of optimism could be discerned on the left, finding its way into the pages of its official journal, the *Congress Socialist*. Bose also took the initiative in trying to mend the Congress's relations with the Muslim League; but although Bose specifically repudiated Nehru's claim that after 1937 there were only two parties in India, namely the Congress and the British government – thereby refusing even to acknowledge the League – Jinnah wanted more than that for the League: he wished it to be recognised as the representative organisation of *all* Muslims in India. To this Bose could not agree because this would have amounted to surrendering the Congress's right to represent Muslims at all; the initiative collapsed. Once again this highlighted the problems of a politics that claimed to represent the 'masses', but had to conduct all major negotiations among 'leaders' whose mandate as leaders was rather dubious.

Subhas Bose announced his intention of running for a second term as Congress president and was re-elected in January 1939. In March 1939, Nehru wrote a series of articles in a weary tone entitled 'Where are We?' for the *National Herald*, preceding the Tripuri session of the Congress. Provincial autonomy, he wrote, had created opportunists, provincialising and narrowing politics and perspectives, and diverting the anti-imperialist struggle into narrow channels. The major problems of poverty, unemployment, land reforms and industry were not being addressed. The possibility of the Congress finally addressing Nehru's concerns seemed to have arrived with Bose's re-election, for in all their public statements there was no indication that they were not on the same side.

But, in 1939, Subhas Bose had stood for the post without Gandhi's backing, and against Gandhi's candidate; the right wing had tried to persuade him not to stand, but failed. He won; the left had succeeded in electing its candidate and, far more importantly, this time against the explicit opposition of the 'Gandhian' right wing, coordinated by Vallabhbhai Patel. This was a new situation. Nehru's presidential terms had been different – he had been supported by Gandhi, and had explicitly been willing to accept a right-wing-dominated Working Committee and a token left-wing presence. Bose, on the other hand, was willing to give Gandhi the respect due to an elder statesman, but not to surrender his mandate; 1939 showed clearly that the right, acting through Gandhi, would not tolerate a majority on the left.

The right now opposed Bose and insisted on his appointing 'Gandhians' to the Working Committee. Gandhi referred to Bose's victory as his defeat, pitting his personal reputation against Bose's electoral victory, and even making barbed remarks about 'bogus' voters on the electoral register. Gandhi, in effect using his tactics of non-cooperation on

Bose, suggested that Bose, since he had won, should appoint his own working committee – which would definitely have precipitated a split in the Congress. Bose, for his part, was unwilling to publicly oppose Gandhi, whom he still referred to as 'India's greatest man'. The cult of Gandhi's personality, not discouraged by Gandhi, was now the yardstick of legitimacy within Congress politics. The Congress president could not function without a working committee, and the Great Soul would not let him have one.

Nehru at first tried to play the mediator, keeping a distance from the controversy; then, after giving the matter some thought, he deserted Bose. The Congress Socialists, having also given the matter much thought, decided not to split the anti-imperialist movement and the Congress, and abandoned Bose as well. Once again, Nehru had lacked the courage to make a decisive difference in a crucial debate. In the acrimony that followed, Subhas Bose justifiably felt that Nehru had betrayed him. Bose angrily referred to defects in Nehru's character and his character-istic weaknesses when it came to the crunch, to Nehru's ambiguous and therefore damaging statements to the press about the period of Bose's presidency, and Nehru's assumption that coalitional politics condemned that coalition to being perennially a coalition led by the right rather than by socialists – the last making it impossible for him to envisage a left-wing victory within the Congress. Nehru, sounding tired and isolated, acknowledged the charges and avoided Bose's direct challenge to him to clarify his position:

> Am I a socialist or an individualist? Is there a necessary contradiction in the two terms? Are we all such integrated human beings that we can define ourselves precisely in a word or a phrase? I suppose I am temperamentally and by training an individualist, and intellectually a socialist, whatever all this might mean. I hope that socialism does not kill or suppress individuality; indeed I am attracted to it because it will release innumerable individuals from economic and cultural bondage . . . Let us leave it at this that I am an unsatisfactory human being who is dissatisfied with himself and the world, and whom the petty world he lives in does not particularly like.[41]

Bose was forced to resign by the end of April 1939 as a result of a campaign against him that was engineered by Gandhi and the Congress right among the so-called 'High Command', effectively a small clique with no legitimate status in the Congress's organisation, ready to abandon any pretence of intra-party democracy once the left had achieved the not unremarkable feat of winning the Congress presidency unaided within five years of organising itself (ironically, one of the issues on which Bose had been re-elected was inner party democracy in the Congress). Having resigned, Bose formed the Forward Bloc, initially within the Congress, then, when he and his group were expelled from the Congress, outside it. The left had been successfully split; the Congress survived, and remained theoretically united under the new president, Maulana Abul Kalam Azad. Azad, for his part, had refused to stand against Bose in the 1939 presidential elections; Dr Pattabhi Sitaramayya, who had been persuaded to oppose Bose on behalf of the right, vanished from the equation with Bose's exit.

WAR AND A LIFELINE

The Congress's internal equilibrium had been severely disrupted. The organisation listlessly limped along, inevitably, continuing with its job of running provincial governments. As an organisation it was already dead for all practical purposes; the 1935 Act had successfully done its job of divide and rule, with politics in the late 1930s being dominated by intra-Indian squabbles and issues. The Congress had been functioning as both quasi-parliamentary government and extra-parliamentary opposition, operating as a left and a right completely at odds with one another; in the Congress-ruled provinces, the only effective opposition to the Congress governments were the organisations affiliated to and controlled by the Congress left. Even that left was beginning to fragment, with the expulsion of Subhas Bose from the Congress being merely the most explicit example of fragmentation. Many anti-communist socialists were resentful of the communists' successful use of the CSP platform – a use so successful, in fact, that in some areas the CSP *was* the CPI, and since the Congress in that region was controlled by the CSP, the Congress was the Communist Party.

And then, once again, the British government stepped in to provide a unifying issue. On September 3, 1939, the long-anticipated war broke out in Europe. The viceroy, Lord Linlithgow, declared war on India's behalf, without consulting any of the 'representative' bodies of Indians now in existence. The viceroy had, however, rescued the Congress from an uncomfortable situation, effectively throwing it a lifeline. His unilateral declaration of war gave the Congress the opportunity to make a principled stand and a public show of unity once more. And in the last confusing years leading up to independence and the partition of India, it would be the British government – who needed the Congress, as an organisation with which to negotiate a transfer of power – that would keep *an* organisation of that name together, and in possession of a rationale for continued existence.

4

THE END OF THE RAJ

Jawaharlal Nehru kept a page from his copy of the *New Republic* on which W.H. Auden announced the close of 'a low dishonest decade' and the beginning of the war. Auden's last stanza read: 'Defenceless under the night/ Our world in stupor lies/ Yet dotted everywhere/ Ironic points of light/ Flash out wherever the just/ Exchange their messages:/ May I, composed like them/ Of Eros and of dust/ Beleaguered by the same/ Negation and despair/ Show an affirming flame.'[1] Feeling increasingly isolated within the Congress's fragmented unity, and seeking some comfort in his never-to-be-lost love of poetry, a throwback to his days of aesthetic contemplation with his Theosophist tutor, Nehru was more likely to see himself as an ironic point of light than an affirming flame; and in September 1939, ironic points of light were easier to find than affirming flames.

By the end of the 1930s, Nehru seems to have been more sure-footed when discussing the international situation than in responding to the domestic one. He was also rethinking his political position. An outside observer might have been justified in saying that Nehru had sought, and found, a moral and personal justification in socialism, but ran away from the practical implications of his ideological commitment. Another, perhaps more generous way of looking at it would be to trace in Nehru, as with others at the time, a general disillusionment with the shibboleths of the socialist movement, but – even when he could see no practical way forward on this count – a continuing and agonised acknowledgement that some form of socialism was still the only way forward. Support for the USSR, for example, was the touchstone of a socialist's legitimacy. While most members of the Congress Socialists put a Nelsonian blind eye to the telescope and praised the economic and technological miracles of the Soviet Union, Nehru had never altogether been an unqualified admirer; and news of Stalin's purges had disturbed him as they had disturbed many others. Personal experiences also played a role in his apparent equivocation: Viren Chattopadhyay, who had been a regular, if critical, correspondent of Nehru's from Europe and the USSR, vanished towards the end of the 1930s in one of the purges. Nehru's anxious letters to Chatto and his associates in trying to trace his friend yielded no responses. Yet if Nehru was more circumspect in his praise of the USSR, as the Congress's main thinker on international matters, he could not slip into an unreasoned anti-Soviet position, unlike many former believers.

But for a while at least, philosophical speculation and ideological correctness were not permissible luxuries. Events were now to speed up to an extent never before encountered in the Indian freedom struggle.

THE IMPERIAL LEAD, 1939

The viceroy's declaration of war on India's behalf, although technically legal, placed a central anomaly squarely in the public domain: self-government, which the 1935 Act's supporters had declared to have substantially arrived, obviously did not apply to the matter of declaring war. The Congress had to respond, or to be seen to respond, although the anomaly was not a new one – reserve powers under the Act had always remained in the hands of the viceroy and his provincial governors.

Given that he was one of the few Congressmen who could understand international affairs, Jawaharlal now had to play a central role in Congress as a whole (when the war broke out, he had been in China on a long-planned solidarity visit, and the Congress's meetings on how to respond to this situation had been put on hold until his return). It was Nehru's demand that the Congress Working Committee put forward on September 15: an immediate declaration of Indian independence should be the basis of support for the British war effort. On October 17, the viceroy repeated the by-now familiar vague promises of future dominion status. He added that after the war consultations would take place with 'representatives of the several communities' and with a consultative group of representatives of Indian politicians and princely states – not elected ones –to review the 1935 Act. This was far from adequate: only a free India, Nehru reiterated, could participate in the war effort. 'We have no intention,' he wrote, 'of shouting *Heil Hitler*; neither do we intend to shout *British Imperialism Zindabad* [Long Live British Imperialism].'[2] Meanwhile, the government was busy putting in place emergency provisions and ordinances suppressing civil liberties and imposing censorship.

After over a month of discussions the Congress came up with its counter-move: its governments would resign from the provinces they controlled, in protest at India's being dragged into a war not of its own choosing. On October 29–30, the Congress ministries resigned (Muhammad Ali Jinnah, for the Muslim League, welcomed the resignations as 'deliverance' for Muslims). The resignation decision, Gandhi later wrote, 'covered the fact that we were crumbling to pieces';[3] it was merely a prelude to the internal struggle on how to respond to the war within the Congress. For now, Congress was back to being a party of opposition. But Linlithgow's apparent blunder was also a good way of regaining British control: with the ministries having resigned, the provinces were now ruled directly by their governors under Section 93 of the 1935 Act, thereby restoring to the British government autocratic control of most of British India. Discussions in official circles in the period leading up to the resignations worked on the assumption that if the Congress ministries did not resign, they would have to be dismissed, while various other measures would have to be taken 'to suppress and muzzle hostile opinion'.[4] Some sections of the Government of India, among whose numbers apparently the viceroy could be counted, believed that the war was an opportunity to reverse the dangerous trend towards giving away India to Indians, regarding this reversal 'not merely as desirable, but also as entirely practicable'.[5]

Soon afterwards, Linlithgow invited Gandhi for talks, along with Jinnah on behalf of the Muslim League. The invitation was a good example of how colonial Indian politics still worked. Gandhi was, from 1934, no longer formally a member of the Congress, and the League could hardly, after its electoral showing in 1937, have claimed to represent the majority of Muslims. Elected ministries did not need to be consulted, but two individuals could be recognised as representatives for the purposes of discussion regardless of their popular mandate or lack thereof.

Nevertheless, it infinitely simplified British negotiations during the war to be dealing with two parties rather than several. For all practical purposes, then, the British position that there were many 'interest groups' and 'minorities' in India that the British had to stay on to protect was replaced by the *de facto* recognition of two parties to represent the two major 'communities'. Jinnah, now armed with British recognition, could bargain with other Muslim groups to operate through the League and through him – because no political settlement was possible without the British being a party to it, and it was with Jinnah that the British had chosen to deal. Viceroy Linlithgow's and Secretary of State for India (from 1940) Leo Amery's private statements make it clear that it was the British intention to use the League as a counterweight to the Congress in an attempt to contain opposition to British policy during the war. Muslims were to be encouraged through the League to keep contacts with the British. Given that the British were anxious to show some form of support for their war effort, they were able to promote the League to the status of sole negotiator and representative of 'Muslim' opinion – the assumption was, of course, that the genie could be persuaded back into the bottle afterwards.

Asked to put his demands on the table, Jinnah now came forward with the resolution passed by a number of Muslim parties at Lahore on March 23, 1940. The Lahore Resolution envisaged territorial units grouped together in North-Western and Eastern India 'to constitute Independent States in which the constituent units shall be autonomous and sovereign'.[6] Retrospectively known as the 'Pakistan Resolution', it mentioned neither the word Pakistan nor the principle of partition. As a compromise formula, however, it was useful by virtue of its vagueness. Internal discussions reveal some desire for a weak central government in an eventually independent India, one rationale being that Muslims in the Muslim-minority provinces needed protection that could only be provided by the newly-created Muslim-majority independent states remaining within an Indian union, however defined. There were other opinions; but nothing clear was about to emerge, and Fazlul Huq, who moved the resolution, was to stand in the 1946 elections against the Pakistan demand.

THE CONGRESS RESPONSE, 1939–41

But the Muslim League was not Congress's main concern as yet. After the ministries' resignations, the question of how next to respond remained to be settled. There were genuine moral and political dilemmas to consider. Nehru and the left were committed anti-fascists; but they would not support a war on the basis of continued subjection to British rule, especially as they did not take British claims to anti-fascism at all seriously. The CPI, still outlawed but still in the CSP – until 1941 – characterised the war as another imperialist war (1939–41 was the period of the Nazi–Soviet Pact). Nehru himself accepted the CPI line: 'the war is a purely imperialist venture on both sides. Fine phrases are being used by politicians as they were used in 1914. It seems to me highly important and vital that we should not be taken in by these phrases and pious protestations.'[7] Nehru undertook the task of explaining the apparent anomaly of the Nazi–Soviet Pact to Gandhi: unable to find an ally in Europe, the USSR had been forced into an illogical and temporary alliance that held off the immediate threat of war and gave them the breathing space to prepare for the inevitable later war to come. Nehru fully expected the imperialist and fascist powers to collectively turn against the Soviet Union and proclaim 'a holy war against communism . . . That would be a calamity from every point of view, quite apart from our agreement with Russian policy or not.'[8]

The Congress right hadn't a clue about how to respond. Gandhi was perhaps more helpful, given that he could at least have a moral, pacifist, position. For those trained in and around the Marxist tradition, the equation of fascism in Europe with imperialism in India and elsewhere had been a useful one in sustaining the Popular Front policy. But things were beginning to lose that clarity now that the imperialists were at war with the fascists: how long would the equation last? Would it not be necessary to choose between the two? This question worried not a few people in leadership positions. Rank and file communists and socialists, distinctions among whom were often far less clear than among the parties who led them, were understandably rather confused by the situation.

In Nehru's view, the dilemma could be solved. Congress was seeking a guarantee from the government that support during the war would this time lead to independence. With such a guarantee, the logical next step would be for Congress to fully support an anti-fascist war (thereby publicly acknowledging that it was one, even if remaining suspicious in private of a war that the Congress believed still had imperialist objectives). Nehru attempted to use his personal connections to sound out British opinion, because the Congress could hardly lower the stakes on its initial demand now that it had been made public. In December 1939, Stafford Cripps visited India – this was the first visit of a man soon to be regarded as an 'expert' on the 'Indian problem' – and met Nehru. Nehru asked for a sign that he could sell to Indian opinion which would enable the Congress to participate in the war effort with honour, and suggested to him that a definite commitment from Britain on Indian independence was essential – no sidetracking through the communal question was now possible if agreement was to be reached with the Congress. Cripps assured Nehru that Linlithgow had promised he would not exploit the Hindu–Muslim question (Linlithgow had either lied to Cripps, or Cripps was being economical with the truth).

Nehru had not been overly optimistic about Cripps's semi-private diplomatic initiative – at the time, Cripps had no official standing, having been expelled from the Labour Party in January 1939, although official opinion in Labour circles hoped his personal diplomacy might have a positive impact – or the prospects of British policy taking any of the discussions on board; in this his political judgement was sound. 'I understand Cripps very well,' Nehru wrote to Krishna Menon. 'His visit will make no difference to us, or very little, but I hope it will help him to understand a little more of the Indian problem.'[9] By 1942, when Cripps reappeared in India, he had been reincorporated within officialdom – the demands of wartime politics had brought a national coalition into being, and Cripps had from June 1940 to January 1942 been ambassador to the USSR before returning to Britain and joining the Cabinet. For the time being, he was engaged in personal diplomacy: in January 1940 he wrote to Nehru from Chungking [Chongqing], 'I want to do all I can to encourage Trading and economic relationships between China and India as in the future for a free India I am sure it will be important. There are masses of openings of every kind from Finance to secondhand machinery. Could your Congress people send a Trade Mission to Chungking . . . ? It sounds awfully capitalist but at the moment it is the only way to start the relationships and also to help China where Great Britain is failing.'[10] The Congress had already sent a medical mission to the Communists' Eighth Route Army; Nehru's China visit was to have included a visit to the Eighth Route Army in the north-western field of operation against the Japanese, and to the Congress Medical Mission there, when his trip was cut short by the outbreak of war, and a trade mission to the Guomindang's headquarters would have been an appropriate hedging of bets for the future. Both Nehru and Cripps had individually been struck by the ineffectiveness of the Guomindang and of the non-functioning of the GMD–Chinese Communist Party's united front against the Japanese.

Meanwhile, the bargaining over possible cooperation continued. In May 1940, Winston Churchill, the old enemy of Indian independence, took control over a wartime coalitional government. On August 8, 1940, during the Battle of Britain, an 'August offer' was made, so hedged about with reservations that all parties in India rejected it. It offered an expansion of the Viceroy's Executive Council to include more Indians, and dominion status within twelve months of the end of the war. The Congress was waiting for a better offer – this was not much more than a repetition of the viceroy's offer of October 17, 1939. A concern for world opinion dictated what was offered to India at the time; but by May 1940, Linlithgow and Home Member Sir Reginald Maxwell had also prepared the Revolutionary Movements Ordinance in case they should need it against a large-scale civil disobedience campaign.

Gandhi now devised what he thought was an appropriate tactic for the Congress's response to British rebuffs: 'individual satyagraha'. This was a curious form of political protest, driven by the need to do something rather than the desire to be effective. His earlier, interim response to the declaration of war had required provincial ministries not to resign but to refrain from providing more than moral support to the war effort; now, 'individual satyagraha' was to oppose government censorship regulations on free speech but not to embarrass the government – so it was to be a symbolic sort of movement, although it was to pick up speed over time. The first person selected by Gandhi as morally disciplined enough to undertake this activity was his close disciple, Acharya Vinoba Bhave. The second was Nehru, who was profoundly sceptical about the usefulness of opposing such minor details of British policy as censorship regulations at such a time. But if this was to be a game of symbolic politics, the government was equally capable of responding with its own, not necessarily symbolic, disciplining apparatus. The satyagrahis were arrested.

Nehru was sentenced on three charges (based on three speeches he made), under the wartime Defence of India Rules, to one year and four

months' rigorous imprisonment for each offence, the sentences to run con-
secutively – making four years in all. The trial lasted three days, although
Nehru had pleaded guilty and refused to defend himself, insisting instead
that the Defence of India Rules were 'the greatest insult that can be
inflicted on the country'.[11] The trial, Nehru's sister Vijayalakshmi
observed at the time, had an 'Alice in Wonderland' element about it;
Nehru agreed that 'but for the prison sentence at the end, one could not
take it seriously'.[12] This was his eighth conviction; he settled quickly into
his jail routine of spinning, reading and *yoga* supplemented by cooking
for and playing badminton with his brother-in-law Ranjit Pandit, who
joined him in prison. He also formed a strong attachment to the prison
dog. This time he found it difficult to avoid being depressed both by his
personal circumstances and by news of world affairs that filtered through
to him. Soon he was mourning the death of Rabindranath Tagore (who
died in August 1941). 'Perhaps it is as well,' he noted, 'that he died now
and did not see the many horrors that are likely to descend in increasing
measure on the world and on India. He had seen enough and he was
infinitely sad and unhappy.'[13] To keep himself occupied, Nehru decided
to work on a second instalment of his autobiography, the first volume of
which had just been published in America and had been acclaimed as a
masterpiece; events overtook the draft and it was never published.

Among the more romantic incidents of the war was the escape of
Subhas Chandra Bose from house arrest in Calcutta in January 1941.
Travelling via Afghanistan and the Soviet Union (where he had hoped
for but failed to obtain support), Bose reappeared in Berlin in April, asking
for German guarantees of Indian independence after the war in the event
of an Axis victory. The Nazi leadership were not averse to allowing him
to make propaganda broadcasts to India, but stopped short of providing
him with any guarantees or concrete assistance. (Having spent nearly
two years in this frustrating situation, Bose made his way to Japan by
submarine to take command of an Indian National Army organised
from among Indian prisoners of war in Japan. He arrived too late: the
moment for an invasion had passed with the loss of momentum of the
Japanese advance, and his having missed the opportunity of the Quit India
Movement.)

The viceroy, meanwhile, sought to work around the Congress if they
would not cooperate. In July 1941, the Viceroy's Executive Council was
expanded, to include eight Indians out of a total of twelve members.

Defence, Finance and Home remained in the hands of 'European' officials; the new post of War Production was given to the British businessman Sir Edward Benthall – the man who had, before the Round Table Conferences, explained to his colleagues that they had nothing to fear from Indians in government as long as Defence, Finance and Home remained in European hands.

JAIL AGAIN, AND OUT OF IT: THE CRIPPS MISSION AND BACK TO JAIL AGAIN

Jail during the war meant respite from the outside world; one's jailors could decide how little or how much one was to have access to information: Nehru requested, and after much delay was denied, access to the papers of the Congress's National Planning Committee that he had hoped to work on while in prison. A limited correspondence was permitted, however, and Nehru could continue to write to interested parties in England who were watching his ideological development with some interest.

In one candid letter, Nehru outlined his ideological state: 'I hate anarchy of all kinds, of the mind, the body, and the social organism. I dislike a mess, and my own predilection is entirely in favour of order. And yet there are worse states than that of anarchy and disorder, and in this mad world of ours, the choice often lies between evils . . . No, I am not a communist, nor indeed do I belong to any other "ism". Having failed to find anchorage in religion, I refuse to give up my mental freedom in favour of any dogma or binding creed. Yet I believe in the socialist structure; it seems to me inescapable if the world is to survive and progress . . . These last five years . . . have had a powerful effect upon me, and my mind's assurance about the future of humanity has been considerably shaken.' Nehru spoke of Indian culture, of its resilience over thousands of years, and of its importance for post-independence India. 'The new culture and civilisation that will come will (or I hope it will) produce a classless society & will make Brahmanas and Kshatriyas of all of us wherever we may be.'[14] This last usage had echoes of Gandhi's argument on the basis of a 'true' caste system: not based on birth, but on moral values. It was a moment of weakness; the image is not typical of Nehru – but it was a moment indicative of a tone of resignation and lack of certainty or control that was beginning to affect Nehru at the time.

Nehru emerged from prison after over 13 months of solitude and isolation in December 1941, to be faced with major changes in the war situation. On June 22, 1941, Germany had attacked the Soviet Union, ending the uneasy peace of the Nazi–Soviet Pact. In December, Japan attacked the United States at Pearl Harbour, and Germany declared war on the USA. Writing for the London *Daily Herald*, Nehru confessed that his prison term had put him out of touch with events and political perspectives: 'Individual opinions may be expressed but they will lack the reality which contact with people and a living situation gives them. I am seeking to regain these contacts.'[15]

The British response to the entry of the USSR into the war on the allied side was to legalise the Communist Party of India. The hope was that its campaign for a 'People's War' against the fascist powers would serve the British need to find some sort of support base for its war effort in India. But officials remained extremely suspicious of the CPI, who they expected to use the opportunity to campaign both against fascists as the immediate and interim enemy and against imperialism as the major enemy to be fought next. The CPI in turn was far from willing to be a puppet of the British government. Moreover, its rank and file membership, at least, if not sections of the leadership, were not altogether willing to fall in behind leads from the USSR at all times, as subsequent events in 1942 were to show.

By early 1942, a Japanese invasion of India seemed impending; the Japanese advance through South-East Asia had absorbed Malaya and Burma in February and March, and seemed inexorably to lead on to India. There was an urgent need for Indian support. This was no longer only a question of supplies, though supplies themselves were important enough (India was the main source of supplies for the Middle Eastern and North African as well as the South-East Asian theatres of war, and the base for airlifts to China, in addition to providing armed forces; since suppliers were mostly in the private sector, the profit motive could be relied upon to keep supplies coming). If India were to be lost, the war seemed all but over for the Allies.

But in the event of a Japanese invasion, it was not impossible that the Indian population would welcome the Japanese as liberators. Refugees among Indians who had worked in South-East Asia had brought back reports of British forces running away from the Japanese rather than fighting; evacuation had been organised on a racial basis with all safe routes and modes of transport reserved for whites, leaving Indians of all classes to fend for themselves. An impending sense of collapse of British rule was in the air. In February 1942 Chiang Kai-shek had visited India along with his wife, Song Meiling (whose sister Song Qingling, Sun Yat-Sen's widow, Nehru had met at Brussels in 1927). Having met Congress leaders, Chiang told his British and American allies that their lack of clear commitment to Indian independence was tantamount to presenting India to the Japanese – an ironic comment coming from him, given that it was widely felt that Chiang's own anti-Japanese campaign was quite feeble, and that the struggle against Japan in China was largely being carried out by the communists.

Towards the end of March 1942, Sir Stafford Cripps was sent to India on a mission to find a formula that Indians could agree upon in order to support the war effort. Once again, Nehru was the major source of hope for negotiations to succeed, and Nehru was with a clear conscience able to seek agreement with Britain in what was now a genuine anti-fascist war. Within the Congress' internal structure, he was by now anointed as leader-in-waiting: in January 1942, Gandhi had confirmed that he thought Jawaharlal should be his 'successor' (this was not a formal handing over of power, because Gandhi himself had no formal leadership role). But Nehru was by no means the only person to consider (Nehru and the Congress president, Maulana Azad, were the appointed negotiators on the Congress's behalf). With a Japanese invasion impending, more pragmatic solutions seemed to dictate that a settlement would need to be made with the Japanese rather than the British. Cripps travelled around meeting Indian 'leaders' of various kinds and making copious notes as to their demands. (Towards the end of March, Nehru was absent from a number of crucial meetings due to the necessity of being in Allahabad for the wedding of his daughter on 26 March to Feroze Gandhi, a young Congress worker of Zoroastrian origin who presented his wife with a name that became a huge political asset.)

On the British side, there was also little unity of purpose, given that Labour and the Conservatives were uneasy co-partners in the wartime coalition. Cripps was sent to India with a brief that he could offer Indians a share in government immediately in exchange for the right to decide their future after the war. American pressures also had a role to play: the grandiose declaration in the Atlantic Charter of August 1941 that the 'United Nations' were engaged in a war for freedom for the world had forced Churchill to declare in the House of Commons the following month that this did not, of course, apply to India or the other British colonies. This was not the American interpretation; and the presence in Delhi from April 3, 1942 of President Roosevelt's personal representative, Colonel Louis Johnson, was a matter of some irritation to the Conservative establishment, who felt that Johnson was encouraging the Indians to demand independence. Immediately upon his arrival, Johnson involved himself in the Cripps negotiations and established a firm rapport with Cripps and, more disturbingly, with Nehru.

Secretary of State Leo Amery believed that America had its eye on the British Empire's markets in a post-war trading world in which the US could play the role of free-trade imperialist that the British had been able to play in the nineteenth century. Amery's view was that even an eventually independent India must be encouraged to remain in a trading bloc based on the British Empire and Commonwealth after the war; he was close to circles in British politics that had long argued that the Commonwealth and Empire should become an economic partnership and a trading bloc rather than a system of political domination – white colonies first, then native dependencies would voluntarily become members as they 'progressed' into self-governing dominions. Churchill's views were not quite so sympathetic. Comforting his fellow Conservative, Linlithgow, on the eve of Cripps's visit to India, Churchill wrote: 'It would be impossible, owing to unfortunate rumours and publicity, and the general American outlook, to stand on a purely negative attitude and the Cripps Mission is indispensable to prove our honesty of purpose . . . If that is rejected by the Indian parties . . . our sincerity will be proved to the world.'[16]

Whether or not the Cripps Mission was actually designed to fail, therefore, in Churchill's eyes it was more a public relations gesture than a concession. The Cripps proposals offered post-war dominion status with the right to secede from the Empire if India so desired. The Cripps proposals also recognised individual provinces' right to opt out of an eventual post-war Indian union – the first official recognition of a potentially divided India – a 'Pakistan'. This was a necessary concession to the Muslim League to secure their agreement in any settlement. For the present, Cripps promised the Congress a quasi-Cabinet; Defence would have an Indian in charge, although actual military matters would still be in the hands of the commander-in-chief. This would, he felt, show sincerity of purpose. But in making such an offer, he had apparently overshot the mark, and was forced to climb down, saying he had been misunderstood. The pressures on him were obvious: the viceroy, Linlithgow, continuously complained to London that his authority was being undermined, and Churchill telegraphed Cripps that he had not been authorised to offer so much. At any rate, the Congress and the Muslim League rejected the Cripps proposals, and the Mission had failed.

AFTER THE CRIPPS MISSION: THE DEBATE WITHIN THE CONGRESS, AND THE QUIT INDIA MOVEMENT

With the Cripps Mission having failed, and the Japanese fast approaching the north-eastern frontiers of British India, the Congress sat down to debate terms of possible cooperation or conflict with the government. This was now a hard debate within the Congress, watched anxiously at every step of the way by the British, whose intelligence services and reporters worked overtime. The working committee was divided on what approach to take. It was, however, generally felt that the British had demonstrated their lack of good faith conclusively; moreover, many had begun to feel that the time for a compromise with the British was over, and the more pressing need was for a beginning of negotiations with the advancing Japanese, who were almost inevitably going to enter India in the near future. Gandhi's succinct statement on the Cripps offer – a 'post-dated cheque' (to which a journalist had added 'on a crashing bank')[17] – summed up the mood. Gandhi himself said that India had no quarrel with the Japanese; it was Britain that was at war with Japan. Such statements were given much publicity by the government's propaganda departments during the war to demonstrate the Congress's defeatist position and thereby to justify the incarceration of the Congress leaders.

But Gandhi's statement represented only one side of the debate; and he was by no means clear about what he anticipated. Paper positions, clarified retrospectively, do not altogether reflect the dilemmas and confusions of those anguished days of debate, in which the old alignments of left and right were no indication of what position someone might take. Gandhi took the most militant line of his career, backed by a combination of the Congress' right wing and some members of the CSP; strong action was opposed by some moderates as well as by the CPI, for different reasons. Nehru, on the latter side, argued that it was not possible to do a deal with fascists, and was against an anti-British move that might in the end lead to a fascist victory. But short of arguing that British imperialism was better than Japanese imperialism, Nehru could no longer insist that some sort of agreement with the government should be the goal. After the failure of the Cripps Mission this position was not tenable. Cripps' reliance on Nehru for the success of his mission had irritated Nehru and placed him in a false position. 'I made it perfectly plain to him [Cripps],' Nehru was to write later, 'that there were limits beyond which I could not carry the Congress and there were limits beyond which the Congress could not carry the people.'[18] Perhaps Nehru's closeness to Cripps and to the Labour Party had led him to believe that Indian independence under a Labour government would be a reality, but for this to happen Britain had to end the war on the winning side, and India had to remain British. At any rate, Nehru's side lost the argument; the Congress decided to launch the Quit India Movement, and in the spirit of democratic centralism, Nehru moved the Quit India resolution himself. The country was waiting for a signal, it was now argued, and three years of dithering, manoeuvring and searching for direction in the hope of some sort of British gesture had come to nothing. On August 8, 1942, the Congress announced that the British were being told to quit India immediately.

Through July and early August 1942 the internal debates of the Congress had been followed with great anxiety and interest by the British. The moment the call to Quit India had been announced, the government acted swiftly. The entire top-level leadership of the Congress was arrested. But if this was intended to retard a potential anti-government movement, it did not work. The government seems to have had more faith in the Congress's ability to command and control the masses than did the Congress itself: the Congress leadership had fully expected to be arrested, and to be reduced to following events through the limited information that would be available to them in prison. Uncharacteristically, Gandhi's call for popular action did not make the usual appeal to non-violence: the movement, once begun, must not be stopped, and could not be stopped; people would have to make judgements for themselves; this was a time to 'do or die'.[19]

The resultant upsurge of popular anger took the British by surprise. From August to September 1942, different local initiatives and circumstances and divergent goals merged and coalesced into popular violence and unrest. Much of this was unorganised activity – there was a large-scale sense of the impending end of British rule. Linlithgow wrote to Churchill at the end of August that the rebellion was 'by far the most serious rebellion since that of 1857, the gravity and extent of which we have so far concealed from the world for reasons of military security.'[20] The Quit India Movement of 1942 has acquired the status of legend in the Indian nationalist imagination, but it is a much disputed legend. Retrospectively it has been described as the 'almost revolution', the expression of collective national consciousness, a spontaneous outburst of anti-imperialist anger. In some versions, this revolution was betrayed by the perfidious Communist Party of India, who refused to support the movement because the Soviet Union was by this time among the allies of Britain in the war. This view was particularly strong among the Congress Socialists, many of whom played an important leadership role once the Congress leadership was in jail, organising popular resistance, including acts of sabotage of communications that lasted far longer than popular protest and violence. In reality, although the CPI's *leadership* decided not to back the movement, so as not to disrupt the anti-fascist war effort, many party members participated in the movement. It should also be remembered that throughout the 1930s, the CPI (having been illegal since 1934) had worked from within the CSP, and many among the primary levels of active political workers were unused to making sharp distinctions between the CPI and the umbrella organisation of which they were a part. A further irony, of course, was that several of the Congress's own leaders, Nehru among them, had argued strongly against anti-British agitation at that juncture.

The British government's response was brutal. Secretary of State Leo Amery decided that one of the best ways to restore order at minimal cost to British manpower was to bomb or machine-gun agitating crowds from the air. Churchill and Amery had pioneered this policy in the 1920s in Iraq during their respective stints as Secretary of State for the Colonies (the airman responsible then for bombing the Kurdish population being 'Bomber' Harris, later immortalised for another bombing of civilian populations in Dresden). Additional forms of chastising the errant natives included imposing collective fines on entire villages from which people had been deemed to have participated in the movement, and public floggings of individuals in order to set an example to others. Amery qualified the punishment regime somewhat: there should be no fines for Muslim villages (Muslim participation was not very high – according, mainly, to British records). The rationale was clear: Quit India was to be described as a Hindu movement, and nothing should be done that might create cross-sectarian solidarity (Muhammad Ali Jinnah, for the Muslim League, did not support the movement, so at least the successful detaching of elite Muslim leadership from potential opposition had been successfully achieved). As in 1857, large parts of the country had to be re-conquered; at the height of the movement, fifty-seven and a half battalions were in action against the internal threat. In 1857, of course, there had been no planes to bomb or machine-gun people from the air, unlike in 1942 when this was done as a legitimate means of crowd control. During and after the Quit India Movement, India was treated not as an ally but as an occupied country.

JAIL 1942–5

As events unfolded, the Congress leaders remained out of the loop. Jawaharlal remained in jail; Gandhi, now in his 70s, was given the more luxurious prison of the Aga Khan's palace, where nevertheless his fast from February 10, 1943, broken after 21 days, managed to become the focal point of British imperial politics: if Gandhi died, would it be possible to hold an India that knew he had died in British custody? Gandhi's fast had been, as he put it, both a self-purificatory exercise and a protest against the government's accusation that he had been personally responsible for the violence of the Quit India Movement. British propaganda had sought to cast the Congress leaders as defeatist and at worst pro-Japanese and pro-fascist. Nehru, in prison, following events on the outside, had time to contemplate the irony of events: he, a premature anti-fascist, was in jail, with many appeasers-turned-opponents of fascism now accusing him and the rest of the Congress of being pro-fascist.

For nearly three crucial years, from 1942 to 1945, Nehru remained in prison. He used the time, as usual, to further his intellectual development, in a burst of activity from April to September 1944 writing his *Discovery of India*. This was a book clearly written in anticipation of independence, and was a clarificatory endeavour as much for himself as for a potential public. It was also Nehru's last major statement of his ideological position made with the benefit of leisure – asked in January 1950 whether he was writing another book, he replied, 'How could I be? I've not been in jail of late.'[21] The text was a strange conglomeration of diverse styles and genres.

It was in part a narrative, in part reflections on his own life and his 'discovery of India' as one who had approached India, with his British educational background, almost as an alien himself; in part an attempt to think through some of the problems of constructing a coherent national identity. Based in part on discussions had with fellow prisoners, who he thanked in the text for their contributions, it reflected on the nature of the positive content of Indian nationalism: the negative content of anti-British or anti-imperialist sentiment would be inadequate cement for holding together a diverse conglomeration of peoples. And of course it had centrally to tackle questions of a unifying national identity in the light of what he felt to be the unnecessary sectarian call for a 'Pakistan'. But by the time Nehru emerged from prison, events had for the most part overtaken him.

The highlight, if one can call it that, of Nehru's time in jail was the great Bengal Famine, which ran its course from 1943 to 1944. This is now the textbooks' central example of a man-made famine. The fall of Burma, a rice-supplying area for Bengal, nevertheless left 90–95% of the normal rice supply. But hoarding in anticipation of shortages, leading to price rises, and further hoarding exacerbated by profiteering traders began to create artificial shortages. The Bengal Provincial Government under the Muslim League was unable and at times unwilling to organise supplies. Shortages were partly the outcome of British attempts at organising an anti-Japanese 'scorched earth' policy. The policy involved 'denial' of resources to the advancing Japanese by removing supplies that might feed an advancing army and included the sinking of boats – absolutely crucial to all transport of men and materials in eastern Bengal, where communication was mostly through the intricate network of waterways that criss-crossed the region. 'Boat denial' therefore also had the effect of denying grain to the population of eastern Bengal. It was clear to many that 'scorched earth' would be bitterly opposed by the population of eastern Bengal who were supposed to make sacrifices not for a clearly understood patriotic cause but for the cause, apparently, of a hated regime whose officials were to arrive in the region to enforce the policy. The necessary corollary to such a policy, the movement of people away from the region, could never have been seriously contemplated: the possibility of Eastern Bengalis retreating westwards from a densely-populated region into equally densely-populated areas could never have been realistic.

Moreover, the British government had set priorities according to the needs of the war effort. According to these, armed forces and urban regions, especially the urban workforce which kept the factories and the ports running, were to get preference in terms of food and essential supplies. Transport bottlenecks also ensured that stockpiles of grain rotted in the humidity of the Bengal climate even as people starved and hoarders made huge profits. Meanwhile, partly due to the government's 'priorities' policy which kept Calcutta supplied and fed, and partly due to wartime censorship, news of the famine reached Calcutta only through hordes of starving villagers appearing on its streets, begging not for rice, but for the froth from the surface of others' rice-pots, then dying on the streets and creating a major health hazard. (Eventually, a Calcutta newspaper, *The Statesman*, defied the government and broke the news to the world; earlier sources of information had been sketches and paintings by artists from the Communist Party who produced some of the most striking and harrowing images of the famine.) Relief, such as it was, was mostly through private initiatives. These, often based on care of the 'community', caused a certain amount of sectarian tension as it was seen that Muslims were excluded from Hindu relief efforts and vice versa.

The new viceroy, Lord Wavell, who replaced Linlithgow during the course of the famine, was genuinely shocked by what he saw, but his requests for relief were resolutely blocked by Winston Churchill, who argued that ships could not be diverted from their essential wartime duties to bring grain to the stricken Bengal population. In the end the central argument that secured relief was a military one. Commander-in-Chief Lord Auchinleck wrote a memorandum explaining the devastating effects of the famine on military morale: troops were seen to be sharing their own rations with the starving Bengal population, and had uneasy consciences as they realised that the priority to keep them fed was directly causing starvation among the people they were living amidst. Relief, though was the proverbial too little and too late; estimates put the number of deaths at 3.5 million to 4.5 million persons, and disease took its toll on the weakened population long after direct starvation had ceased.

BACK IN THE OUTSIDE WORLD

On June 14, 1945, Nehru and other members of the Congress Working Committee were released from jail. The British wanted to do business with them again. The war in Europe having ended with the German surrender on May 7, other matters could now reappear on the agenda. It had become apparent, in the course of the war, that Britain did not have the will or the military resources to hold India by force after the war, and the viceroy, Lord Wavell, as a military man, now saw the virtues of an orderly transfer of power to a government that Britain would be able to deal with after the war, rather than risk popular initiatives that led in unknown directions. This seems to have been the British position from at least late 1944, if not earlier. The problem now, as the British saw it, would be to create enough agreement among the two main players in the negotiations, the Congress and the Muslim League, to effect such an orderly transfer. Wavell now decided that the time had come to agree terms; to this end, he arranged a conference at Simla.

One of the major outcomes of the Congress leadership's long period in jail during the war was that when they re-emerged into the outside world they were not fully conversant with the political situation. Events had moved along quickly in their absence. Most importantly, the Muslim League had made great advances in their political strength. Whereas at the beginning of the war, they were a small part of an uneasy coalition in the provincial government of Bengal, by the end of the war they had emerged as a major political force, with much of India's Muslim population rallying round their slogan of Pakistan. Admittedly, 'Pakistan' was not properly defined; it was a deliberately vague slogan that could by its very vagueness accommodate the aspirations of every Muslim dissatisfied with his lot. Nevertheless, the Muslim League's gains in the wartime period were undeniable. In this they were substantially helped by the British shopping around for allies who would back them in the war effort. The Muslim League was able to offer cautious and conditional support to the British, winning in turn the right to represent Muslims to the British. Thus in large measure, it was due to *British* recognition of the Muslim League as representing Muslims that the League could, post-ex facto, gather the support of Muslim groups behind itself, and thereby also inherit the supporters of these other Muslim groups.

The Congress, and Nehru, missed this part of the plot. For them, the League was the major failure of the 1937 elections, where they had failed even to win Muslim seats. A hard-line, uncompromising position against the League could still be viable as far as they were concerned, because, even as it was admitted that the Congress itself had to work harder to bolster its Muslim support base, it was taken as self-evident that the League did not have much of a support base itself. The last testing of the electoral waters had, therefore, not prepared the Congress at all for the situation, and the incarceration of its leaders had left them unable to follow developments during the war with any accuracy – to which developments they had also a propensity to be blind. At any rate, the endgame was to be played on the basis of negotiations between three main players – the Congress, the League and the British; the 'people' were to be invoked by all sides in different ways, but the 'will of the people' was a mysterious entity to all concerned.

Negotiations, nevertheless, now began in earnest. In May 1944, Gandhi had been released from prison; soon afterwards, in July, he had met Jinnah for talks. With most important Congressmen in jail, in 1943 the South Indian Congress leader Chakravarty Rajagopalachari had proposed a formula for an eventual Pakistan: Muslim areas should be defined, followed by a plebiscite of the areas with a Muslim absolute majority to determine whether they would prefer a separate Pakistan. The proposals envisaged important subjects such as communications and defence remaining in the hands of some sort of union government even in the event of some separation. Gandhi based his talks on the Rajagopalachari formula; Jinnah preferred the separation of Punjab, Sind, Baluchistan, the North-West Frontier Province, Bengal and Assam, and refused to accept what he referred to as a 'maimed, mutilated and moth-eaten Pakistan'.[22] This hardly augured well for Simla, at which haggling over formulae, territories, reassurances to minorities and the Muslim League's wish to be identified with all Muslims took centre stage.

Wavell's hope at the Simla Conference (June 25–July 14, 1945) was to bring Congress and League into government. Muslims and 'caste Hindus' were to be equally represented in a new Viceroy's Executive Council, with other minorities also represented, on the basis of the existing constitution, but with a new one to be drawn up after the war. Negotiations broke down on the League's refusal to allow Congress to appoint any Muslims to the Council and the Congress's refusal to be further reduced in stature to that of a 'caste Hindu' party. Maulana Azad, the Congress president, himself a Muslim, was continuously derided by Jinnah as the Congress's window dressing. 'This was the first time,' Azad later wrote, 'when negotiations failed, not on the basic political issue between India and Britain, but on the communal issue dividing different Indian groups.'[23] Perhaps Wavell's major achievement had been to convince Churchill of the need for such an initiative; at any rate, in July 1945, the landslide Labour victory in Britain removed Churchill from the equation. In August 1945, elections were announced for the coming winter in India.

The Labour government had a concrete commitment to Indian independence, with the obvious corollaries that had been discussed with Nehru at Filkins in 1938: a transfer of power would have to safeguard some long-term British interests, otherwise no British government could support it. Within the Congress, it was clear who Labour would prefer to deal with: Jawaharlal Nehru. But Nehru was not himself, by this time, the best possible negotiator. Still thinking in terms of principles, and often refusing to surrender the moral high ground, Nehru could make blunders that a more pragmatic negotiator could avoid.

If Nehru was, as most people accepted, going to be a main protagonist in the endgame, he had to be briefed by persons more in touch with the outside world than someone just emerging from prison. During the Simla conference, on June 27 and 28, 1945, Z.A. Ahmad of the Communist Party of India was delegated to brief Nehru on what had been going on, and to sound him out on his views. Ahmad drew attention to Nehru's description of the CPI's refusal to support the Quit India Movement as due to their being virtually Soviet agents. Nehru was distinctly uncomfortable; he averred that he had not intended to make such a statement but had been cornered by the press into saying something. Breaking through the discomfort barrier, Nehru put his cards on the table: he was influential in the Congress partly due to his mass popularity and partly because he was 'internationally better known' and had 'better contacts than anyone else'; nevertheless he was 'in a sense quite alone'. On his side, he felt that the CPI, who had accepted the demand for Pakistan, wanted the Congress to surrender to all Jinnah's demands; but Jinnah did not actually want a settlement, and was not making a concrete demand that could be responded to. (Nehru's distrust of Jinnah led him to refuse to concede honourable intentions to any of Jinnah's pronouncements; and this distrust seems to have been well-founded: he did not say what he meant, put his cards on the table or conduct transparent negotiations.) Moreover, concessions to Jinnah on Pakistan – and here Nehru was at his most disarmingly honest – would split the Congress: 'There is a strong anti-Pakistan Hindu opinion inside the Congress which would go over to the Hindu [Maha]Sabha.'[24]

This was a telling statement. In 1940, members of the Congress were told they had to choose between Hindu Mahasabha membership and that of the Congress, because membership of a communal organisation was not compatible with Congress membership; apparently, not all Hindu communalists had decided to leave, because the Congress could accommodate a Hindu right-wing position as long as it was not publicly proclaimed. (Consequently, the Hindu Mahasabha's poor electoral showings could be attributed to its natural supporters still voting for the Congress.) Nehru himself practically described himself as an isolated individual tolerated by the Congress because of his popularity and international reputation. Now, in 1945, it was the communists who were excluded from the Congress, using the leverage gained from the 1942 divergences that had, in fact, divided opinion in Congress as much as in the CPI, though neither side was willing to acknowledge this publicly. Nehru confirmed that the CSP and the Congress right were no longer willing to have the communists work through the Congress.

Ahmad sought to clarify the communists' position to Nehru. The CPI had, at the time of its legalisation, decided not to fight against the tide of sectarianism, but to ride it and then attempt to divert it – an early realism that acknowledged the widespread appeal of 'Pakistan' as an undefined utopia in which poor Muslims would find their problems solved. Accordingly, its position on 'Pakistan', published in 1942, modelled itself on Soviet nationalities policy: India was not one nation, or even two, but many; there were, indeed, several Muslim nationalities – 'as soon as we grasp that behind the demand for Pakistan is the justified desire of the people of Muslim nationalities such as Sindhis, Baluchis, Punjabis (Muslims), Pathans to build their free national life within the greater unity of the all-Indian national freedom, we at once see there is a very simple solution to the communal problem in its new phase.'[25] Once the right of individual nationalities to their separate existence was recognised, there would be no reason for an actual separation of provinces or areas from an Indian union, which could then be a multinational state. (This formulation had allowed the CPI to continue its work on a class basis while working around the 'communal problem': indeed, in Bengal it was able substantially to strengthen a left wing of the Muslim League that was through the CPI able to appeal to peasants, and the CPI was able to appeal to Muslim peasants as peasants.) The CPI further argued that it made no sense to talk of Pakistan based on provinces separating, either, because existing provinces and states were not congruent with nationalities. But these intellectual distinctions made far more sense to a leadership than to followers. Nehru found them unviable.

Ahmad's report to the CPI noted that Nehru had temporarily lost his sense of perspective because of his admiration and respect for the underground activists of 1942, but that his respect for the CPI as a party of principle still remained. Ahmad concluded that Nehru would still have to be educated: he would have to be sent Party literature regularly, and would benefit from conversations with the main CPI theoreticians, but that the CPI should not give up working through Nehru.

This was logical enough, because by 1945 Nehru was for the first time unquestionably being pushed forward as the leader of the Congress and of an independent India – not merely as a leader of the left, with whom he had been identified in his years of equivocation. Gandhi had more or less by now anointed Nehru as leader-in-waiting, and as his own spiritual and moral successor, despite their political differences that were in many cases overt by this time: Nehru had no time for the Gandhian ideal of self-sufficient village communities, as he refused to compromise a modern and industrial India by a return to the idiocy of rural life. Equally importantly, the British would deal with him (he was 'internationally better known', as he politely put it), a pattern strengthened by the Labour victory in Britain, so the Congress right would deal through him. Although Vallabhbhai Patel would have dearly loved to be the leader, a choice that would also have been welcomed by many of India's big business lobby, Gandhi could persuade them that Nehru would be a more useful leader. This set up a pattern to follow through to independent India. Nehru would be a leftish leader of a mainly right-wing party that was forced, because it was led by him, to appear to be left wing in terms of rhetoric, and held back from its more right-wing tendencies by Nehru and by the public support commanded by Nehru. The left slowly left the Congress – first the CPI was edged out, then the CSP left, soon after independence. As a result Indian politics would look particularly radical in the post-independence years: an *apparently* centre-left party in power (the right hiding behind Nehru's image), the opposition almost entirely to the left of this, and a mostly empty right wing.

TAKING COMMAND?

From August 15, 1942 to November 11, 1945, Nehru's paper, the *National Herald*, had not been published – as Nehru explained it, the *National Herald* refused to submit to the conditions of censorship and control imposed upon it by the government. The fanfare reopening editorial, written by Nehru, was headlined '*Jai Hind*'.

This was, of course, an appropriation of the rallying call of the Indian National Army led by Subhas Bose. Bose's INA had failed to seize the moment; militarily speaking they were a failure, and Bose himself was dead, killed in a plane crash on the island of Formosa. It is not clear how many people in India had even known of the existence of the INA. Now that the war was over, INA prisoners were returning to India, censorship regulations had lapsed, and the British military establishment wanted to make an example of the INA as traitors. Suddenly the country was faced with news of an army they had not encountered before (if they had been reading *People's War*, the CPI's journal, they would have read that Bose was a fascist who was a puppet of the Nazis and the Japanese, but this would not have given them a clear idea of what he was doing there, nor of the INA itself).

Slogans and appropriations were now the order of the day. The *National Herald*'s last editorial of August 15, 1942, before its self-imposed silence, had been headlined '*Bande Mataram*' – the title of a prayer to the nation-as-mother by the Bengali novelist Bankimchandra Chattopadhyay that had become something of a national hymn for the Congress and its sympathisers from the days of the Bengal *swadeshi* movement. The only problem was, the novel of proxy nationalism from which the song was drawn cast Muslims as the alien outsiders resisted by Hindu nationalists. The song had become something of a political battleground, leading to its overtly anti-Muslim verses being culled, but many Muslims felt that the whole song was offensive, and that the Congress should abandon it. With regard to slogans, '*Jai Hind*' was infinitely crisper, and solved the problem of sectarian tendencies: in simple Hindustani, it declared 'Victory to Hind', a term that still preserved the geographical rather than the sectarian meanings of the word.

And of course the INA trials had raised passions that nobody could have anticipated. The Indian Army had been the foundation of British rule in India: if their loyalty was suspect, as Wavell and other military sources now believed, British rule could not survive. It was decided that the INA should be made an example of, the government holding public trials for several thousand INA prisoners, detaining without trial a few thousand more, and arranging a show trial for three INA officers, Shah Nawaz, Sehgal and Dhillon, at the Red Fort in Delhi. They had, it was argued, betrayed not only Britain but their own countrymen, against whom they had fought as part of an advancing Japanese army. But this was a difficult case to sell to the public at the time. To many people, the INA were heroes; they had failed, but they had risked their lives for their country.

This was a strategic blunder by the government, especially given that it was particularly anxious at the end of the war, anticipating that another large-scale Congress movement could easily cause large-scale disruption. They listened with particular alarm to Nehru's speeches as he toured the country praising the heroism of the 1942 rebels and martyrs and denouncing the government's repression, while criticising the opportunism of businessmen who had used the war years to make massive profits instead of supporting the national cause. (Patel and the Congress right also appealed to 1942 as a legitimating event in their speeches, but made no references to businessmen as collaborators.) The INA trials potentially cut across sectarian tendencies: a Muslim, a Hindu and a Sikh were being put on trial. The symbolism of the Red Fort was also portentous: the seat of Mughal sovereignty, it was here that the rebels of 1857 had come to demand of Bahadur Shah Zafar, the last Mughal emperor, that he accept leadership of the revolt.

The INA issue forced a response from political groups. For the Congress, as for the CPI, the INA was not exactly their favoured issue. But now, in the situation of unrest and anger that accompanied the end of the war, an issue that seemed to evoke so much popular feeling could not be ignored. The INA issue made its dutiful way into the Congress's manifesto for the 1945–6 elections, although some Congressmen privately admitted that if the Congress came to power it would also purge the army of the INA men. Popular politics at times seemed to be in a position to set the agenda – or rather, *elite interpretations* of the 'people's will' could set agendas. The post-war situation had led to massive cuts in employment levels as soldiers and auxiliary staff were demobilised across the country. The anger and bitterness of the Quit India and famine years had not receded. To this were added further causes for concern by the day. It is difficult to disaggregate the various motivations for popular unrest even now; at the time, it was particularly difficult. What political leaders saw was unrest, strikes, violence of various kinds, and almost millenarian expectations of momentous change.

The Congress took up the cause of the INA officers. Nehru and Bhulabhai Desai were on the INA defence committee, along with the liberal, Tej Bahadur Sapru, who had so recently been able to accept a seat as one of the eight Indians on Linlithgow's Executive Council, Nehru revisiting his past to dig out his barrister's robes. In the outside world, unrest attributed to the perceived persecution of members of the INA was severe. In November 1945 and February 1946, there were serious anti-European and anti-Eurasian riots in Calcutta. Processions through the streets of several Indian cities alarmed the British by their show of cross-sectarian solidarity, carrying flagpoles on which the flags of the Congress, the Muslim League and the hammer and sickle of the CPI had been tied together. In February 1946, the Royal Indian Navy mutinied, protesting, among other things, differential pay rates for its white and Indian members. Once again, a reluctant Congress was forced to provide moral support retrospectively. The RIN mutiny underlined the fact that the armed forces could no longer be relied upon to underpin British rule. When the government decided to drop proceedings against the INA, they were making a considered, strategic retreat; both sides had made their symbolic moves; as head of the interim government, Nehru diplomatically accepted a compromise on the issue of the remaining INA prisoners from the new viceroy, Lord Mountbatten: a few individuals accused of specific crimes rather than the generic charge of 'waging war against the King' remained in prison, the others were released.

Those who hoped for a united independent India saw this period as a hopeful sign of a true popular nationalism replacing the 'communalism' of the kind promoted by the Muslim League and the Hindu Mahasabha, but this may well have been wishful thinking. This was another instance of the mutual unintelligibility of elite and popular politics, even as their paths diverged, interlocked or crossed over.

ENDGAME: CLUMSY NEGOTIATIONS, POPULAR VIOLENCE

The tone for the Congress's election campaign in 1945–6 had been set by Nehru's speeches, although the organisational work of selecting candidates was taken over by Vallabhbhai Patel. In the elections, 442 out of 509 of the Muslim seats in the provinces went to the Muslim League, as did all 30 of the reserved seats in the Central Assembly. These electoral gains took Congress by surprise, but gave the League greater political legitimacy at the negotiating table. The six provinces that Jinnah had demanded as 'Pakistan' had not all obliged by returning League governments: in the North-West Frontier Province and in Assam, Congress was in government. Campaigns had been opportunistic, and often cynical: the Congress had appropriated the INA issue; in Punjab, the League had campaigned on the basis of the distinction between *din* and *duniya* – religion and worldly things – with *maulvis* playing a strong role in their campaigns, threatening recalcitrant Muslim voters with excommunication or divine vengeance. In Bengal, by contrast, where a left wing of the League had working relationships with the CPI-run Kisan Sabhas, the rhetoric was far more economics and class based. Witnesses to the *Tebhaga* movement, an agrarian movement of sharecroppers demanding a fair share of the produce, and led by the Kisan Sabhas, reported the presence of Muslim peasants at meetings carrying Muslim League flags onto which had been painted the hammer and sickle.

A three-member Cabinet Mission was now sent to India with a plan for the transfer of power. Sir Stafford Cripps, the Cabinet Mission's main negotiator on the basis of past experience, offered, on April 16, 1946, a three-tier scheme of provinces, groups of provinces and a weak federal centre to look after matters of vital importance. Provinces were categorised as Group A (the four north-western Muslim-majority provinces), Group B (the Hindu-majority provinces) and Group C (Assam and Bengal, the Muslim-majority provinces in the east). Cripps offered Jinnah this plan with the other option being a partition of Bengal and Punjab. Jinnah did not commit himself. In May, Nehru and Azad, the Congress's negotiators, accepted the three-tier scheme; but details were far from worked out, a familiar sticking point being Jinnah's insistence that the Congress be denied the right to appoint any Muslims in an interim government.

Nehru, however, was far from content with a plan that set out the pattern of a post-independence India in this awkward way. Given that he was committed to strong central government, and to centralised economic planning, a centre with limited powers or even jurisdiction over some areas of the country was not particularly to his liking. In a number of speeches, once again as Congress president (to which post he returned in July), he criticised the provincial grouping aspect of the Cabinet Mission Plan and declared that the Congress would be free to modify it in the future. 'We are not bound by a single thing,' he declared, 'except that we have decided to go into the Constituent Assembly.'[26] This gave Jinnah an opportunity to repudiate the Cabinet Mission Plan. Jinnah now raised the stakes substantially by calling for a day of direct action to show Muslims' support for Pakistan. The date was set for August 16, 1946: the date now remembered as that of the 'Great Calcutta Killings'.

Nehru's fellow negotiator, Maulana Azad, later blamed Nehru's speeches for this turn of events. Had he not made them, Jinnah would not have rejected the Plan, would not have called for a Direct Action Day, and the events of Calcutta and subsequent violence might have been avoided: 'The turn that events had taken made it almost impossible to expect a peaceful solution by agreement between the Congress and the Muslim League.'[27] Calcutta inaugurated a chain of violence that spread across India, which lasted well past the actual transfer of power, a bewildering series of events, and an enormous degree of carnage. Azad's retrospective account, however, never questioned, nor found worthy of mention, Jinnah's opportunism in calling for something that he might well have anticipated, especially in the context of the uneasy and tense environment of 1946, would lead to violence; it would seem that Jinnah's lack of principles could be taken for granted.

But if Jinnah was cynical enough to risk or even incite violence, neither he nor anyone else had much control over subsequent events. The intensity of the 'communal' violence in Calcutta took everyone by surprise. The communal solidarity of the INA trials and the post-war industrial unrest in Calcutta had not prepared anyone for what happened. The Bengal prime minister, H.S. Suhrawardy, made some incautious and provocative remarks in his speech on August 16 in Calcutta, a day on which many Muslims had come in to Calcutta from the countryside. Sporadic violence began, with the occasional looting of shops by Muslims in a state of agitation. It then transpired that neighbourhoods had organised local 'defence groups' and militia in anticipation of violence on August 16, and because violence had been anticipated from Muslims, these defence groups tended to be Hindus, but they were organised according to localities rather than in a massive collective communal organisation.[28] Insecurity had bred violence, 'defence' turned easily into offence, and many more Muslims than Hindus died in the three days of violence that followed in Calcutta. This was certainly far from what League leaders anticipated.

The response to the scale of slaughter was one of disbelief. Nehru was aghast at what he saw. '[T]he conflict is between humanity and inhumanity, between ordinary decency and bestial behaviour,' he declared. 'This has ceased to be merely communal or political. It is a challenge to every decent instinct of humanity and it should be treated as such. What has led up to this, the incitements to violence, the direct invitations to the shedding of blood, are worthy of enquiry.' Clearly referring to instigators, he stressed the responsibility of every citizen to calm things down and to cooperate with the police to isolate 'anti-social elements'. Localities, he advised, should organise themselves for self-protection irrespective of party, religion or profession, as should villages – which, indeed, was something like what happened in Calcutta. People should not respond to trouble from other areas. They should not rely on 'peace committees' composed of the very elements who had indulged in the violence, as had been the practice in previous instances of communal riots.[29]

Such advice had little effect. In October, violence spread to Noakhali, where the slogan 'We Want Revenge for Calcutta' was heard, but violence was largely muted in comparison to Calcutta and to subsequent events, restricted to what amounted to a local act of revenge against a Hindu *zamindar*; the rioters were mostly content to ritually humiliate Hindus by making them eat beef, recite the Islamic creed, the *Kalma*, and wear a *lungi*, a sarong-like garment associated in Eastern Bengal with poor Muslim peasants.[30] Then the violence spread to the north and west of India, where any question of restraint was quickly lost.

By this time, Nehru was the head of the Interim Government, inaugurated by Wavell on September 2, 1946. The Interim Government was to work on the principles of communal representation: Hindus, Muslims and Sikhs, Scheduled Castes (as the Backward Castes were now called after the 1935 Government of India Act had named them in a special Schedule) and the smaller minorities of Indian Christians and

Parsis would be the 'communities' represented. (The Backward Castes' spokesman, Dr B.R. Ambedkar, when he expressed his surprise at not being asked to join the government, was told his chances would have greatly improved had he been a Christian.) When presented with the *fait accompli* of a functioning government, the League decided to join it, despite the fact that it was not permitted to appoint all the Muslims in the government. Jinnah delegated to Liaquat Ali Khan, soon to be the first prime minister of Pakistan, the job of Nehru's deputy in the government – the League decided, however, to boycott membership of the Constituent Assembly (the Central Assembly that came into being as a result of the 1946 elections was to become the Indian Constituent Assembly).

Liaquat Ali Khan held the Finance portfolio, and was therefore the first Indian Finance Member to present a budget, in March 1947. This should have been a historic moment: Liaquat's budget contained radical proposals to tax businessmen for the profits they had made in the war years. But the Congress right now came forward with an objection: since Liaquat knew that most businessmen were Hindu, his proposals to tax businessmen were 'communal', and an attempt to deliver a parting kick to Indian developmental aspirations before Pakistan separated off from India. However absurd this sounded, the Congress right successfully had its way. Liaquat justified his budget by reference to Nehru's radical speeches after his release from prison, in which Nehru had made very similar proposals; and indeed Liaquat had cleared the budget with Nehru before presenting it. Nehru, as usual, when faced with determined opposition, backed down and disowned the budget. It was passed in drastically modified form, and provided more evidence for the League that the Congress had no intention of sharing power. During the recriminations over the budget, Nehru was taking advice from Dr John Matthai, at the time in the Interim Government as a representative of Indian Christians, but also an employee of Tata Sons. Matthai, Nehru claimed, had both economic expertise and business experience; but the principle of conflict of interest was clearly not observed on this occasion, for the Tatas had much to lose from Liaquat's budget.

The budget crisis illustrated the deadlock that had now arisen. Lord Wavell censured both Nehru and Liaquat for failing to agree on the budget, always a central aspect of government policy; if this was a reminder of British paternalistic attitudes to Indians' ability to govern themselves, there was also a sense among all concerned of being locked

Plate 1 'Joe' Nehru at Harrow, 1906
© Hulton-Deutsch Collection/CORBIS

Plate 2 Strained relations: Nehru and Gandhi before the launching of the Quit India Movement, 1942. Gandhi's secretary, Mahadev Desai, whispers something to the Mahatma

© Bettmann/CORBIS

Plate 3 An icon in the making: Lord and Lady Mountbatten looking at the portrait of Nehru after its unveiling at India House, London, on Nehru's birthday, November 14, 1947
© Bettmann/CORBIS

Plate 4 Nehru, in protective glasses, as potential buyer of farm tractors for India, Chicago, October 30, 1949
© Bettmann/CORBIS

Plate 5 Jawaharlal Nehru and Zhou Enlai in Beijing, October 26, 1954
© Bettmann/CORBIS

Plate 6 Nehru with Khrushchev and Bulganin in Delhi, December 1955. In between the two Soviet leaders is his daughter, Indira Gandhi
© Bettmann/CORBIS

Plate 7 The Dalai Lama and Jawaharlal Nehru, September 1959
© Bettmann/CORBIS

Plate 8 A visibly strained Nehru at a press conference, November 1962

into a pathological pattern of mutual psychological dependence – the British position as the arbitrating authority encouraged appeals to that authority on the part of the League and the Congress, and the viceroy could imagine he was dealing with two quarrelsome siblings.

There was also the anomaly of the position of the Muslim League boycotting the Central (Constituent) Assembly while remaining in government. On February 5, 1947, a letter to the viceroy drafted by Nehru and signed by the non-League members of the Interim Government claimed that by rejecting participation in the Constituent Assembly, the League had rejected the Cabinet Mission Plan and therefore should not continue in the Interim Government. On February 21, Nehru met Wavell and agreed not to press the issue of the League's resignation from the government; but he also brought up the question of partitioning the provinces of Bengal and Punjab, rather than surrendering them entire to an eventual Pakistan.

On February 23, Nehru wrote to Krishna Menon in London outlining the situation: as long as the League remained outside the Constituent Assembly, the Assembly had more freedom to 'do what it likes for the parts of India it represents'. The anticipated problem that the League would press for giving only limited powers to an eventual central government would thus not arise. But Punjab and Bengal were of course, by the tenets of democracy, not properly represented as a consequence of the League boycott; western Bengal and south-east Punjab were, because of their non-League representatives still being in the Assembly. Since these two areas wanted to remain in the Union, '[i]nevitably this means a division of Punjab and Bengal, bringing the richer parts of both these provinces, including the city of Calcutta of course, into the Union. The truncated Pakistan that remains will hardly be a gift worth having.'[31] This was, in fact, conventional wisdom among non-partisans: Pakistan was an economic anomaly with no possibility of a successful independent existence.

Meanwhile, the British prepared to leave, destroying incriminating or embarrassing documents – Nehru's protests to Wavell were met with the disingenuous claim that these were routine and unimportant documents; Nehru retorted that as the head of the government, it was surely he who should be the judge of what was or was not useful. And despite Nehru's protests, it was the British Indian Army that did much of the work of restoring British, French and Dutch imperialism in South-East

Asia – with an avowed anti-imperialist at the head of government. Wavell had done to Nehru in government what Gandhi had been accustomed to doing to him in the Congress: imprison him in a system that made him powerless to do any more than formally voice his protest.

Nehru could, however, survey the carnage of sectarian violence that was to be the backdrop of all events from now on, with a certain lack of comprehension. 'What the Muslim League people told us was wrong and exaggerated here and there,' Nehru wrote to Patel from Bihar in November 1946, 'but the real picture that I now find is quite as bad and sometimes even worse than anything that they had suggested . . . there has been a definite attempt on the part of Hindu mobs to exterminate the Muslims.' Most participants in the violence were 'ordinary peasant folk', who seemed full of remorse for what they had done, and had shouted 'Mahatma Gandhi *ki jai*' [Victory to Mahatma Gandhi] when Nehru addressed them at public meetings. Inexplicably, everyone had turned into animals; 'a madness has seized the people'. Obviously there were instigators – 'some educated people of the Hindu Sabha variety', or 'some Marwaris in Monghyr [district]', or landlords who were partly attempting 'to divert the attention of their tenantry from agrarian problems'. But what disturbed Nehru most was that the people had to a very large extent responded to the instigators.[32]

The timetable for British departure was now greatly sped up. All three negotiators had by now painted themselves into a corner: they were in effect negotiating details while claiming to represent people who were dying all around them with nothing they could do to stop this, and all the bargaining about details of various schemes seemed more and more like the vanities of old political rivals who were carried away by the logic and momentum of their negotiations. On February 20, 1947, Attlee announced that power would be transferred by June 1948 at the latest; in March 1947, the new viceroy, Lord Louis Mountbatten, announced upon his arrival that he was to be the last viceroy of British India. The end came even sooner than announced, at midnight on August 15, 1947.

There has been some speculation that there was a special magic between the Mountbattens and Jawaharlal that somehow led to Jinnah being cut out of the dealings. In some versions, this was allegedly due to an affair between Lady Mountbatten and Nehru; in other (oral) versions, this was due to an affair between *Lord* Mountbatten and Nehru. Although evidence of relations of a sexual nature are hard to come by, limited by the historian's inability to get into other people's bedrooms or private spaces retrospectively, it is undeniable that close personal relationships did exist among the three. (A mutual liking for one another had been evident from the time of their first meeting the year before Mountbatten took over as viceroy, when as head of South East Asian Command (SEAC) he and his wife met Nehru on the latter's visit to Singapore.) There was a definite closeness between Lady Mountbatten and Nehru – their relationship is one of the best-known open secrets in Indian history – as well as between Lord Mountbatten and Nehru. It is also clear that Mountbatten did not find Jinnah congenial company (very few people did).

Such questions, however, are largely irrelevant to the larger political picture. In the course of the interminable negotiations and discussions that accompanied the transfer of power and partition negotiations, interspersed, as diplomatic etiquette demanded, with space and time for civilised social intercourse, Nehru seems to have rediscovered in the Mountbattens' company something of the pleasant sociability of his Cambridge and London days. But it would be far too simplistic to suggest that this had a bearing on long-term British plans. Britain's geopolitical and economic interests lay in an undivided independent India as an ally. So it was in their interest to try and prevent a Pakistan that involved dividing India – and Mountbatten appears to have tried, and failed, as Wavell had before him. If partition did have to take place, it was in Britain's interest to have a strong India as an ally, with Pakistan and India maintaining as harmonious relations as possible.

Mountbatten modified the Cabinet Mission Plan to give the Muslim-majority provinces the option of staying out of a union altogether (the third tier had vanished), and in London it was suggested that provinces should be given the right to independence severally instead of as one or even two entities. This variation, in both its forms, was referred to as 'Plan Balkan'; realistic expectations of a united India had vanished. The 'Balkanisation' of India was not acceptable to Nehru. But Nehru had by now accepted a division of India as a distinct possibility. Gandhi, on the other hand, was completely opposed to a partition, and in April 1947 came up with his own plan. To assuage minorities', and especially Muslims', fears of the majority, Jinnah should be asked to form a Cabinet as leader, with the Congress refraining from using its majority in the Assembly to stop any League measures, provided they were in the interest of the country as a whole. Mountbatten would be the judge of the sincerity of such measures not as viceroy but in his personal capacity (in effect, Gandhi granted Mountbatten for this purpose the moral status of a *satyagrahi*). Private armies that had been involved in the violence of the past months should be disbanded, and Jinnah was to do his best to ensure the parties represented in his Cabinet would do their best to preserve peace in the country. If Jinnah rejected this offer, the same offer would be made to the Congress.

This Caucasian Chalk Circle gesture won little support from anyone; by April the practicalities of a partition were already being seriously discussed: how to phrase the questions to be asked the voters of Punjab and Bengal – firstly, whether they wished the provinces to be partitioned; and secondly, whether they wished the whole or parts of the provinces to remain independent, to adhere to the Indian Union, or to join Pakistan. Nehru pointed out there that figures from the 1941 Census were not very accurate in parts of India, especially in parts of Bengal: 'Separate electorates gave a great temptation to "cook" numbers, particularly of women in purdah.'[33] Other questions that emerged included whether the North-West Frontier Province really needed a plebiscite given that it had voted for the Congress and its allies in the 1946 elections, or whether it could realistically have a fair plebiscite given the movement of refugees fearing being caught on the wrong side of the new border.

By May, all that was left to argue about was the details of exactly where boundary lines were to be drawn. The Bengal Hindu Mahasabha leader, Shyamaprasad Mukherjee, wrote to Nehru expressing concern that Sarat Bose was talking to Suhrawardy about an independent, sovereign Bengal, and he opposed this, demanding the partition of Bengal regardless of whether Pakistan was created or not. Nehru replied that he did not 'appreciate' the idea of a sovereign Bengal unconnected with the Union altogether, but that details of a partition would have to be decided by a boundary commission. By this point, the best available option in the absence of the possibility of agreement among Indian political groups seemed a British-administered partition of India – an option that the Congress would have vehemently rejected in earlier years; in a final, ironic twist, the British claim to being referee between two antagonistic communities had *de facto* been conceded to them when they least wanted it. It can only be a matter of speculation what exactly Jinnah's hopes were in terms of his ideal Pakistan; but it seemed clear that what he would now get was what he had once dismissed as a 'mangy' and 'moth-eaten Pakistan', and what Nehru had described as 'a gift not worth having'. Nehru and Patel, for the Congress, and as members of the Interim Government, accepted partition on the understanding that there needed to be no more negotiations with Jinnah once he had been given this last, major concession. In later years Nehru spoke of everyone's tiredness in 1947; at the time, he reportedly summed up the situation as 'cutting off the head we will get rid of the headache'.[34]

Power was, in the end, to be transferred to two entities, temporarily the Dominions of India and Pakistan. The Princely States, allied to Britain under the principle of 'paramountcy' – they were theoretically independent and sovereign, but Britain was the 'paramount power' to which all the states conceded crucial powers – were informed that the paramountcy agreements would lapse with the British departure, and they would have to join one or other of the new dominions. The actual boundaries of the crucial provinces of Bengal and the Punjab were drawn up by a Boundary Commission effectively comprising one man, Sir Cyril Radcliffe, who was brought to India and advised not to visit the areas he was about to tear asunder; he was given maps and census figures and some office space. Radcliffe set out to draw his lines after the matter had been put to vote in the Assemblies of those provinces, whose Hindu and Sikh members tilted the vote in favour of a partition of those provinces rather than a complete incorporation of both provinces into Pakistan. Even the vehemently anti-partition position of the Hindu Mahasabha altered when the alternatives were so formulated. The award of the Boundary Commission was kept secret until August 15, 1947, but in anticipation of partition many areas tried to cleanse themselves of their minorities, adding to the already serious carnage. The western areas were the worst affected – the Punjab was, for instance, a region with ready access to arms due to its high levels of army recruitment – and organised massacres of Hindus and Sikhs by Muslims and of Muslims by Hindus and Sikhs, accompanied by apparently gratuitous mutilations of bodies, by rapes, abductions, and communities killing their own women to protect their 'honour', continued well past the date of actual transfer of power.

For ordinary people, diverse responses to fiercely disruptive events over the past few years – which probably had in common only feelings of confusion and insecurity – had been interpreted simplistically to mean that Hindus and Muslims needed to live in separate states. This spurious neatness hid many diverse tensions and fractures, lines of solidarity and conflict. It was far from clear that anyone had wanted such an outcome – and it is clear that it suited none of the three main parties to such negotiations, the Congress, the British, or even the Muslim League, whose cause had been best served in that they had achieved *a* Pakistan, albeit a somewhat 'moth-eaten' one. It was also clear that events, as they finally took shape, had much more to do with elite negotiations, and with Muhammad Ali Jinnah's negotiating skills in particular, than it had anything to do with popular will; partition was encountered with a sense of bewilderment by many.

Nevertheless, independence had arrived, and this was the end of a long hard road. There was a necessity for optimism. And it was now up to Jawaharlal Nehru to put it in words, and to find words to express joy but not to draw attention to the fact that events had run away from those to whom power was given. The words were carefully selected, for they would remain indelibly imprinted on the Indian collective consciousness, the moment of the birth of an independent state:

> Long years ago we made a tryst with destiny, and now the time comes when we shall redeem our pledge, not wholly or in full measure, but very substantially. At the stroke of the midnight hour, when the world sleeps, India will awake to life and freedom.[35]

The voice crackled on the radio – the speech was delivered in Nehru's characteristically crisp English, with perhaps a touch of exaggeration on the vowels. It was also, perhaps, too perfect a speech, for violence and carnage still continued throughout the country, amplified and intensified by the partition and population movements that accompanied it. Gandhi, typically perverse in the hour of his anointment as father of the new nation, refused to celebrate, or to be in Delhi. He had spent the last months travelling through India using his moral authority and presence to try and halt the violence where he could. The old man now preferred to observe a day of prayer and fasting in Calcutta.

INTERLUDE – ENVISIONING THE NEW INDIA

At the stroke of the midnight hour, India awoke to freedom of a kind, as well as to a host of unresolved problems that had only been discussed theoretically before. In political and intellectual circles, there had for some time been a deeply felt need to anticipate the nature and content of the post-independence Indian state. With formal independence achieved, the need for a definite programme and direction for the new Indian state now became a matter of urgency; there was a need to order various contending ideas into manageable forms and to find at least an interim closure to the debates on the nature of the new India.

The debates, when recounted in terms of their particular arguments, have a spurious rationality and calmness about them: they took place against the very turbulent backdrop of the violence and population transfers of 1946–8, the problems of accession of states to the new Union (notably Kashmir and Hyderabad), armed conflict with Pakistan, and continuing economic and political pressures from the former colonial power. But the debates need to be recounted here in that spurious calmness; because that was the way they were invoked, as legitimising principles for the actual politics of the independent Indian state. We must therefore examine the roots of what came to be called the 'Nehruvian vision' or the 'Nehruvian model' in India, describing thereby what might be called the political culture of post-independence India.

We might profitably ask whether this political culture took shape in the crucial period of transition from the temporary Dominion of India to the inauguration of the Republic of India on January 26, 1950. This was a time when a creative intellect had great scope for imprinting itself on the state. Jawaharlal Nehru was the intellectual for that moment; to a large extent the contours of a vision of the new India were shaped by him. He was not altogether in a position to write the script himself. But he was nevertheless able very effectively to intervene in the foundational debates at crucial points; and the vision of a new India at its most attractive is one that probably most deserves the epithet 'Nehruvian'.

POLITICAL LEGITIMACY: VISIONS AND FORMULAE

The retrospectively-named 'Nehruvian consensus' was often no more than an obligatory but fragile language of legitimacy. It had in part come into being in the course of forging the delicate coalition that was the Congress in the 1930s and 1940s; it was further framed in the debates in the Constituent Assembly, which sat from 1946 to 1949 to draw up a constitution for India. The component parts of that vision – secularism, equality before the law, and democracy based on universal adult franchise; economic self-sufficiency, 'development' as a rationale for the government's legitimacy, the importance therein of technology and of a technocracy to run it; the social concerns which the government claimed to represent; the desire to find an international voice for India and the importance of playing a world role – all bore the imprint of Nehru's energetic interventions: in the debates of the Constituent Assembly, in his speeches, in print, and in the public discussions, often initiated by Nehru, on the consequences of partition and on Hindu–Muslim relations in the new Indian state. It was a most humane, rational and inspiring vision; but we must also ask whether it was a vision ever realised, or whether it was its fragility or impossibility that made it so attractive.

To some extent, too, the 'Nehruvian' vision was based on a pre-existing set of formulae. The formulae can be baldly stated; they are easily recognisable in public debates at least from the 1930s. Claims to 'socialism' – or to some social concern for the poor and downtrodden – were obligatory, and were by the 1940s made by capitalists and avowed socialists alike (capitalists were extremely worried that socialism was in the ascendant and decided that the best way to protect themselves was to appear to concede 'socialism' while maintaining the 'essential features of capitalism'). Also invoked were 'science', technology and technical expertise as ways of achieving 'modern' social and economic goals – even by the Gandhians, who tried to redefine the 'modern' in such a way as to justify a decentralised, village-based and labour-intensive socio-economic order as more in keeping with 'modern' trends. To achieve these goals, a good deal of 'national discipline' was required, and the 'masses' were to have to make some sacrifices in the short term, or in the 'transitional period'. And lastly, all solutions to social, economic or political problems had to conform to 'indigenous' values: borrowings from 'foreign' systems were to be treated with suspicion. This was a particularly useful tactical argument used against socialists and communists by Gandhians and by the right (often strategically merging with the Gandhians); but it was also used by socialists to argue that communists were 'foreign' elements controlled from Moscow. The appeal of the 'indigenist' strand of argument in a colonised country was rhetorically powerful, and could often put people who counted themselves in the 'progressive' camp on the defensive. These views could all be contained within a general view of 'development' as 'progress', and of India as a 'modern' country with a rich 'tradition'.

And yet, to call them 'formulae' is not to suggest that they were meaningless. As ideas that formed the basis of the accepted political rhetoric of public arenas, they defined the boundaries of public standards to which people were expected to conform. This created the basis for public debate and the standards for acceptable action. Claims to political legitimacy had to be made in terms of a rhetorical appeal to the norms enshrined in the formulae. Deviations from such norms needed to be hidden, or justified as only apparent deviations, ultimately assimilable within the bounds of the norms. Those who disagreed strongly with the norms had to hold their peace or to find other ways of getting what they wanted in practical terms, while purporting to uphold the norms. So it was a set of constraining and framing boundaries for arguments and ideas; all arguments that hoped to claim any legitimacy had to place themselves within those boundaries; there was limited room for manoeuvre.

IN THE END IS THE BEGINNING: THE INDIAN NATIONAL CONGRESS AND THE STATE

The institutional framework within which Nehru had to work was in a state of flux, as the Congress searched for a role and a rationale to keep itself together. In the years running up to independence, the Congress had increasingly sought to identify itself with the nation as a whole, and through the nation with the state. So the equation the Congress-is-the-nation-is-the-state was to form the basis of its leadership in defining the nature of the new state, in shaping its institutions, and in mapping out policy directions.

But the Congress was a conglomeration of different forces, pulling in different directions – a platform for anti-imperialist struggle, not a party, as many of its own members had said on many occasions. Its main objective since December 1929 had been that of *'purna swaraj'* – 'complete independence' – which had now formally been achieved, although post-dated to a future period when a constitution had been drawn up and temporary dominion status ended. What was now needed was a party, not a platform. Given the lack of agreement on several basic political questions, this seemed an unrealistic expectation: apologists for capitalism, socialists and Gandhians of varying description and levels of commitment or opportunism had shared the Congress in an uneasy coalition of forces held together only by common opposition to British rule in India.

The Mahatma's suggestion was that the Congress should now dissolve itself. But the abandonment of the security and legitimacy of the Congress label was uncongenial: it was a point of orientation at a bewilderingly disorienting time. The Congress Socialist, Ram Manohar Lohia, argued in 1947 that power could only be transferred to Congress because no other party was capable of receiving it.[1] Ironically, the Socialists first dropped the word 'Congress' from their name, in 1947, and then, in 1949, seceded from the Congress altogether.

Logically enough, therefore, the anti-imperialist coalition that was the Congress broke apart with the achievement of independence. Former allies on the left were divided into three groups: Nehru and a vestigial left in the Congress, the Socialists outside, and the Communists rapidly becoming the main opposition party. Thereafter, if Nehru was to have his way in his own party, dominated by the right, he had to use Gandhian tactics to morally blackmail his colleagues – go over their heads by threatening to resign, in effect threatening them with the 'people', for they knew that without Nehru the party's electoral appeal dwindled to next to nothing. The extent to which Nehru was able to impose his vision on his colleagues had much to do with these tactics: he was staking his personal standing against them. But he could, occasionally, rely on cross-party support outside the Congress.

The Congress had, therefore, to be built into a party, with an organisation and discipline, and to find equations to run the state apparatus inherited, more or less intact, from the British. Institutional continuity was stressed by Vallabhbhai Patel. It was Patel who promoted the cause of the successor institution to the Indian Civil Service, the Indian Administrative Service (IAS); the latter was almost entirely modelled on the former, complete with the horsemanship test that had been the bane of many Indian candidates who had been successful in the written part of the ICS examination. The IAS, the police and the army (with its regimental trophy cabinets continuing to celebrate victories in colonial wars and massacres of colonial peoples) provided strong links with a colonial past. Government departments changed hands but not organisations; in many cases the change of crest from the imperial coat of arms to the Indian national emblem – the capital of one of the third century BC Mauryan Emperor Ashoka's famous pillars – on government stationery and publications was the most tangible indication of change.

THEORETICAL UNDERPINNINGS

The Congress's need for a coherent policy for the party and the state became inextricably linked up with the need for a national identity. The Congress had projected itself as the sole representative body capable of speaking for the nation as a whole. With the creation of Pakistan this claim could, if anything, be intensified: those who did not agree with the Congress's vision of India should now have left, and those who remained were by default those who agreed. But the Congress had no coherent vision of India. Behind the scenes, the Congress right, led by Patel, argued, after the partition of India, that the matter had been decided: Pakistan was a Muslim state; the residual India would therefore be a Hindu state.

Nehru disagreed strongly. Quite apart from the fact that he himself would not have found it congenial, as a non-believer, to live in an India so defined, this would have reduced Muslims in India to the implicit status of foreigners. The cross-border movements following partition and the accompanying violence had made it clear that great insecurity existed. And if this insecurity was amplified, violence would continue until complete population exchange was complete – which was unviable, undesirable, and would retrospectively make a mockery of all for which the Congress had publicly stood for so long. It would also retrospectively justify Pakistan by making explicit what many Muslim League and other Muslim publicists had often said: that the Congress's claim to being a secular party ought not to be taken seriously. And what of other minorities? In a 'Hindu' state, their position would be ambiguous. It was therefore imperative that the principles of secular democracy and equality before the law be observed.

It had long been the contention of Nehru and the Congress left that 'communal' identities were not true identities; they were made possible by the poverty of the people and their consequent search for resources of hope, manipulated by elites with a vested interest in sectarianism for their own narrow ends. 'Communalism', by this definition, was both a false nationalism and a false consciousness. The preferred way of overcoming this was by economic means: greater prosperity for the masses would lead to greater awareness that real issues were economic, not communal.

With this in mind, the left had been concerned to plan a future for India that included economic development and prosperity. The justification for a national state rested on the fact that a national state, as opposed to an economically retarding imperialist one, would have the interests of its own nationals at the centre of its vision. After independence, the Congress, which was in its own eyes the whole of the national movement, and was now also in charge of the state, would take control of economic development. In this way, it could claim legitimacy as the custodian of the national state.

This, in part, was a short cut: it gave the Congress the right to speak for the 'nation'. The rule of the Congress was assumed: universal adult franchise, when it came, would underline that fact. But the problem of a positive content for Indian nationalism remained to be solved. Too many pre-1947 versions of Indian-ness ultimately relied on versions of Hinduness, with tolerance towards minorities thrown in – or not, as was often the case. Typically, these versions drew their sustenance from a history that harked back to a 'Hindu' golden age of civilisation, ironically leaning heavily on the writings of early British Orientalist scholarship, even when placed in a newly nationalist argument. This was not necessarily thought of as a central problem as long as the cement of anti-colonialism could be relied upon to bind diverse elements together, and dissenting voices could simply be dismissed as 'communal'. But an agreed-upon, non-sectarian version of the Indian past had to be found.

Nehru had put his mind to this problem while in jail during the war. It was not a subject to which he was naturally inclined: he would have preferred to argue that nationalism was too narrow a creed whose time had come and gone – as indeed he had done in the 1930s, when expounding the need for socialism. In *The Discovery of India*, published in 1946, Nehru stated, as he often had at various public fora, that an obsession with nationalism was a natural response to the lack of freedom: 'for every subject country national freedom must be the first and dominant urge.'[2] With the achievement of freedom the obsession would vanish; wider groupings of nations and states, and wider solidarities on the basis of internationalism would be possible. But the emotional pull of nationalism could not now be wished away. How could one find a common cultural and historical heritage for India that would serve to build a sense of the nation?

'The roots of the present lay in the past,' Nehru wrote, and so he was to concern himself with trying to understand the history of India.[3] This would be 'a process similar to that of psychoanalysis, but applied to a race or to humanity itself instead of to an individual. The burden of the past, the burden of both good and ill, is over-powering, and sometimes suffocating, more especially for those of us who belong to very ancient civilisations like those of India and China.'[4] So the anxieties generated by the past in relation to the present had to be confronted and resolved.

Nehru confronted the 'Hindu' view of Indian-ness: 'It is . . . incorrect and undesirable to use "Hindu" or "Hinduism" for Indian culture, even with reference to the distant past.'[5] The term 'Hindu' was used in a geographical sense to denote the Indian land mass by outsiders, derived from the river Sindhu or Indus. The 'Hindu golden age' idea had been crucially shaped by the needs of Indian nationalism. This was understandable. 'It is not Indians only who are affected by nationalist urges and supposed national interest in the writing or consideration of history. Every nation and people seems to be affected by this desire to gild and better the past and distort it to their advantage.'[6] But it was a version that was, he argued, historically false (he could not have been blind to the fact that he was himself attempting something not dissimilar; to narrate an acceptable past for the 'nation', retrospectively to justify his own commitment to that 'nation'). Although he acknowledged that some basic ideas and continuities had been preserved in popular and elite cultures, it was impossible to attribute this to one group of inhabitants of India.

Historically, India was 'like some ancient palimpsest on which layer upon layer of thought and reverie had been inscribed, and yet no succeeding layer had completely hidden or erased what had been written previously.'[7] Each layer had enriched Indian culture, and had a place in a new national consciousness; the great rulers of India were the synthesisers who looked beyond sectional interests to bring together different layers. The crux of the alien nature of British rule was that it never adapted itself to India, never accepted India geographically as a home, and exploited India economically for the benefit of outside interests.

Nehru also warned against a view of India that over-glorified the past – a danger, he noted, that was also present in China. He agreed that both civilisations had 'shown an extraordinary staying power and adaptability'.[8] But not all ancient things were worth preserving: caste discrimination, for instance, had to be struggled against – in its origins, he reminded his readers, this had been based on colour. India was at present 'an odd mixture of medievalism, appalling poverty and misery and a somewhat superficial modernism of the middle classes'.[9] What was needed was to bring modernism to the masses, by the middle classes understanding and promoting the needs of the masses – he stressed his admiration for Russia and China in their attempts to end similar conditions (writing before the victory of the Chinese Communist Party, Nehru apparently backed the CCP's vision of a new China).

'Culture' remained a tricky question for an inclusive nationalism, and Nehru's solutions to the problem of Indian cultural unity were not altogether satisfying. He himself claimed to have experienced this unity emotionally rather than intellectually, in his travels through India. On the intellectual side, however, he tended to fall back on stereotypes. Nehru's own language, then and later, tended to be imbued with some of the prevalent language of race and eugenics, as well as a patronising and at times paternalistic attitude towards the 'masses': he spoke unself-consciously of 'sturdy peasants' and 'good stock'. ('Good stock' was, for Nehru, the result not of ethnic or racial *separation* but on the creative intermingling of the races that made up India.) His accretion-and-synthesis view of Indian culture fitted in well with cultural practices such as the worship at Sufi shrines of both 'Hindus' and Muslims. In other cases, this view did not work quite so well: the peasants, he wrote, had in common oral versions of the great epics, the *Ramayana* and the *Mahabharata* – this was, perhaps, true even of some Muslim and Christian 'sturdy peasants', but was not true, for instance, of the north-eastern 'tribal' territories of India that were to be inherited by independent India because they had been within the borders of British India. The difficulty of finding an inclusive 'culture' that would encompass class, regional and religious differences was an insuperable one – the communist-preferred model of an India of many nations and a multinational Indian state might have solved this problem better.

However, despite its problems, Nehru's version largely succeeded in becoming the dominant left-secular master narrative of Indian history. Its major achievement was to disarm the view of Indian culture as 'Hindu'. It could, of course, be argued that this was a matter of *naming*: a Hindu majoritarian ethic could hide behind the secular view of an overarching Indian culture, in which 'Hindu' culture, no longer so called, was given a large space, with any attempt to assert the particularism of a Muslim or any other minority culture being regarded as 'communal'. This allowed Hindu sectarianism to survive behind a veneer of political correctness, even within the Congress. But this banishing of Hindu sectarianism into an outer darkness, in which it was the 'ism' that dare not speak its name, was in itself an achievement.

COMPROMISES AND THE CONSTITUTION

The practical business of defining future directions for India was, however, not in Nehru's hands; it was the responsibility of the Constituent Assembly, where Nehru's ability to obtain his desirable outcomes were constrained. 'I feel greatly how much out of touch I am with the present sentiments of the Hindus,' he wrote to Krishna Menon. 'Over many matters we rub each other the wrong way and I fear that the Constituent Assembly is not going to be an easy companion.'[10] Nehru's natural allies in the cause of building a progressive constitution, the Congress Socialists, had boycotted the Constituent Assembly as it had been based on the old communal electorates and property franchise of colonial India, which they believed was no basis for framing a democratic and progressive constitution for the nation as a whole.

The Constituent Assembly met from 1946 to 1949 to frame a constitution for the new state – temporarily a self-governing dominion under the British Crown. Nehru had an over-optimistic time-frame in mind for the preparation of a constitution: he thought dominion status would only last a short time, until June 1948 at the latest – the projected date of British departure according to Attlee's announcement – by which time an Indian constitution would be written. Lord Mountbatten had, on Nehru's request, agreed to stay on as governor-general of the new and temporary Dominion of India to ensure continuity of administration and smoothness of transition (Mountbatten held this post until June 1948). At any event, the document produced by the discussions turned out to be the longest written constitution in the world, reflecting awkward compromises and containing frankly irreconcilable principles that had to be reconciled by hiding them in minor sections of the constitution.

The composition of the Constituent Assembly, with its Congress majority, reflected the Congress's strength in the 1946 elections – elected not under universal adult franchise but a limited property franchise, it did not represent the social forces that might potentially have supported a consensus to the left. Its president was Dr B.R. Ambedkar, long a voice of dissent from the nationalist mainstream, having been willing to use the interested assistance of the British administration to safeguard the position of the backward castes, and from August 1947 a member of Nehru's first Cabinet. This Cabinet was itself a balancing of divergent forces in what was effectively a national coalition. Notably, Vallabhbhai Patel and Rajendra Prasad within the Congress, and Shyamaprasad Mukherjee, also in the Cabinet though a member of the Hindu Mahasabha, together represented right-wing upper-caste Hindu opinion; Patel also remained a central pro-capitalist voice within the Congress.

The unresolved nature of the debates on what an independent India was to look like was reflected in the debates of the Constituent Assembly. Minoo Masani, former Congress Socialist and soon to be the main spokesman of Indian capitalist interests, classified opinions in the Assembly along two axes: 'modernists' and 'traditionalists', 'socialists' and 'non-socialists'. Even this is shorthand; it did not nearly reflect all the interests and points of view to be reconciled. Moreover, the arrangement of political opinion did not divide neatly along parallel axes: both 'modernist' and 'traditionalist' opinion divided along socialist and capitalist lines. Matters were not made any simpler by many followers of Gandhi claiming, as Gandhi himself was occasionally, though not consistently, wont to do, to be socialists themselves – the boundaries of 'socialism' were fuzzy and there was no agreed-upon adjudicator to decide who could claim to be within them. Gandhi, regularly invoked in the debates of the

Assembly now that he had been anointed as 'Father of the Nation', was not a member of the Assembly or a participant in its debates, although the occasional remark from him might produce resonances therein. His assassination on January 30, 1948 added to and amplified the tendency of debates to claim a Gandhian lineage as legitimating principle.

The question of minority rights loomed large in the discussions – not only in the context of the movement for and creation of Pakistan, but possibly more urgently in relation to other and smaller minorities and the very large numbers of Muslims remaining in India after partition. The transition from British rule to Indian self-rule had not abolished the 'interest groups' that had been carefully nurtured by the British or had grown up in the interstices of colonial power and nationalist resistance; many of these had claims to special representation entrenched in the existing colonial constitution. 'Modernists' had an uncomfortable relationship with these special interest groups: their attempt to deal with individuals as individuals seemed to be undermined by collective bargaining by groups acting as groups. And yet, the question of minorities and their genuine insecurities had to be dealt with. Nehru had often said that a majority community had special responsibilities to assuage the insecurities of minorities; therefore the principle of minority representation and 'safeguards' had to be acknowledged. This eventually involved special representation for 'backward castes' and 'tribes', recognised (as they had been under the 1935 Government of India Act) under specific Schedules of the Indian Constitution (giving rise to the awkward Indian political expression 'Scheduled Castes and Scheduled Tribes', or SC/ST for short). Such provisions were intended to be temporary forms of social protection and positive discrimination; economic and educational advancement, as Nehru put it, would quickly end the conditions in which they were necessary. The special provisions still exist today, with various accretions over the years – if this seemed dangerously akin to colonial enumeration policies, it also illustrated that a category that became the basis of claims to resources was extremely difficult to abolish later. It might have been different if power had been seized by a revolutionary nationalist force; but in an orderly transfer of power designed to protect mutual interests and based on mutual fear of the 'masses' among British and Indian elites, such continuities were logical. These continuities enabled various interpreters to conclude that the newly independent India was going to be British India with a few adjustments.

'As evidence of the enduring quality of the 1935 Act,' Alan Campbell-Johnson, Mountbatten's press attaché noted in his diary after a conversation with Ambedkar, 'he [Ambedkar] said that some two hundred and fifty of its clauses had been embodied as they stood into the new constitution.'[11] While to Campbell-Johnson this was evidence of a positive British legacy, for others it was proof of an inability to break free of colonial shackles – a mood which showed itself again later on, in the anguish felt by many in the Assembly that despite all the rhetoric of independence and sovereignty, India was going to remain in the British Commonwealth.

The Constituent Assembly began its work on December 8, 1946. On December 13, Nehru's speech on the Objectives Resolution invoked the American Constitution, the Tennis Court Oath of the legislators of the French Revolution's National Assembly, and the experiences of the USSR. He insisted that a future Indian political order would be based on the principles of democracy and socialism, called for a republican form of government, and rejected 'an external monarchy'. He stressed the principle of popular sovereignty: in the princely states, the people, not their monarchs, would decide on their future (a principle that Patel, in his negotiations with the states' rulers, in effect ignored in order to persuade them to surrender sovereignty to the Indian Union). As always, Nehru offered the route of compromise: the constitution would be based on basic principles that were 'fundamental' and 'not controversial'.[12] But he also hinted at the possibility of revolution and of the impermanence of the constitution, gently prompting more conservative elements to accept gradual, top-down change as a better solution than revolution from below.

The implicit tensions that were part of the constitution-making discussions were enshrined in the written version. These tensions remained unresolved – between the principles of equality before the law and various minority rights and forms of positive discrimination; between the Fundamental Rights guaranteed by the Constitution (equality, freedoms of various kinds 'against exploitation' of various description) and various exceptions to the Fundamental Rights; and between the Fundamental Rights and the 'Directive Principles' of state policy, which were not a legally enforceable part of the Constitution but were said to be desirable goals or aspirations that would justify future legislation. The central principle of 'secularism' was negatively defined: everyone would have the freedom to 'practise and propagate' their religion, but the State and its organs would neither recognise nor support particular religions or religious organisations. The 'Directive Principles' were the box placed in a corner of the Constitution to which were banished principles that were undesirable to reject altogether given the demands of political legitimacy, but were impossible or undesirable to make a part of the actual legal framework of the state. These included proposals to abolish poverty, commitments to redistribute wealth and establish social equality, to establish a total ban on alcohol consumption (among the so-called 'Gandhian principles'), as well as the more sectarian demand to ban cow slaughter; but the possibility of opening that box to justify diverse political agenda was always present.

ECONOMIC VISIONS: RETREAT ON 'SOCIALISM'; THE 'TRANSITION PERIOD'; THE COMMUNISTS

The vision of India to which Nehru remained publicly committed depended upon the disarming of sectarian tendencies through the delivery of economic progress for everyone, 'irrespective of caste, creed, religion or sex', as the phrase went; it remained committed to state intervention in economic matters through economic planning. This involved, therefore, both a productive and – perhaps more importantly – a redistributive imperative. However, Nehru had more or less conceded, by the time of his days as chairman of the Congress's National Planning Committee, that socialism was to be deferred to some time in the future. He continued to distinguish his own commitment to socialism from the political goals of the 'nation' as a whole. He had accepted 'the fundamentals of socialist theory' – 'the Marxian thesis' 'successfully adapted' by Lenin – although he 'had little patience with leftist groups in India, spending much of their energy in mutual conflict and recriminations over fine points of doctrine'.[13] The 'nation', on the other hand, had not altogether accepted socialism. Thus, the link between economic planning and socialism (identified with Nehru since the exit of Subhas Bose from the Congress) had to be loosened.

Consequently, there was much talk of a 'transitional period' of indefinite length before socialism could be considered. Nehru was certainly not the only person on the left involved in this deferral. The Socialist Party's 1947 programme, before it seceded from the Congress, declared that 'where democracy and civil liberties are in existence, the transition to socialism must be peaceful and through democratic means'. There was much emphasis on the 'transition period' to 'a society in which all are workers – a classless society', in which human labour would not be subject to exploitation for private profit, and all wealth would be 'truly national or common wealth'. The transitional period, however, was essential, because 'socialist society is not created in a day'.[14]

Planning was, however, not to be abandoned. State intervention *per se* had no necessary connection with socialism, and no particular negative connotations even for industrialists as long as it was not accompanied by nationalisation of existing industries. Nehru was able to link up the commitment to economic planning and industrialisation with a broader 'modernist' trend; his public roles as socialist and moderniser could be adjusted to prioritise the latter. 'Modernity' was understood then in unproblematic terms as scientific and technological advance and industrialisation. Meanwhile, the rhetoric of social commitment could be pushed even by industrialists who wished to pre-empt a move too far towards radical socialism: they believed that *some* 'socialist demands' could be 'accommodated without capitalism surrendering any of its essential features'.[15]

Detached from the socialist imperative, the economic programme for the new India could be reduced to the goal of 'national self-sufficiency' as an escape from what Nehru described as 'the whirlpool of economic imperialism',[16] and industrialisation as a central plank of that self-sufficiency as India attempted to 'catch up' with the advanced countries. This could draw on an older tradition of economic nationalism that could trace its genealogy back to the nineteenth century. Economic nationalists demanded protection for 'infant industries' so that they could, with time, compete with foreign industries; they pointed out that political dependence was a necessary concomitant to an economic relationship that relied on foreign sources of supply of essential manufactured goods, and that the employment and wealth-building potential of agriculture on its own was limited. This was an argument that could be built upon by Indian industrialists in later years: they wanted more space in which to operate, to be protected against foreign competition, to start new and profitable industries rather than be confined to the low end of the industrial spectrum – cotton and jute textiles, sugar and so on. Within the nationalist movement, to the extent that a businessman's demand was a demand for national industry, it was a national demand that the left wing of the movement could also support. This was again able to provide a coalitional space in the post-independence period: industrialists were nervous about the details of Nehruvian policy, but most could live with the whole. An Industrial Policy Resolution of 1948 stressed that heavy industry and industries of national importance would be established under state control: in effect, the long-term investments in infrastructure were to be taken care of by the state, while existing industries under private capital would remain in private hands.

In effect, then, the post-independence political economy was set up as a protected national economy, run on capitalist lines with a strong state sector. And with socialists committed to a 'transition period', it could be all but admitted that the shared goal was one of achieving a relatively successful capitalism rather than anything that could be recognised as 'socialism' – but the obligatory language of political legitimacy dictated that this was a step too far.

Planning was therefore constructed as a 'technical' process in which 'experts' with 'scientific' knowledge would take decisions on the basis of technical, and therefore apolitical, criteria. Nehru himself, as is evident from a number of his public statements, did not believe that there were such things as purely apolitical criteria; but he found this to be an enabling myth: an appeal to purely technical criteria depoliticised an area of activity that could therefore run parallel to the political arena of elected repre-sentatives, giving Nehru and a team of carefully selected 'technical experts' more or less loyal to him greater capacity for autonomous political action.

Even for the minimalist programme of Nehruvian economic and social engineering to work, the first steps would have had to be abolishing vested interests – some would have said 'feudal' remnants – in the countryside; in effect dismantling the 'feudal–imperialist alliance': *zamindars*, *talukdars* and various other intermediaries who exacted various kinds of payments from the actual producers. Land reforms were the basic minimum for this. Potentially, this could lead to agrarian capitalism, but social justice was to be administered through land ceilings: an upper limit on the amount of land that could be owned by an individual. Cooperative farming was envisaged among policy-makers, especially in areas where land holdings were too small to be productive.

In a way, Nehru's theoretical scenario – economic man replacing sectarian man – had been tested by events elsewhere in India, in which the Communist Party of India was extremely important. The *Tebhaga* movement in Bengal in 1946 had demonstrated ambiguities in class and community identities, with pro-Muslim League and pro-CPI loyalties co-existing among the peasantry; but this test case was not quite conducted in the best possible ground, given the strong sectarian context of the times, and the implications of the ambiguities were not acknowledged officially by the CPI itself. The movement for Pakistan had been strong enough to force the CPI to concede the importance of Pakistan as a rallying point for almost millenarian aspirations among poor Muslims, and to try and work within rather than against that movement. But the capacity to direct or control changes in the incomprehensible world of colonial negotiating tables remained beyond the capacity of ordinary people or the leadership of agrarian struggle. On the other hand, in the Telengana region of Hyderabad state, agrarian discontent and linguistic solidarities were organised from 1946 under the communist banner in solidarity against the (Muslim) ruler's attempt to split the movement on communal lines even as he claimed the right to independence or to accede to Pakistan rather than India. But here, solidarity had partly been due to agrarian conditions, partly due to language and regional loyalties – the CPI's own narratives of Telengana point to the eventual reorganisation of Indian states on linguistic lines as one of the movement's real gains. The simple dichotomy of 'communal' versus 'economic' man did not work: identities and solidarities were based on a far more complex mixture of factors. (In the end, the Telengana movement surrendered not to the Nizam of Hyderabad but to troops fighting it in the name of independent India who had in September 1948 invaded Hyderabad State in a so-called 'police action' against the recalcitrant ruler.)

NON-ALIGNMENT: ASSUMPTION OF SPACE TO MANOEUVRE

In one area at least, the identification of Nehru with the policies of his government would not be inaccurate: Nehru was to a very large extent able to mould Indian foreign policy, to make, and thereafter justify, the major decisions, and to leave a strong impress of his personal style upon India's international image and reputation – a personal style which, it must be said by way of qualification, owed much to the firm hand of Krishna Menon, whose London-based Independence for India League had already done so much to provide India its international diplomatic profile.

It has been customary to separate Nehru's domestic policy from his foreign policy. This is largely unjustified; domestic difficulties can often be seen as connected with international pressures. Nehru himself insisted that foreign policy was the external reflection of domestic policy and particularly of domestic economic policy – he said this publicly and often – but it was perhaps as often the other way round. As he put it on other occasions, a country's independence consisted basically of the right to conduct its own foreign relations. 'External affairs', as it came to be called, was a particularly important concern for India, involving defining political and economic relations with Britain, with the superpowers, with other colonies and former colonies in Asia and elsewhere, and with its neighbours in the region. For a young state just emerging from formal colonial control, the overriding concern was with finding an independent voice in international politics and retaining effective independence for India. Nehru's external problems were reflected in internal equations. Internally, the Indian political system aimed at being consensual and non-confrontational, and the Congress was effectively a coalition of the moderate left and the centre-right, which meant that the Cold War, at the very least, impinged on the internal relations of the party.

Of the higher ranks of the Congress leadership, Nehru had the most international experience; force of circumstance had found him outside India, in Britain and Europe, at crucial points in the history of the twentieth century: the Oppressed Nations' Conference in Brussels in 1927; the Soviet Union in 1927 before the beginning of Stalinism proper; Europe in the mid-1930s, during the rise of fascism and the Spanish Civil War; and again in 1938, at the time of the Munich Crisis. By the end of the 1930s, Nehru had succeeded in establishing his hegemony over the Congress's foreign policy. As the only person acceptable to a Congress mainstream with an understanding of international politics and an international standing, he was able – although not without resistance – to make his own foreign policy. As a result, Indian politics, viewed from outside India, often appeared more 'progressive' than it actually was, viewed from inside India.

There were, of course, few things that could be considered purely 'external' affairs. A number of grey areas fell between domestic and foreign policy. Many of these were legacies of the peculiarities of colonial rule in India: the problem of the princely states, of Junagadh and Hyderabad, but in particular of Kashmir; later of the Portuguese colony of Goa; and of course international border questions. Of these issues, Kashmir came to be an international one and came to dominate the question of Indian relations with Pakistan – although perhaps Junagadh and Hyderabad, involving similar issues of principle but dissimilar geopolitics, could theoretically also have done. And of course relations with Pakistan were also to be implicitly or explicitly linked within India to the 'communal question' of relations between Hindus and Muslims. The decisive question, however, which placed items on the international agenda and forced the Government of India to deal with them as 'external', tended to be their importance to the Cold War.

Nehru himself was in charge of foreign affairs in the Interim Government from September 1946. The Interim Government did not have significant powers. Nevertheless, it was necessary for Nehru's claim not to be in government by the invitation of the viceroy but 'by our right and by our strength'[17] that he used the position to think ahead, to achieve international recognition and to set up diplomatic links with the world in anticipation of independence. (He made it clear that the Muslim League, although part of the Interim Government, could not expect to be included in foreign policy delegations and discussions, especially as they were not cooperating with the rest of the government, and had reserved the right not to be part of an eventual Indian Union.) The paradoxes of a still dependent Indian foreign policy were continuously present: Nehru sent sympathy messages to the Indonesian freedom struggle – at a time when Indian troops, under British command, were still in Indonesia, attempting at the request of the Dutch government to restore Dutch rule. (Nehru assured the Constituent Assembly that Indian troops would be withdrawn immediately – 'we are not going to tolerate any delays or any subterfuges,' he stated – but he admitted his powers in this respect were limited.[18])

The central plank of Nehru's foreign policy was outlined by him within a few days of the inauguration of the Interim Government. 'We propose, as far as possible, to keep away from the power politics of groups, aligned against one another, which have led in the past to world wars and which may again lead to disasters on an even vaster scale.'[19] Non-alignment was at least as much a pragmatic as a principled position: military advisers had pointed out that the Indian Army could at best expect to hold its own against the forces of a similar-sized regional enemy, and provoking Great Power rivalries in the region was not the best way forward. The Polish economist Michal Kalecki was later to describe non-alignment as a strategy of sucking two cows.[20] 'It is a difficult position,' Nehru confessed to the Constituent Assembly, 'because, when people are full of fear of one another, any person who tries to be neutral is suspected of sympathy with the other party.'[21]

Nehru made it clear that India would cooperate with the newly formed United Nations – it was, he believed, still feeble, and had many defects, but ought to be supported. He was particularly critical of the Great Powers' veto rights in the Security Council, which he believed defeated the purpose of a world forum in which states could participate as equals. Nehru was also keen to disassociate India from British Indian foreign policy. He was aware of the twin dangers of Indian delegates becoming Anglo-American 'satellites' at the UN, and of irritating them by 'partiality towards Russia'. Non-alignment did not preclude leaning to one side at times, but required an avoidance of 'entanglements with groups'. 'Personally,' he wrote to his sister, Vijayalakshmi Pandit, the head of the Indian delegation to the General Assembly (and soon to be the Indian Ambassador to the USSR), 'I think that in this world tug-of-war there is on the whole more reason on the side of Russia, not always, of course.' Nevertheless, '[w]e have to steer a middle course not merely because of expediency but also because we consider it the right course.'[22]

Non-alignment did not rule out cooperation or trade with the superpowers, particularly the USA. Such contacts were to be approached pragmatically. 'We are likely to have dealings with them in many spheres of activity, industrial, economic and other,' Nehru wrote to Asaf Ali, shortly to be the Indian representative in Washington. Nehru envisaged an inflow of capital goods from the USA to India, as well as many technical experts. 'All these dealings will of course not be for humanitarian reasons but because they are to the mutual advantage of both parties concerned.'[23] But he expected US pressure on India to be particularly acute in a number of ways – his own 1927 prophesy, restated in 1946 in *The Discovery of India*, and British wartime fears that the USA would be the main imperialist power of the future had come true. 'We have to be exceedingly careful in our dealings with the State Department,' he wrote to Asaf Ali in Washington. 'The United States are a great Power and we want to be friendly with them for many reasons. Nevertheless I should like it to be made clear that we do not propose to be subservient to anybody and we do not welcome any kind of patronage. Our approach, while being exceedingly friendly, may become tough if the necessity arises, both in political and economic matters. We hold plenty of good cards in our hands and there is no need whatever for us to appear as suppliants before any country.'[24]

In October 1946, Krishna Menon took the initiative to establish links with the USSR. He met Molotov in Paris, and in informal conversation Molotov regretted that at the present time the USSR could not offer to ease India's food shortage, because the USSR had shortages of its own to deal with; but he offered India the USSR's technical and military assistance. This was too much and too fast for the British government, especially at the beginning of the Cold War – India was not yet independent. Nehru advised Menon to go slow for a while. By November he asked Menon to make a formal approach to Molotov for diplomatic links, and requested him to make informal approaches to other European countries.

As part of his policy of laying out India's foreign policy before world public opinion, Nehru also denounced South African race policy and maintained his principle of supporting anti-imperialist movements, in Burma (where Nehru's expression of support was complicated by Indians being seen as occupiers and as part of the ruling classes themselves), in Indonesia and in Indo-China: he refused to provide overflight rights for Dutch aircraft in the Indonesian conflict and French aircraft in the Indo-Chinese conflict, and openly declared his support for Ho Chi Minh. Although he was still corresponding with Song Meiling, Chiang Kai-Shek's wife, he avoided committing himself to taking sides in the Chinese Civil War, noting to the new Indian Ambassador to China, K.P.S. Menon, that the communists 'have no bad case'.[25] (By the end of 1949, Nehru's government had recognised the People's Republic of China.) He noted that the USA had a 'Negro problem' in which Indian sympathies were with the Negroes. The Indian Ambassador to the USA was told not to hide this sympathy, but not to get entangled in the issue either. By January 1947, US Secretary of State John Foster Dulles was already denouncing Soviet Communism's influence on India through the Interim Government; Nehru repeated that India reserved the right to an independent foreign policy, and stated that Dulles had showed 'lack of knowledge of facts and want of appreciation of the policy we are pursuing'.[26]

Non-alignment with the superpowers did not preclude other forms of state groupings. Writing in the *National Herald* in 1940, Nehru had stated that the era of small countries was at an end. An 'Eastern federation' was a desirable group for the future. Such a group must contain China and India, and could include Burma, Ceylon, Nepal, Afghanistan, Malaya, Siam, Iran and possibly others: 'That would be a powerful combination of free nations joined together for their own good as well as the world good.'[27] The idea of pan-Asian solidarity was not a new one in India, and had once included Japan as a potential member and source of inspiration as a powerful late industrialiser; but Japanese expansionist tendencies had alarmed those who had once assumed benign motives on Japan's part. In August 1939, Nehru met Rabindranath Tagore – as it turned out, for the last time – in Calcutta en route to China. The poet asked him to go to Japan as well to express solidarity with the Japanese people and to ask them 'not to lose their soul in the present adventure in China', while at the same time condemning Japanese militarism and imperialism and their atrocities in China.[28] Nehru had had few illusions about persuading the Japanese to change their minds. But the idea of a pan-Asian fellowship of nations survived for him as an ideal despite its appropriation by Japanese imperialism.

In April 1947, Delhi hosted an Asian Relations Conference, organised by a non-official body – the Indian Council for World Affairs – but with implications for future policy since it was organised with Nehru's support. The conference had a ceremonial value as the first large international conference organised by an almost-free India. Nehru's speeches at the conference made no explicit reference to non-alignment. He spoke instead of 'some deeper urge' bringing Asian countries together. Sarojini Naidu, minor poetess and sometime Indian nationalist, also mystically invoked Asian-ness (in the 1920s she had asked, from a Congress platform, that East Africa be handed over to Indians for colonisation, because as a great nation India was entitled to colonies – and had been rapped on the knuckles for it by Gandhi).

Pan-Asian solidarity, however, did not get off to the best possible start. The Malayan delegate, Dr John Thivy – an Indian lawyer who had been in Subhas Bose's movement and who later took Indian citizenship and was appointed Indian ambassador to Syria and Italy – suggested that the gathering discuss the formation of a 'neutrality bloc' to refuse assistance in terms of raw materials, dockyards, arms, etc. to British imperialism as the only way to secure Malayan independence. This was not intended 'to start a movement', Thivy clarified, but to prevent aggression by alien powers. The suggestion was not taken up at the time; Nehru seemed unnecessarily cautious, and with Indian troops at this time being used or having been recently used to recapture imperial territories for Britain in Malaya, the Dutch in Indonesia and the French in Indo-China, suspicion of his motives was understandable. There was criticism of Nehru from all these countries, and a sense that smaller Asian states were wary of India and of China – both were suspected of harbouring ambitions to regional leadership.

If such ambitions did exist on Nehru's part, they seem to have been more in terms of moral leadership and expectations of world status than ambitions to power. On November 8, 1948, in a speech to the Constituent Assembly, Nehru stressed the important part to be played by India in world affairs, and the inevitable responsibility this entailed in connection with the promotion of world peace and the welfare of mankind: 'we dare not be little,' he declared.[29]

FINANCIAL DEPENDENCY, 'DEVELOPMENT', THE COMMONWEALTH AND THE COLD WAR

Indian membership of the British Commonwealth seemed, in the context of keeping away from 'the power politics of groups', to be a complete anomaly. Pragmatism rather than principles dictated India's acceptance of Commonwealth membership, albeit in a Commonwealth whose formal structure had been specifically altered to include a republic. India's acceptance was pushed successfully by Nehru against much opposition. Here is a good example of the triumph of *Realpolitik* over principle; and it was Nehru as the man of principle who could successfully pilot such a clearly anomalous project.

Political, economic and military ties with Britain remained far stronger, even after formal independence had been achieved, than should have been comfortable for a country whose rationale for independence had been self-sufficiency. The primary ties remained, as Nehru had always suggested, economic – a galling situation for a nationalist movement that had set great store by freedom from economic dependence as a necessary condition of political independence. From the British point of view, there were wider fears that connected with Indian problems. From 1946 onwards, Britain's panic over its financial and military capability world-wide led to a scaling down of economic and military commitments. US pressures for convertibility of sterling, the British need for US loans, and *quid pro quos* related to Marshall aid, were also strong influences on British policy as Britain tried to preserve a world role with limited resources by trimming commitments and by looking for reliable allies. Transfer of power to 'responsible Indians', as hoped for, tended to mean to those who could be persuaded to remain on Britain's side in strategic – and with time, Cold War – calculations. Exactly what these calculations were became apparent only over time, even to the main protagonists; but the necessity of maintaining some sort of leverage over India remained central, belying the claims that power was in the process of being, or had been, altogether 'transferred'.

The economic relationship between India and Britain had significantly altered during the Second World War: from being a debtor of Britain's, paying interest on capital that was lent to the Government of India without necessarily being sought by Indians, India became a creditor. Private producers in India had been enlisted to produce not just the simple things like textiles for military uniforms, but also light aircraft, chemicals and more sophisticated products – creating the inadvertent industrialising effect that accompanies disruption of the normal links between colony and metropolis. Indian producers were willing to invest in new areas in exchange for promises of post-war tariff protection for these industries. This merged with a demand for state-protection-led industrialisation after the war, shared by Indian capitalists and socialists. Production had been paid for in paper currency, printed in large amounts, with obvious inflationary effects, especially at a time of scarcity of goods for civil-ian consumption. This increase in currency was backed up at first by cancelling India's debt to Britain, and then through the building up of the so-called sterling balances in the Reserve Bank of India's London branch against goods and services provided during the war under the same principles as the Lend-Lease Agreement.

After the war, the extent of Britain's debt to India and to the various constituent parts of the Empire and Commonwealth in the form of sterling balances led to searches in Britain for schemes to prevent these balances from being drawn upon too quickly. It gradually became clear that the demand for capital goods for their development schemes from holders of the sterling balances (as payment in goods for these balances) would outstrip Britain's post-war ability to spare such capital goods for export, especially while at the same time aiming at a planned economy with full employment at home. This gave rise, after the war, to a British policy of maximising dollar- or hard currency-earnings in the sterling area as a whole, and inducing dollar-saving by ensuring, when possible, sterling area sources of supply of goods for countries within the area. (Britain's short-lived attempt to accede to US pressure in the summer of 1947 and have a convertible pound had swiftly had to be ended due to a massive flight from the pound into dollars.)

In India, the idea mooted in some business circles that India should look to the USA instead of Britain for economic assistance was, however, not particularly congenial either. Offers of loans from the USA came with conditions attached that seemed suspiciously like mechanisms of control not particularly different from earlier colonial bonds; US policy-makers frankly set out terms for the easy access of US goods and capital to Indian markets. 'We are going to permit no control of our industry by an outside agency,' Nehru wrote to Asaf Ali in Washington in May 1947, 'though we shall gladly cooperate on terms of mutual advantage with outsiders.'[30]

There was much resentment in India at the situation: Britain was unable to provide vital capital goods after the war, but was not willing to release Indian sterling balances in dollars to enable India to obtain supplies from outside the sterling area. This amounted to continued colonial financial control after formal independence had been achieved – and to a forced loan from a poor country that was now told that the money was needed in Britain and therefore could not be returned. The (not unjustified) sense that Britain was building a social security network and a welfare state – ideas that had been equally considered in India before independence – with colonial loot, while India could not finance such measures herself added to the sense of injury.

Negotiations with Britain on the sterling balances also ran into claims by Winston Churchill, now in the Opposition, that Britain had defended India during the war and ought to allow Britain to give itself at least a discount on the balances. The official view, however, consistent with financial advisers' fears for confidence in Britain's creditworthiness, was that Britain should honour her financial commitments. The question remained as to how quickly the balances would be released, in what form and at what exchange rate. The last question was resolved by retaining the exchange rate link between the rupee and the pound that had been set by imperial statute (the rupee–sterling link, in fact, outlived Nehru); but the rest was the subject of much hard bargaining.

Inevitably, it was Stafford Cripps, who became Chancellor of the Exchequer in November 1947, who had to negotiate with India. The cordial relationship between Nehru and Cripps had by now been replaced by irritation on Nehru's part. '[T]he India Office crowd and the British Cabinet still move in the old grooves,' Nehru had remarked in May 1947. 'They are completely out of touch with recent developments in India, but they consider themselves experts who can lay down the law, especially Stafford Cripps.'[31] Both in 1942 and in 1946, Cripps had appeared not to have dealt with him honestly, and attempts now to put pressure on India to accept British terms were not appreciated. During the bargaining over the balances, Britain threatened to expel India from the sterling area, but it was always doubtful whether this was a plausible threat. India would then have had no compunctions about spending in dollars, and Britain would have had no authority to prevent this. Moreover, it became clear that British military and strategic considerations required India to remain in the Commonwealth, which meant that an overuse of blackmail was counterproductive. (At the time, Britain was looking at the possibility of having airbases in Northern India as 'forward bombing centres' to target the Soviet industrial heartland; eventually, Peshawar in Pakistan won the privilege of hosting these.) The eventual agreement in June 1948 indicated the superior bargaining power derived from actually holding the money in one's hands: the gradual release of a scaled-down sum from the balances, with only a small part of this to be in dollars was secured by the Indian finance minister, Shanmukham Chetty, and was widely criticised.

The British still needed the Commonwealth as an international power centre and an economic bloc, remodelled in the ways suggested by Conservatives like Leo Amery so as to appear to be a partnership of equals (this was a difficult task while many countries remained formal colonies, but sought to be achieved by the claim that these colonies were to be 'developed' before they were fully trained for and capable of freedom). By 1943, it was realised that a post-war Commonwealth was the only possible basis of British power in a post-war world dominated by the USA and the USSR. There was a military aspect to this as much as a purely economic one. Could British troops remain in India after a transfer of power? Stafford Cripps had suggested in 1945 that Indian forces might be available for internal security, but British troops could indeed remain. There was some talk of treaties for mutual defence. Mountbatten's instructions, as the last viceroy of India, had been clear: he was to encourage India to stay within the Commonwealth.

Mountbatten's record of his first conversation with Nehru on March 24, 1947, soon after arriving in India, provides evidence that he lost no time in attempting to settle this question. 'Nehru said that he did not consider it possible, with the forces which were at work, that India could remain within the Commonwealth. But basically, he said, they did not want to break any threads, and he suggested "some form of common nationality" (I fear that they are beginning to see that they cannot go out of the Commonwealth; but they cannot afford to say that they will stay in; they are groping for a formula). Nehru gave a direct implication that they wanted to stay in; but a categorical statement that they intended to go out.'[32] (In May 1942, after the failure of the Cripps Mission, Nehru had in a long note to Louis Johnson left the possibility of future Commonwealth membership open to an independent India; but he said that such a Commonwealth would have to 'undergo a complete change after or even during this war'.[33]) This is consistent with the difficulties inherent in what, if Nehru played it, was always going to be a tricky card to play: Nehru's history of commitment to breaking formal links with Britain, from his rejection of dominion status in 1927 onwards, made his insistence on the value of Commonwealth membership a clear anomaly. This was also a potential constitutional problem – India as a proposed republic would find it difficult to maintain a Commonwealth connection as long as the head of the Commonwealth was the King of England. It was also a difficult commitment to reconcile with the principle of non-alignment. In the run-up to the making of the new Commonwealth in 1949, most of the negotiations were centred on wrangling about finding a status for the King in the Commonwealth which did not involve one for him in the Indian Constitution. The tricky and emotive issue of sovereignty combined with nationalism was at stake. Eventually it was agreed that the King would be accepted by India 'as the symbol of the free association of its independent member nations and as such the

Head of the Commonwealth'.[34] ('The fact that even Winston Churchill should fall into line', Nehru noted, raised suspicion in India that some strange and unsavoury deal had been done behind the scenes.[35]) Nehru's proposal on common citizenship was, unsurprisingly, not accepted by Britain.

Nehru sold Commonwealth membership to a reluctant Constituent Assembly by insisting that the connection was extra-constitutional and affected neither substantive questions of Indian foreign or domestic policy nor her republican status: 'it is an agreement by free will, to be terminated by free will.'[36] It was of course untrue that the British connection was not a constraining one. At the January 1950 regional conference in Colombo, Ernest Bevin, British Foreign Secretary and the Labour cabinet member most committed to an imperialist future for Britain, agreed with Nehru that he opposed a regional defence pact in Asia on the lines of other emerging Cold War pacts. This was good diplomacy. Nehru for his part agreed to the bland rhetoric of what came to be called the 'Colombo Plan' for mutual technical and economic assistance; it placed before the British and Indian publics, and the publics of the region of South Asia (this was to become the acknowledged shorthand for the region) a vision of benign collaboration in a shared project of 'development'. Nehru and Bevin both knew that this was far from the truth – in private everyone admitted that the conference had been prompted by the need to protect the sterling area and by fears of communism in Asia – but both seemed to feel that this public stance was more palatable according to the emergent rhetoric of 'development': it would conform to the aspirations of Indian public opinion as well as projecting an image in consonance with the new British rhetoric of being in charge of a benign imperialism that was engaged in a progressive project to undermine its own existence. This benign project was engaged at the time in what has aptly been referred to as the 'second colonisation' of Africa: attempting to sort out British balance of payments problems by making sure African countries were 'developed' to become dollar-earners.

By 1950, moreover, British policy-makers were convinced that for all his anti-imperialist rhetoric, Nehru was reliably anti-communist and would acquiesce in British activities in Malaya, the major dollar-earning country (through rubber and tin) that had at all costs to be held by Britain. The Malayan Emergency had begun in 1948, a brutal war above all against Malayan communists, who were to be butchered in large numbers by British 'special forces' while a battle for the 'hearts and minds' of the population was to be undertaken at the same time. For this to continue, British policy had to tread carefully. According to the British view, the USA was too unsubtle in its approach to Cold War problems: a little more subtlety and a little less rhetoric worked far better. Nehru had recognised the People's Republic of China; he would nonetheless refrain from interfering in Malaya. British sources believed that Nehru would recognise that they had a mutual enemy in communism, given that he had communist problems at home himself, and believed that with proper steering he could be relied upon to let them deal with the Malayan Emergency without making too much noise.

AUTHORSHIP

The normative significance of the 'Nehruvian model' can with some justification be seen as a central feature of the political culture of post-independence India. The question is whether the vision fully deserves the qualifying adjective: how far was Nehru its author? The answer we might provide points to the fact that he was, to a large extent, its author; it may have been his most enduring achievement. But it may also never have been an effective vision, capable of being fully implemented.

The Congress, after the departure of the socialists, was a centrist party with a leftist rhetoric, dominated by right-wingers but fronted by a moderate left-winger with relatively little power to deliver major changes. This was a situation partly of Nehru's own creation; he had failed to win the confidence of the left due to years of prevarication, and he did not have the goodwill of the right. In the first few years after the formal transfer of power, both the Hindu right and the capitalist right were in the Congress as well as outside it, although for the time being neither of the two rights, nor the rights inside and outside the Congress, were identified with each other. Minorities tended to cluster round the Congress because it was publicly committed to social equality and to the protection of their rights. The population's expectations, after two hundred years of colonial rule, rested upon the new government, expectations stirred up by the revolutionary rhetoric of the left wing of the nationalist movement. But a commitment to major social change was notably lacking on the part of that government. The Congress' cautious left rhetoric in the 'Nehruvian period' worked on the vaccination principle: a dilute strand of what many in the Congress openly regarded as a disease, 'socialism', administered to the body politic, helped to prevent the disease itself from taking root.

International pressures, too, should not be underestimated. The unfinished business of empire and the emerging business of the Cold War collaborated in putting pressure on colonies and former colonies. The British expectation and the US desire that empires would be folded up after the Second World War in anticipation that the US economy's strength would be best served by 'free trade' and their consequent ability to penetrate markets across the globe without the need for formal political control did not quite materialise. The new reality of Soviet power, the Soviet Union's willingness to express support for anti-colonial movements around the world, and the dangers of communism in colonies or former colonies, led to a contingent and uneasy alliance between the European colonial powers and the USA: the USA would consent to the continuation of empire, the colonial powers would allow the USA greater influence in their colonies; if independence had to be conceded, there would have to be a transfer of power to a successor authority that could be relied upon to act as a bulwark against communism. In this context, non-alignment can be seen as a useful counter-manoeuvre on the part of Nehru, who also had his own internal Cold War to fight, in addition to the problems of transition and stabilisation of the new state.

If, moreover, these principles as laid down seem to imply that post-independence India was a relative oasis of political rationality and democratic calm once the partition violence had died down, that would be wrong. The atmosphere in India in the 1950s was one of Cold War paranoia, as elsewhere. Indians with relatives visiting from Pakistan were regularly harassed and subject to police surveillance. The Chilean poet Pablo Neruda records that when he visited India in 1950 as a protagonist of the world peace movement, and acting as messenger for the French nuclear physicist Joliot-Curie to his fellow physicist C.V. Raman and to Nehru himself, his baggage was searched, his documents confiscated and photographed, and every person in his address book visited and interrogated by the police. Neruda was, of course, a communist, as was Joliot-Curie. However, he had not expected to be treated as a semi-criminal in a country in which he had once lived, and whose freedom movement he had participated in: he was followed by the police, and both in Bombay and Delhi was told he could not leave the city limits. Nehru himself, when Neruda met him, was completely unsympathetic to a man he had last met in India in the 1920s as a comrade. 'I thought perhaps,' Neruda noted, 'the silent man before me had in some subtle way reverted to a "zamindar" and was staring at me with the same indifference and contempt he would have shown one of his barefoot peasants.'[37] Whether Neruda had met Nehru at a time when the latter was particularly cornered and isolated in his own party is a question worth asking.

5

CONSOLIDATING THE STATE, c. 1947–55

On August 15, 1947, Nehru, referring to himself as the 'First Servant of the Indian People' (invoking in his rhetoric the Soviet People's Commissars of the early days of the Russian Revolution), outlined the many problems that faced the new state. The predominant problems, he reiterated, were economic: the country was faced with inflation, the people with lack of food and clothing and adequate shelter. 'Production today is the first priority,' he explained; but on its own it would not be enough – the key social question would be one of distribution.[1] But these priorities would have to be deferred. For Nehru, the early years after independence, from 1947 to 1950, were ones of struggle, as he sought to maintain his political authority within his own party, and his government tried to maintain the stability and effective independence of the new state.

STABILISATION: 'COMMUNAL HARMONY'

The problem of stabilisation was in the first instance one of ending the disorder and violence associated with partition. Vallabhbhai Patel, the central negotiator with the Indian States, and deputy prime minister and Home minister in Nehru's first government, formed with Nehru the second part of what came to be called the 'duumvirate'. As Home minister, Patel was in charge of suppression of rioting and revenge killings, and dealing with problems of the influx of refugees from West and East Pakistan.

But it was Nehru, not Patel, who played the conciliator and the voice of reason, arguing against defining India as 'Hindu', touring riot-affected areas and intervening in public disorder in person. 'Communal' disorder cast a long shadow into the early years of the newly-independent state. There was a continuation of transfer of populations between India and Pakistan after partition (about nine million Sikhs and Hindus entered India, five million from West Pakistan and four from East Pakistan, while six million Muslims left India for Pakistan, in the period 1946–51). Atrocity stories spread by refugees increased tensions and the desire for vengeance, and helped to accelerate violence; casualties from the period of partition and post-partition violence were estimated at between 200,000 and 800,000.[2] 'Spontaneity' of popular anger – often used as an explanation of the intensity of such violence – was not always an accurate explanation. Desire for the property of the departing community, whose departure ought therefore to be sped up, was also an important motivation. Organised violence was also an extremely important contributory factor in the carnage. When the partition of Punjab had been mooted, Sikh violence on Muslims had been organised, among others, by the leader of the militant Sikh organisation, the Akalis, Tara Singh, who had only recently been a member of the Viceroy's Executive Council during the war (he was eventually arrested in February 1949). After partition, Hindu fundamentalist paramilitary organisations such as the Rashtriya Swayamsevak Sangh (RSS) were involved in organised killings – in September 1947 in Delhi, Sikhs and Hindus organised large-scale killings of Muslims. In Pakistan, it was widely (and not implausibly) believed that despite the sincerity of Gandhi and Nehru in attempting to stop violence against Muslims in India, Patel in the Congress, and right-wing Hindu opinion outside it, had welcomed or encouraged anti-Muslim violence.

The situation left Nehru extremely demoralised. 'I feel particularly helpless,' he wrote to Mountbatten, in a letter that he could think of no better reason for writing than 'to unburden my mind a little'.[3] He noted that the army had resorted to firing indiscriminately at refugees as large-scale violence continued. '[T]here was still an odour of death, a smell of blood and of burning human flesh,' he wrote to Mountbatten from Lahore, describing what he had seen in the Punjab in the course of his tour with Liaquat Ali Khan, now the Pakistani prime minister. 'I am sick with horror.'[4] (Nehru's personal ties with the Mountbattens, and particularly with Edwina Mountbatten, were cemented in this period of close contact. Lord Mountbatten did his best, with the forces at his disposal, to try and help Nehru stop the bloodshed, and Lady Mountbatten actively involved herself in relief measures for refugees.)

An aggressive Hindu revivalist frenzy had appeared in the open. 'I find myself in total disagreement with this revivalist feeling,' Nehru had written to Rajendra Prasad in response to Prasad's request that Nehru ban cow slaughter on August 15, 'and in view of this difference of opinion I am a poor representative of many of our people today.'[5] This was not, however, an offer to resign; as he explained in public, to run away from the responsibilities of leadership at a time of crisis would have been an act of cowardice. And if Nehru had one strongly held belief, it was that sectarian politics based on religion was wrong; he would have to try and control the situation, staking his reputation and his popularity against much popular anger and against many of his colleagues' ideological propensities. He repeatedly made appeals, during the Delhi slaughters and after, that Muslims must not be victimised. He also objected strongly to the proposals of large-scale transfer of populations being considered on either side of the border, and was disturbed that many Muslims who had originally wished to stay in India were now changing their minds. '[W]e cannot encourage this business of Muslims leaving India,' he wrote to Patel. In the first place, Pakistan could not possibly 'accommodate all the Muslims in India'; the consequent 'political and economic difficulties' for both India and Pakistan would be immense. But there were reasons larger than the merely practical to prevent such a situation from arising. 'I feel convinced,' Nehru wrote, 'that culturally India will be the poorer by any such divorce and all wrong tendencies will hold the field then.'[6]

While the right wing of the Congress and the Pakistan government scored political points from killings on either side of the border, Nehru tried to create an area open for non-sectarian discussion. India had 'degraded herself' by violence, he said repeatedly. The more murderous aspects of the post-partition disturbances were of more pressing concern, but little acts of political discrimination and public humiliation directed against Muslims, carried out with the consent of members of his government, had also to be curbed. Nehru was outraged that Muslim men and women were being singled out from other passengers and separately searched at airports in India, and demanded to know on whose orders – he implied, in a letter to Patel on October 18, 1947, that the orders had been Patel's. (The Home Ministry under Patel conducted a campaign of petty harassment not merely of Muslims, but also of communists; conveniently, as in some cases in which Nehru intervened, the communist in question was also a Muslim.) Nehru's continued insistence that a minority was entitled to be nervous about the activities of a majority, and that it was therefore the majority's duty to assuage the fears of minorities, was a more plausible approach to the problem than demonstrations of official power that could be construed as 'Hindu'; he was able to persuade Patel that he should, at least publicly, take this position.

Nehru was in no doubt that the violence had been planned and orchestrated by communal organisations. '[W]e have had to face a very definite and well-organised attempt of certain Sikh and Hindu fascist elements to overturn the Government or at least to break up its present character,' Nehru wrote to Patel. 'It has been something much more than a communal disturbance.'[7] Meanwhile, the practical business of bringing violence to an end ultimately boiled down to a question of law and order in which the army and the police were the main instruments – consternation at the number of deaths in army or police firings was balanced against a sense of the numbers that otherwise might have been lost in communal violence. Of greater concern, however, were the sectarian activities of some police forces who seemed to have been infiltrated by the Rashtriya Swayamsevak Sangh, the stormtroopers of the Hindu Mahasabha and its ideological allies. The government eventually resorted to colonial measures such as collective fines, used not so long ago during the Quit India movement. Nehru himself announced this measure on September 28. On the night of September 29, armed men from neighbouring villages attacked a ward in a hospital in Delhi, killing four Muslim patients and wounding twelve. The district magistrate imposed a collective fine of ten thousand rupees on each of the two villages.

By October the worst of the violence in Delhi seemed over. About 120,000 Muslim evacuees from Delhi had been placed in refugee camps at the Purana Qila, recently the site of the Asian Relations Conference, and at Humayun's Tomb. Nehru recognised that they would have to be resettled in Delhi in a way that did not isolate small groups of Muslims in non-Muslim areas – reluctantly, therefore, he was forced to accept a ghetto principle. The crisis had also reinforced differences between Patel and Nehru. Nehru had several times intervened in matters within Patel's jurisdiction as home minister, largely because he could not trust Patel to be non-sectarian, even as he denied allegations in the press that there were serious differences between the two men.

Gandhi, the creator of the 'duumvirate', was no longer involved in the government's activities, except for the occasional, and often idiosyncratic, intervention on what he believed to be a matter of principle. In the last months of his life, the Mahatma, in his late seventies, poured an immense amount of energy into the cause of reconciliation between Hindus and Muslims. Events had passed him by, he believed, and the best he could now do was to contribute to a cause he had always held to be central to India's future. Holding prayer meetings in the cause of communal harmony became a central activity for the man anointed in his own life-time as a saint and as the father of a 'nation'; yet there were limits to his abilities. At the height of violence, Nehru had appealed to Gandhi to go to the Punjab from Bengal, but Gandhi did not feel that would be useful at the time. He came to Delhi from Calcutta on September 7, 1947, but his presence there did not have the expected magic touch.

On January 13, 1948, Gandhi began a fast to attempt to restore peace between the communities. 'I urge everybody dispassionately to examine the purpose [of my fast] and let me die, if I must, in peace which I hope is ensured. Death for me would be a glorious deliverance rather than that I should be a helpless witness of the destruction of India, Hinduism, Sikhism and Islam.'[8] To Muslims who complained to him of the Home Minister Vallabhbhai Patel being anti-Muslim, he merely replied that Patel was no longer a 'yes-man' (leaving open the question of whose 'yes-man' he believed Patel had previously been); but he denied that his fast was intended as condemnation of the Home Ministry's handling of the communal situation. During the armed conflict with Pakistan over Kashmir, he urged the government not to attempt to blackmail Pakistan by withholding payments due to it as a consequence of the division of Indian finances. His public appearances were increasingly becoming a security concern for the new government, as Hindu fundamentalist groups such as the RSS publicly blamed Gandhi for having 'emasculated' Hindus by his ideology of non-violence and having thereby 'surrendered' Pakistan to Muslims, and Hindu extremist papers published exhortations to their readers to murder Gandhi and Nehru. (Nehru had responded emotionally to a young man who had shouted 'Death to Gandhi', stepping forward to confront him and declaring 'kill me first'.[9]) But Gandhi refused to take his own security seriously. Having called off his fast on January 18, following assurances from Hindu and Muslim leaders that there would be no further violence, he had a hand grenade thrown at him two days later by a Hindu refugee from West Punjab; it exploded without injuring anyone. Then, on January 30, 1948, the old man made his final contribution to the cause of Indian unity. At his prayer meeting at Birla House on Akbar Road in New Delhi, he was shot three times at point-blank range by Nathuram Godse, a Hindu and a member of the RSS.

As the news of Gandhi's death spread, public anger began to build up, and Hindu groups, assuming that he had been killed by a Muslim, began to gather. The news that Gandhi had been killed by a Hindu was as disarming as it was unexpected; when the news of the RSS's involvement in his murder became known, angry mobs destroyed RSS and Hindu Mahasabha offices and attacked its members. While this directed violence away from Muslims – and was a reminder that violence had become a feature of the times that had haunted India since 1946, and would take different forms at different times – it also underlined the fact that the atmosphere of violence could not be allowed to continue unchecked. On the evening of January 30, 1948, Nehru, on the radio, appealed for calm. 'Friends and comrades, the light has gone out of our lives and there is darkness everywhere,' he said simply;[10] and for him, this was the end of a long, intimate and agonised relationship with a man who had genuinely become an alternative father figure, one with whom he had conducted his essential political and emotional dialogues for the last thirty-two years of his life, one whose closeness had made political disagreement a painful and personal matter on both sides. Neither ever gave up the hope of bringing the other round to their way of thinking. 'I know this,' Gandhi had said in January 1941, in naming Nehru as his chosen successor as Congress leader, 'that when I am gone he will speak my language.'[11] For all their political disagreements, neither man had doubted the other's sincerity. As a man who had been forced to live most of his life in public fora, Nehru had not had much time to develop close relationships with very many people; Gandhi had been an exception and his death left Nehru awkwardly bereft of personal support.

In the days that followed Gandhi's assassination, Nehru reiterated what he now declared to be the Mahatma's central message: unity between Hindus and Muslims, and opposition to sectarian violence. 'It is a shame to me as an Indian . . . It is a shame to me as a Hindu,' Nehru said of Gandhi's assassination, speaking, strategically, as a Hindu himself.[12]

On February 12, Gandhi's ashes were immersed at the sacred confluence of the Ganga and the Yamuna rivers at Allahabad, coincidentally Nehru's home town. Nehru's speech, in Hindustani, warned of the dangers of idolatry of Gandhi, and reminded the vast gathered crowd to consider his message of tolerance and of non-violence instead.

Gandhi's murder helped to dampen down the atmosphere of communal violence. It also provided the government an opportunity to ban 'communal organisations' – the RSS, the Muslim National Guards (the 'volunteer unit' of the Muslim League) and the Khaksars, a paramilitary Muslim unit modelled, like the RSS, on the Nazi stormtroopers. On February 5, 1948, Vinayak Damodar Savarkar, former Hindu Mahasabha president and main ideologue of Hindu race theory, was arrested. The awkward question was what was to be done about SP Mukherjee, Industries minister in Nehru's Cabinet and president of the Hindu Mahasabha. Throughout the period of violence, Nehru had asked him to stop flying the saffron flag of the Hindu Mahasabha above his ministerial house, and to make a statement clarifying his position on the RSS's murderous activities and on the death threats against Gandhi and Nehru himself – the last such request having been written on January 28, 1948, two days before the murder of Gandhi. Now, Gandhi's assassination forced the issue, but the response was unexpected and disarming. On February 15, 1948, the Hindu Mahasabha, by a resolution of its Working Committee, liquidated itself – or more precisely, suspended its political activities in favour of 'cultural' ones (its political wing was shortly to reappear under the innocuous name of the 'Jan Sangh', translatable, in conformity with the obligatory populist language of the time, as 'people's organisation'). On the same day, the UP Parliamentary Muslim League also liquidated itself, post-dating the end by two weeks, and also reappeared under a new name. Other banned organisations tended, similarly, to regroup and reconfigure themselves over time.

Effectively, this had only dealt with the overtly sectarian organisations, and with overt expressions of sectarianism. Those whose sentiments or goals were not very different from the Hindu Mahasabha's, for instance, could still hide in the Congress. And by pushing the tendency into an enforced silence, problems had been made more difficult to identify. Nehru suspected, for instance, large-scale collusion by the police in suppressing evidence of larger RSS involvement in Gandhi's murder; but his Home minister, Patel, assured him that only a few 'extreme elements' of the RSS had been involved. Here, indeed, was a good example of a deferral of a problem rather than its solution. But at the time the deferral was more than welcome.

JUNAGADH, HYDERABAD, KASHMIR

There was of course a way in which anti-Muslim sentiment could be equated with reasons of state, where 'Pakistan' could take the place of 'Muslims'. Pakistan, by attempting to define itself as a Muslim state that was not Islamic in a religious sense – a state in which the Muslims of the Indian sub-continent did not feel persecuted – in effect made its self-definition a negative one, dependent on the fact that it was not India. There was a danger of India following suit, and of mutually reinforcing definitions of national boundaries and identities bound to each other in intimate antagonism. This was almost facilitated by the question of Kashmir, where by the end of 1947, hostilities had broken out between India and Pakistan over that state's accession to one or the other state. Pakistan's sponsorship of the so-called 'tribal incursion' into the kingdom of Kashmir, and the maharaja's decision to accede in haste to India, abandoning his earlier position that he wished to secure independence for Kashmir was the beginning of a long and agonised conflict.

Compared to the problems of Kashmir, the other recalcitrant states that by August 15, 1947, had not yet acceded to one or other of the new dominions of India and Pakistan posed far less of a problem. Junagadh, a small state in the Kathiawad region with a Hindu-majority population but a Muslim ruler, decided it wished to join Pakistan. After a brief stand-off with Indian troops outside the state, the maharaja lost his nerve and ran away to Karachi; his dewan ('First Minister'), the Muslim League appointee Sir Shah Nawaz Bhutto, was unable to continue, as his maharaja had emptied the state treasury on his departure. In February 1948, a referendum was held in Junagadh that showed an overwhelming desire to join India. The non-accession of Hyderabad to India was considered an anomaly given that the state was surrounded entirely by Indian territory (although by that reasoning East and West Pakistan were themselves anomalies, and the potential accession of the North-West Frontier Province to India given the 1946 election results could have been achieved). The Nizam of Hyderabad could claim a lineage and a tradition of independence from late Mughal times, but geopolitics were against him – on September 13, 1948, the Indian Army conducted what was referred to as 'police action' in Hyderabad state, incorporating it into the Indian Union. Kashmir, on the other hand, desiring, with its Hindu maharaja and Muslim-majority population, to be independent, and geopolitically in an easily contested border area, was more problematic. Kashmir's borders were more or less artificial – bits had been added on after the British conquest of Punjab in the 1840s and parts of Punjab had been sold to the Dogra ruler of Kashmir. Sir Cyril Radcliffe had awarded Amritsar to East Punjab (India) because of its sacred significance for the Sikhs; British opinion agreed that parts of Gurdaspur District, in which Amritsar fell, should go with it to India. This gave Kashmir a border with India, and a more practical option of joining India should this be desired.

The Congress's policy before August 1947 had been to attempt to guide Kashmir towards India, as opposed to its maharaja, Hari Singh's desire to have an independent Kashmir – which was an option that also had substantial support in Kashmir. In September and October 1947, Pathan 'tribals' from the North-West Frontier Province invaded Kashmir. Some observers see this as a relatively spontaneous – to the extent that any conscious activity can be 'spontaneous' – response to massacres of Muslims in Jammu that had been part of the post-partition violence on the Indian sub-continent (it is also alleged that the maharaja of Kashmir colluded in this violence). But the Pakistan government was not opposed to the incursion, and was soon providing logistical, and eventually formal military support in the form of conventional troops. The British governor of the North-West Frontier Province, Sir Olaf Caroe, also colluded with the Pakistan government. September 13 saw the first 'tribal' incursions; by October 25 a full-scale invasion was clearly underway, with non-Muslims targeted by the invaders; Srinagar was threatened, and Maharaja Hari Singh fled to India. On October 27, India airlifted troops to secure the capital. In the interim, Hari Singh acceded to India.

Here was a strange situation. British officials knew of the support provided to the invaders by Pakistan, but did not bring it into the open for fear of exacerbating conflict. These officials – governors of provinces in Pakistan, armed forces personnel on both sides, and Mountbatten – regularly exchanged information that they could then decide whether or not to share with their governments. At the outbreak of hostilities, Jinnah, the governor-general of Pakistan – who now denounced Hari Singh's accession to India as the result of 'fraud and violence' – had wanted to send regular Pakistan army troops into Kashmir, but was dissuaded by army sources. British officers in both armies were bound to resign in the event of a war between the two dominions – constitutionally, India was a Dominion from 1947 to April 1949 and Pakistan remained a dominion until 1956 – and the Pakistan army was far more dependent on British personnel than the Indian and had a much more British-dominated officer corps.

For Nehru, there was much personal prestige associated with his own Kashmiri origins and Kashmir was a test case for his understanding of a secular India: if a Muslim-majority state could accede to India, the legitimacy and rationale of Pakistan would be undermined, at the same time as strengthening Nehru's vision of India as a non-sectarian society rather than a 'Hindu' nation. But there was of course another point of principle raised by the maharaja's accession. If the monarch alone could decide the question of accession to India or Pakistan, Junagadh or Hyderabad might have had equally good claims to make up their own minds. Patel's negotiations with other states had tended to ignore the question of popular will. Nehru, on the other hand, wished to base the accession of Kashmir to India on democratic principles. Therefore, a popular and democratic government would also need to be installed, and the maharaja's accession could not be accepted without a plebiscite: Nehru believed that the Maharaja alone could not carry through accession to India. The plebiscite could of course only occur if peaceful conditions were restored – which meant the withdrawal of the 'tribesmen'.

In Kashmir, the logical political organisation that presented itself as the defender of democratic principles was the National Conference led by Sheikh Abdullah. Abdullah's National Conference was built up during a successful movement for political rights against Hari Singh in the 1930s, associated with the Indian National Congress through the States Peoples' Movement that Nehru had coordinated in his days on the Congress left (the Congress had always restricted its support for movements inside the princely states to agitational and moral support rather than active participation). The National Conference was the only political organisation in Kashmir that had a credible mass base and was also a secular, non-sectarian organisation – although, in a mirror-image situation to that of the Congress, it was dominated by Muslims (in a Muslim-majority state). Nehru's policy was therefore to get the maharaja to release Sheikh Abdullah from jail, and to seek the National Conference's cooperation. Nehru hoped that the National Conference would lean towards India rather than Pakistan. Fortunately for him, at the time Abdullah (a personal friend of Nehru's) believed that accession to India was the lesser evil, and closer to the independence desired by Kashmiris than accession to Pakistan would be.

It was Mountbatten who persuaded Nehru to place the Kashmir case before the UN. Nehru agreed; it was to be an appeal to the Security Council for condemnation of Pakistani aggression. 'We have refrained [from attacking Pakistani bases near the Kashmir border],' Nehru wrote to Mountbatten, 'because of our desire to avoid complications leading to open war. In our avoidance of this we have increased our own peril and not brought peace any nearer.'[13] When the case was referred to the Security Council in early 1948, however, the terms of reference were extended. Pakistan brought up the question of atrocities against Muslims (the undeclared war continued). Mountbatten was put in a false position; having persuaded Nehru to go to the UN, he had not anticipated conflicts within British official thinking. Foreign Secretary Ernest Bevin's continued hope that Britain could still offer an alternative to US power required him not to antagonise Pakistan. According to him, Pakistan could take the lead in organising the Arab states in the Middle East (or West Asia, as Nehru insisted on calling the region instead) on Britain's behalf. Bevin's attempt to preserve British power in the Middle East came into play: the Palestine question, that of the creation of the Jewish state of Israel, now occupied the UN, and the British did not want to look anti-Muslim and align Muslim opinion against Britain (thereby providing an opportunity for a communist or Soviet takeover); in addition, many British officials now working in Pakistan took up a pro-Pakistani position. Therefore, it was quite impossible simply to provide a verdict on Pakistani aggression.

On the military front, a stalemate had been achieved in Kashmir by 1948. In September 1948, Muhammad Ali Jinnah died of tuberculosis. On December 23 and 25, 1948, UN plebiscite conditions were accepted by India and Pakistan, respectively; a ceasefire was to come into effect from New Year's Day 1949, along a line of actual control. (Militarily the Pakistan army was incapable of defeating the Indian army both in terms of size and equipment; the best they could hope for was a stalemate helped by geography. This is eventually what happened: the 'line of actual control' that divides 'Indian Kashmir' from 'Pakistan-Occupied Kashmir' or 'Azad Kashmir' is such a line.) The desired plebiscite was never held. Jinnah had contended that no fair plebiscite could be conducted with Indian troops and a government sympathetic to India in place – soon after accession to India, the National Conference formed the government in Kashmir – and later, with Kashmir divided between India and Pakistan, this would hardly have been practical. By late 1948, Nehru had abandoned the idea of a plebiscite, and had said so to Sheikh Abdullah in January 1949, but he never publicly abandoned the idea until 1954. Kashmir's accession to India had been loose and partial rather than one of complete incorporation into the new federation: constitutionally, the subjects of defence, external relations and communications were the only three on which the Indian Union was empowered to legislate for Kashmir. This constitutional position has never been respected. (Nehru himself was later to be complicit in putting his friend Sheikh Abdullah in jail, and the autonomy of Kashmir was gradually eroded.)

DOMESTIC BATTLES: NEHRU'S SEARCH FOR POWER

Through all this, the 'duumvirate' was engaged in what effectively was an internal Cold War. There was a brief thaw after Gandhi's assassination in which Nehru and Patel appeared to stand together on the issue of communalism and to have overcome differences: in his address on All-India Radio, following Nehru's, after Gandhi's assassination, Patel referred to Nehru as 'my dear brother'.[14] But this was illusory. Patel, the man who increasingly felt in control of the Congress's organisational politics and who had done so much to set up the continuity and functioning of the institutional mechanisms of the new Indian state, wished to have a larger say in political matters. Representing the Congress right, he also commanded the allegiance of a large section of the party, possibly, he believed, the majority; especially after he had engineered the transformation of the Congress into a more disciplined party, had engineered the exclusion of the CPI from the Congress after the war, and had seen the secession of the socialists in 1949. Nehru was definitely indispensable to the Congress as the most popular and recognisable figure both on a world stage and within India that the Congress could present in public. But the attempted disempowerment of Nehru in terms of day-to-day practical politics was to continue, if possible. Patel hoped he could work Gandhi's old trick of placing Nehru in a position of formal responsibility from which he could not exercise power.

Gandhi, however, had been able to work this tactic because of Nehru's undoubted reverence and respect for him. Patel could command no such respect from Nehru, who would publicly praise him when necessary, but made no particular secret of their differences. Nevertheless, Patel was firmly in control of the Congress organisation and the leader of the right wing of Congress, supported by surviving members of the 'old guard' such as Rajendra Prasad, who if anything was more anti-Muslim than Patel himself. These members of the Congress right, increasingly sensing their potential for achieving effective power, no longer felt it necessary to hide behind the legitimating rhetoric of Gandhism. Genuine Gandhians, whose discomfort with a centralised state apparatus and large-scale industry as envisaged by Nehru had long been apparent, now withdrew to the background. J.B. Kripalani, who had been the Congress president at independence, resigned his presidency in November 1947, raising uncomfortable questions about corruption in the party and in the civil service inherited from British rule, and warning of the dangers of 'investing the State with the monopoly of political and economic exploitation, which is what happens in the centralised economy of a communist or a fascist state'.[15]

Meanwhile, Nehru's natural constituency within the Congress, the old Congress Socialist Party, were by now beginning to feel he had ignored or betrayed them too often. At its conference in March 1948, the Socialist Party announced its intention to secede from the Congress. Surveying the post-independence situation, the Party's resolutions noted that the partition of India, with its emphasis on religious communities, negotiations by an elite of leaders, and the integration of the princely states on the basis of the sovereignty not of the people but of the princes, had moved the emphasis of politics towards communalism and against popular sovereignty. The Congress, now in government and completely identified with it, dominated by the vested interests of 'finance capitalists', refused to support the 'social struggles of the masses' and could therefore not be relied upon to 'sustain its revolutionary tradition'; it was, 'because of its authoritarian bias', in danger of 'being overwhelmed by anti-secular, anti-democratic forces of the right'. The communists, on the other hand, were accused of 'adventurism', of insufficient respect for 'democracy, and of being agents of powers outside India.[16] It was therefore up to the

Socialist Party to take up the cause of socialism. As part of its farewell to Congress, however, the Socialist Party expressed the hope that the Congress would ultimately 'remain a progressive organisation sharing common political ideals, loyalties and memories with the Socialist Party'.[17]

This farewell had something in common with the initial stand of the CPI, the party that the socialists now considered their sworn enemy after its gains at the expense of the old CSP in capturing left organisations in India – student unions, the trade union movement, the *Kisan Sabhas* and other front organisations. In June 1947, the CPI passed a resolution offering support to the 'national leadership in the proud task of building the Indian republic on democratic foundations', and urged all progressive Congressmen to rally behind Nehru.[18] The CPI's position was, however, contradictory. From February 1948, after the Calcutta 'Conference of Youth and Students of Southeast Asia Fighting for Freedom and Independence', the CPI took a strong anti-Nehru line. After the establishment of the Cominform on September 22, 1947, the Andrei Zhdanov line had been adopted by the communist movement – there were now two camps in the world, imperialist and anti-fascist. The CPI stepped up its campaigns in India, much to the alarm of Nehru's government (it was officially at war with the Indian state until October 1951, when the Telengana struggle was called off). At the same time, the CPI's members clearly recognised the situation in India for what it was: if the Congress was to rule, it would be Nehru who could prevent it from ruling as a right-wing party, or taking a pro-US position in the emerging Cold War; to that extent, they had to strengthen Nehru's hand – as the lesser evil. Many members of the Congress, and senior figures in civil service positions, were resolutely reactionary as well as anti-communist, and would have gladly seen India closely aligned with the USA – which Nehru, despite the changes in his views over the years, still identified as an imperialist power. Nehru, for his part, intervened – it became part of his ongoing struggle with Patel – in what he saw as unnecessary persecution of communists *qua* communists, deciding instead to use the forces of the law only against particular communists who broke particular laws. He regarded communism as an ideology rather than an international conspiracy led by the Soviet Union; therefore, in what might be seen as a classical liberal position, he believed communism should be allowed to compete with other ideologies on a level playing field.

This hyper-democratic tendency was in contrast to the reputation Nehru was beginning to develop for being irritable, impatient and autocratic – tendencies of Napoleonism or Caesarism that he had identified in himself in his anonymous self-assessment for the *Modern Review* in 1937. Politically at least, he honourably fought against this side of himself, patiently and laboriously explaining and justifying his policies before legislatures and electorates. Ironically, he might have used this tendency to good measure more often, by allowing himself to be more assertive within his party and government, staking his personal standing and popularity against his colleagues' obstructions.

Nehru was also under considerable pressure and working very long hours, to the consternation of those close to him. He found their attentions and concern somewhat annoying. 'Everybody seems to be anxious to look after me as if I was some kind of a cripple,' he wrote to his sister Vijayalakshmi in Moscow.[19] Despite the attentions of members of his family – his daughter Indira was effectively living with him in Delhi from 1947 onwards, while her husband Feroze ran Nehru's paper, the *National Herald*, in Lucknow – Nehru's personal life in his period as prime minister was one of relative isolation; to some extent this mirrored his political life. Nehru does not appear to have found many people whose social and intellectual company was genuinely fulfilling. Until their departure in June 1948, Nehru found some comfort in the company of the Mountbattens; thereafter, he availed of the opportunities provided by his visits to Britain as prime minister to see 'Dickie' and Edwina, and Edwina's later role as a volunteer for the Red Cross in Asia enabled her to make occasional visits to India. Edwina's death in February 1960 was strongly felt by Nehru.

As the socialists moved inexorably towards their exit from the Congress, Nehru was able to recognise the dangers of his own potential vulnerability and isolation. In August 1948, Nehru pleaded for understanding from his old friend Jayaprakash Narayan. 'I cannot, by sheer force of circumstance, do everything that I would like to do. We are all of us in some measure prisoners of fate and circumstance. But I am as keen as ever to go in a particular direction and carry the country with me and I do hope that in doing so I have some help from you.' Along with this plea, he warned Narayan that any attempt at 'premature leftism' might lead to a further move to the right, as, he claimed, had been the case in Europe – he also directed the charge of premature leftism against the CPI, which mirrored the socialists' own position on the communists.[20] Narayan was unconvinced; he had told the Socialist Party conference that the Congress as it now stood was a far cry from the common anti-imperialist platform it had been, and that it was necessary for political campaigners to give it no special deference on account of it having in effect inherited a recognisable label – this was the very label whose safety many were now seeking. As for Nehru staying with the Congress, this was another example of his inability to back what he stood for by concrete action. 'You want to go towards socialism,' Narayan sarcastically wrote to Nehru, 'but you want the capitalists to help in that.'[21] Narayan made no secret of the fact that he believed Nehru to be trapped in a right-wing party.

The socialists perhaps erred in not giving Nehru adequate credit for his major contributions, and his principled opposition to Patel and the right, on the 'communal question'. Patel believed that supporters of the erstwhile Hindu Mahasabha as well as members of the RSS logically belonged in the Congress, and that steps should be taken to attract them in – a strange position for a 'Gandhian' to take, soon after Gandhi's assassination by an RSS man.[22] Nehru strongly opposed this tendency. When communal violence broke out in East and West Bengal in the winter of 1949, Patel's preferred solution was once again large-scale population exchanges. Instead, in April 1950, Nehru was able to persuade the Pakistan Prime Minister Liaquat Ali Khan to sign the 'Delhi Pact' with him, which asserted the right of minority communities in both India and Pakistan to equality of citizenship irrespective of religion – an underlining of Nehru's victory over Patel on the issue of nationality for Muslims in India.

With the socialists' departure from the Congress in 1949, Patel's followers could attempt to disarm Nehru and gain control. The 1950 Congress presidential elections saw seven candidates enter the fray. Three of them (J.B. Kripalani, Purshottam Das Tandon and Shankarrao Deo) contested the elections; the other four (among them Nehru himself) withdrew. Tandon, a Hindu communalist and a close follower of Patel's, beat Kripalani by 246 votes (1,306 to 1,052) and was elected Congress president in August 1950. Nehru, clearly aware that this was now a matter of his own political survival, refused to join Tandon's Working Committee, without which the president of Congress was powerless (Nehru's tactics recalled Gandhi's non-cooperation with Subhas Bose in 1939). A stalemate followed; Nehru eventually, in October, joined the Working

Committee, but voiced his disapproval of Tandon's views and his selection of Congress Working Committee members. Then, on December 15, 1950, Patel, the power behind Tandon's candidacy, died, having been ill. He received the obligatory tributes from his colleagues, Nehru included. This was not altogether hypocrisy. Patel and Nehru had for over thirty years been colleagues in the Congress, and had acquired a certain respect for each other despite their strong disagreements. Nehru could hardly deny that Patel's organisational skills had contributed to the building up of a strong state apparatus, and whatever their other disagreements the two men had shared a belief in a strong, centralised state. To the extent that the state was to be identified with the nation, both men were nationalists; but they had very different views of that nation.

With Patel's death, the balance of power shifted slightly. But the ascendancy of the Congress right was still underpinned by the president of India, Rajendra Prasad, who had attempted to block land reform legislation relating to his home state, Bihar, in 1950, and had opposed his prime minister by presenting his personal views on the Hindu Code Bill to Parliament in 1951, causing a minor constitutional crisis. On both occasions Nehru had threatened to resign as prime minister, and Prasad had retreated. (On the latter, Nehru had been forced by the surprisingly strong conservative opposition to compromise, diluting and splitting the Bill up into four separate pieces of legislation on marriage, divorce, succession and adoption passed between May 1955 and the end of 1956.) The president had also, in April 1951, against Nehru's advice, inaugurated the rebuilt Somnath temple, in the erstwhile Junagadh state, which in Hindu nationalist mythologies was an emotive symbol due to its having been destroyed by 'Muslim invaders' almost a thousand years before. Patel, as deputy prime minister in November 1947, had announced that Somnath would be rebuilt. Nehru had felt that official support for the rebuilding of a temple whose history was directly connected with anti-Muslim sentiment was unwise. Prasad, however, and Patel posthumously, won this battle.

Nehru was also under pressure from the *secular* right, represented by Rajagopalachari. Nehru had earlier sought out Rajagopalachari as an ally against communal forces within the Congress; now he was faced with a home minister who felt that communalism was far less of a problem than communism. In February 1951, Rajagopalachari opposed Nehru's commuting of death sentences on communists in connection with the

Telengana uprisings, and led a chorus of objections in Parliament, from inside and outside the Congress, to accepting Soviet wheat in India – at a time of food shortages verging on famine, and of US blackmail on food aid in connection with India's role in the Korean War negotiations – of which more shall be said later.

Meanwhile, Kripalani and Rafi Ahmed Kidwai, the latter a close associate of Nehru's, left the Congress and formed the Kisan Mazdoor Praja Party (translatable, in what was by now a recognisably populist format for party names, as the 'Peasants', Workers' and Subjects' Party'). Nehru was disappointed; this further narrowed his potential support base in Congress. In September 1951, Nehru decided to force the issue, staking the vast capital of his own reputation and standing against the opportunists and factionalists within the Congress, resigning from all Tandon's committees and asking the party to choose between him and Tandon (offering to resign was his tactical equivalent to Gandhi's fasts). Consequently, Tandon, outmanoeuvred, resigned.

Having recaptured the presidency of the Congress, Nehru appealed to Congressmen who had left the party due to its rightward drift to return. Notable among the prominent returnees was Rafi Ahmed Kidwai, who abandoned the party he had so recently helped to found. After this, Nehru was the acknowledged and largely unchallenged leader of the Congress. From September 1951 to November 1954, Nehru himself was both prime minister and Congress president (he was succeeded in the latter role from 1954 to 1959 by U.N. Dhebar, an administrator unimportant in actual politics, then by his daughter, Indira Gandhi from 1959 to 1960). But the character of the Congress itself did not substantially change; it rhetorically took on a form more in keeping with Nehru's views.

All these internal agonies did not appear to affect the standing of the Congress before the 'masses'. Nehru, unsurprisingly, was the central figure in the Congress election campaign for the first general elections on the basis of universal adult franchise in 1951–2, travelling the country and making innumerable speeches and public appearances. The heroic, elegant figure of Jawaharlal Nehru, the Mahatma's anointed successor and the Congress's most articulate spokesman for so many years, was a familiar figure across India; he was of course the successful leader of a victorious movement for national liberation. Nehru was no orator; he could be hesitant and flat in his delivery, but his speeches to large public gatherings were disarmingly direct and straightforward, giving the impression of candour and intimacy. He came across to diverse audiences, to sophisticated intellectuals and landless peasants alike, as a man of great integrity amongst lesser mortals: it was easy to trust him, for here was a prime minister with whom one could imagine mutually shared concerns.

The Congress emerged from the elections as the single largest party in the Lok Sabha, the lower house of parliament, with 364 seats out of 489; it had contested all the seats, winning 74.4% of them in a first-past-the-post system with 46% of the vote. The CPI emerged as the main opposition party; it contested 49 seats and won 26 of them, concentrating on its areas of strength, gaining 5.3% of the seats with 3.3% of the vote share. The Socialist Party, by contrast, contested 256 seats but won only 12, that is 2.5% of the seats, with 10.6% of the national vote. The Kisan Mazdoor Praja Party contested 145 seats and won nine, that is 1.8% of the seats, with 5.8% of the national vote. Together, the two non-communist socialist parties outside the Congress had won 16.4% of the vote (the KMPP and the Socialist Party merged in 1952, after the elections, to form the Praja Socialist Party). The Jan Sangh, the Hindu fundamentalist party led by S.P. Mukherjee that replaced the Hindu Mahasabha, contested 93 seats and won three; that is, 0.6% of seats, with 3.1% of the national vote. Altogether, 105,944,495 people voted.[23]

Simultaneous elections were held in the federal units, now called 'states', with the old distinction between provinces and princely states having been abolished. Altogether, the Congress contested 3,153 seats (of a total of 3,283) and won 2,246 of them, which made 68.4% of the seats, with 42.2% of the votes. The CPI contested 465 and won 106, 3.2% of the seats, with 4.38% of the vote share; the Socialist Party contested 1,799 and won 125, 2.8% of the seats, with 9.7% of the vote. Corresponding figures for the KMPP were 1,005, 77, 2.3% and 5.11%; and for the Jan Sangh, 717, 35, 1.2% and 2.76%. A total of 103,801,199 votes were cast in the state assembly elections. The 'largest democracy in the world' – a phrase that would soon become a cliché – had been inaugurated.

THE NEHRUVIANS AND THE NEHRUVIAN PROJECT

With the consolidation of his position in the Congress, and with the endorsement of Congress by the electorate, Nehru could try and get his project of state-led social engineering off the ground. What exactly this project was going to be was not immediately apparent. The phrasing of the Congress's statement of its economic objectives had not exactly been precise; it spoke of the need for 'social justice and equality', the importance, 'as far as possible', of 'national and regional economic efficiency', and the necessity to ensure that 'democracy extends from the political to the social and economic spheres'. References to effective control over local affairs by village-level committees or *Panchayats* could be seen as a concession to the Gandhians. The statement maintained that 'democracy in the modern age necessitates planned central directions as well as decentralisation of political and economic power, in so far as this is compatible with the safety of the State, with efficient production and the cultural progress of the community as a whole.'[24] The rhetoric of the period strongly stressed the need for collective and disciplined national progress, for production before distribution could be achieved, and consequently for harmonious industrial relations. Change would come, but it would be relatively gradual, consensual, and rely on the education of the masses and the initiatives of the state. Vested interests would be chipped away by the authority of the state, represented by the national government, which in effect was the Congress.

Integral to these plans was the acceptance of the myth of a benign state. The characterisation of the state as an organ of class rule, and consequently the importance of identifying who the ruling classes were in a given state, could not afford to be brought out into the open. Instead, 'national' solidarity and 'nation-building', both of which had been important concepts under imperial rule, were to be invoked. The national state, as opposed to the colonial state, was assumed to have the interests of its citizens at its core; the Congress, which was the legitimate heir of the national movement, would automatically embody these interests – or so the myth ran. Nehru himself, if one goes by the views he expressed in the *Discovery of India*, did not believe either in the nationalism that this implied or in the necessarily benign nature of the state: nationalism for him was an obsolete idea and only survived in the absence of national freedom, and he was clearly conscious of divergences in class interests. But in public he accepted, and promoted, the myth.

With the emphasis placed on 'nation-building', industrialists and workers were asked to work together for the collective good. Nehru acted as intermediary, declaring that 'indiscipline among labour' was indeed a problem, but that industrialists had to stop blaming labour, or agitators among labour, for their problems,[25] and asking industrialists to set up

industries for the benefit of '400 million Indians and not a few industrialists and capitalists', even as he called for workers to refrain from strikes.[26]
Some of his rhetoric was beginning to sound dangerously as if drawn
from Gandhi's 'trusteeship' theory, which Nehru and the left had once
so ridiculed. In March 1947, an Industrial Disputes Act was passed, which
called for the setting up of tribunals for the prevention and settlement
of disputes. The Act cast the government as mediator – a paternalist, or
at least avuncular, presence in industrial disputes. Industrialists and
trade unions were both suspicious of the government. The trade union
movement by this time had split – the old All-India Trade Union
Congress (AITUC), now more or less dominated by the CPI, refused to
accept the validity of government mediation; the Indian National Trade
Union Congress (INTUC), a Congress-sponsored body, accepted the
paternalist claims of government. The socialists, who also opposed
government mediation, stood at the time outside both the AITUC and the
INTUC.

Nehru knew that getting even mildly radical legislation through
parliament or state assemblies was a difficult route to take towards social
change. A case in point was that of land reforms. The first step towards
this, the abolition of *zamindari*, or the rights of superior landlords who had
controlled the land and paid taxes directly to the British government,
had been initiated by legislatures both in the 1937–9 period and in the
1940s and 1950s, only to be blocked by vested interests – often by
zamindars – who were strongly represented within Congress. *Zamindari*
abolition was the only stage of land reforms to be properly carried through,
but this was not particularly radical. Already in the late 1930s, British
government reports had called for the abolition of *zamindari*, though
not for reasons of social justice: land revenue, fixed 'in perpetuity' for the
permanent settlement areas, no longer yielded adequate returns for
the government. Post-independence land reform was a relatively mild
form of social engineering, given that the principle of private property
was resolutely observed and that compensation payments were made
to dispossessed *zamindars*. The legislation lacked bite, however. Overall,
there was to some extent a shift of power in the direction of better-off
'caste peasants'. Partially dispossessed landlords were allowed to keep the
best of their lands, joined the ranks of the rich peasantry, and circum-
vented the laws against sub-letting land by employing sharecroppers;
a landowner could also avoid the ceiling on the amount of land he was

entitled to possess by the nominal redistribution of his land within his own family.

From Nehru's point of view, these blockages required him to seek the power to act effectively outside the structures of party and legislature – even as, paradoxically, Nehru remained the most committed and scintillating of parliamentarians, addressing the House in impassioned words and defending his policies in frank and logical terms. For the greater goal of national development, the Planning Commission existed from 1950 onwards, almost a parallel Cabinet, with Nehru himself as its chairman, in which 'experts' would be able to pronounce on issues of national importance, allegedly from a non-political perspective, thereby disarming and bypassing opposition to its measures. Governing by Planning Commission rather than by Cabinet lost Nehru his Finance minister in June 1950 when John Matthai, formerly and thereafter of Tata Sons, then the largest business house in India, resigned in protest against what he thought were the excessive powers of the Planning Commission.

The Planning Commission was far from the ultra-socialist or quasi-communist body that it was depicted as in the propaganda of the emergent Indian right. And if Nehru's governments acquired a reputation for Fabian socialism, the Planning Commission was to a large extent responsible for the impression. 'Fabianism' was less a philosophical choice than a tendency retrospectively named: here was a system that worked by gradualism, by permeation, by compromise, and by advice from think tanks, academics and technocrats. It was these clusters of learned men who were Nehru's best support base: the 'Nehruvians'.

This was the goodliest fellowship of knights ever to be assembled in the service of a new state: intellectuals, men of distinguished education and good breeding, whose commitment to socialism or to social change in less grandiose terms hinged on their sense of being the harbingers of modernity and the custodians of the future of the nation. Their allegiance to Nehru was in some cases based on a throwback to Nehru at his romantic best: the fiery revolutionary and the self-reflexive progressive and fellow intellectual of the 1930s, whose urbane sophistication combined with radical social comment and international renown was an inspiring example of the possibilities of a Cambridge-New Delhi axis (which several of the Nehruvians had in common), at a time when an education in the metropolis was still a large helping of social capital, ensuring high social status and employability. Many of those committed to Nehru's 1930s *avatar* were disappointed by the prime minister's now infinitely more cautious, even conservative, behaviour. But the Nehruvians were also divided along lines defined by those who had been drawn to the socialist in Nehru and those who had been drawn to the moderniser in Nehru. At any event, in a gradualist system, they could well afford to co-exist in the same spaces: the interim goal of socialists, and a desired goal of modernisers, would have to be a viable national capitalism first, state-led and capitalist-assisted, or perhaps vice versa, but necessarily different from the poorly-industrialised and famine-prone country left behind by British rule.

Intellectuals' allegiance to Nehru can be traced to the consequences of Nehru's interventions into the political arena from the late 1920s onwards. The space opened out by him provided scope for the reinstatement of intellectuals in the Indian nationalist movement; they had been displaced since the moderates had been eclipsed by extremists and their populism. After Gandhi's insistence on an anti-intellectual position and the privileging of peasants, this reinstatement was more than welcome. It was not possible, after Gandhi, to go back to an avowedly elitist politics (although Gandhi's own reliance on a moral elite was in its own way resolutely elitist as well). The commitment to enlightenment, modernity and social change that Nehru represented seemed to avoid that pitfall, while providing a central role for intellectuals in the life of their nation. What this amounted to was a vulgar Leninism without Leninist goals: the intellectuals, collectively, would be the vanguard party that would bring 'progress', only they were not a party either in discipline or in coherent ideology. The 'people', they agreed, would be served, but by those who knew better; in return, they would be expected to produce the required efforts for the 'nation'.

Among the cluster of people who gathered around Nehru was P.C. Mahalanobis, the physics teacher turned statistician who was the author of the Second Five-Year Plan and the eponymous model associated with it (he was responsible for the First Plan as well, but did not set much store by it). Mahalanobis had spent his early years as a statistician dabbling in eugenics-related work, and had switched to economic surveys at first under the British government's patronage. In 1939, he had offered his services to the Congress's National Planning Committee. Mahalanobis's institution, the Indian Statistical Institute, was to become one of the showcase institutions in India; it had no precise brief and could therefore interpret its work any way its director saw fit. Apart from the obvious work implied by its title, it invited scientists and economists from around the world to spend time in India and work on various projects. Mahalanobis, resolutely patrician, was no socialist except in a distant and paternalistic sense, although he came to be associated with many socialists; but there were others who worked with him or under him who were. Indeed, many ideologues of the left thought working with Nehru's planning team was important: they were building an independent and self-sufficient nation-state that would be able to withstand the pressures of foreign interests seeking markets or spaces to invest excess capital – a phenomenon that was soon to be given a proper name – neo-colonialism. Even the CPI's official opposition to Nehru was tempered by a sense that the technocrats were doing important work; communists or their sympathisers were able, in these circumstances, to offer their services to the state in that role.

In building the new 'nation', 'expertise' and the 'scientific temperament' were given privileged positions ('scientific research' was one of the ministerial portfolios that Nehru retained for himself in the first government of independent India). India was a country that had to be made modern, its people dragged, sometimes kicking and screaming, into modernity. 'Backwardness' of all kinds had to be fought. In the new India the glorious potential achievements, and the universality, of science and technology were universally praised. 'Science and technology know no frontiers,' Nehru declared. 'Nobody ought to talk about English science, French science, American science, Chinese science. Science is something bigger than the countries. There ought to be no such thing as Indian science. So also with technology.'[27] 'Science', however, was easily confused with the pervasive importance given to technology, which was well short of 'science' as its professional practitioners might have understood it. This tendency was soon to be reflected in the educational and career aspirations of several generations of post-independence Indians: engineering was among the most important professions of the post-independence generation, to which might have been added that of economists.

The stress on technology and technical expertise could be seen to be borrowed from the influential Soviet model of planning – in which, especially in its borrowed version, 'socialism' was not a necessary component. A member of the National Planning Committee, formerly one of the USSR's 'technical experts' himself, summed it up: '"Industry and technique solve all problems," rightly said Comrade Stalin.'[28] The Nehruvians would not altogether have disagreed; it is certainly true that this was the route they attempted to use towards development, as more radical routes were considered impassable or unviable. The Nehruvians hoped to use state power, via the justificatory potential of the 'national' idea, to arrogate to themselves several roles: of administering social justice, producing wealth and refereeing social conflict – which at best implied a rather naive view of the manipulability of society, politically and otherwise. Nehru presided over this, finding, in his inimitable style, the language to justify and glorify it.

From the point of view of this intellectual elite, the First Five-Year Plan (1951–6) was most unglamorous. The First Plan (although it began a longer-term commitment to capital goods production) aimed at achieving self-sufficiency in food, and consequently spent most of its outlay on the agricultural sector, notwithstanding the widespread desire for industrialisation among the planning classes. The First Plan also put into operation the projects for big river valley dams that are now the bane of environmentalists but were then the starting adventures of underdeveloped countries in building large projects. These schemes for dams had been put on the books by the late colonial government – largely as an exercise in economic public relations, because it was frankly admitted by colonial officials that they neither wished to spend nor had the resources to get these projects off the ground. Made concrete – literally – by the government of independent India, these became truly *national* projects: Nehru promised that the Damodar Valley Corporation scheme for damming the river Damodar would be 'bigger than' the Tennessee Valley Authority, that great achievement of the New Deal. For all the tentativeness of the First Plan, it was a relative success: the plan had envisaged an increase in national income of 11% but had achieved 18%; foodgrains production increased from 52 million tonnes to 66 million tonnes; of the envisaged total investment of 35 billion rupees, only 31 billion had been spent. But this success was deceptive, and would create longer-term over-optimism among planners who at any event sought to create greater things. 'The first five-year plan is an anthology,' P.C. Mahalanobis believed, 'a plan has to be a drama.'[29]

THE RETURN OF THE 'VILLAGE COMMUNITY'

Received wisdom, corresponding with the emphases recognisable in the public statements of the Congress under Nehru, is that India in the 1950s was obsessed with heavy industry, technological change, machinery and centralised planning. But there was also the recognition of the importance of decentralised initiatives and rural welfare, an obvious concern in a country whose population was still predominantly rural and agricultural, and where employment had to be created. These were embodied from 1952 in the so-called 'Community Development' schemes, which incorporated Gandhi as a crucial legitimating icon; thus, even as the remaining genuinely ideological Gandhians gradually began moving into the opposition to the Congress, the Congress discovered new uses for Gandhian ideas.

Such schemes required local officials to encourage villages to organise their own local initiatives for welfare or developmental purposes, hopefully to be expressed in the organisation of rural cooperatives and some form of voluntary collectivisation that might solve some of the problems of landholdings too small to be economical (even by the Second Five-Year Plan this had not got very far, but already 'creeping collectivisation' was being denounced by some). They might also organise cottage industries based on local labour power, under-employed due to the seasonal nature of agriculture or disguised unemployment in the area. Community Development acknowledged its debts to both public and private 'village uplift' or 'rural reconstruction' initiatives under colonial rule. These predecessor schemes, which had much in common with Gandhian attempts at rural social engineering, also shared with the latter a benevolent paternalism that was most often well-meaning, if at times misdirected and out of joint with the wider political economy. The genealogy of the idea of the 'village community' and its alleged ancient autonomy can be traced back to early British attempts to understand Indian history. Allegedly, India was a country of autonomous 'village republics' which ran their own affairs and changed little even as the wider political world changed around it: dynasties came and went, but the 'village community' remained unscathed. For the Orientalists, this demonstrated that if the 'village community' (as they understood it) could be preserved, ruling the larger entity that was India could proceed with less friction. Later versions, from the nineteenth century onwards, built on what was in the main a misunderstanding of the 'autonomy' and 'self-sufficiency' of the village community; when this idea entered the nationalist imagination (it found a place, notably, in Gandhian thinking), it evoked schemes to revive this ancient and glorious tradition of 'local self-government' of an authentic and indigenous kind. But the harmonious and self-regulating idyllic village, ruled by the village *panchayat*, its own council of five village elders, was a myth. The reality of local inequalities, class and caste stratification did not lend themselves to the 'restoration' of a mythical idyll: the village was, in the words of B.R. Ambedkar, 'a sink of localism, a den of ignorance, narrow-mindedness and communalism'.[30]

The First Plan had envisaged land reforms and panchayats as the economic and political prerequisites for Community Development programmes. But as the Nehruvian state was unable – or unwilling – to challenge the social order in the countryside, progress in this direction was slow at best. In 1956, Malcolm Darling, who as a pioneer of rural reconstruction and the cooperative movement in colonial Punjab had been considered a sympathetic colonial official, was invited back to India to report on the progress of the cooperative movement in India under Community Development; his progress report was far from encouraging. It could be said in its defence that the remarkable survival of Indian traditions of craftsmanship and the development of handicrafts in independent India owed much to the Gandhian defence of small-scale industry that was strengthened by Community Development. It also provided, in the longer term, a language of legitimacy in which rural communities could make claims on their own behalf, demanding the right to take developmental initiatives of their own – as envisaged by the ideologues of 'self-help'. But this was a long time coming.

Against the backdrop of the stalling of land reform measures, there appeared what seemed to be a striking victory for the Gandhians: Acharya Vinoba Bhave's *bhoodan* (land donations) and *gramdan* (village donations) movement. The *bhoodan* movement, dubbed a 'revolution through love', involved the ascetic figure of Vinoba Bhave roaming the countryside in search of alms in the form of land, and receiving large tracts as voluntary donations from landlords whom the force of law had not managed to dispossess. In the religious tradition of giving alms or donations to holy men, some had been encouraged to give of their plenty. Much publicity was given to this movement, especially among Cold War-motivated observers, who encouraged this non-confrontationist and non-communist trend towards redistribution. There was at the time much concern among Indian anti-communists as well as US India-watchers (a growing breed, with the beginnings of Cold War-related 'area studies' soon to swell their numbers further) that India might be headed in a communist direction: the CPI was the second-largest political party in Parliament and some of the socialists like Jayaprakash Narayan, a former member of the Communist Party of the USA, were far too militant for comfort. What most observers neglected to mention was the poor quality of much of the land, and in some cases the uncultivable land that had been donated.[31] But the legitimating possibilities of such donations were not lost on the donors, as they had not been lost on other opportunist donors to Gandhian causes before.

There then occurred a most unexpected political event: in 1953, Narayan, along with several prominent socialists from the PSP, withdrew from formal politics to pursue the Gandhian route of 'work amongst the people', joining Vinoba Bhave's *bhoodan* movement. As he retrospectively described it in 1957, in his narrative of a pilgrim's spiritual and intellectual progress, Narayan was getting increasingly frustrated by the politics of independent India, which he believed to be too centralised, and based on the passive participation of ordinary people, leading to their becoming 'politically emasculated'. He moreover had come to believe, he said, that 'morality', as offered by the Gandhians, was a powerful incentive for human behaviour, and that Gandhians could educate the people 'about a balanced or whole view of life' and disciplining the bodily appetites, thereby enabling 'socialism' to 'merge into *sarvodaya*' (the uplift of all). He declared that he had made a 'final break with Marxism'.[32]

These shifts in political allegiances muddied the political waters. Were the Gandhians to be regarded as agrarian conservatives or Tolstoyan socialists? (Gandhians would, indeed, crop up right across the political spectrum thereafter, from the 'Gandhian socialists' of the strange constellation now developing, to the right-wing and pro-US *Swatantra* Party – the name, ironically, is loosely translatable as 'self-reliance' – in the 1960s.) Although Narayan himself was cautious to point out that he was not simply advocating 'indigenist' solutions and declaring all 'foreign' forms of socialism evil, an 'indigenist' rhetoric was now amplified and used – although more subtly – by those who used to be its biggest opponents, reflected in the Hindi neologisms that came to dominate political life: '*rajniti*' ('power politics') was to be replaced by '*lokniti*' ('the politics of the people'), and so on. 'Socialism', which had once been declared foreign by Gandhi, could, indigenised by the introduction of Gandhism and stylistically revamped, also lend to Gandhism the aura of 'socialism' and shift the pressure of foreignness onto the communists, cast as agents of a foreign power.

In 1953, Narayan had proposed a Gandhian–socialist alliance, while advocating Congress–Praja Socialist Party cooperation in some spheres; this was opposed by other PSP leaders. The 'democratic socialist' camp, as it was called to distinguish it from the communists, began to split. Ram Manohar Lohia, who himself had engaged creatively with Gandhi in his political thinking, was not, however, content to be mystical; on December 28, 1955, he formed the 'Socialist Party of India'. Lohia was acutely conscious of the continued polyvalence of Gandhi and the possibility of appropriating him for a variety of causes. As he saw it, slightly retrospectively (in 1963), Gandhism after the death of Gandhi had 'branched off into the "priestly" and "governmental", and priestly Gandhism got so well integrated with the governmental that it has not struggled against any kind of injustice'. A third variant, 'heretic Gandhism' had found its home in the Socialist Party, but had been disowned by 'priestly Gandhism'; nevertheless, it was this variant that had some progressive potential, for '[b]y its very nature, heresy should be more responsible than orthodoxy'.[33] Among Lohia's followers, as among other non-dogmatic left-wing political thinkers in India, there was also a muted but very present admiration for China; Nehru certainly shared this admiration. China, like India, was an agrarian country that had, unlike India, moved along a revolutionary path of its own choosing, prioritising the needs of the peasantry – or so it was then believed. The knowledge that urban standards of living improved faster, and that despite the rhetoric, the countryside lost out once the Chinese Communist Party had come to power, was not widely available at the time.

Meanwhile, the central aspect of Gandhians' disagreement with the rest of the nationalist movement – that of a centralised and industrialisation-oriented economic policy – remained unresolved in political rhetoric. Congress policy, armed with Community Development, now played both the Gandhian and the industrialising card: the village would look after its own needs, especially in much-need consumer goods sectors, while the larger business of industrialisation, requiring the production of capital goods, was dealt with elsewhere. In January 1955, Nehru was able to take the offensive, after a fashion: the Congress's 'Avadi Resolution', at its annual conference, declared its goal to be a 'socialistic pattern of society' (parliament had already endorsed this goal in late 1954) – the word 'socialism' was avoided. The realignments among oppositional forces, meanwhile, had to a large extent strengthened the Congress, and Nehru's position in it: if *everyone* claimed some form of 'socialism', then Nehru could safely claim the same, with the clear understanding that those in his party who opposed him had no publicly legitimate basis on which to oppose him; there was as yet no organised right outside the Congress. Rhetorically, at least, Indian politics had an overpopulated left, a sparsely populated centre and an almost empty right, as religious and sectarian parties had successfully been cornered and contained in a delegitimised zone.

THE INTERNATIONAL ORDER

'We have talked,' Nehru had said in the Constituent Assembly, 'so much about British imperialism that we cannot get out of the habit of it.'[34] He was presenting to the House the need for political realism and a practical as well as a principled foreign policy. But of course he knew that British imperialism was not dead – it had nonetheless to be downplayed – at first if the objective of joining the Commonwealth was to be carried through, and thereafter to sustain some delicate negotiations in which Britain was considered the lesser evil to the greater evil of the USA. Nehru was far from enamoured of the American approach to world politics; in private, he observed that President Truman was a mediocre man who ought not to be trusted and who could not carry out his international responsibilities as the man in charge of a superpower. It is possible to see the Commonwealth link as important to Nehru: the Commonwealth was a compromise that prevented political isolation, without implying a corresponding commitment to the Western bloc.

But there were moments, with the pressures of world politics apparently getting to him, at which Nehru contemplated temporarily breaking his principles, quietly and without fanfare. There was an explicit element of opportunism in this. In 1948, Nehru speculatively asked Krishna Menon, 'why not align with the USA somewhat and build up our economic and military strength?'[35] Menon firmly refused to let his colleague take that route. The Soviet Union was already suspicious of

Nehru's anti-imperialist credentials, which had not been improved by his decision to keep India within the Commonwealth, seemingly indicating a leaning to the Western side; non-alignment could better be sustained by inviting the suspicions of both sides rather than only one.

Meanwhile, Britain, increasingly dependent on and therefore sub-servient to the USA, was able to use its 'Commonwealth' commitment to argue that it had to tread softly in matters of foreign policy: it could not afford to annoy or alienate key allies such as India. That this was less out of respect for the Commonwealth as a partnership of equals and more out of a need to find space to manoeuvre and to behave less like the global bull-in-a-china-shop than the USA did was quickly apparent to Nehru. He was unwilling altogether to rely on the British as an ally – the Kashmir issue at the UN was a good example of why this would have been unwise – but found the British to be more reasonable than the Americans.

There was, of course, the crucial issue of anti-communism. Indian anti-communism had its own concerns and genealogy, and it was irritating to have it appropriated by the USA's spurious rhetoric of 'democracy', which many Indian anti-communists did not for a moment take seriously, given the pro-imperialist causes that the USAs was willing to defend internationally. Domestically, Nehru's own views, at least publicly, tended towards opposing what he saw as the undemocratic or adventur-ist nature of some communist activities, while refusing to condemn communists *per se*. Internationally, Nehru, despite his insistence on non-alignment, had professed his own anti-communism in various ways to US and British sources, perhaps a little more strongly than he might have to other audiences. In October 1949, on his first trip to the USA, he had said that in China nationalism would emerge stronger than communism (in effect, that the CCP was more nationalist than it was communist), thereby amplifying a trend in US China policy that hoped for a Chinese 'Titoism' along the lines of Yugoslavia's staying aloof from the Soviet bloc. Nehru also assured the Americans that the communist strategy in India of first aligning with the left wing of nationalism and then attempting to control it had failed. At the same time, Nehru managed to deflect the issue of aligning with the USA: 'the most intimate ties,' he told journalists in New York, somewhat mystically, 'are ties which are not ties.'[36] (India was among the first powers to recognise the People's Republic of China, established October 1, 1949 – India recognised the PRC on December 30, 1949, and Britain on January 6, 1950, shortly before the Colombo

Conference, at which Britain's strategic attempt to contain communism by developmental and technical assistance was inaugurated).

The USA for its part disliked Indian attempts to organise international diplomacy without reference to metropolitan interests, bringing together countries of the periphery; the rhetoric of Asian solidarity was disturbing. The independence of Burma in January 1948, of Ceylon in February 1948, and the anti-imperialist struggles in Indonesia, Indo-China and Malaya had made the Western bloc extremely nervous about communism in Asia; neutralism of the Nehruvian variety was disturbing. In January 1949, following Dutch attempts to recapture the Indonesian republic, Nehru intervened (in 1946 he had in similar circumstances, as head of the Interim Government, been unable to do so). Tiring of the Security Council's handling of the question for the previous six months, where the Western bloc had persistently blocked the demand for the Dutch to withdraw their forces, he called an Asian conference of twenty countries in New Delhi. This included Pakistan and several Arab states, as well as Australia and New Zealand. In the case of Indonesia, Nehru was willing to stick his neck out and provide actual support (there might also have been personal reasons for this; Nehru had first met the then prime minister of Indonesia, Mohammed Hatta, at the Brussels Congress in 1927). The Interim Government in 1946 had demanded the withdrawal of Indian troops from Indonesia; later, Indian aircraft had broken the Dutch blockade of the Indonesian Republic and carried food, medicines and other supplies (perhaps not excluding arms) to republican forces, All-India Radio in Delhi functioned as the official radio station of the Indonesian republic, and Nehru had even offered Delhi as a base for a government in exile if the need should arise. Politically, this was not entirely unsafe, as the Dutch were relatively isolated internationally and the Indonesian republic was not communist. The 1949 Conference in Delhi asked the Dutch to withdraw troops from occupied areas, to release Indonesian leaders from prison and to allow the formation of an interim government, but did not ask for sanctions against Holland.

As far as Cold War India-watchers were concerned, however, the more disturbing trend was that Nehru appeared to be bringing into being a separate bloc, outside of Soviet or US control; the invitation to Australia and New Zealand raised the suspicion that Nehru was trying to detach them from the 'West'. Both the USA and the USSR were suspicious, the USSR because it felt that this was a second anti-communist bloc in the making. To a certain extent the USSR's nervousness was justified. Nehru was very careful to separate anti-imperialism from communism; the first he would support, the second he would distance himself from, even if its main goals at a given point were anti-imperialist. But Nehru was careful to insist that the conference was not an alternative Asian bloc, nor was it directed against either existing bloc, though he was more careful to soothe the West. However, several delegates at Delhi proposed that such meetings should continue as they could eventually provide a forum for resisting the demands of either bloc.

Soon afterwards, the Korean War brought Nehru into international negotiations again. The Korean peninsula had been partitioned along the 38th Parallel in 1948; on June 25, 1950, a UN Security Council resolution (in the absence of the USSR, boycotting the Security Council in protest against the Chinese place being occupied by the Taiwan government, not the Beijing one) condemned North Korea for crossing the 38th Parallel. On June 26, Truman pledged the USA to military intervention against further communist expansion in Asia – outside Korea, the US 7th fleet was sent in to protect Formosa, and military aid was provided to the French in Indo-China. Nehru refused to accept the US view that the USSR was behind the outbreak of hostilities in Korea, and to tolerate US support for a renewal of European imperialism in Asia. The British were also somewhat alarmed at the USA's extreme position and sought instead to defuse the situation.

Nehru's neutralism now meant that he was well positioned to mediate. When hostilities began, he strongly advised against the USA entering North Korea, especially after it had already created tensions by bombing Chinese territory in Manchuria – this, he said, would escalate the conflict with China entering the fray. US Secretary of State Dean Acheson thought this was a bluff on the Chinese part and ignored these warnings; but by November Chinese forces had joined the war and had inflicted heavy defeats on US forces. Soon things were looking to get out of hand. Now it became essential to get an intermediary to defuse tensions – in November 1950, feelers were sent to India by British and American diplomatic sources, asking for Indian mediation; US Assistant Secretary of State, George McGhee, explicitly linked this to an offer of US food aid for India, a request for which had been made earlier that year due to a severe drought. The offered incentive of the aid package was opposed by the US Treasury in January because, as one US official put it, 'aid should be given

[only] to those who are demonstrably on our side and willing to fight for it'.[37] Dean Acheson and George McGhee, however, used the prospect of food aid as a lever to demand a settlement of the 'Kashmir issue' and a closer integration of Indian foreign policy with the USA's, including on the question of Korea. Nehru refused to be intimidated; therefore, it was not until June 1951 that US food aid was finally agreed upon. From British sources, Nehru would have been aware of the acute need for an intermediary on the Korean question, and therefore able to withstand US pressures; he became the main diplomatic channel between the 'West' and China as the conflict continued. It was not, however, until early summer in 1952 that substantial progress towards an armistice, pending further negotiations, had been made according to Nehru's early suggestions.

The sticking point thereafter remained the repatriation of North Korean and Chinese prisoners of war: Truman suggested it was immoral to repatriate to a communist country anti-communist soldiers who did not want to be repatriated. The resolution passed in the UN General Assembly on December 3, 1952, had been substantially drafted by India: force would not be used either to return POWs or to prevent their return. This phrasing of the repatriation question, in its evenhandedness, reflected the Indian position on the necessity for compromise: it was important not to highlight that too many soldiers did not want to return. The clinching success for the resolution was the USSR's opposition to it, believing it to be too pro-Western bloc; therefore the USA had to accept it.

By this time Nehru and Krishna Menon, the central Indian diplomatic figures, were seen by US policy-makers as enemies. Britain wanted India to be present at the eventual peace settlement talks, but the US-supported South Korean dictator, Syngman Rhee, opposed this. He claimed – as the USA wanted him to – that India was pro-communist, pro-Russian and anti-American; the USA, armed with this statement, asked India to stay out of the UN delegation to the Korean conference, and pressured other countries not to back India's candidature. 'Some countries who had openly stated that they would vote for us had to back out,' Nehru observed. 'Not only that, but American Ambassadors brought this pressure on countries in their respective capitals. It really has been an extraordinary experience to see how a great Power behaves.'[38]

Nevertheless, Nehru's India now had an independent international standing of its own, and Nehru was highly regarded as a world statesman of principle and talent. This regard was not always entirely positive; in time, it would create some resentment among newly-emergent independent 'nations' who felt that Nehru was claiming a dominant role wholly unwarranted by the mere fact that India was the earliest country to achieve independence from colonial rule. India, and Krishna Menon, played a crucial role at the Geneva Conference in July 1954 that ended the fighting in Indo-China and recognised the successor states of Cambodia, Laos and Vietnam (the last of which was partitioned along the 17th Parallel). Non-alignment, an idea of which Nehru had come to be regarded as author, was gathering to itself a number of adherents: Indonesia, Burma, Laos, Cambodia, Egypt, Nepal, Ceylon, a number of Arab states, and soon, newly independent African states; but 'non-alignment' was less a clear policy decision than a residual category that could comfortably accommodate those that did not or would not, for a variety of reasons, fit in the superpowers' blocs (Yugoslavia's non-alignment, for instance, was an accident of its leader's heresy against Stalin). India's sometimes implicitly assumed leadership role emanated, probably, more from Nehru's personality and his tendency of patronising those he felt to be his intellectual inferiors than from any genuine attempt by India to dominate the emerging 'Third World'; the presumption on Nehru's part that he was entitled to scold 'junior' politicians for their failings was a potential cause of diplomatic tension.

The two Asian powers who were most likely to come into conflict by virtue of size and of that tricky question of vanity, unfulfilled national aspirations, were of course India and China. But for the time being, this seemed unlikely. Their interests did not seem likely to come into conflict. A potential conflict was avoided in 1950, when Chinese troops entered Tibet and claimed what successive Chinese governments regarded as theirs by right. Vallabhbhai Patel had wished to denounce this as communist expansionism; Nehru had not been particularly concerned, even though India had become the heir to British interests in Tibet (the British Mission in Lhasa had in fact been converted in 1947 into the Indian Mission in Lhasa without so much as a change in personnel). Tibet, which had been a part of the late Qing empire, but had from 1913 effectively been under British control, had never been acknowledged as independent even by the government of Republican China, which was too weak to assert effective control over the region even if it claimed *de jure* sovereignty over it. (There is, of course, an inherent tension between a *legal* position and the *right to self-determination* and consequent claims to sovereign statehood on the basis of being a 'nation'; a problem that did not arise before the rise and naturalisation of nation-states. Under the late Qing, Tibet enjoyed effective autonomy, in conditions of limited communications links and non-centralised state power, when the rules of all international intercourse were not quite so nation-state oriented.) Now, Nehru, unlike the British, found it unnecessary to continue to control Tibet or to encourage it to assert its independence. He also advised the British and Americans against bringing up Tibet as an issue at the UN Security Council, especially at a time when the Korean War was happening. The Indian position, as expressed to the Americans, was that 'India was the heir to British policy which had sought [to] achieve a buffer state in Tibet against Russia and China. [The] G[overnment] O[f] I[ndia] however was not disposed [to] create or support buffer states . . . throughout the centuries[,] Chinese influence and control in Tibet had fluctuated with the strength of the regime in power. Weak Chinese governments lost nearly all influence, strong governments regained it . . . it was inevitable that the present Chinese government should gain control over Tibet.'[39]

Against this backdrop, India's early relations with the People's Republic of China were nothing if not warm. On December 31, 1953, India began negotiations in Beijing for what became the 1954 'Agreement on Trade and Intercourse in the Tibet Region of China' – which is the term India and China were henceforth to use in all references to Tibet. The Preamble to this agreement contained the *Panch Sheel* or Five Principles of Co-Existence which were to govern Indo-Chinese relations, and which were to be Nehru's contribution to the theory of non-alignment and, he hoped, world peace: mutual respect for each other's territorial integrity and sovereignty; mutual non-aggression; mutual non-interference in each other's affairs; equality and mutual benefit; and peaceful co-existence.[40] (The last phrase foreshadowed a later stage of the Cold War in which the Soviet leader Nikita Khrushchev adopted it; the Soviet leadership actually claimed to have borrowed the phrase from the *Panch Sheel*.) The euphoria and hyperbole of the great fraternity of Asian nations was expressed in the slogan '*Hindi Chini Bhai Bhai*' (Indians and Chinese are brothers); Zhou Enlai visited Delhi in June 1954, and later that year, in October, Nehru returned the compliment by visiting Beijing, where he met Mao Zedong and was paraded in triumphal splendour through the city in Zhou's company. Indo-Chinese friendship was celebrated as both modern and correct and – in a mystical flourish that would pander to nationalist sentiment – 'ancient' and 'cultural': from the time, as Nehru put it, of the Mauryan emperor Ashoka in the third century BC, when India had sent out the first Buddhist missionaries to China.

The apparent success of Nehru's policy of refusing to align with the superpowers, and particularly his refusal to submit to US pressures, needs to be connected to another, related, story: that of outside influences, secret and behind the scenes, seeking to lend a directing hand to Indian political developments. The extent to which the Cold War actually reached Indian soil and affected everyday domestic politics is as yet largely unknown. A few fragments are known, however, and they are in themselves worth noting. The United States' encouragement, at least from the early 1950s, of opponents of communism in India – the US definition of 'communism' was notoriously broad, with Nehru himself not being above suspicion in this regard – was in part organised through its CIA-funded 'cultural front', the Congress for Cultural Freedom. The CCF's promotion of the Western side of the Cold War in the domain of culture consisted mainly in funding academic and cultural activities, acting as a showcase for Western 'freedoms'. This organisation was headed, in India, by Minoo Masani. As a skilled propagandist, Masani was an excellent choice for the job. He had made an effortless transition from socialism within the old CSP – where he was its most strident anti-communist voice – to the capitalist camp. During the Second World War he joined Tata Sons, a shift facilitated by communal and family connections with the Parsi community, among whom the Tatas counted, and was an extremely useful presence in their public relations department, even dressing up the industrialists' 'Bombay Plan' of 1944, a set of proposals that sought to direct a post-independence Indian political economy towards preserving 'the essentials of the capitalist system', as 'socialism', and persuading Oxford University Press to publish a version of it as a children's picture book.

The CCF, however, operated without divulging its source of funding, which was important to its success in a country like India: to many people the acknowledgement of taking CIA money was tantamount to declaring that one had betrayed the nation's independence (when in 1967 the CIA's 'cultural' game was revealed to the world, many who had worked under the CCF banner were acutely embarrassed; others, it would seem, had known all along – Masani certainly had). The CCF did not necessarily require blatantly pro-American voices; it simply amplified as many non-communist and anti-radical voices among intellectuals and politicians as it could. (Among the political trends the CCF adopted wholeheartedly was the *bhoodan* movement; Jayaprakash Narayan, Masani's old comrade from the CSP, joined both the *bhoodan* movement and the CCF. There is a delicious irony in the CIA and CCF sponsorship of an 'indigenous' movement: 'It is the colonialists who become the defenders of the native style'.[41])

Such funding as the CCF provided did not actually procure pro-American opinion, the centrality of Minoo Masani in both the right-wing opposition to Nehru and in the Indian branch of the CCF notwithstanding. However, in a country with limited resources, funding and work opportunities, it had a central role in the career and prospects of many persons, and enabled an anti-communist agenda to occupy a disproportionate amount of space. Many prominent academics and intellectuals – people of high status in the Nehruvian order – were also attracted by a novel situation: Indians were being taken seriously and funded to present their opinions before a potentially wide audience. This was seductive for persons accustomed to the marginalisation that was the lot of intellectuals from the colonies. Given that the CCF had among its larger circles various members of Nehru's Cabinets at different times, the constraints on Nehru's left-wing tendencies, or those of them that remained, would be maintained, and pressure to align more closely with the USA was never too far away. But it was not merely through the CCF and 'cultural' activities that the CIA operated in India; details are now beginning to emerge that some extremely prominent members of Nehru's inner circle were working with, and possibly for, the CIA.

DEFERRALS: NATION-BUILDING AND ITS DISCONTENTS

The relative success enjoyed by Nehru in the foreign policy realm obscured continuing problems, or potential problems, on the domestic front – indeed, critics were prone to accuse Nehru of spending too much time and energy on foreign policy, to the detriment of domestic policy. Nowhere were the domestic problems more evident than in that delicate project of 'nation-building'. 'External affairs' were usually less contentious than internal affairs, because they were conducted on behalf of the 'nation' against outside entities, which provided the required contingent solidarity around the national idea, and because much of it was conducted outside of public scrutiny. Generally, the unresolved problems of defining an Indian nation were usually avoided by the conventional conflation of the state and the nation – common to all international (which, when one thinks about it, actually means inter-state) as well as national (which actually means intra-state) discourses. In the Indian case, however, it was impossible to wish away the continuing problems of 'nation-building'; India was a problematic entity. And it is possible to see in retrospect that the Nehruvian state preferred to defer problematic questions of identity and difference rather than highlight them – because they did not lend themselves to easy resolutions.

Paradigmatic 'nations' have often been able to base their nationalisms on a common language. According to the CPI-adopted position, India, as a multinational state and a federation, would have nothing to lose by acknowledging the rights of linguistic 'nationalities' to self-determination of sorts, within an Indian union. However, if the official view was that India was composed of one nationality (and that Pakistan was an aberrant division of one nation into two), to raise the possibility of reorganisation of boundaries of states was a delicate one. Nehru was uneasy about this question. He preferred, if he could, to defer a problem which stressed particularisms rather than the collective unity of India. The first concession was made in 1953, when the state of Andhra Pradesh was created from the Telugu-speaking areas of Madras and Hyderabad; in effect a success for the CPI, which had raised the question during the Telengana struggle and had thereafter been able to draw on the movement's momentum in electoral terms, showing its strength in these areas in the state elections of 1951–2.

Once accepted in principle, the process had to continue. From 1953 to 1955, a States Reorganisation Commission met to decide principles of the redrawing of boundaries, and the 1956 States Reorganisation Act enabled boundaries to be redrawn. Nehru's own impatience with what he contemptuously referred to as 'provincialism' remained. Although he was willing to acknowledge that there might be groups within a country that felt the need to organise separately against exploitation or perceived exploitation, as someone sceptical of strong forms of nationalism, he was even less sympathetic to smaller fragmentary identities. 'While sectarian interests eat at the roots of our national unity,' he declared somewhat wistfully on his return from China in 1954, 'China has no such problem . . . any decision taken by the central government is the nation's decision and accepted all over the country.'[42] The process of redrawing state boundaries was by definition incomplete and in some cases not entirely logical, leaving future claims waiting to be made. In 1960, the old Bombay Presidency was divided (this had not been envisaged by the 1956 Act) into Gujarat and Maharashtra, after much acrimony, and not without pain as proponents of Maharashtra and Gujarat rioted over the fate of Bombay city – it stayed with Maharashtra. But Nehru would not compromise on overall 'national' unity, and consistently opposed the creation of new states on ethnic or religious lines, for Sikhs, Jats or Rajasthanis. At any event, linguistic states and other particularistic sub-divisions had political and electoral implications not dissimilar from colonial enumeration policies: vested interests were being created in particular linguistic, and potentially ethnocentric, identities that could be exploited for narrowly sectarian purposes. In an electoral system already marked by 'bloc voting' of particular communities or language groups for particular parties, this was a negative trend; the Nehruvian dream of a democratic India of rational individuals making informed decisions was deferred into the distant future – yet to be arrived at.

The question of a 'national language' on its own was a problematic one. The claims of linguistic surveyors that India was a country of a few hundred languages had been ridiculed by Nehru in his *Discovery of India* as academic quibbling: he claimed that 'Hindustani' was intelligible across much of North India, and that the 'few hundred' idea was the invention of a colonial imagination intent on describing India as a fragmented society. Nehru regarded 'Hindustani' as a potential national language for India: 'it must not be too Sanskritised or too Persianised which would divorce it from large masses of people.' Although Hindi and Urdu had 'developed separate literary forms', he believed that 'no great language can grow up if it is based on literary coteries'.[43] Earlier, Nehru had argued that Hindi and Urdu were not mutually conflictual and should come closer together to 'develop into one language, with two scripts, for India', to form 'our great national language', while at the same time the 'present literary forms' of Hindi and Urdu 'represent a certain individual genius and background' and should therefore 'be allowed to develop without interference from the other'. 'This seems,' he acknowledged, 'to be [a] mutually contradictory process but I do not think it will prove so.'[44] (It was not clear from this whether he was not in fact making a case for three languages: 'Hindi', 'Urdu' and 'Hindustani'.) After independence, Nehru protested against the difficult and over-Sanskritised Hindi words used in provincial administration and on All-India Radio. At the same time, he believed that for the time being, English would need to continue as the language of official communication.

The defence of 'Hindustani' as opposed to 'Hindi' as a national language was an attempt not to acknowledge what was potentially a sectarian position. Literary Urdu was generally considered the language in which all poetic and literary production had operated in northern India; Hindi's over-Sanskritised form owed much to its having been modelled on modern Bengali, itself a self-consciously 'classicising' language that had Sanskritised itself, attempting to purge itself of its Arabic and Persian words in its *bhadralok* and therefore implicitly high-caste Hindu version. From the latter part of the nineteenth century, sectarian movements had come to claim 'Hindi' in the Devanagari script as a 'Hindu' language; Urdu in the Arabic script had come to be associated with Muslims. In everyday language, the script was the only difference between the two languages; this made no difference to the majority of people who were illiterate anyway. Teaching Hindustani in the Roman script had been supported by various people at various stages; early on Gandhi had lent his voice to this – which might have made sense, in the tradition of Kemal Ataturk's choice in Turkey of a 'modern' script to modernise a language. By 1946, Gandhi opposed this idea, preferring to keep both scripts. The Hindi question was a recurrent theme in Nehru's time. The language would not, it was always insisted, be imposed on anyone who did not want it; and the southern Indian states, whose languages were in a completely different linguistic group, did not want Hindi.

More problematic still were the peripheral areas of India that were only accidentally a part of the Indian Union – an accident of colonial history and its arbitrary borders. The 'tribal areas' of North-East India were a case in point. Under colonial administration, they were administered differently, designated as 'tribal territories', and separated from the rest of India by an 'inner line'; the 'outer line' then divided it from the outside world. Potential secessionist tendencies had been identified in the Naga areas of the north-east early on by Nehru, at the time of the Interim Government. At the time of the separation of Burma from India in 1935, British administrators had toyed with the idea of attaching these areas to Burma rather than India. There was no particular reason why such areas should have shared an Indian nationalist sentiment, as Nehru himself acknowledged: 'Our freedom movement reached these people only in the shape of occasional rumours. Sometimes they reacted rightly and sometimes wrongly.'[45] (By this, apparently, Nehru applied to the behaviour of the 'tribals' a yardstick of legitimacy that was based on a 'right' attitude to Indian nationalism.) After Indian independence, Nehru believed, the Naga areas ought to be a part of India and of Assam. He offered concessions: 'It is our policy that tribal areas should have as much freedom and autonomy as possible so that they can live their own lives according to their own customs and desires.' They could expect protection from being 'swamped by people from other parts of the country' and consequently from being exploited.[46] He seemed quite unconscious of the patronising language and the colonial rhetoric of his pronouncements. In March 1952, Nehru visited the north-east and made paternalistic assurances: the tribals would be protected, but would not be treated as anthropological specimens. In April 1953, Nehru, now accompanied by the Burmese prime minister, U Nu, attempted to address a gathering of Nagas; they turned their backs on the two prime ministers and walked out of the meeting. Rhetorically, Nehru could afford to be tolerant: 'The tribal people of India are a virile people who naturally went astray sometimes. They quarrelled and occasionally cut off each other's heads . . . It is often better to cut off a hand or a head than to crush and trample on a heart. Perhaps I also felt happy with these simple folk because the nomad in me found congenial soil in their company.'[47] This tolerance, in effect, was making a virtue out of necessity. A modernising agenda that depended on the prior interpretation of that agenda by outside agents, and thereafter its application to its alleged beneficiaries, was bound to be resisted.

Nehru's 'Naga problem' was not solved – there was insurgency throughout the 1950s, ending in the formation of a new Naga state within the Indian Union, conceded in 1960 and inaugurated in 1963 – the ethnic principle of redrawing the map had had finally to be conceded. Meanwhile, Indian attempts at 'nation-building' by force of arms, with the Indian 'defence forces' in culturally alien territory indulging in large-scale killing and rape, were hardly the best ways of demonstrating to the Nagas the warm and enveloping joys of belonging represented by Indian nationhood. But Nehru's centralised state could not afford to have fuzzy edges. It was in the north-east of India that the Nehruvian vision took on its most brutal and violent forms.

Kashmir, equally, was now both an internal and an international issue, especially with Pakistan raising Kashmir as a central issue in international fora and with the USA, incorporating Pakistan into its system of international alliances through the Baghdad Pact and the South-East Asian Treaty Organisation (SEATO), having to support Pakistan's claims to Kashmir. Nehru's Kashmir policy had been built around Sheikh Abdullah's commitment to an Indian connection rather than a Pakistani one. Now, Abdullah's position had begun to shift towards independence for Kashmir. India's interference in Kashmiri affairs beyond the three subjects of defence, external affairs and communications, the basis of Kashmir's accession to India, had been gradual but steady, and was beginning to be the cause of some resentment in Kashmir. In India, there was, on the other hand, some resentment at Kashmir's special status, which S.P. Mukherjee, now leader of the Jan Sangh, sought to exploit.

Abdullah had been quite frank with Nehru: however much he sympathised with Nehru's attempts to build a secular state, and agreed that Kashmir's connection with India was an important part of achieving this goal, he also saw clearly that communal forces were constantly working against Nehru's vision of India. He, Abdullah, as a Kashmiri leader, could not afford to subordinate Kashmir's future to an Indian project, however desirable. At the end of 1952, Mukherjee and the Jan Sangh led a coalition of sectarian forces to challenge Kashmir's special status within the Indian Union, and to detach the Hindu-majority Jammu area from the rest of Kashmir. Nehru attempted an exercise in damage control by trying to prevent cross-party support for Mukherjee, requesting socialists not to support the movement, and at the same time trying to get Abdullah to look like an Indian nationalist, among other things by flying the Indian flag alongside that of the Kashmir state; he failed. When Mukherjee crossed into Jammu without a permit in March 1953, Abdullah had him arrested; Mukherjee then died in prison on June 23.

In the face of Abdullah's public call for Kashmiri independence, it was useful to be able to claim that Abdullah no longer had public support in Kashmir and in his own party. Whether this was the case or not was less important than the fact that on August 9, 1953, his government was dismissed, and the new prime minister of Kashmir, Bakshi Ghulam Muhammad, promptly had him arrested. Nehru accepted the course of events; they were of doubtful legality, given that the constitutional provision for the dismissal of state governments should not in the first place have applied to Kashmir. But this, effectively, set a precedent from which the special status of Kashmir within the Indian Union never recovered. Over the next few years, he wrote sympathetic and philosophical letters to Abdullah in jail, where he was held without trial; one could have imagined such letters being written to Nehru himself by a sympathetic British imperial official, lamenting the impersonal forces of politics that had brought about the situation.

THE INDIAN STATE: THE END OF A BEGINNING?

If we were to let 'tribals' illustrate the potential problems with definitions of nationhood and the explicit and implicit exclusions that were still at work – 'castes' and 'women' would also be good illustrative examples of this problem – we might provide a foreshadowing of some of the problems that would be carried into what we might call the 'mature' stage of Nehru's prime ministership; for the period from formal independence to *circa* 1955 was what we might well regard as a formative period in state-building. It was easier to get the *state* to function than to produce a viable version of the necessary myth of the *nation* with an identifiable *positive* content, especially as its stronger, negative form, expressed as anti-colonialism, waned with the loss of its explicit counter-image, British imperialism. It should be pointed out that there is no state that has produced a version of nationalism perfectly congruent with its boundaries, linguistic, ethnic or historical character; this is an impossible demand. But as Nehru himself might have put it, mature states can afford not to take their national myths too seriously; the need for a cementing idea of India was still strong.

Nevertheless, the future looked bright. Nehru was at the peak of his powers; the stabilisation of the Indian state had been achieved; the sectarian forces had been held at bay largely due to Nehru's efforts; and he had succeeded in gaining if not decisive control over his party and government, at least effective control on most issues, and the authority to present his own positions as the standards of public legitimacy. The great developmental project was underway; India, as a model for colonial nations struggling for independence, and as a country willing to stand up to the superpowers, had acquired an international role and standing; Nehru himself was almost permitted, in the public eye, to personify all these achievements – even to the extent that if a certain resentment might have simmered in some quarters, that too was a compliment. Hopes of rapid economic development and of emergence from poverty could be realistically held. Despite the fact that the struggle for effective independence was, as Nehru knew, far from over and would in fact be an ongoing process, and that his proclaimed goal of economic democracy had miles to go before it was even partially realised, there might be time to draw a quick breath of relief.

6

HIGH NEHRUVIANISM AND ITS DECLINE, c. 1955–63

The ascendancy that Nehru had achieved in Indian politics by 1955 had a disturbing corollary. In a manner of speaking, people were now willing to let Nehru win; it was too difficult to oppose him, given both his international prestige and his domestic popularity. Moreover, the lack of a coherent counter-ideology to Nehru's meant that it was easier to concede that vision as the legitimate one for India. This, in effect, was the consensus of the left and centre in Indian politics – and criticism, such as there was, could be largely confined to Nehru's failure to deliver on Nehruvian promises. There also opened out a strong divergence between politics at the centre, in which Nehru's leadership was largely unchallenged, and regional politics, where various divergent trends that pulled away from the centre became apparent: regional, linguistic, caste, community or a combination thereof. These trends were not allowed to become dominant: Nehru's India was a federal system with a strong bias towards central authority; the strong centre was a prerequisite for the success of the central plank of Nehruvian policy: planned economic development.

Nehru was, perhaps, a victim of his own success: the lack of legitimacy given to openly sectarian arguments was largely a result of his own personal victory in a debate involving the higher ranks of the Congress Party in the early years after independence, centred primarily on the category 'Hindu', but arguing more generally for an open-ended and inclusive definition of Indian-ness. One result of this victory was that the only place for Hindu sectarians to continue to operate was under the protective umbrella of the Congress itself, where Nehru's leadership and their paying lip service to the ideals of Nehruvian secularism provided the legitimising cover of political correctness. These problems were perhaps aggravated by the fact that Nehru was becoming an iconic figure in his own lifetime. Although an adulation of Nehru was not incompatible with a few electoral defeats for the Congress, there was a tendency, as there had been with Gandhi and the (then) Congress right, of making excuses for Nehru himself while attacking the Congress.

But there was a definite space to the right of Indian politics that called out for someone to occupy it. Once again, it was Nehru's early victories that prevented this space to the right from being taken up by explicitly Hindu sectarian positions. (Nehru always acknowledged that there were Muslim sectarians in India as well; but for reasons of their lack of strength of numbers, he did not take them as seriously.) The right had to organise outside the Congress in terms of secular politics – most conventionally, as expected, around the interests of capitalists, and around that staple of Cold War rhetoric, 'freedom'.

THE EMERGENCE OF ASIA? COLD WAR BREEZES AND NON-NON-ALIGNMENT

Two conventional views of the Cold War have shown a remarkable resilience that a wealth of historiography has been unable to decentre: that the Cold War was not really fought except diplomatically and that 'non-alignment' or 'neutralism' was a way of keeping out of it. The first is a product of a Eurocentrism that saw Asian wars as less important, Great Power intervention in anti-colonial struggles as logical, and Asian communists or suspected communists murdered on an unimaginably large scale in countries like Malaya and (later) Indonesia as no more than a problem of counter-insurgency. The second promotes the myth that a country like India was not really involved in the Cold War. But it was impossible not to be involved; even the mere act of trying to keep out of the way was a very active process. And for Nehru, who in many ways led the battle for the right of countries not to decide their external *and* internal policies purely with reference to the Cold War, the process was a very active one. (Those who criticised Nehru for the attention he paid to foreign policy probably either chose to ignore, or were ill-informed about, the extent to which foreign affairs, and the Cold War in particular, impinged on Indian domestic affairs.)

The year 1955, which we might be justified in treating as the highest point of Nehru's career, was in many ways the year of Bandung. Here, in a small town in Indonesia in April and May, the ideal of Afro-Asian solidarity, of the need for an alternative focus of politics to superpower rivalries, was finally to be put to the test. Plans for such a conference had been laid at two conferences among the five prime ministers of Pakistan, India, Ceylon, Burma and Indonesia, first at Colombo in April 1954 (for a brief period these five countries were referred to as the 'Colombo Powers'), and then at Bogor, Indonesia, in December 1954. These meetings did not necessarily augur well for future solidarity. The middle years of the 1950s saw the struggle in Asia by the USA to gain adherents to the South East Asian Treaty Organisation (SEATO); on February 24, 1954, the 'Baghdad Pact' had been signed between Turkey and Iraq, and most Asian countries were under heavy pressure to align with the Western bloc on the basis of the 'communist threat'. Tensions in 1954 were high over the Indo-China conflict; French planes had been denied transit permission when carrying reinforcements for the war by India, Burma and Indonesia, but had been granted permission by Pakistan and Ceylon. Therefore, Colombo and Bogor, unsurprisingly, reflected these Cold War tensions. At both meetings, Pakistan and Ceylon wished to make 'communism' a central issue; Nehru was unwilling to condemn the strange beast called 'international communism', which he regarded more as an invention of the USA than as a reality. The Indonesian prime minister, Ali Sastroamidjojo, also said he had no difficulties in allowing communists of the domestic variety to operate. Tensions between India and Pakistan manifested themselves; Nehru was in no doubt that by this time Pakistan was 'practically a colony of the United States'.[1] Pakistan was keen on raising the Kashmir issue (that is, Pakistan wished to stake its claim to Kashmir) and Nehru was convinced that this assertiveness was a direct consequence of US military aid to Pakistan. Despite Nehru's self-conscious avoidance of anti-Pakistani rhetoric – it would have been too much of a cliché – these tensions spilled over into his relations with Pakistani representatives at negotiating tables. At Colombo, Nehru had allegedly said to Muhammad Ali, the Pakistani prime minister, that he was 'nothing but an American stooge', to which Ali had replied – quite unfairly – that Nehru was 'nothing better than a Russian stooge'. Nehru also allegedly said he would 'tear to pieces' Muhammad Ali – it was quickly clarified that he meant his arguments, not his person.[2]

Invitations to Bandung were sent out selectively and diplomatically. The USSR had hinted that they wanted their Central Asian republics to be invited, but Nehru had decided that the USSR should be taken as a whole and counted as a European country. Only four 'African' countries – Ethiopia, the Gold Coast, Liberia and Sudan – were invited; Libya and Egypt were considered 'Arab' (Bandung was to be Colonel Nasser's first international conference). Israel was not invited so as to avoid offending Arab states – India had recognised Israel, but Nehru had proved adept at postponing the exchange of diplomatic personnel. Everyone agreed that China should be invited because of her importance in Asia – and even to Asian anti-communists, 'international communism' meant the USSR, possibly demonstrating an implicit Eurocentrism. As a result, Bandung provided the People's Republic of China with its first international forum and consequently the first large-scale endorsement of its legitimate statehood and its place in international politics. This was largely Nehru's achievement; his had been the most influential voice arguing for a recognition of and normal diplomatic relations with the People's Republic since the early years of its establishment. Outer Mongolia, North and South Korea were not invited; nor, because it was based on the continuing claim to being China, was Taiwan. For this last discourtesy, an airplane that was carrying an advance Chinese delegation from Hong Kong to Bandung was blown up by Taiwanese saboteurs; Zhou Enlai was unfortunately for them not on that plane. The conference also only invited independent countries (or almost-independent countries, in the case of the Gold Coast, an invitation which provoked immediate British protests) – representatives of the Mau Mau in Kenya or the Malayan Communist Party were therefore excluded from a conference that was intending centrally to discuss anti-colonialism.

The 'Bandung Spirit', referred to later with satisfaction, sought to present a picture of great solidarity and collective good spirits. The actual diplomacy was less clear. Holding the Bandung Conference implied criticism of the United Nations' handling of anti-colonial questions – that at least, was UN sources' view of the conference, although of course this was nowhere stated. More to the point: the Cold War had reduced the UN to stalemate. It was to create a similar stalemate at Bandung. The central issue turned out to be non-alignment versus non-non-alignment. This should have been anticipated in the differences among the original five prime ministers who were the organisers – to some extent setting themselves up as an alternative set of Permanent Members (without formal veto powers), but reflecting similar divisions that had frozen the dealings of the original.

To Nehru, the intellectual, Cold War alignments required states and their representatives to surrender their reason: 'I am not prepared, even as an individual, much less as the foreign minister of this country, to give up my right of individual judgement to anybody else in other countries.' And the Cold War was nothing if not crude: as a result of 'this exhibition of mutual abuse' among the main protagonists, 'we are being coarsened and vulgarised all over the world'.[3] Nehru offered his 'Five Principles' as an alternative to alignment: the alternative to backing 'peaceful co-existence' based on 'mutual respect' was to support potential and actual wars. Aligned Asian nations – those who felt threatened by Russia or by communism, whether or not they used the rhetoric of 'freedom' – saw it differently. Iran, still largely feudal and controlled by the Western powers, feared its Russian neighbour and joined the Baghdad Pact of February 1955 (which became CENTO, the Central Treaty Organisation, after 1958) and the South East Asian Treaty Organisation (SEATO); Pakistan joined both, because, as its diplomats were prone frankly to put it, Pakistan really wanted arms and political support against India on the Kashmir issue. Thailand joined SEATO for fear of China and the Vietnamese; the Philippines were a US ex-colony, still very much within its sphere of influence and had little choice.

It was evident that what the USA really wanted was not Asian military allies – their powers were insignificant – but military bases, in order to surround the Eurasian land mass's communists. Nehru opposed the new military pacts in Asia as dangerous for world peace, creating tensions in Asia and posing the risk of proxy wars being fought. The issue was almost personalised into a conflict between Nehru and John Foster Dulles; Nehru regarded Dulles as somewhat stupid, short-sighted and crude, while Dulles regarded Nehru and non-alignment as immoral and anti-American. The 1954 Geneva Agreement on Indo-China had been unsatisfactory for the USA, and Dulles sought to repair the effects of that defeat with SEATO. But to cordon off China and communist North Vietnam required Laos, Cambodia and South Vietnam to become SEATO members; Laos and Cambodia preferred non-alignment. This was seen in some circles as Nehru's victory over Dulles; but the pacts were still enough of a concern for Nehru to seek to address the danger. Bandung, for Nehru, had at least in part been prompted by the desire to mobilise separately, or at least differently, from SEATO.

Another significant victory of Nehru's, even before Bandung had taken place, was the announcement on February 8, 1955, by Foreign Minister Molotov on behalf of the USSR that the Soviet government accepted Nehru's 'five principles' or *Panch Sheel*. This was probably a feeler to encourage Nehru to invite the Soviet Central Asian republics to Bandung; at any event, the Soviets were not churlish after the event. The USSR was clearly warming to the idea that non-alignment was not necessarily support for imperialism. Those who wished to read the policy of the Communist Party of India as a direct reflection of directives from Moscow could with satisfaction note that the CPI decided to back Nehru's foreign policy from August 1955, after Bandung, and after the Soviet Union had accepted the *Panch Sheel*.

The Bandung Conference itself, however, had little success in passing even elementary resolutions, such as that condemning colonialism. Divergences quickly appeared with aligned countries such as Ceylon and Pakistan wishing to discuss Soviet 'imperialism' in Eastern Europe and including Soviet Eastern Europe in a definition of colonialism. Pakistan was quick to clarify to its powerful neighbour that this definition did not apply to China, which, Pakistan averred, had no expansionist tendencies and did not suppress any other nationalities. Nehru opposed this broader definition of colonialism: Russia's influence in Eastern Europe was not the same thing, he argued, although he did not clarify exactly why not.

As Bandung's pre-eminent personality, Nehru deliberately stayed in the background and would not play too prominent a role in the proceedings. This was intended to be diplomatic; but since his importance was widely recognised, there were times at which his silences came across as patronising and his interventions as abrupt. The space he graciously vacated was best filled by the Chinese premier, Zhou Enlai. Zhou did not always win friends, but he did influence people, paradoxically by casting himself as mediator in conflicts between the aligned pro-Western and non-aligned countries. At what was the People's Republic of China's first large conference on an international scale, Zhou came across as reasonable and unaggressive. Amongst the quibbling on definitions of 'colonialism', it was Zhou who proposed that the principle of racial equality be added to the *Panch Sheel*; this suggestion made it to the 'ten principles' that were adopted by the Bandung Conference as a whole – but the conference members did not find time to discuss it adequately. This was a strange outcome, given that Nehru had on several occasions condemned racism in the colonial policy of British and other European powers, and in South Africa. It reflected, perhaps, the deflections from the anti-colonial agenda that had occurred at Bandung and the self-assertion of the Cold War agenda.

The ten Bandung principles were variations on a number of principles thrown up by various participants: among them were Nehru's five and Zhou's seven. All of them were open to various interpretations. The best that could be said of Bandung was that a stalemate had been achieved between aligned (with the West, since Nehru and the other 'Colombo Powers' premiers had kept out all the communists except China) and non-aligned powers. The lack of agreement did not seem to affect the 'Bandung spirit', that mythical entity that was to be periodically invoked in the years to come, for it had been a great achievement to get so many countries together. Bandung's 'psychological impact' was therefore praised by Nehru.[4] Among those who came along to observe proceedings was the Yugoslavian leader, Josip Broz Tito, who was interested in a grouping of states that could end Yugoslavia's isolation from both blocs; he was photographed along with the leaders of the non-aligned countries, the sole white man present at the gathering. (There were, it might be noted, no women among the 340 delegates present at Bandung.)

Bandung was in many ways a culmination of Nehru's idea of bringing the non-European world together, although the Burmese and Indonesian governments could also lay claim to have desired such a meeting. In a limited way, a triumph for Nehru had quietly been achieved before and at Bandung; only at Bandung itself, it had not quite been publicly acknowledged by all present. Peaceful co-existence, based at least loosely on the *Panch Sheel*, had been endorsed, notably, by the USSR and China. In this way, a shift in the Cold War itself had been facilitated, at least as far as the Eastern bloc's attitude to non-alignment was concerned.

If one were to see this instrumentally, the Soviet assumption that the USSR could be friends with India without requiring India to detach itself from all its other diplomatic connections, in the spirit of 'peaceful co-existence', was immensely important for India and by implication for the emergent 'Third World', who could now expect Eastern bloc assistance without aligning with it – and there were fewer strings attached to Eastern than to Western assistance. The USSR's new respect for India quickly translated into economic assistance and technical collaboration. Negotiations had begun in November 1954 for a steel plant to be set up with Soviet help; the agreement, envisaging a plant with an annual capacity of one million tons, was agreed in February 1955. In the summer of 1955, after Bandung, Nehru was given a very warm reception in Moscow, comparable to the heroic reception he had received in China – retrospectively, it might have been said that the USSR and China were competing for Nehru's favour.

In December 1955, the Soviet leaders Bulganin and Khrushchev visited India, to great public interest and popular acclaim – and also to great apprehension from anti-communists and pro-capitalists (the two were not entirely the same in India, we should remind ourselves). Nehru used the opportunity to ask for assurances that the USSR would not support the Indian communists against his government. Khrushchev agreed, claiming that the USSR had no connections with the CPI and pointing to the dissolution of the Cominform as proof that the Soviet Union was not intent on fomenting world revolution. The USSR would also proffer tactical support for India on the Kashmir issue and on the tricky issue of Goa remaining a Portuguese colony (in 1954, the French had amicably agreed to hand over Pondicherry and other remaining territories in India that still were their colonies; Nehru had hoped that Goa would similarly be handed over, and he even appealed to the British, the USA and the Vatican for intervention; but this did not materialise).

The USSR now quickly became a major trading partner and developmental collaborator of India's. At the Twentieth Congress of the Communist Party of the Soviet Union in 1956, Khrushchev's famous de-Stalinisation speech also praised new nations such as India. Soon the USSR had admitted the possibility of other routes to socialism than the Soviet model. They were to be extremely interested in the Indian planning project – as of course were Western scholars, for whom in the new discipline of development economics, nothing as exciting and ambitious was being attempted anywhere else – what was more, this was within a democratic and non-communist framework. Non-alignment seemed to have won a great victory; but of the two cows seemingly about to present themselves for milking, the Eastern cow seemed far more forthcoming.

World politics, however, refused to stay calm to allow Nehru to take full advantage of the situation. In 1956, the twin crises of Suez and Hungary were cause for concern. Suez could be interpreted as a culmination of Nehru's prophecy of the dangers of dividing the world in terms of military pacts. Colonel Nasser had seen the Baghdad Pact, signed on February 24, 1955, as potentially hostile to Egypt; consequently, he bought arms from the USSR. The Americans responded by withdrawing US aid for the Aswan High Dam. Nasser responded by the nationalisation of the Suez Canal. In the crisis that followed, Nehru and Krishna Menon went about their now familiar task as mediators, Nehru appealing for calm but making it clear that he would not take a stand against Egyptian sovereignty. Nehru at first advised Nasser not to place the problem before the United Nations if he expected support – he had seen too much horse-trading there to feel this was a safe route. He sought to push for a compromise – other users of the Canal would be represented as a minority on the Egyptian corporation for the Canal. This proposal died a natural death, and Egypt was not particularly enamoured of it in any case. Nehru then advised going to the Security Council, if only to defer potential violence. Krishna Menon and Nehru continued to try and play an intermediary role until the Israeli invasion of Egypt in October 1956 and the British and French ultimatum to Nasser – at which point Nehru spoke openly of 'clear aggression and a violation of the United Nations Charter', and of the spectre of a revived wave of imperialism.[5]

The Suez Crisis raised strong passions in India, and temporarily rallied divergent elements in domestic politics around Nehru. India threatened to withdraw from the Commonwealth in protest – this was not just Nehru's threat, but was backed by conservatives in India such as Rajagopalachari; the spectre of a revival of colonialism certainly brought back the unity around anti-colonialism that had been the hallmark of the Indian nationalist struggle. At the time, the Soviet Union, Egypt and China called for a reassembling of the Bandung countries to discuss the situation, but Nehru rejected this as impractical – he probably had a more realistic assessment of what the 'Bandung spirit' really meant, despite the rhetoric. Britain and France eventually backed down in the face of its ally, the USA, refusing to underwrite this adventure.

When the USSR invaded Hungary, however, the principled denunciation everyone expected from Nehru was some time in coming. India abstained in the UN from voting to ask the USSR to withdraw troops and to back UN observers in elections – it would set a bad precedent, Nehru claimed, to have foreigners overseeing elections; this would damage Hungarian sovereignty (since the Russians were there anyway, this did not sound very convincing). A concern for Kashmir appears to have been behind this. Nehru and Menon felt that the implications would eventually be that the same conditions of foreign intervention might be applied there. But Nehru made a strong informal protest through the Indian ambassador in Moscow. Nehru's later vocal condemnation of Soviet aggression in Hungary before the Indian Parliament and before a world awaiting his words – he referred to the Hungarian revolt as a 'nationalist uprising' – brought from the Russians a gentle reminder of Kashmir, on which issue they hinted they might withdraw their support.

'DEVELOPMENT' AND ITS FATE

Two basic commitments were constantly reiterated by Nehru – to economic independence as the necessary corollary to political independence, and to economic democracy as the necessary corollary to political democracy. The fate of 'development' was thus at the heart of the self-definition of the Indian state, and at the heart of the legitimacy of Nehru's government. But the two commitments addressed two different units of relevance: the first – the 'nation' (that is, the state); and the second, the 'masses'. The first was far more consensual – after all, Indian capitalists, whether or not or to whatever degree they had been 'collaborators' with British rule in India, had always complained bitterly about the dependent nature of their opportunities to do business, the various forms of unfair competition from foreign goods, and discriminatory legislation they were subjected to. So the economic independence of the 'nation', amounting to a protected national economy, was something to be desired.

Conflicts inevitably arose on the social goals. Land reforms, economic controls on the activities of private capital, and redistributive or collectivisation measures, however gently put forward within the framework of democracy and free will, would come into conflict with powerful interests. Philosophers of capitalist freedoms have always tended to point to the incompatibility of centralised planning and freedom; socialists argued similarly that the autonomy of private capitalists had the potential to wreck the assumptions and predictions of the planners. More importantly, the question of the amount of social control that planners had to exercise to get the plans to work was based on the answer to the underlying question: would existing vested interests militate against changing social relations in the country? And if this was the case, would the best-laid plans of economists and statisticians be insufficient to achieve significant results?

It can be said that there was a continuous conflict between liberal market urges and control urges, represented among policy-makers by separate camps that tended to work against each other. During the First Plan various voices spoke in favour of an ultimate goal of removing controls over the price and movement of food-grains. An earlier attempt to do this, in 1947, supported idiosyncratically by Gandhi at a time of food shortages, had been a great disaster, leading to spiralling price rises, and controls had had to be swiftly put back in place in 1948. But the results of the First Plan had given cause for celebration; total production of cereals for 1953–4 was three million tonnes higher than the target fixed for 1955–6; consequently, the state abolished all controls on food-grains. Also, despite the rhetoric of self-sufficiency a liberal import policy had been followed, with the result that foreign exchange reserves were used up fast – the sterling balances, for instance, were gone far sooner than expected, by 1956. Nehru, although chairman of the Planning Commission, was not in touch with its day-to-day duties; his best wishes were with his planners, and he co-wrote some important policy statements, but on the details he relied on the 'experts'.

A degree of impatience with – and an over-reliance on results achieved in – the First Plan could be observed among planners, in their desire to get on with what they considered the main business of industrialisation. By 1954, the Second Plan was already in preparation; the First had only been approved by Parliament in late 1952. The First Plan had given rise to a tendency to believe that the agricultural sector would continue to provide for the rest: cheap food and cheap labour. 'Institutional constraints', as the euphemism put it, were of course acknowledged – the Second Plan contained an important chapter that stressed the importance of 'land reforms and agrarian reorganisation', pointing the way towards an eventual cooperative system of farming. Politically, as everyone knew by this time, this was always going to be difficult. But, as Mahalanobis put it, 'a plan has to be a drama'. This drama was to be the Second Plan.

Social justice, to some extent, was something for which the Nehruvians believed they could plan. From 1955, the Congress had declared, and

Parliament had accepted, a commitment to a 'socialistic pattern of society'. The 1956 Industrial Policy Resolution replaced the gentler-on-private-entrepreneurs Industrial Policy Resolution of 1948 – it envisaged the dominance of the public sector, and a complementary private sector preferably organised on cooperative lines. Rapid economic growth through industrialisation, especially through the development of heavy industries – machines to make machines (to make machines) – was set as the goal. The Second Plan was to operate on the basis of these principles.

More ink has probably been spilt in praise or discussion of the Second Plan than on Mr W.H. of Shakespeare's sonnets, so perfect was it seen to be by its supporters. Nehru co-wrote the introduction with Mahalanobis; it is a tight, tense piece of writing that expresses the excitement of the project. The total outlay envisaged was to be distributed across four sectors: investment goods or capital goods; industrial goods; agricultural and cottage industries; and services, education, health, 'etc' – the 'etc' was an indicator of the lack of attention to the items before it in the planners' imagination, despite their frequent resort to the language of welfare. One-third of total investment was to be made on investment goods. The rest was to be divided between industrial goods; agricultural and cottage industries; and services, education, health, etc. Given the philosophy of 'jam tomorrow' that the investment-goods-first strategy required, a shortage of consumer goods was envisaged. Cottage industries, which required low capital investment and were highly labour intensive, were to make up for this shortage as well as provide extra employment. Raising employment would itself create higher demand for consumer goods, to be met by pursuing lightly capitalised methods of production – that is, cottage industries. Following from the inauguration of the revamped 'village community' of the 'community development' programmes, it was possible to invoke Gandhi as the spiritual patron of this strategy, thereby implying, in a system that was intended to be consensual, that both the 'modernising' industrialising agenda and the 'Gandhian' tradition of the Indian national movement were represented in the Second Plan. Gandhi, of course, had based his rural idyll in large measure on individuals' voluntary limitation of their wants, a self-sufficient village community, and harmony between man and nature – hardly what the planners envisaged, given that their village was intended to support and supplement their urban industrial landscapes; limitation of wants to most people was a ridiculous idyll to promote given that they were already constrained to limit their basic needs. But self-control in terms of consumption was useful to invoke in the education of urban and/or higher income groups, especially when consumer goods were not widely available. (The Indian developmental model has been seen by some as indicative of a mixture of Fabianism, Gandhism and Soviet planning; how far any of these were consistently present except implicitly and in passing is questionable.)

The assumption made by the planners was of a nearly totally closed economy. Trade, it was reasoned, could perhaps take off later, with the development of industrialisation and of capital goods and consequently of the diversification of manufactured goods available for export. There was no strategy of focusing on textile exports, which might have been plausible given that textiles were an established industry in India. The reasons for this were, perhaps, political – the left-ish consensus among the planners was that there was no need to further strengthen Indian industrialists; textiles fell strongly in the category of established private sector industry, and small numbers of large business houses had a disproportionate share of them. (This consensus at times owed as much to the patrician and somewhat Brahmanical disdain that the Nehruvians, who of course regarded themselves as intellectuals, had for people who merely 'made money' as to a commitment to social justice.)

Political responses to the Second Plan now opened up the basic pattern of the politics of high Nehruvianism. Allegedly, many socialists now wished to return to the Congress, but Nehru discouraged this, ostensibly on the grounds that there was still a need for a proper opposition – a different position from his having invited them back in after defeating Tandon in the Congress's internal struggle in 1951. The question of whether he knew of shifting and strange alliances among people who still called themselves socialists is worth raising. However, the 'socialistic pattern' – which many simply shortened to 'socialism' – attracted significant support for Nehru from outside his party. Ram Manohar Lohia's socialists at the time took a soft line on the Congress and even some in the CPI advocated this. (As mentioned before, the 'national' work of planning the economy was already something that had attracted CPI supporters and members, some to Mahalanobis' Indian Statistical Institute, some to other fora for 'experts' where they could contribute something constructive.) For those sceptical of the claims to 'socialistic patterns' or 'socialism' achievable through the Congress or through planning, the approach was simple, perhaps even sensible: the *avowed* project was to be welcomed, but at the same time the impossibility of its achievement under the directorship of the Congress, with its own entanglement in the classes it would need to dispossess or attack, would be stressed. In effect, the opposition to the left of and outside the Congress accepted the Nehruvian version of socialism, but claimed to be better Nehruvian socialists themselves: better, even, than Nehru, as long as he operated from within the Congress.

This space for 'socialism' also provoked into being an explicit right wing in Indian political life. The now much more explicit rhetoric of socialism gave them the space to claim once again – in a direct link to the Cold War that was often more than simply ideological – that India was in danger of communist takeover. In 1959, the Congress declared that cooperative joint farming would be a desired goal – despite the fact that several imperial officials had made similar suggestions in the 1920s, and that cooperatives of various description had existed in India for some time, this was now declared by some to be an attempt to foist Soviet-style collectivisation on India by stealth. Meanwhile, the government was accused of an unreasonable hostility to all private enterprise, and the enforcement of land ceilings and the public distribution system for food-grains that had been seen as necessary corollaries of cooperative farming were resolutely attacked.

This would have seemed, to any reasonable observer, rather absurd. Land reforms had been assiduously avoided by Congress governments in the states; there was no agricultural income tax (there still isn't), although there were clearly rich farmers, thereby allowing everyone who worked the land to claim 'peasant' status, with its accompanying implications of struggle and poverty. Taxation as a whole was regressive: indirect taxes were relied upon rather than progressive direct taxation – to the benefit of higher income groups. Some planners, officials or politicians were, it is true, not keen on a further strengthening of the private sector, or an excessive space for a private sector in a planned economy; that could only have meant distorting a planning process that relied on being able to exert centralised control over the economy. But the Plans did not boil down to a simple question of the private sector versus the public sector – it was only strategic points of production that had to be in state hands. And capitalists had less cause to complain than they made out. The government looked after capital goods production –requiring longer-term investment and low returns, both unattractive to private investors. The building of infrastructure was a government duty that most industrialists were rather willing to see in its hands. Buying power was generated by government spending – there were fears that this could lead to inflation, but here the private sector could be the corrective, providing consumption goods which yielded quick returns – or, perversely, not providing them, as the case often was. In a situation of protected oligopoly, industrialists could decide to keep capacity idle and maintain artificial shortages to make artificial profits, even from selling sub-standard goods – there was no competition. This was to remain an anomaly of the so-called 'mixed economy', a term that was applied to the Indian economy at the same time as that of the 'socialistic pattern'. Some industrialists, at least – notably the Birla group – decided that the Congress umbrella was worth their while; others, notably the Tata group, at the time the larger of the two giants that dominated the Indian economy, chose to oppose the Congress. With time, the former overtook the latter, without surrendering its traditional commitment to the Congress. And though the Planning Commission agonised at various stages over inequality of income, they had little ability to change things.

In a system born out of compromise, negotiation and suppression or deferral of conflictual situations such as that of post-independence India, such contradictory trends might have been expected. An influential account of the emerging class coalition that governed India in and after the Nehruvian period has offered this picture: the class base of the new state was a three-fold coalition – of capitalists, of landowners, and of bureaucrats, intellectuals and technocrats – the last-named category including the Nehruvians, but also others not specifically sympathetic to the Nehruvian project.[6] This may be a good starting point – one may wonder whether 'class' here might be a misnomer, and 'status group', at least for the last-named, might be a better category to use – although it may also be too schematic. The last category of bureaucrats, intellectuals and technocrats would lump together a group of people whose political allegiances were extremely difficult to predict; they were those from whose numbers the 'political class' was drawn; they occupied positions right across the political spectrum. It is therefore easier to identify the beneficiaries than the supporters of the Nehruvian project: in the towns businessmen and the professional classes gained visibly, as did to a lesser extent small-town middle- and upper-middle-class groups from the new industrial and commercial classes that came into being after independence. In the countryside, landowning dominant castes made some gains at the expense of the large landlords, as did superior tenants.

THE SLOW REVERSAL: THE RE-EMERGENCE OF THE RIGHT AND THE 'FOREIGN HAND'

The 1957 general elections, in which once again Nehru had been the main campaigner and the central figure for the Congress, had underlined the Congress's supremacy: it won 371 of 494 seats in the Lok Sabha – 75% of the seats, with 48% of the vote, a marginal increase from the previous general elections. (Many journalists wrote – as they had in 1952, only now more strongly – that without Nehru's leadership, the Congress would have done far worse: voters' open contempt for some of its candidates was offset by the fact that they were voting for Jawaharlal Nehru, and were therefore willing in practice to cast their vote for the sometimes pathetic figures placed before them.) The CPI, meanwhile, now operating under the constraints of the Indian Constitution, won 27 seats, which in the slightly larger Lower House was a smaller percentage of the seats (5%), but its vote share had almost tripled, from 3.3% to 9%. The Praja Socialists won 19 seats, with 10% of the vote. At the other end of the political spectrum, the Jan Sangh won four seats, with 6% of the vote; and the Hindu Mahasabha won one seat, with 1% of the vote. So the old Hindu right was still not doing particularly well, but it had doubled its vote share as compared with 1952.[7]

The simultaneous State Assembly elections of 1957 returned Congress majorities in most states; but opposition parties, many of these drawing on communal, regional or linguistic loyalties, increased their strength relative to the Congress. Most states had Congress governments; in Orissa, the Congress had to combine with independents to form a ministry that commanded a majority. In West Bengal, an electoral alliance of left parties strongly increased their electoral showing; and right across the country, the CPI did far better than it had done in the previous round of elections. But it was Kerala that produced the most difficult results: a communist government, led by E.M.S. Namboodiripad, came to power. Namboodiripad had been a major figure in the Malabar branch of the old Congress Socialist Party at the time of the United Front – Malabar was now the major part of the new, linguistically-defined, state of Kerala

– where the communist tactic of 'capturing' party units in the 1930s had been so successful that the Congress in effect was the CSP, which in turn was the CPI. The communists' successes had been based on a significant commitment to social justice in everyday situations, protecting lower castes against the more explicit forms of discrimination, and coordinating resistance to oppressive landlords. All of this was, it might have been remarked, well within the 'Nehruvian' project, and within the parameters envisaged by the Indian Constitution; indeed, it might be said that the CPI's successes were built on implementing Nehru's comparatively moderate social goals – because they were not constrained, as he was, to operate within a centre-right party with a commitment to the *status quo*.

Sources within the Congress, assessing the electoral showing, showed dissatisfaction at these results. The lesson they drew was that the Congress could no longer rely on rhetoric alone and would have to deliver on some of its promises in a more concrete manner. The Gandhian, Shriman Narayan, pointed out that 'conflict of class interest' had to be acknowledged by the Congress, that the interests of the poor and of the 'privileged and richer sections' of society could not indefinitely be harmonised, and that 'socialism', albeit 'through persuasion and democratic legislation', had to be made a priority.[8] Internal voices, seeking to justify their actions through statements made by Nehru at various points, organised a Congress Socialist Forum within the party – providing a fleeting sense of *déjà vu*, perhaps – but Nehru was most discouraging.

Nehru's campaign speeches against the CPI in the 1957 elections had hinged on the fact that they were obsolete and thought in categories that no longer applied to the world and to India. This criticism was somewhat inaccurate and itself obsolete: the positions he attacked were, if they had ever been held in the forms described, no longer held. In any case, the communists in India, contrary to the propaganda surrounding their status as agents of a foreign power, had always been quite adept at interpreting directives from on high – Moscow or, before 1947, the CPGB – in ways that were suitable for what its own leaders believed would be right for the situation. 'Official' policy could thus often be observed in the breach – the Popular Front line had been interpreted as one against imperialism rather than fascism because India did not have a particularly strong fascist movement; the placing of India in the imperialist camp after 1947 had been tempered by the CPI's effective participation in 'national' work. This was made much easier after 1955, when Khrushchev's visit to India and his endorsement of Nehru's regime allowed the CPI to abandon its position that 'independence' in 1947 had been a false dawn – 'yeh azadi jhuta hai' – with India unable to achieve actual freedom from imperialist control. Thereafter the CPI was pledged to work within the Indian Constitution of 1950; it used the radical statements present in the Constitution to justify their policies. Caste uplift and freedom from discrimination became central planks of the CPI's programme and won many adherents.

In 1957, Kerala provided a large issue that allowed pressure on Nehru from the Congress right wing, for some time successfully suppressed, to emerge again. E.M.S. Namboodiripad, the Kerala chief minister, had declared soon after forming his ministry that the CPI would implement the policies that the Congress governments in the state and at the centre had made promises to implement but failed to do. But Govind Ballabh Pant, the home minister, had no intention of allowing communists to govern on any programme whatsoever. Namboodiripad's amnesty for political prisoners, his commutation of death sentences and his banning of the eviction of tenant farmers by their landlords were not appreciated; Pant's instrument in Kerala was the governor of the state, Ramakrishna Rao, a fellow anti-communist. Nehru, who himself was against the death penalty but had refrained from speaking out against it in the constitutional debates or afterwards, could only support these measures; but, still playing intermediary, he intervened to prevent Namboodiripad from nationalising foreign-owned plantations in Kerala. Nehru was also in agreement with the Namboodiripad government's proposed land reform programmes and education policies (the state of Kerala is the first and only state to have achieved nearly 100% literacy in India). All of this was most moderate and Nehruvian, although the CPI's willingness to take on the vested interests that the Congress was entangled in and therefore unable to deal with made these measures appear far more radical. Opposition to the CPI in Kerala was with some justification characterised as a combination of upper-caste Nairs and Catholics, powerfully supported by the church – through which, it is alleged, the CIA channelled funds to anti-communists – and backed by the Congress.

Nehru's initial support of the CPI's democratic right to rule Kerala was quickly vitiated by the disruptions engineered by his own party, and by Cold War pressures that took the state of Kerala to be a prophesy of

things to come in India. The influence can be read in his public statements: from an initial endorsement of the moderate and constitutional
nature of the Namboodiripad government to the expression of misgivings
about the lack of toleration of dissent in 'communist' Kerala. While the
Kerala Congress used all resources at their disposal to disrupt the
administration of the state, Namboodiripad's letters to Nehru requested
his intervention in preventing Congress-led violence; Nehru expressed his
disapproval and did nothing.

The eventual dismissal of the Kerala government on July 30, 1959,
by the governor on the advice of the prime minister implicated Nehru
in a most significant act of destruction of constitutional propriety,
ranking alongside the dismissal and imprisonment of Sheikh Abdullah
in Kashmir. The Constitution of India provided regulations for the
declaration of an 'emergency' in a state and its temporary takeover by the
centre; the continuities with the 1935 Government of India Act had
always been considered disturbing (Section 93 of 1935 and Article 256
of 1950 which provide for this are largely indistinguishable). But the
actual use of this provision was considered improper; it had to be used
sparingly or it would open the floodgates to its abuse by central authority
against opposition governments in the federal units (Article 256 had been
used before, notably in Kashmir, where it was illegal to use it, but never
in so flagrantly partisan a manner as now). Nehru, in surrendering to his
party's right wing and to external pressures, had struck a blow against the
propriety for which he had always stood.

The decisive role in this dismissal has always been attributed to the
new Congress president, Indira Gandhi, Nehru's daughter, who was
elected in January 1959, allegedly without support or encouragement
from her father (though it was clear that no one could have become
Congress president if Nehru had actively disapproved). It might be said
that at a crucial juncture, over a political issue, Nehru's personal life and
long-term yearnings caught up with him. From very early on in the life of
his daughter, he had always wanted to be close to her. But he was often
in jail and had to be satisfied with writing letters to her, or at least to his
idealised image of her, or she was abroad (in Oxford or in Switzerland, as
a student or an invalid). Then, from about 1947, Indira had begun to
spend much of her time with him as a sort of personal assistant on his
trips abroad and as social organiser and hostess at home, living with him,
along with her two sons, at Teen Murti Bhavan in New Delhi. (Indira had

become increasingly distanced from her husband, Feroze, but remained married to him until his death in 1960; Nehru had disapproved of their marriage, but according to his own principles of romantic love and freedom of choice could hardly have opposed it too strongly – a victory, ironically, of his own principles over his personal wishes.) This was for Nehru the closest he ever came to a fulfilling domestic life: living with his daughter and two grandsons. Indira's presence on his overseas diplomatic visits from early on in Nehru's prime ministership had invited some adverse comment in the political press; her control over access to Nehru at Teen Murti Bhavan had also been noted – in his early years as prime minister, Nehru would meet members of the public and accept petitions and comments from them in person. Now, even members of his party were said to need to go through Indira as an intermediary. Most observers were therefore content with the attribution of guilt to Indira over the Kerala episode. The fact remained, however, that Nehru had at a crucial juncture supported his party, and his daughter, over his principles. For those who chose to see patterns, this could be another in his long line of surrenders, allegedly despite himself, to right-wing opposition.

The strongest exoneration of Nehru came, paradoxically, from E.M.S. Namboodiripad himself. Namboodiripad pointed out the deep internal differences within the Congress, the dangers of the triumph of the trends opposed to political democracy that had led to the dismissal of his government, and the increasing divergence under Nehru's government of India's political and economic path from 'the goal set by him and all of us'. But he listed Nehru's achievements: 'development' had progressed as far as it could 'in the circumstances', and Nehruvian secularism was a great achievement, especially when seen 'in contrast to the medievalism, obscurantism and ideological backwardness shown by the leaders of certain other newly-independent but underdeveloped countries'.[9] Here was a judgement that made explicit the differences between Nehru himself and his party. (In the mid-term polls following the dismissal of the Kerala government, the allegedly secular Congress had allied with the Kerala Muslim League to keep the communists out of power.)

It was around this time that the hitherto sparsely populated right wing of Indian politics began to look a little more crowded. A strong leftward shift in Indian politics, or at least an apparent one, became the catalyst for the emergence of a conservative force. The 1950s were seen as a period of communist 'unrest' throughout the country; the CPI victory in Kerala was considered a culmination of that trend. In 1959, the Congress's Nagpur Resolution on cooperative farming – albeit within a 'mixed economy' – was denounced as 'communism' by, among others, Rajagopalachari, Minoo Masani and N.G. Ranga. These were the figures at the core of the Swatantra Party, established in the late 1950s, and which was, after the fourth general elections in 1967, to emerge as the main opposition party in Parliament. The Swatantra Party was established under the ideological banner of a reasoned and non-communal conservatism by Rajagopalachari, and was supported at its establishment by landlords, princes, traders and retired ICS officers. Among its other leading lights was N.G. Ranga, an academic who had in the 1930s been one of the main founders of the *Kisan Sabha* and had therefore counted as one among the Congress Socialists (he had seen his organisation captured by the communists by the 1940s). He now counted among the agrarian conservatives who were uneasy about Congress's economic and in particular agrarian policies, accusing the Congress of having been captured by the Communist Party. Perhaps the most articulate of its members was Minoo Masani, who had mastered the language of the Western side of the Cold War, organising a Forum for Free Enterprise and chairing the Indian branch of the Congress for Cultural Freedom. In addition to its legitimating rhetoric drawn from the Cold War, it required a suitably 'indigenous' idiom; it claimed, therefore, a lineage drawn from the nineteenth century economic nationalism of Ranade, Naoroji and Gokhale, further enabling a self-description of 'liberal' (because these economic nationalists had, at a time of high liberalism, also linked their legitimating rhetoric to liberalism) – others' readings describe the Swatantra Party as 'conservative'. There was also, inevitably, the whiff of Gandhism that always went down well as legitimating rhetoric.

If it was Nehru's influence that prevented the Congress from finding its natural equilibrium as a party of the centre-right, Kerala can be seen as the beginning of a gradual slippage of Nehru's authority to do this. Nehru's ascendancy within the Congress assumed the energetic and cogent interventions of a prime minister whose only hope of continued success depended on an unfailing energy and an ability to oversee and anticipate everything with which his government might be concerned. But Nehru, who turned 70 in November 1959, was beginning to recognise the limits of his physical and mental energy. In April 1958, pleading exhaustion, he had asked for a spell as a 'private citizen', only to be refused by his party and greeted with anguished messages from Eisenhower and Khrushchev that extolled his virtues and declared his indispensability for the stability of the world. The best he could manage was a few weeks off in the Himalayas, in touch with Delhi but temporarily away from it. Nehru appears at this time to have entered another of his self-reflexive phases, unfortunately not, this time, shared with the world. He was also now at the head of a government populated increasingly by men of inferior rank and ability: Maulana Azad died in 1958, making Nehru the last representative of the giants of the nationalist movement left in government. Krishna Menon, who joined the Cabinet in 1956 after various overseas assignments, recalled that there was seldom a major debate in Cabinet because of everyone's great respect for Nehru; Nehru would tactfully dictate Cabinet minutes to the Cabinet Secretary summarising 'discussions'. And on foreign policy issues in particular, other Cabinet members 'would say something and then the Prime Minister would more or less educate them'.[10]

The disadvantage of what was effectively a personalised government was that what might be seen as the smaller things were left to be handled by the lesser mortals, whose conduct was not always above board. By the late 1950s, the first public rumblings of dissatisfaction at governmental corruption around him were beginning to emerge, and although they did not affect Nehru himself, they were indicators that Nehru's reputation was not likely to be a permanent shield against his colleagues' activities. More dangerously, however, Nehru was unwilling to take seriously charges of corruption levelled against those close to him, believing them to be indirect attacks on him. When his personal secretary, M.O. Mathai, was accused of corruption in February 1959, Nehru defended him in public, although an informal enquiry revealed he could not account for his disproportionate wealth and had almost certainly been paid by both Indian businessmen and the CIA for information. Mathai's resignation was accepted. 'It can safely be assumed,' Nehru's official biographer notes, 'that from 1946 to 1959, the CIA had access to every paper passing through Nehru's secretariat.'[11]

The CIA: these three letters crop up repeatedly in this period. Initially dismissed by many as paranoia, fears of CIA intervention now look increasingly as if they were severely understated. Prominent members of Nehru's inner circle were working with and for the CIA from at least 1955; among them Bhola Nath Mullik, who was director of the Indian

Intelligence Bureau from 1950 to the year of Nehru's death, 1964. Mullik was an advocate of alignment with the USA in the Cold War, trained under him large numbers of anti-communists as Indian intelligence agents, and worked closely with the CIA to sponsor Tibetan guerrillas in India. Intelligence sources' warnings to Nehru of the 'Chinese danger' seem to have been in keeping with their anti-communism, and may have eventually turned out to be a self-fulfilling prophesy. Regardless of whether Nehru approved of these activities, that he knew of at least some of them and acquiesced in them is in itself significant: what were the pressures that made him accept the situation? The entire strategy of non-alignment can only have been irrevocably compromised by these activities.

Nehru's foreign policy interventions in the late 1950s may provide a clue to his recognition of failure: the tone of upbeat optimism that marked his early years as prime minister was notably absent from the later period. In 1958, asked by the USA to mediate over Soviet-American disarmament talks (the USSR had rejected Western inspections of its nuclear sites but was willing to accept Indian inspections), Nehru refused, on the grounds that neither side was serious about disarming or limiting nuclear tests. Nehru more or less kept his head down even when maintaining his 'progressive' and anti-colonial line in foreign policy. At the 1961 Belgrade Conference of non-aligned countries he said to the gathered delegates, even as he condemned further Soviet nuclear tests, 'we must not over-estimate our own importance'.[12] Nehru, at Belgrade, was out of joint with a movement that was in large part his creation, and also with the new African states, clustering around ideas of the 'African personality' and pan-Africanism, and led by Ghana's Kwame Nkrumah, who consciously cast himself as a counter-Nehru, even as he modelled himself on him. For the new African states, Nehru's studied intellectual approach seemed strangely patronising. The grandeur of Nehru's principles sounded strangely hollow to Nehru himself: 'co-existence' was interpreted entirely differently by each member-state, and the increasing number of border skirmishes between India and China from 1959 had made Nehru himself quietly shelve the *Panch Sheel* from his political vocabulary.

THE 'NATION' AND THE CHINESE SHADOW: DISPUTE, WAR, CAUSES AND CONSEQUENCES

The skirmishes with China were a long-standing result of simmering disagreements between the Indian and Chinese governments over where exactly the borders between the two countries lay. Initially, both Nehru and Zhou Enlai deferred the problem; Nehru believed it would be a minor issue of readjustments and comparisons of incompatible Indian and Chinese maps to determine where the borders between India and China actually stood. This was a vexed question that had its origins in the machinations and disputes of predecessor governments of an imperial era that neither the People's Republic of China nor the Republic of India necessarily wished to claim as theirs; in the heady days of Sino-Indian friendship, neither side was keen to bring up an issue that might lead to disagreement.

The border dispute with China and the eventual 'China War' in 1962 had major consequences for both Indian domestic and foreign politics and did great damage to Nehru's position and reputation, making him far more vulnerable to attacks from the right than ever before. In retrospect, the whole affair might even appear a little bit ridiculous: the dispute was largely about uninhabited territory of little importance to either side. However, the implications for nationalist pride in a new state that had internally unresolved problems of defining its nationhood must be taken into account: it was relatively simple to manipulate public opinion around the idea of defending the 'national borders'.

But there were several intertwined issues, leftovers from an era of Great Power rivalries, which made the border question difficult. On the Indian side, if its borders were acknowledged as resulting from arbitrary imperial actions, there were implications for Nagaland and the 'tribal' territories in the North-East. The claim that imperial borders were arbitrary and had no connection with the intrinsic integrity of the Indian 'nation' could not be admitted without damaging the process of 'nation-building' or forcing an acknowledgement of the multinational instead of the national character of the Indian state. At the North-Western end, China's borders with Kashmir were a major part of the dispute, and Kashmir's attachment to India for the purposes of communications, external affairs and defence empowered India to negotiate on Kashmir's behalf; but by this time significant sections of Kashmiri opinion were in favour of Kashmiri independence.

Then there was Tibet. Much of the disputed border was actually one between India and 'the Tibet region of China': Chinese governments were understandably nervous about Tibet and potential foreign activities to destabilise Chinese claims to Tibet. At the Asian Relations Conference in Delhi in 1947, the Chinese delegation (still represented by the Guomindang) had insisted that questions of Tibet's political status should not be discussed. Tibetan representatives were to be included in the list of Chinese representatives and treated merely as 'cultural representatives'. Right through the border dispute, Indian documents maintained the reference to the 'Tibet region of China'; but part at least of the problem was the arbitrary boundaries sought to be imposed for the purposes of Tibet's buffer state status in between Russia, China and India, and the need to detach it from China and encourage its 'independence'. There were fears that this game was continuing, and some Indian officials did indeed wish to detach Tibet from China – in 1950, a British official had suggested that to pre-empt a Chinese takeover of Tibet, India should invade Tibet itself. Nehru had refused to contemplate this, but Chinese suspicion of India's intentions with regard to Tibet continued throughout the 1950s.

In the North-East of India under British rule, from 1873 an 'inner line' had demarcated the plains from the 'tribal' territories, a sort of no-man's-land, or rather no-country's-territory, which had been off limits to plainsmen without necessary licences to travel. The 'outer line' was the international frontier. But there was uncertainty as to exactly where this was. From about 1900 to 1910, during a period of Manchu 'modernisation' in Tibet that had attempted to replace Tibet's ancient theocratic institutions and *inter alia* reduce British influence, British viceroys of India had responded by unilaterally pushing the 'outer line' northwards. After the Chinese Revolution of 1911, the weakness of the Chinese government had provided Tibet with *de facto* independence from China, but not from Britain.

The so-called 'McMahon Line' was sought to be imposed at a conference in Simla from October 1913, based on the British decision to leave Tibet formally in China while controlling Tibet from India; the line had never been accepted by the Chinese government (even in the late 1950s, the Guomindang in Taiwan continued to protest that the McMahon Line had no legal validity) and the Tibetan representatives seem not to have noticed that the line had moved progressively northwards as the conference progressed through late 1913 to 1914. Later British claims to the 'Tawang Tract', a sliver of territory then a part of Tibet but extending onto the plains, had been based on *their own* claim that the McMahon Line had no validity. By 1947, Britain had occupied the Tawang Tract, and in 1951 India took it over without protest from China.

Nehru had told the Lok Sabha in 1950 that he stood by the McMahon Line; by 1950, the 'tribal areas' below the McMahon Line were being administered as the North-East Frontier Agency (NEFA) under Nehru's dual conciliatory-disciplinary framework for the 'tribals' that had been put in place with the assistance of the anthropologist, Verrier Elwin. With the establishment of NEFA, the gap between the 'inner line' and the 'outer line' and consequently the territory south of the McMahon Line was, in contrast to earlier years, being actively administered by India – *de facto* Indian influence had moved northwards; the Line was no longer as theoretical as before, and from 1956, following an intensification of Naga 'insurgency', Indian troops were present in larger numbers.

In the North-West, on the other hand, the border had been arbitrarily drawn by the British in the mid-nineteenth century to prevent the Dogra ruler of the new British-created Kashmir state from invading Tibetan territory. This theoretical line was incomplete; it did not extend as far as the territory of Aksai Chin – which later became the basis for conflict – because it was uninhabited and barren and, it was reasoned, a line was therefore unnecessary. (It was on an ancient trade route between Tibet and Xinjiang, 17,000 feet above sea level.) In the 1890s, China claimed Aksai Chin; thereafter, due to a 1907 Russo-British undertaking to stay out of Tibet, the British decided that Aksai Chin was in Xinjiang in case they needed to take over the territory. After 1911, China was considered too weak to protest, so Aksai Chin was shown as British territory; but in 1914, at the Simla Conference, British maps accompanying the attempted agreement that would have endorsed the McMahon Line – it did not – showed Aksai Chin as part of Tibet. Through all these machinations, the mountain kingdoms of Sikkim, Bhutan and Nepal had been caught in a web of shifting 'spheres of influence' and were handed round indiscriminately, although they maintained formal sovereignty.

There was a fundamental incompatibility between the Chinese and Indian positions. China apparently wanted, simply, to settle its borders. In 1955, at Bandung, Zhou Enlai had said openly that some Chinese borders were not yet clear and that they had to be determined in discussion with its neighbours. Part of his diplomacy was to assure neighbours of China's non-expansionist aims; he was willing to discuss delimited and demarcated borders without preconditions. (Borders with Nepal and Burma were settled on this basis in 1960, in the latter case on the basis of the McMahon Line: also, more controversially, with Pakistan in May 1962 – there is actually no Sino-Pakistani border; there is a Chinese border with Kashmir, but as a result of the Pakistani occupation of western Kashmir, pragmatism required China to discuss borders with Pakistan. The implicit recognition of Pakistan's right to at least that part of Kashmir was not the intention; both sides regarded the boundary as provisional pending a settlement of the Kashmir dispute.)

The problem, however, was that there was a strong Indian tendency to claim that its borders were not negotiable; this left no room for compromise and turned the entire dispute into quibbling over obsolete treaties or agreements of doubtful legality. With a history of the imposition of 'unequal treaties' by foreign powers, such preconditions were not likely to be accepted by China; the Chinese distaste that independent India should base its claims so strongly on an era of imperial treaties was strongly expressed. On the Indian side, there seemed to be a singular lack of appreciation that China could offer negotiations without preconditions, and remain flexible on the actual boundaries even to the extent of conceding to India exactly the same territory as delimited by the McMahon Line; but China could not concede the legality of the Line itself without implying that Tibet, whose delegates had been the only ones to accept any version of the Line, had been sovereign in 1914, and therefore were possibly so now.

In 1954, Indian maps abruptly changed to show concrete and delimited international boundaries in place of earlier provisional ones and Aksai Chin was placed firmly within the Indian Union, on the basis that the Indian side wished to argue that India's boundaries were already determined and not open to negotiations. This principle was especially to be observed, as Nehru's directive stated, 'in such places as might be considered disputed areas'.[13] Clearly, the intention was to present China with a *fait accompli*. From 1954 to 1956, China began to build a road across a corner of Aksai Chin, connecting Xinjiang and Tibet. Since China argued that the Indian maps did not accord with reality, and the Indian side did not even discover the Aksai Chin road until 1957 or 1958 (there are conflicting accounts), it would be fair to say that Aksai Chin was not a necessary part of Indian territory. But the Government of India's note to Beijing on October 18, 1958, claimed that the road was across territory that had been 'part of the Ladakh region of India for centuries'. This was a completely spurious claim: Ladakh had been captured by the Dogra ruler of Kashmir from *Tibet* in the mid-nineteenth century, and this had been recognised by his British overlords, who had thereafter contained him within their arbitrary line, while they themselves played with Aksai Chin in a positional war with Russia.

All of this was made far more tricky from March 1959, when Tibet was in rebellion and proclaimed itself independent; the Dalai Lama fled Lhasa and crossed the McMahon Line into India to (the monastery of) Tawang. (The United States 'requested' Nehru to provide asylum to the Dalai Lama; CIA operatives conveyed the Government of India's acceptance by radio to the rebels in Tibet, and on March 30, 1959, the Dalai Lama crossed into India with 200,000 Indian rupees provided by the CIA.[14]) There was some sympathy for the Tibetan cause in India, and this was taken up by the Socialist Party who, in April 1959, organised a portrait of Mao Zedong to be pasted on the wall of the Chinese consulate in Bombay and organised a crowd of people to throw eggs and tomatoes at it. Nehru, once again attempting his balancing act, tried to reconcile hospitality towards the Dalai Lama with gestures of correctness towards the Chinese – he refused to denounce the Chinese occupation of Tibet, but his reception of the Dalai Lama and the latter's access to the press to publicise the case for Tibetan independence annoyed China greatly.

Moreover, the Chinese government knew that Kalimpong in the hills of West Bengal in eastern India had become a centre of exiled Tibetans and CIA agents and plots, supported by persons prominent in Nehru's administration. Members of Nehru's government were prone to say in private that the formulation 'the Tibet region of China' was merely a realist concession. What would have been clear to observers in India, though not necessarily to foreign observers, was that this was not the only issue on which the Government of India seemed to pull in different directions. Yet as far as China was concerned, it had no reason to give Nehru the benefit of the doubt.

From August 1959, border skirmishes between Indian and Chinese troops occurred not infrequently, with troops on both sides having advanced up to the McMahon Line. The 'Longju incident' on August 25,

1959, marked the first clash of border forces – Indians usually had the worst of these encounters. From late 1959, China dominated Parliamentary proceedings and inflamed passions. The China issue led to a progressive erosion of Nehru's dominating authority in Parliament. Attacks on China were easily connected to criticism of the government's China policy, and spread swiftly to non-alignment and thence to Nehru's 'socialist' economic and domestic policy. Socialists were keen to play on the idea of Chinese 'expansionism', as the Praja Socialists put it – it was a stick to beat the communists with at home. The non-communist left therefore joined in the verbal attacks on China, and the right – both within and outside the Congress – took this forward into a general attack actually aimed at Nehru's economic policy. After the first border raids, officials became wary of supporting cooperative farming too openly – they had frankly looked with envy at the Chinese agricultural cooperatives, but then 'everything Chinese became taboo'.[15] State trading in food-grains – considered desirable in connection with cooperatives – also encountered obstacles. Attacks from the Swatantra Party and Jan Sangh on the socialist principles of planning became much simpler.

The paradoxical manoeuvres of Nehru tied him up into an even more complicated knot than usual. Nehru at first tried his best to hold a moderate line on China – in Parliament, on occasion, he admitted that the borders were vague and needed further discussion – especially Aksai Chin. Nehru also said frequently that it was not worth going to war to claim barren mountain peaks. But such open-mindedness was never expressed in communication with Beijing – trapped by the increasingly hysterical nationalism surrounding the border issue (not so much a popular sentiment as one among the 'political classes'), Nehru felt it best to hold his peace. There were also indications that he was getting annoyed with what he saw as Chinese arrogance. It became a matter of personal – and by projection national – pride: China was undermining his foreign policy and damaging his reputation as the architect of a pro-People's Republic policy. Meanwhile, Dr S. Gopal, then the director, Historical Division, Ministry of External Affairs, son of the then vice-president, Dr S. Radhakrishnan, and later Nehru's official biographer, was despatched to London to the India Office and Foreign Office archives – he returned to declare that India had a better claim to Aksai Chin than had China. After this, Nehru's openness regarding the possibility of negotiations vanished from his internal pronouncements as well.

On September 8, 1959, Zhou Enlai wrote to Nehru, explaining his position: no border, western or eastern, had ever been delimited. A reasonable solution therefore depended on bilateral negotiations. Zhou's letter, however, also contained the first claim by China to the no-man's-land between the McMahon Line and the foothills that was now mostly NEFA, and to everything beyond the Brahmaputra river. This was a tendentious claim, but possibly a raising of the stakes since the Indian side was so intransigent. But he still offered to negotiate –Indians kept missing clues in the Chinese correspondence that not all the territory China might *theoretically* have a claim to would *actually* be claimed by them. Further clues that China might be flexible in the North-East in return for Indian flexibility in the North-West were also ignored.

Meanwhile the right attacked non-alignment and demanded that India join various military pacts against China. The opposition was always more bellicose than Nehru, forcing him, if he wasn't to look unpatriotic, into a more and more aggressive posture. If war came, Nehru now found himself declaring, India would be ready. The assumption always remained that the choice of whether to go to war or not would be in Indian hands; alongside these remarks, Nehru's claims that India was fundamentally non-violent, even 'Gandhian', sat uneasily. From 1958, however, Nehru had begun taking precautions. With the military dictatorship of Ayub Khan in Pakistan inaugurated with American support and further arms sales, a potential two-pronged military threat had to be considered; in 1959, when Eisenhower visited Delhi, Nehru sought from him a guarantee that in case of a dispute with China, Pakistan would not attack India – this Eisenhower believed he could promise, which amounted to an admission that Pakistan was indeed controlled substantially by the United States.

On April 25, 1960, Zhou came to Delhi, still offering to negotiate on the basis of no preconditions and a 'line of actual control' principle. Nehru said later there was no question of 'barter' on the boundary question. When asked after a closed session whether the Indian negotiators had talked of Chinese 'aggression', Zhou said India had not: if they had, it would have been both untrue and unfriendly. But Nehru, when pushed by the press, said he could not remember whether he had used the word 'aggression' or not – the Indian press clearly thought he ought to have – but he had referred to the Chinese entering Indian territory 'which we consider aggression'. Zhou Enlai, now in Kathmandu, was not amused:

'He did not say it to our face but as soon as we had left he attacked the Chinese government as aggressors. That is not an attitude to take towards guests. We were very much distressed by such an attitude, particularly as we respect Prime Minister Nehru.'[16] These were, perhaps, the last civil words on Nehru to emanate from Chinese sources. The Chinese view up to 1960 – largely correct – was that Nehru was a captive of reactionary forces he couldn't control, but that he might just break free and become a progressive influence. By 1962, this had given way to denunciation of Nehru as a representative of the big bourgeoisie and landlords. China also correctly identified US pressures on India regarding aid, therefore explaining why India was having to move closer to the USA; it related the USSR's support for India on the border question to the recent Sino-Soviet split. China thus found herself isolated in international opinion, with both the capitalist and socialist side backing India. Ironically, one of the reasons the USSR took India's side was that its foreign policy observers found it impossible to believe that any country as weak as India would challenge or provoke China; the Soviet Union's public support for the Indian side encouraged the militancy of the Indian position.

By this time the argument between India and China was rapidly degenerating in standards – the Indian side was resorting to claiming a 'mystical affinity' with the Himalayas, and N.G. Ranga of the Swatantra Party declared that the Chinese were 'soiling our motherland with their cancerous fingers'.[17] The 1960 summit was destroyed largely by Indian intransigence; on the same trip, Zhou arrived at amicable boundary agreements with Nepal and with Burma – on the basis of the McMahon Line. Officials' consultations between India and China simply produced two contradictory reports in 1961: the Indian side paraphrased the Chinese position as 'India, like Britain, had invaded and occupied various portions of Chinese territory along the Sino-Indian boundary'; they then rejected this accusation, 'since these areas were correctly part of India'.[18]

Now, a 'forward policy' – a provocative sending of adventurous border patrols into disputed territory, to imply *de facto* Indian control – was inaugurated by the Indians. This absurd policy could even be seen as a *satyagraha* of the Gandhian kind, claiming the moral right not to face Chinese retaliation – but 'the *satyagrahis* would be armed troops'. 'We thought it was a sort of game,' an Indian army officer recalled in November 1962; indeed, Defence Minister Krishna Menon called it 'a game of chess'.[19] An ill-equipped and poorly-funded army – raising the military budget was opposed even by those in the Lok Sabha who hysterically advocated the use of force against China – was courting disaster.

Some of the more adventurous acts of the 'forward policy' occurred without Nehru's knowledge. It is reasonable to suggest that in the run-up to the January 1962 general elections, this was considered a popular policy to follow. From the autumn of 1961, the invasion of Goa was planned. The timing of the invasion was the subject of some comment: many saw it as a way for the government to appear decisive when they looked anything but decisive when faced with China. This was a soft target, and relatively consensual: Goa's continuance as a Portuguese colony had long been considered an anomaly; India had broken off diplomatic ties with Portugal in 1955 following the firing upon and killing of *satyagrahis* campaigning for Goan independence. The Portuguese were not likely to retaliate, and the international community would not make too many noises; the so-called 'police action' was carried out in December 1961. Nehru, to give him credit, had vacillated till the end: 'he had a complicated temperament; he didn't like the vulgarity and the cruelty of it, but at the same time he wanted results,' was Krishna Menon's retrospective view.[20] Nehru recognised that it would take pressure off him with regard to the China situation – although it contradicted his policy on peaceful and negotiated solutions. At any event, Goa, in stirring up national feeling against the residual coloniser, appears to have been a surrogate for China. But disturbingly, after Goa more far-fetched and explicitly threatening remarks were directed towards China – even by Nehru. In the election campaigns, home minister Lal Bahadur Shastri threatened China with a similar fate to that of Goa, and the Congress president, Sanjiva Reddy, talked about forcing Pakistan out of Kashmir. The restraint shown by China on the border was interpreted as a sign of weakness.

The January 1962 elections, predictably, kept the Congress in power: it won 358 of 491 seats in the Lok Sabha, 72.9%, with 44.78% of the vote share, and managed to hold on to the states. But the results did not strengthen Nehru's hand. The right showed impressive gains: 18 seats and 7.89% of the vote to the Swatantra Party, 14 seats to the Jan Sangh, with 6.43% of the vote. The Praja Socialist Party won 12 seats, with 6.81% of the vote share, and Lohia's Socialist Party six seats, with 2.83% of the vote share. With the secular and communal right having worked together throughout the previous parliamentary session, and the position of the PSP, working closely with Masani through the Congress for Cultural Freedom, remaining ambiguous, this was a disturbing trend for Nehru, especially when the Congress right's hostility to him was taken into consideration. Meanwhile, the CPI increased its seats from 27 to 29, 5.9% of the seats, raising its vote share to 9.94%.[21]

The China crisis continued. There were still occasional glimpses that Nehru was not unable to be sensible – in May 1962, he told the Lok Sabha, 'If you start thinking as the Chinese do . . . on the assumption that the territory in Ladakh, especially in the Aksai Chin area, is theirs and has been theirs, well, everything we do is an offence to them. But if we start on the basis of thinking that the territory is ours, as it is, then everything the Chinese do is an offence. It depends on with what assumption you have started.'[22] The almost throwaway line 'as it is', indicated that Nehru could not afford to be seen to be making concessions – the opposition, as it was, refused even to see talks with a Chinese delegation as anything short of surrender to an aggressor. Yet things were now beginning to look dangerous. In July 1962, the USSR asked the two sides to negotiate; China promptly agreed, but the Indian opposition would not agree to any softening of India's stand: the boundaries were not negotiable.

It was surprising that open armed conflict took so long to begin. On September 9, 1962, the decision to evict Chinese troops from south of the McMahon Line was taken – although there had long been Indians north of the line, in territory even the extreme Indian position did not claim. This decision was taken by Krishna Menon in Nehru's absence in London at the Commonwealth Prime Ministers' conference. Military officers knew this was disastrous and delayed action as long as they could – they knew their troops would be slaughtered. Still the hope remained that the Chinese would not retaliate – but on October 10, their first retaliation alarmed the generals in command. On October 13, Nehru responded to reporters' questions: 'our instructions are to free our territory' – this was interpreted worldwide as his declaration of war. On October 20, the Chinese assault began – it was swiftly clear that they could go anywhere they wished across any lines they cared to cross.

As the military defeats built up, Krishna Menon swiftly became the scapegoat; by November 8 he had been dropped from the Cabinet after pressure led by the president of India, Dr Radhakrishnan. Nehru had tried to avoid sacrificing Menon by first effectively demoting him and then by offering to resign himself – this tactic had always worked in the past, but this time it did not. During the conflict, the non-aligned movement did not particularly back India – only Ethiopia and Cyprus explicitly did so, and the rest reserved judgement. The Soviet Union again advised negotiations, and on October 24 China renewed its offer of negotiations without preconditions and of a ceasefire and withdrawal of troops on both sides. This was rejected by India, but Nehru's tone was noticeably gentler than before (he could not rely at this point on effective Soviet intervention; Russia was busy elsewhere, with the Cuban missile crisis from October 14).

A nationalist hysteria gripped India, with unparalleled outpourings of emotion and collective solidarity visible in large numbers of students volunteering to join the army and fight the invaders. The ultra-nationalist hysteria now also began to take an explicitly Hindu tone, with various public speakers and pamphleteers resorting to mythological analogies of Indian invincibility and strength. Chinese shops and shopowners were attacked in Delhi and Calcutta. Alongside these were organised and unorganised attacks on Communist Party of India offices across the country. The hysteria reached government departments: Indian citizens of Chinese origin were interned and later expelled to China. This was a complete destruction of one of Nehru's central principles – which he had so successfully maintained by refusing to equate Pakistanis and Muslims, offering the latter the full protection of Indian citizenship.

It was now that Nehru discovered an unlikely ally: the Communist Party of India. Themselves placed in an awkward situation, the CPI backed the Indian 'response' to Chinese 'aggression' and fell back on a version of nationalism themselves. Many at the time called for the arrest of communists and the suppression of the CPI. It was therefore necessary to support the war, as communists were always vulnerable to the charge of being anti-national, because internationalist. Among communists, therefore, there was much talk of the 'nation', even the 'motherland', and the need for unity despite political differences. The CPI reiterated its commitment to non-alignment despite some Congressmen wishing to abandon it. (Non-CPI members could shout '1942' in the House as a response.) Before an audience of alleged socialists and progressives, the CPI also backed Nehru; they listed his achievements and his progressive credentials – the *Panch Sheel* in 1954 (which even Nehru was less keen on being reminded of at this juncture); Bandung 1955; his anti-imperialist credentials denouncing aggression in Egypt (Suez 1956); his acclamation of the Cuban revolution in 1959; his support for the Algerian freedom movement, the Congolese and Angolan people; his liberation of Goa. For the duration of the China conflict, the CPI agreed to curb trade unions' activities to ensure productivity for a war. 'The working people of this country realise the gravity of the situation. The working people on their side will never repudiate their responsibilities.'[23]

The CPI now attacked Nehru's opponents and defended his policies far more strongly than Nehru could afford to do: 'under cover of a call to patriotic resistance' some people now wanted 'to lead India into the Western imperialist military alliances'; the Chinese attack had 'given a hearing to those who formerly had no hearing at all in this country'.[24] They attacked suggestions that a change of leadership was required, stressed the need for unity behind a 'national leader', and successfully placed the Swatantra Party and Jan Sangh on the defensive, forcing them to deny that they had made such suggestions. Communists ridiculed the Congress for saying they were behind Nehru when there were many in the Congress against his foreign policy, against non-alignment, against planning and against the goal of socialism. The CPI declared that despite differences with Nehru on domestic policy, they had no differences with him on foreign policy. This was for Nehru a welcome respite from the relentless attacks he had suffered in Parliament over the previous weeks and months.

On October 29, the US ambassador, John Kenneth Galbraith, offered India US military aid; a few weeks before, Nehru had rejected an offer, but now he accepted – military supplies were landing in India five days later from West Germany. From the Chinese point of view, it became more important therefore not to let the conflict drag on. By November 20, no organised Indian military force was left in NEFA. There was now nothing between the Chinese forces and the plains. Panic set in in Delhi; orders were sent out to arrest pro-Chinese members of the Communist Party of India, but this order was muddled and many centrist or pro-Moscow CPI members were arrested; they had to be let out one by one to avoid drawing attention to the error. That night, Nehru panicked and – this from the father of non-alignment – requested US military intervention: unknown to others, he asked for American-manned bomber and fighter squadrons to go into action against the Chinese.[25]

And then, just before midnight on November 20, the Chinese announced a unilateral ceasefire and withdrew from NEFA. Clearly this was meant as a punitive expedition, not an invasion. On November 21, Zhou Enlai announced the details: a 20-kilometre withdrawal by both India and China on both sides of a November 7, 1959, line of actual control – much further than anything the Indians had demanded before – then discussions on an amicable settlement should begin. China would put this into effect even if India did not respond. On US Ambassador Galbraith's advice, Nehru played for time – indirectly telling Zhou through the good offices of the Sri Lankan prime minister that India would not move back to the McMahon Line, but refusing to answer the Chinese call. At talks in Colombo, India avoided an explicit settlement; it was impossible even now to acknowledge the simple reality that, on the ground, the Chinese victory had settled the issue. On the Chinese side, a generous willingness to allow Nehru to save face prevented their forcing an explicit agreement; but the border issue remains, theoretically, unresolved, as it was before 1962.

THE FRAYING OF NEHRUVIANISM

The last years of Nehru's prime ministership were haunted by the ghosts of the China War. From the very early years of his government, he had always been a prime minister at war with significant sections of his government. But now, both within and outside his party, he came under attack. Nehru was accused of undermining national security; he had been forced to drop his major adviser on foreign relations, Krishna Menon, and increasingly he appeared to be on the defensive. The China crisis appeared to have undermined the very basis of the Nehruvian system. The central plank of Nehru's foreign policy, non-alignment, came under attack, and Nehru himself had, though clandestinely, completely surrendered the principle. In early 1963, Tibetan guerrillas trained in the United States were flown into India, not clandestinely as before, but openly to an Indian Air Force base, where the Indian armed forces welcomed them.[26] By 1964, Nehru had given free reign to the CIA to use Indian territory in its war against China in Tibet, and US spy planes were given refuelling rights in India on their way into Tibetan airspace.

Leading the attack on Nehru from the outside was the Swatantra Party. But internal opposition within the Congress, always present, also emerged openly, and the open swing to the right that Nehru had held off for so long became more evident. The CPI's leading parliamentarian Hiren

Mukerjee's spirited defence of Nehru in the Lok Sabha and his profession of loyalty and patriotism had been one of the central features of the China crisis. Now, in what was both a holding operation, given the rightward drift of Indian politics at the time, and a survival tactic, given the aspersions cast on the CPI's patriotic credentials during the China crisis, the CPI seemed Nehru's most loyal support base in Parliament.

The China War and the patriotic frenzy that followed cast Nehru, the idealist, as one whose idealism had betrayed the country. Nehru – trying at times to hold the balance and find a rational way forward – eventually realised this was not possible. Not too long before, he had written to the philosopher Bertrand Russell pointing out the usefulness of nationalistic feelings in producing in India some of the solidarity required to carry through economic policies that would eventually lead to self-sufficiency. But this attempt at an instrumental use of nationalism had as a result of the China conflict been amplified 'to such an extent that it is quite out of hand'.[27] It had also been diverted in directions that were no longer conducive to the uses to which Nehru wished to put it. The Swatantra party had turned the China war into a propaganda call – a war between communism and democracy. Nehru's foreign policy and domestic policy could be attacked – non-alignment, planning and socialism. Nationalism, in this scheme of things, belonged at least for the moment to those who opposed communism, and Nehru's policies could now be associated with communism. This was, for the time, completely paradoxical given his surrender of non-alignment and his effective alliance with the Western bloc; if anything, he could now be more realistically accused of being the 'running dog of imperialism' that some Chinese voices had claimed he was. A return to non-alignment from this position would be difficult. The effective independence that Nehru had made the central plank of his domestic and foreign policy looked more damaged and impossible of achievement than ever before.

Nehru, on his part, had allowed himself to be manoeuvred into a position in which – however, we may assume, reluctantly – the sceptic and rationalist found himself trapped and carried onwards in a cycle of aggressive, patriotic fervour to a disastrous policy of confrontation with a neighbour who desired no such confrontation, and which confrontation could only damage his policies and greatly ease the agenda of his enemies within and outside his party. Non-alignment; the social concerns of planning; Nehru's command over Parliament; his international reputation: all of these had taken a battering as a result of his reluctance to translate his misgivings into action. Nehru operated through a coalition of forces, headed by himself due to his peculiar prestige, his intellect, his energy, and the respect and cooperation even his enemies were forced to give him. He had at best been a clumsy coalitionist, failing to recognise and work with his natural allies, and finding himself bound up in a coalition of his natural opponents: businessmen, right-wingers and corrupt bureaucrats and colleagues. Now, his refusal to seek these natural allies had isolated him more than ever before; it remained to be seen whether they could reach out to him despite himself.

The question of succession to the prime ministership was also by this time in everyone's mind. In 1959, as Nehru had celebrated his seventieth birthday, speculations about the future leadership of Congress began to emerge from offstage whispers to open speculation in the press and in political circles. There was an international dimension to this as well: for the Eastern bloc, Nehru was as progressive a third world leader as could be expected in Indian political conditions; for the Western bloc, he was a necessary bulwark against communism. Such speculation was amplified by the China conflict, which had simmered since 1959 – at the end of which India was, in the phrase then emerging, 'bi-aligned', buying arms from both the United States and the Soviet Union. Then, in the spring of 1962, Nehru suffered his first major illness, and was thereafter obliged to rest every afternoon and to reduce his work schedule from seventeen hours a day to twelve. The China 'War' itself was a turning point: Nehru appeared to be demoralised – he had swiftly turned from a sprightly 70-year-old to a slow and tired 73-year-old, less sure of himself and altogether more vulnerable. He appeared to have lost much of his authority, and talk of finding successors to the prime minister was now everywhere.

Nehru still had a mandate to rule (it might well be said that an election at the end of 1962 would have looked very different from that at the beginning of 1962, but elections then might equally have endorsed Nehru: electoral popularity and parliamentary authority were two separate things). Nevertheless, opposition to him within the Congress was mounting. Nehru's Finance minister, Morarji Desai, was anti-Nehru and very anti-socialist. Congress corruption was the subject of much discussion. The Congress had proved to be a means of social mobility for new groups – not altogether or always legally; it was widely talked about that the Scheduled Caste leader, Jagjivan Ram, used the Railways Ministry to further the interests of his caste, not to mention his personal fortunes. In 1963–4, defence expenditure doubled as a result of the China affair, and the process of planning was directly affected by this reallocation of resources. With the Third Five-Year Plan going badly, and food shortages appearing, the issue of Congress's internal corruption was beginning to be raised more loudly than ever before.

Symptomatic of Nehru's loss of power was the passing of the 1963 Official Language Act – Hindi was to be the sole official language of India, although allegedly it would not be imposed on any states. The promotion of Hindi had of course long been a central theme of Hindu nationalists and fundamentalists. But the potentially sectarian implications of this went against Nehruvian political tenets. Nehru provided an extremely obfuscating defence of Hindi in Parliament, attempting to downplay the sectarian aspects of the proposed legislation: if India had had only two or three languages, all of them could have been national languages; but the Constitution recognised fourteen languages. Hindi was the only possible 'link language',[28] but it had to 'grow into' one; meanwhile, English would have to continue to be the link language. He now claimed that Urdu was 'about 75–80% Hindi'.[29] He nonetheless said that regional languages also had to develop, and he defended the continuance of English for official purposes in some form, even removing the earlier clause that after 1965 no further use of English would be made for official purposes.

But now a major problem was beginning to emerge. Nehru had been central to the Congress's legitimacy in Indian politics. From outside the Congress, it had always been easier to focus criticism on the lesser lights in the Congress rather than on Nehru himself. Within the Congress, Nehru was usually above criticism, both due to his reputation and his personal integrity, which no one questioned, even when they might question his judgement. In this respect he had been a worthy successor to Gandhi. Now, undermining Nehru was in many respects a suicidal strategy for the Congress, exposing to clear public light what from its point of view best remained hidden: the Congress was a party of mediocrity, corruption and intrigue, with a leader who had, with almost Olympian disdain, not paid enough attention to these mere details as he spoke instead of high principles and moral standards.

CONCLUSION: DEATH, SUCCESSION, LEGACY

The Nehruvian aura was beginning to fade by the end of 1962, and with it the legitimacy that he had for so long lent to the Congress under him: he appeared now as a mere man. In the spring of 1963, there were three important Lok Sabha by-election defeats for Congress, in Amroha, Farrukkabad and Rajkot. The victorious candidates were J.B. Kripalani (standing as an independent), Ram Manohar Lohia (the leader of the Socialist Party) and Minoo Masani (of the Swatantra Party) – all three of them had been defeated in the 1962 general elections. Kripalani immediately served notice of a no-confidence motion against the government. This was of course defeated; but it was understood by many to be a general attempt at censure of Nehru, rather than an attack on specific policies. Nehru conducted his own, powerful defence: he stood by India's economic record under planning, defended the *Panch Sheel* and non-alignment as correct (at a time when he had abandoned both), and he welcomed the no-confidence motion as an opportunity to defend his policies. But he recognised it as a personal attack. What had brought the opposition together on the motion, he noted, was 'a negative, not a positive attitude, not only a dislike of our Government, but – I am sorry to say – perhaps a personal attitude against me'.[1]

As Nehru's weaknesses and the Congress's lack of legitimacy without him became apparent, the urgency of moves to cleanse the Congress of corruption clearly emerged: for it was the issue of corruption that had been least satisfactorily dealt with. For this purpose, there emerged the

'Kamaraj Plan', named after a quiet, soft-spoken Congressman, the Madras chief minister, K. Kamaraj Nadar, but attributed to Biju Patnaik the Orissa chief minister, Kamaraj and Nehru himself, and originating with Patnaik. As an attempt to stop the decline in Congress's moral standards, it suggested – inevitably invoking Gandhi – that self-sacrificing members had to renounce high office to concentrate on 'grass-roots' politics (a phrase that meant an attempt to reconnect with ordinary people and in doing so acknowledged that those connections had been lost). Some senior Congressmen in government would therefore resign their posts and take up full-time organisational work to revitalise the party. A visibly old and tired Nehru publicly accepted the Kamaraj Plan in August 1963 and asked permission to resign himself. This he was not allowed to do, as his colleagues proclaimed his indispensability as head of government. Nehru then suggested a committee be set up to implement the Plan, but this was also turned down – he himself should be the judge of the moral standards of the party and the main executor of the plan. Clearly, the intention was to place powers in Nehru's hands to use his own legitimacy – damaged but not broken by the China war – to re-legitimise the Congress, as well as to remould the upper ranks of the party to his liking.

THE LAST RECOVERY

The All-India Congress Committee endorsed the Kamaraj Plan on August 10. Many Union cabinet ministers and state chief ministers submitted their resignations, and the Working Committee set up three committees to deal with organisational matters, corruption charges and the collection of party funds, respectively. The Kamaraj Plan was activated on August 24, after many days of behind-the-scenes lobbying and bargaining. Its Gandhian rationale – that the Congress was not for people attracted merely by office and the power it brought, but was for people who respected the Congress's tradition of service – disarmed the internal opposition, which could not afford to look as if it was acting in a self-interested manner. But with Nehru not getting any younger (he was almost 74), many Congressmen knew that these activities could affect the succession to Congress leadership.

The list of those who were to take the temporary path of renunciation contained six Cabinet ministers – including Morarji Desai (Finance),

Jagjivan Ram (Transport and Communications), Lal Bahadur Shastri (Home) and S.K. Patil (Food and Agriculture) – and six chief ministers – including Kamaraj himself (Madras), Biju Patnaik (Orissa) and Bakshi Ghulam Mohammed (Jammu and Kashmir). Nehru hinted that he might add to the list later, but he did not, leaving the possibility suspended like a sword of Damocles. The ability to reorder and reorganise the Congress's upper ranks placed back in Nehru's hands some of the initiative to lead the Congress that he had lost over China. But the press, at least, remained sceptical. The process of the Kamaraj Plan provoked some amount of irreverent comment: those who resigned were referred to as the 'Kamarajed men', some of whom were later 'deKamarajed'; the 'politics of Kamarajerie' was much discussed. By this time so many in the higher ranks of the Congress hated each other that it was fair to say they were held together only by prospects of power, under the comforting canopy of Nehru's persona.

Observers could point out that some of these men were clearly tainted by corruption charges, while others were on the list so as not to make the singling out of the corrupt men too obvious. Among the 'Kamarajed men' were also those dropped to redress the balance of power in the Cabinet following the departure of left-wing Congressmen such as Menon. There were two genuine cases of resignation to follow up a 'grass-roots' agenda, or who were not under suspicion of corruption or right-wing deviation: Kamaraj himself and Lal Bahadur Shastri. The 'Kamaraj Plan' removed main players in the bid for the succession from the centre of power and manoeuvre – the Cabinet – at a crucial juncture. Shastri, S.K. Patil, the food minister who had become notorious even among the Swatantra Party members for periodically asking for American wheat, and Kamaraj himself were later 'de-Kamarajed'. As a rescue operation for the Congress, it was not very successful; but the Kamaraj Plan clearly affected the succession.

On January 6, 1964, at the annual Congress session in Bhubaneshwar, Nehru suffered a stroke that affected his left side. Considerably weakened, he continued to work a reduced schedule; those close to him recognised that he was near the end. Advisers and journalists pressed him to name a successor. Nehru ploughed on with his work. Meeting his old friend Sheikh Abdullah in April, just out of jail at Nehru's request (facilitated by the Kamaraj Plan that had removed the Kashmir chief minister), his was a philosophical counterpoint to Abdullah's bitterness. Nehru hoped for reconciliation and spoke of his understanding for 'an old friend and colleague and blood brother',[2] but this sounded a little hollow. With Nehru's consent – even if he had occasionally protested at the lack of respect for legal procedures – Abdullah had been imprisoned without trial for the better part of a decade, with a brief respite for three and a half months from January to April 1958, while the state of Kashmir had been ruled by a corrupt Indian loyalist who was comfortable with rigging elections, of whom even Nehru had said that if he 'lost a few more seats to bona fide opponents' it would be to his advantage.[3] Nehru understood Abdullah's fears that India had alienated Kashmir, and he blessed his forthcoming trip to Pakistan, expressing the hope for better relations between Pakistan and India as well. All that remained was for the two old comrades divided by *Realpolitik*, to Nehru's mind, was that they should find the equivalent symbolic act to Nehru and Churchill singing the Harrow School Song together at an old boys' reunion, less than a decade after Churchill had had his schoolfellow incarcerated in an imperial prison.

At his last press conference on May 22, those present remember his slow and deliberate words in response to the inevitable question: was it not time to name a successor? 'That,' said Nehru, 'is a leading question.' 'It is on everybody's lips,' the journalist replied. There was a long pause and then Nehru's voice cut through the silence: 'They may be talking like that. My lifetime is not ending so very soon.'[4] On May 26, he completed his correspondence for the day and cleared his desk of pending papers. In the early morning hours of May 27, he suffered a rupture of the abdominal aorta; pain-killing injections enabled him to sleep until two o'clock in the afternoon, and then he died. On his bedside table, on a small notepad, was found scrawled in his own rather shaky hand the last stanza of Robert Frost's 'Stopping by the Woods on a Snowy Evening':

> The woods are lovely, dark and deep,
> But I have promises to keep,
> And miles to go before I sleep,
> And miles to go before I sleep.[5]

SUCCESSION MANOEUVRES

Symbolic of the isolation of the man in his last days, Nehru lost control even of his last request. Nehru's funeral was a public pageant and a spectacle, replete with Vedic hymns sung and Hindu priests chanting – in flagrant disregard of his express wishes that no religious rites be performed at his funeral. 'I wish to declare with all earnestness that I do not want any religious ceremonies performed for me after my death,' Nehru had written in his will. 'I do not believe in any such ceremonies, and to submit to them, even as a matter of form, would be hypocrisy and an attempt to delude ourselves and others.'[6] His daughter, Indira Gandhi, knew about this, but was either persuaded, or chose, to ignore it. As part of the pageantry of succession and an attempt at building legitimacy, one of Nehru's main opponents within the Congress, Morarji Desai, staked his claim to succession over the corpse of Nehru, placing himself in a prominent position near the body, displayed in state: the nation would see him as close to the dear departed leader as possible. The Hindu side of the Congress was reasserting itself, and Nehru was in death to be its symbol: the process of appropriation of Nehru was already under way. The route of the funeral procession was more or less the same as Gandhi's had been; the pyre was lit by Indira's younger son, Sanjay. The people, so the rationale went, were religious; so it would be religion that they would get. Mammoth crowds lined the route of the funeral procession and huge numbers watched the cremation.

A residual spiritualism, perhaps, had remained in Nehru; he had requested a scattering of his ashes from the air over the countryside, his fantasy of oneness with an India that he had been unable to mould to his liking. A small handful, however, he requested be disposed of in the river Ganga: 'a symbol and a memory of the past of India, running into the present, and flowing on to the great ocean of the future.' 'I do not wish,' he wrote, 'to cut myself off from the past completely.' This was to be his 'last homage to India's cultural inheritance';[7] but it was not intended to be a 'return' to a 'Hindu' religion that he had never practised or believed in. That was not how it was displayed to the public. 'In something like the delirium of grief, the scattering of the ashes took place with pomp and ceremony which had near revivalist overtones he had warned against. However, it was a lapse which could be related to a kind of temporary mental atrophy which overtook many as he died.'[8]

There was a strong sense that a noble era had ended and that what followed was bound to be petty in comparison. Nehru had often been encouraged to speak out on the question of succession: the very language had the ring of monarchy about it. Later in his life, admittedly, he had been more inclined to a certain authoritarianism – not institutionally, but due to his personal abilities and reputation. He had, however, held his peace: a democrat did not name an heir. Since Nehru's illness, from about January 22, 1964, Gulzarilal Nanda, Lal Bahadur Shastri and T.T. Krishnamachari had been dividing responsibility for his duties, with Kamaraj just behind and a shadowy 'caucus' slightly further behind. Shastri as Minister without Portfolio and acting as assistant to the prime minister was, however, considered – popularly as well as in the party – to be Nehru's designated successor. But Nanda was acting prime minister after Nehru's death pending the appointment of a new prime minister by the Party – this was unconstitutional, according to some. In the days after Nehru's death, Morarji Desai made a determined bid for power. Contemporary observers believed that had he not been 'Kamarajed' so recently and had he still been in the Cabinet holding the Finance portfolio, he would have won. (He had his chance eventually – after Indira Gandhi's 'Emergency' from 1975 to 1977, he came to power at the head of the Janata (People's) coalition, which however did not last long.)

Within less than two years, however, the prime minister's office had seen a succession and a succession's succession. In 1964, Nehru's daughter, Indira Gandhi, told K.D. Malaviya, one of Nehru's close allies on the left of the Congress, that she was not a candidate for the prime ministership. Malaviya had felt that as a man on the left he should ask her – because she was the best chance for 'socialism' (this was, in time, to appear particularly ironic). Lal Bahadur Shastri was elected successor, largely due to the Kamaraj Plan and to Kamaraj's continued prestige. Shastri himself, after a tenure that saw a major food crisis, a second war with Pakistan and a sometimes violent anti-Hindi movement in South India, died less than two years later, on January 11, 1966, the day after signing a Soviet-brokered peace with Pakistan. This time Indira Gandhi took the job; she had been Shastri's Information and Broadcasting Minister, having been elected to Parliament for the first time in a by-election in 1964. Could this be considered dynastic rule? Perhaps; there is no indication that she was a reluctant entrant – and in her swift elevation there was an element of the instrumental use of the Nehru name (in later elections it was found that her name combined the uses of both the icons of Indian nationalism – Gandhi and Nehru; not everyone knew she was Nehru's daughter and unrelated to the Mahatma). A now-struggling Congress party could use the Nehruvian mystique to maintain its legitimacy; Mrs Gandhi had been a compromise candidate, but it was soon discovered that she was not inclined to let others control the administration. In the end she split the party, and was willing to do more to have her way than her father had ever been, without necessarily having her father's agendas.

PARADOXES OF 'LEADERSHIP'

For historians, Nehru remains a much-admired enigma. The private views of Nehru disappeared so completely from the public domain in the post-independence years – and remain so out of reach for researchers even now – that writers have tended to project the philosophical, self-reflexive intellectual of the 1930s into the later years, with the necessary qualification that his radicalism was tempered by the practical responsibilities of office. But it is unclear how much of the radicalism survived into the 1950s and 1960s. Nehru's speeches were still inspiring, and the general assumption of his good intentions given his early years stood him in good stead as he posed as the voice of reason against socialist and communist 'extremism' while pushing for socialism himself. At the same time, he stood at the head of – and tolerated the presence of – tendencies that he would certainly have called 'reactionary' in his earlier avatar. If we assume that he exercised self-censorship out of party loyalty – the party had not fully accepted socialism, as he might have put it – we miss the question as to why he did not find himself a more congenial party to head, which he certainly might have attempted to do. (It can always be said of Nehru's governments that they were largely coalitions, and they were therefore unable to be as effective as governments that spoke with one voice.) More unpalatable possibilities – that Nehru himself saw his role as that of administering the anti-socialist vaccine of socialist rhetoric, or to transpose a later joke about Deng Xiaoping's China, signalling a left turn and turning right – have been avoided by historians. It is therefore only possible to raise questions that will continue to be debated.

Paradoxes abound: Nehru, the eternal coalitionist, appears to have been particularly adept at locking himself into coalitions with his opponents rather than his allies. Given the confusions of the socialists after they departed from the Congress, an alliance in that direction might have been ruled out later on – but that was in the 1950s; the moment had come and gone earlier, in the 1930s and perhaps the 1940s. It is possible that Nehru remained in the Congress and at the head of the government as a sort of holding operation against right-wing tendencies. 'Most of my Ministers are reactionary and scoundrels,' the scientist, J.D. Bernal, records Nehru as saying to him when they met in Beijing in 1954, 'but as long as they are my Ministers I can keep some check on them. If I were to resign they would be the Government and they would unleash the forces that I have tried ever since I came to power to hold in check.'[9] This would certainly have been an accurate assessment of Nehru's major triumph against the anti-Muslim communalism of the Congress right wing. Thus it is tempting to believe that the Nehruvian coalition was *acknowledged* as that between the right and left within the Congress, but that the real Nehruvian coalition consisted of the left in the Congress and the communists outside it, with various socialists occasionally weighing in with their contributions, and Nehru remaining in the Congress to prevent, or at least retard, a strong move to the right. This could of course never be acknowledged either by Nehru or the CPI, and it is uncertain whether they were aware of this at any point except during and after the China war, because if such a coalition had been acknowledged, it would have added fuel to the fires of both internal and external Cold Warriors, who at any rate already did their best to keep Nehru honest and away from communism.

Thus it was that Nehru was perhaps at his most perceptive when he noted that non-alignment would be at the core of independence, and an internal distance from the CPI was integral to the external distance from the superpowers. (Those who accused Nehru of being an internationalist at the expense of the merely domestic tend to miss the point that the domestic and the international could not be separated.) The leadership of Nehru instead of anyone from the right or the left can be seen as a cause of a certain degree of effective independence being maintained by India in the context of the Cold War and its concomitant pressures: neither West nor East could find enough faults with the Indian system to justify explicit intervention. (This does not of course account for the fact of the secret machinations of organisations such as the CIA in India; it is clear now, and constantly getting clearer with the emergence of new evidence, that these interventions strengthened or even brought into being a coherent right-wing opposition to Nehru in the end. How far Nehru knew of these activities, and how far he opposed or was in a position to oppose them, we are not yet in a position to judge.)

However, if we rule out the role of foreign pressures in the day-to-day working of the government – in, for instance, the details of the Hindu Code Bill, which could hardly have excited CIA observers too much – there is of course another argument to consider: that Nehru could have sought to push his governments' and his country's politics further towards the left despite the constraints of working within a centre-right party, had he been inclined to do so, because as the central vote-winner for his party he could have used the 'masses' against the 'reactionary forces'. Here it might be said that he encountered what could be considered a generic problem of parliamentary democracy. Nehru's moral authority and popularity with the 'masses' only came into play during elections, and therefore could only be ascertained or drawn upon once every five years, or if he was willing to precipitate elections and resort to direct democracy by threats of resignation more often than he actually did. Therefore this weapon of the 'masses' was only available to him occasionally. In parliament itself, it was difficult to use it on a day-to-day basis.

Behind this might be detected another potential reason – a paradoxical distrust of the 'masses' in the 'largest democracy in the world' and in the political thinking of a democrat. In the expectations of political leaders in the years leading up to and following independence, the 'masses' were cast in the role of supportive followers: they were expected to participate in production, to endorse the national leaders, and – before independence – demonstrate to the colonial rulers the importance of those leaders; but their judgement in distinguishing various strands of policy could not altogether be relied upon. Fears of mass irrationality on the lines of the partition riots reinforced this tendency or converted ardent democrats to a general tendency of not trusting the voters to think the right thing. This perhaps explains the obligatory and somewhat formulaic rhetorical populism that sometimes dominated Indian politics, and the related danger of an iconography of great leaders emerging as legitimating formulae in the place of reasoned debate. Nehru could not have been unaffected by the misgiving that what he considered some sort of false consciousness was actually a strong motivating factor. If he maintained his original formulation that economic uplift eroded sectarian or primitive values, he would also have had to admit that this remained an untested hypothesis: the gains of economic development had failed to reach the 'masses'.

In January 1956, asked to comment on the differences in his politics from his earlier years, Nehru replied, 'one tones down in a position of responsibility. One has to carry people with one. I am constantly facing the difficulty of not being able to carry people with me. And apart from everything else, my pride is hurt that I cannot convince a person, that I cannot carry him with me.'[10] In some ways, Nehru might be said to have had a Trotsky problem: as an intellectual, he did not tend to build up practical alliances within his party, appearing to believe that his being correct would bring colleagues round to his position. This depended, of course, on those colleagues having shared concerns with him, which Nehru often admitted – certainly in private – was not the case.

MILES TO GO: UNFINISHED BUSINESS

The Nehruvian project contained an emphasis on secularism, democracy and state-led developmentalism; a containment of religious nationalism and obscurantism; and an obligatory rhetoric of social justice which, although called 'socialism', was unable to deliver social justice. Its international corollary was non-alignment, which was considered essential to effective independence. How far we can properly identify Nehru himself with the Nehruvian project is a question we have already raised. We could also remind ourselves that it was to a large extent a failure.

There is a tendency, of course, to judge Nehru by standards far beyond those applied to most politicians. Perhaps this is because he himself set the standards so high, and also perhaps because, as Nehru was and regarded himself as an intellectual, subsequent writers engage with him in the full splendour of intellectual combat, delighting in his inconsistencies and revelling in revealing his compromises. Even by these standards, however, Nehru is owed a somewhat positive assessment.

The flagship of the Nehruvian project, development planning – at least the first three Five-Year Plans – had definite successes to show for itself, even if after the First Plan the Plans all failed to meet their own rather over-optimistic targets. There was, as desired, a sharp jump in industrialisation – industrial production doubled between 1950 and 1960, and went up another 40% between 1960 and 1964. Heavy industry did best, although the cotton textile industry, the oldest-established industry in India, stagnated. (Whether it was in fact necessary for the cotton textile industry, in the private sector, to increase production or whether they could simply produce less but continue to make abnormal profits due to the oligopoly of a few industrialists, is a question that has been raised.) Consumption, it has been said, was limited by a slow rise in per capita incomes, and incomes rose mainly for the urban population and rich peasants. Agriculture did worse, and eventually began to hold back the developmental process. (After Nehru's death, US President Lyndon Johnson was able to threaten to withhold shipments of grain to India unless a policy shift to 'betting on the strong' was inaugurated. This was to become the basis of the so-called 'Green Revolution' strategy, where high-yielding seeds and increased fertiliser use by richer farmers on larger plots of land led to increased production – only in wheat areas, not elsewhere. Instead of cooperatives, there was an increased polarisation of rich and poor farmers in the countryside.)

Thus, most importantly, as Nehru admitted at the time of the drafting of the Third Plan, the redistributive agenda had largely failed; over half the Indian population lived in poverty. India was still a capitalist economy; socialism required more than just a large public sector. Nehru frankly stated that the private sector was expanding with state help, that a group of leading capitalists had taken over the economy, and with it controlled politics and society. Not enough attention had been paid to human development in the form of education, apart from at the higher end of the spectrum – scientific and technological education, or higher education in general, to the detriment of primary education. No proper social security provisions were in place, despite the fact that, as far back as 1938, the Congress's National Planning Committee under Nehru's chairmanship had put together a package of extremely radical provisions.

The social corollary to developmental planning, 'modernisation', was also noticeably lagging behind. Many of Nehru's failures in this regard were due to a conservative opposition that he was unwilling or unable to confront by strongly asserting his own views. In 1948, a senior civil servant had protested against the appointment of women to the Indian Foreign Service because they would ultimately need to get married; Nehru had declined to make not appointing women a legal principle, but he attempted to assuage the gentleman's anxiety by suggesting that it was highly unlikely that women would join the Foreign Service in large numbers. The Hindu Code Bill had been opposed by conservatives, and delayed for four years before Nehru was forced to compromise. On 'Muslim law', Nehru's principle of not giving the impression that a Hindu majority was enforcing anything on the Muslim minority led to a fossil-isation of that category of 'personal law': as late as 1959, Nehru refused to touch Muslim personal law, and would not place monogamy on the agenda, at a par with the Hindu Code Bill that had made polygamy illegal for Hindus (both 'Hindu' and 'Muslim' personal law were legacies of the colonial imagination). In both cases, what his reluctance achieved was that women's representation was left in male hands: the custodians of the rights of a 'community' were its 'leaders', self-appointed and male. In most arenas, a few elite women appointed to or earning high office – among the most prominent such examples being Nehru's sister, Vijayalakshmi Pandit – stood as token representatives of the wider agenda of liberation for women.

In the end, the greatest betrayal of Nehru's policies came from Nehru himself, in compromising non-alignment and becoming the 'American stooge' of his own rhetoric and his Chinese interlocutors' acid pronouncements. To Nehru, the rationalisation was simple: the Chinese had 'betrayed' him: he had been their friend, recognising the People's Republic, pushing for its international recognition, providing it with its first international forum at Bandung and continuously backing its right to a place in the United Nations. Yet for all his acuteness in understanding Cold War pressures and politics, he appears to have been quite unable to understand the pressures and imperatives of Chinese foreign policy: it was impossible for China to accept the Indian refusal to negotiate on the borders without the Chinese themselves appearing as if they had given in to 'unequal treaties'-style blackmail: there was no point in negotiations where one side had already declared that there was nothing on which to negotiate. There is therefore a good case for arguing that Nehru betrayed China rather than the other way round; it is impossible to understand why Nehru and other seasoned Indian policy-makers believed Indian troops' border brinkmanship would be tolerated in the spirit of 'peaceful co-existence'. As Nehru became trapped in an Indian nationalism that he refused to disown even in its nastiest and most illogical form, he was forced away from his principles into a disastrous war, and saw his policies collapse around him.

The tale of the sabotage of the Nehruvian project is a predictable one for which Nehru's 1930s avatar might have written the outline: progressive intentions in the absence of the realignment of class relations and in the presence of imperialist interventions are bound to fail to achieve much. But philosophers of defeat can also be too pessimistic. Nehru's one unambiguous triumph, that of having held the sectarian forces at bay and of successfully defining India as a secular state, is now in some circles beginning to be devalued. This is in many cases a variation on the 'Westernised' versus 'indigenist' argument: Nehru's version of secularism is considered unviable in a country that is allegedly 'fundamentally religious' or 'spiritual' – an emphasis on the alleged separateness and uniqueness of Indian 'culture' based on the facile stereotypes 'Eastern' and 'Western' that to some extent have been internalised by many Indians. Anti-Nehruvians who are also anti-fundamentalists seek to draw on Gandhi's version of tolerance instead: routing their idea of tolerance through a religious and spiritual appeal to the equality of all religions. It is a caricature of Nehru's views to claim that he left no place for religion at all. On the other hand, he had a definite distrust of religion as a motivating factor in politics. And Nehru himself used Gandhi's version of the message of tolerance when he felt it would go down better. The problem was, and is, that Gandhi's polyvalent messages were never very consistent. 'Hindus' can claim that Gandhi's position as a Hindu proves the essential tolerance of 'Hinduism' and the need for others to line up behind them.

Success or failure of a 'project' apart, the consequences of the Nehruvian period for the long-term language of political legitimacy in India have been tremendous. Although many of his principles worked through deferral – what, for instance, was the positive content of Indian nationalism, other than an impossible-to-define 'composite culture'? This very deferral was the source of its strength: 'Indian-ness' could be what one wished to make of it. Unsolved problems and unresolved questions surfaced, of course: towards the end of Nehru's life, in particular, the exclusion or marginalisation of some groups from the alleged 'Nehruvian consensus' became apparent. For all the rhetoric of social justice, poverty remained a problem; women, though placed in some prominent positions by Nehru himself, were far from in the position of equality that he had envisaged; caste- and tribe-based job reservations had created new vested interests in a set of perpetuated sectarian identities instead of leading to more egalitarian social and economic interactions. 'Communal riots' still occurred in the 1960s, albeit with less frequency and virulence than in the pre-independence and immediate post-independence years. Indeed, various divergent kinds of sectarianism emerged: linguistic, regional, 'tribal' and so on. These undoubtedly would have been seen as failures by Nehru himself: a perpetuation of the 'medieval' and a failure to embrace the 'modern' (in Nehru's day, these terms were far less problematic than they are considered today). However, more positively, a commitment to secular democracy, and to social justice, became integral to public standards of legitimacy in independent India, even if they were not always followed. And it was these public standards that gave many otherwise marginalised groups the hope that some form of redress was indeed possible. These were the standards that were and would be invoked in the post-Nehru years to describe the essential values of India's democratic, secular society. This returns us to an earlier point about the 'Nehruvian vision': however impossible it was to materialise, it was an enduring set of goals – its legacies, the disputes and defences conducted in its name, were more important than its failures. And in the absence of a clear content to an Indian 'nationalism', it provided direction and coherence to an Indian ideal that was otherwise no greater than the sum of its fragments.

And yet, whether Nehru succeeded altogether in being a Nehruvian or not, the debates about the validity of Nehruvian ideas are to a large extent independent of him: the author, in several senses, is dead. We might wish to separate what might be considered an iconography of Nehru – which operates not by a serious consideration of his ideas, but by linking the necessity of nationalist adulation of a hero of the 'freedom struggle' with a policy – and a reasoned debate regarding what the Nehruvian legacy can provide by way of resources for the present and the future. And we may look back at the life and career of an intellectual and politician whose political activities tended constantly to undermine the possibility of the achievement of his vision as an intellectual.

NOTES

PREFACE

1 Hiren Mukerjee, *The Gentle Colossus* (Manisha Granthalaya, 1964; new edition, Oxford University Press, 1986), pp. 222–3.

INTRODUCTION

1 H.N. Brailsford to Jawaharlal Nehru (JN), March 8, 1936, Jawaharlal Nehru Papers (JNP), Nehru Memorial Library (NML), volume 10, p. 15.
2 Fenner Brockway to JN, 30 June 1938, JNP, NML, volume 10, p. 131.
3 Figures cited in Mushirul Hasan, 'Introduction', *The Partition Omnibus* (Oxford University Press, 2002), p. xxxi; Dick Kooiman, *Communities and Electorates* (VU University Press, 1995), p. 44.

1 THE MAKING OF A COLONIAL INTELLECTUAL

1 In Mughal practice, *zamindari* is not ownership of land, but the right to collect its revenues and carry out local administration. The landlord, in this sense, remains the emperor. Calcutta was a city set up by the East India Company; the emperor simply recognised and gave a legal basis to the British control over Calcutta, but *not* as landowners.
2 *Pandit* is the customary title given to a man of learning, and sometimes more specifically a teacher of Sanskrit. This should not be confused with the title *Panditji* – the *ji* being an honorific – that many used for Nehru. The term *pandit* was used generically for the Kashmiri Brahmin community, and as Brahmins were traditionally supposed to be men of learning, it was possible to conflate the two meanings.
3 Jawaharlal Nehru, *An Autobiography* (Bodley Head, 1936), p. 8.
4 M.K. Gandhi, *An Autobiography, or The Story of My Experiments with Truth* (Penguin, 1982) (first published 1927–9; translated from the Gujarati by Mahadev Desai), pp. 76–7.
5 JN, *An Autobiography*, p 15.
6 Motilal Nehru (MN) to JN, November 16 1905, in Ravinder Kumar and D.N. Panigrahi (eds), *Selected Works of Motilal Nehru* (SWMN) (2 volumes, Nehru Memorial Museum and Library, 1982–4), volume 1, p. 89.
7 JN, *An Autobiography*, p. 7.
8 MN to JN, October 20, 1905, from Marseilles, *SWMN*, volume 1, p. 79.
9 JN to MN, October 22, 1905, from Harrow, in S. Gopal (ed.), *Selected Works of Jawaharlal Nehru* (first series, 1972–82) (*SWJN*), vol. 1, p. 3.
10 JN to MN, December 11, 1905, *SWJN*, volume 1, p. 6. The infant had

already died on December 2; Jawaharlal did not hear of the death until his father's next letter.

11 MN to JN, January 18, 1906, *SWMN*, volume 1, p. 101.

12 By this time, under British administration, a *zamindar* was a large landowner, recognised as a proprietor by, and paying land revenues to, the government.

13 See MN to JN, December 27, 1906, *SWMN*, volume 1, p. 115, and JN's protest in reply, February 8, 1907, *SWJN*, volume 1, p. 19. The word 'oily' has been editorially omitted from MN's letter in *SWMN*, volume 1, but appears in JN's reply in *SWJN*, volume 1.

14 JN to MN, June 4, 1908, *SWJN*, volume 1, p. 58.

15 JN to MN, November 7, 1907, *SWJN*, volume 1, p. 37.

16 MN to JN, February 21, 1907, *SWMN*, volume 1, p. 121.

17 JN to MN, January 30, 1908, *SWJN*, volume 1, p. 44.

18 JN to MN, December 3, 1908, *SWJN*, volume 1, p. 62.

19 MN to JN, December 23, 1910, *SWMN*, volume 1, p. 156.

20 MN to JN, August 30, 1909, quoted in editors' introduction, *SWMN*, volume 1, p. 17.

21 JN to MN, March 18, 1909, *SWJN*, volume 1, p. 66.

22 JN, *An Autobiography*, pp 19–25. The quote is from p. 25.

23 JN to MN, October 29, 1908, *SWJN*, volume 1, p. 59.

24 JN to MN, June 17, 1910, from London, *SWJN*, volume 1, p. 74.

25 JN, *An Autobiography*, p. 25.

26 JN to MN, January 30, 1907, *SWJN*, volume 1, p. 18.

27 JN to Swarup Rani, May 7, 1909, *SWJN*, volume 1, p. 67, in Hindi (editor's translation).

28 JN to Swarup Rani, March 14, 1912, *SWJN*, volume 1, p. 97, in Hindi (editor's translation).

29 JN, *An Autobiography*, p 26.

2 THE YOUNG GANDHIAN

1 MN to JN, October 5, 1911, *SWMN*, volume 1, p. 164; MN to JN, December 22, 1911, *SWMN*, volume 1, p. 166.

2 MN to JN, December 22, 1911, *SWMN*, volume 1, p. 167.

3 JN, *An Autobiography*, p. 31.

4 JN, *An Autobiography*, p. 35.

5 JN, *An Autobiography*, p. 37. The chapter is called 'My wedding and an adventure in the Himalayas'.

6 The statement is reproduced in Bipan Chandra *et al.*, *India's Struggle for Independence* (Penguin, 1988), p. 168.

7 Quoted in Sumit Sarkar, *Modern India 1885–1947* (Macmillan, 1983), p. 196.

8 Quoted in BR Nanda, *The Nehrus: Motilal and Jawaharlal* (Allen & Unwin, 1962), p. 175.

9   JN, *An Autobiography*, p. 44.
10 JN, *An Autobiography*, p. 46.
11 Judith Brown, *Gandhi: Prisoner of Hope* (Yale University Press, 1989), p. 154.
12 M.K. Gandhi, 'Hind Swaraj', in A. Parel (ed.), *Gandhi: Hind Swaraj and Other Writings* (Cambridge University Press, 1997), p. 28.
13 S.A. Dange, *Gandhi versus Lenin* (Liberty Literature Co., 1921).
14 JN, *An Autobiography*, p. 73.
15 JN, *An Autobiography*, p. 75.
16 *Young India*, February 16, 1921, June 15, 1921, quoted in Sarkar, *Modern India*, p. 208.
17 *Young India*, January 19, 1921, quoted in Sarkar, *Modern India*, p. 207.
18 JN, *An Autobiography*, p. 57.
19 S. Gopal, *Jawaharlal Nehru: A Biography*, volume 1 (Jonathan Cape, 1975), p. 53.
20 JN, *An Autobiography*, pp. 57, 61.
21 Sarkar, *Modern India*, p. 226.
22 An oft-quoted remark: see Sarkar, *Modern India*, p. 1.
23 *SWJN*, volume 2, p. 14 ff.

3   'INEFFECTUAL ANGEL', 1927–39

1   Quoted in S. Gopal, *Jawaharlal Nehru: A Biography*, volume 1, (Jonathan Cape, 1995) p. 104.
2   Quoted in G.H. Jansen, *Afro-Asia and Non-Alignment* (Faber, 1966), p. 31.
3   These articles were published together in 1928 as *Soviet Russia: Some Random Sketches and Impressions* (Kitabistan, 1928).
4   Leaflet reprinted in A.G. Noorani, *The Trial of Bhagat Singh: The Politics of Justice* (Konark, 1996), p. 31
5   Motilal Nehru to M.K. Gandhi, August 14, 1929, reprinted in B.N. Pandey (ed.), *The Indian Nationalist Movement 1885–1947: Select Documents* (Macmillan, 1979), p. 63.
6   JN *An Autobiography*, p. 121.
7   JN, *An Autobiography*, p. 189.
8   JNP, NML, Part III, No. 166.
9   JNP, NML, Part III, No. 166, p. 20.
10 JNP, NML, Part III, No. 166, p. 106.
11 JN, *An Autobiography*, pp. 246, 247.
12 JN, *An Autobiography*, p. 259.
13 Vithalbhai Patel to JN from Vienna, July 22, reporting a conversation in Berlin, where he had met Viren Chattopadhyay and A.C.N. Nambiar. But he added, by way of comfort, 'They are I am afraid not prepared to appreciate the practical difficulties in our way and the odds against which we have to fight.' JNP, NML, volume 81, p. 95.

14 Reprinted in *SWJN*, volume 6, pp 1–31; quote from p. 16.

15 Abdur Rahim to Nehru, October 26, JNP, NML, Vol 1, p. 24.

16 Quoted in S. Gopal, *Jawaharlal Nehru: A Biography*, volume 1, p. 186.

17 Copy of note accompanying application form of Indira Priyadarshini Nehru, dated May 20, 1934, signed Jawaharlal Nehru. JNP, NML, volume 21, pp. 161–5.

18 Cedric Dover to JN, 'Sunday' [1936], JNP, NML, volume 18, p. 123.

19 Dover to JN, May 18, 1936, JNP, NML, volume 18, pp. 125–7.

20 JN to Amiya Chakravarty, March 4, Montreaux, JNP, NML, volume 11, p. 189.

21 Subhas Chandra Bose to JN, Badgastein, Austria, March 4, 1936, JNP, NML, volume 9, pp. 7–9.

22 JN, *An Autobiography*, p. 164.

23 Jayaprakash Narayan, *Why Socialism?* (All-India Congress Socialist Party, 1936), pp. 136, 143, 154–60.

24 JNP, NML, volume 110, Subject Files No. 19 (Part I), pp. 2–3.

25 Prospectus of the Socialist Book Club, copy in All-India Congress Committee (AICC) Papers, NML, 21 (Part I)/1936, pp. 661–3(b).

26 Speech at the Left Book Club Rally, Queen's Hall, London, July 6, 1938, *SWJN* volume 9, p. 34.

27 Gandhi to Agatha Harrison, April 30, 1936, copy in JNP, NML, volume 24, p. 55.

28 Quoted in Bipan Chandra, 'Jawaharlal Nehru and the Capitalist Class, 1936' in *Economic and Political Weekly* x (33–35), 1975.

29 George Joseph to Jawaharlal Nehru, July 18, 1936, JNP, NML, volume 37, pp. 57–8.

30 Nehru to George Joseph, August 7, 1936, JNP, NML, volume 37, p. 59.

31 *Modern Review*, November 1937, copy in JNP, NML, Part II, Sl No. 54 and JN's letter to Krishna Kripalani at Vishwa Bharati University, June 26, 1938, JNP, NML, volume 41, pp. 5–6, in which he confirms he wrote it himself.

32 JN to Nawab Mohammad Ismail Khan of the Muslim League, February 5, 1938, JNP, NML, volume 39, pp. 131–2.

33 Syed Mahmud to JN, December 9, 1939, JNP, NML, vol 97, pp. 159–65.

34 JN to Syed Mahmud, December 12, 1939, JNP, NML, vol 97, pp. 166–7.

35 Report dated August 29, 1938, India Office Records (IOR): L/P&J/12/293, f. 136.

36 Partha Sarathi Gupta, *Imperialism and the British Labour Movement* (Macmillan, 1975), pp. 258–9.

37 Chairman's Note on Congress Policy, December 21, 1938, reprinted in KT Shah (ed.), *Report: National Planning Committee* (Bombay, 1949), pp. 35–7.

38 *National Herald* editorial, copy in JNP, NML, Part III, Sl No. 52, September 27, 1936.

39 Jayaprakash Narayan to JN, Calicut, November 23, 1938, JNP, NML,

volume 54, p. 58. Narayan had been particularly close to Nehru, and addressed him as 'bhai' (brother).

40 Subhas Bose, quoted from 'Report of an interview with R. Palme Dutt, published in the *Daily Worker*, London, January 24, 1938', reprinted in Sisir Kumar Bose and Sugata Bose (ed.), *Netaji Collected Works, volume 9: Congress President: Speeches, Articles and Letters, January 1938–May 1939* (Oxford University Press, 1995), p. 2.

41 Nehru to SC Bose, April 3, 1939, JNP, NML, volume 9, p. 211.

4 THE END OF THE RAJ

1 W.H. Auden, 'September 1939', *New Republic*, October 18, 1939, p. 297, in JNP, NML, Part V, Nos 46–55, p. 3.

2 *National Herald* editorial, October 19, 1939, reprinted in *SWJN*, volume 10, p. 197.

3 Quoted in J.H. Voigt, 'Co-operation or Confrontation? War and Congress Politics, 1939–42', in D.A. Low (ed.), *Congress and the Raj* (South Asia Books, 1977), p. 354.

4 Personal and Most Secret: letter dated September 29, 1939, R.A. Cassels to G. Laithwaite, Private Secretary to the Viceroy, file entitled 'Suggestions for dealing with a break with Congress if it occurs under Sec. 93', IOR: L/P&J/8/593, f. 18.

5 Note by G. Laithwaite, Private Secretary to the viceroy, IOR: L/P&J/ 8/593, f. 2. Laithwaite had strong misgivings about this approach, and placed his misgivings on record, deploring an attempt to return to 'a Constitution based apparently on the principles of the Act of 1858'.

6 The Resolution is reprinted in full in a number of sources: see for instance S.S. Pirzada and Syed Sharifuddin (eds), *Foundations of Pakistan: All-India Muslim League Documents 1906–1947* (Metropolitan Book Co., 1982).

7 JN to Gandhi, January 24, 1940, JNP, NML, volume 26, p. 5.

8 JN to Gandhi, January 24, 1940, JNP, NML, volume 26, p. 6.

9 JN to Krishna Menon, December 2, 1939, *SWJN*, volume 10, p. 263.

10 Cripps to Nehru, January 14, JNP, NML, volume 14, pp. 221–2.

11 Statement to the court, in Prison Diary, *SWJN*, volume 11, p. 491.

12 Prison diary, entry for 14 November 1940 (Nehru's fifty-first birthday), *SWjN*, volume 11, p. 495. He was arrested on October 31, and tried on November 3–5, 1940.

13 Entry for August 7, 1941, prison diary, *SWJN*, volume 11, p. 671.

14 JN to J.C. Wedgwood, April 23, 1941, JNP, NML, volume 103, pp. 32–3.

15 JN, article for *Daily Herald*, London, typescript dated December 9, 1941, JNP, NML, Part III, Sl No. 85.

16 Prime Minister Winston Churchill to Viceroy Lord Linlithgow, March 10, 1942, in N. Mansergh (ed.), *India: The Transfer of Power 1942–1947* (TOP) (12 volumes, HMSO, 1975–83), volume I, p. 395.

17 The amendment to the quote is noted in S. Gopal, *Jawaharlal Nehru: a Biography*, volume 1, p. 279.

18 Nehru to Evelyn Wood, June 5, 1942, quoted in Peter Clarke, *The Cripps Version: The Life of Sir Stafford Cripps 1889–1952* (Allen Lane, 2002), p. 305.

19 The text of the speech is available in M.K. Gandhi, *Collected Works* (88 volumes, Navajivan, 1958–), volume 76, pp. 384–96. For a summary see Bipan Chandra *et al, India's Struggle for Independence*, (Penguin, 1988) pp. 459–60.

20 Linlithgow, personal telegram to Winston Churchill, August 31, 1942, *TOP*, volume II, p. 853.

21 Dorothy Norman (ed.), *Nehru: The First Sixty Years* (2 volumes, Bodley Head, 1965), volume 1, p. ix.

22 Quoted in Ayesha Jalal, *The Sole Spokesman: Jinnah, the Muslim League and the Demand for Pakistan* (Cambridge University Press, 1985), p. 121.

23 Maulana Abul Kalam Azad, *India Wins Freedom* (Orient Longman, 1959/1988), p. 117

24 Z.A. Ahmad's talk with Jawaharlal Nehru, June 1945, 'not to be shown to anyone else without P.C. Joshi's [General Secretary, CPI] permission', 1945/9, P.C. Joshi Archive, Jawaharlal Nehru University, New Delhi.

25 G. Adhikari, *National Unity Now!* (People's Publishing House, 1942), pp. 5–6, P.C. Joshi Archive, Jawaharlal Nehru University, New Delhi.

26 AICC speech, July 7, 1946, quoted in S. Gopal, *Jawaharlal Nehru: a Biography*, volume 1, p. 326.

27 Maulana Abul Kalam Azad, *India Wins Freedom* (1959/1988), p. 170.

28 Sulagna Roy, 'Communal Conflict in Bengal, 1930–1947', unpublished PhD thesis, University of Cambridge, 1999, Chapter Four.

29 Statement to the press on the Great Calcutta Killings, August 26, 1946, JNP, NML, Part III, No. 345.

30 Sulagna Roy, 'Communal Conflict in Bengal, 1930–1947', Chapter Four.

31 S. Gopal (ed.), *Selected Works of Jawaharlal Nehru, Second Series* (Delhi 1984–) [hereafter *SWJN II*], volume 2, pp. 44–5, quote from p. 45.

32 JN to Patel, November 5, 1946, JNP, NML, volume 81, pp. 93–4.

33 Minutes of the 6th Miscellaneous Meeting of the Congress, New Delhi, April 22, 1947, *TOP*, volume 10, pp. 363–5.

34 Quoted in Alan Campbell-Johnson, *Mission with Mountbatten* (Hale, 1951; edition cited 1985), entry for June 1, 1947, p. 98.

35 S.L. Poplai (ed.), *Select Documents on Asian Affairs: India 1947–1950* (Oxford University Press, 1959; reprint, New York, 1970), volume 1, p. 2.

INTERLUDE – ENVISIONING THE NEW INDIA

1 Ram Manohar Lohia's note (1947) 'Fifteen-Point Note on Congress and the Socialist Party', AICC Papers, File 6/1947, pp. 467–77.

2 Jawaharlal Nehru, *Discovery of India* (Meridian Books, 1946), p. 52.

3   JN, *Discovery of India*, p. 25.
4   JN, *Discovery of India*, p. 36.
5   JN, *Discovery of India*, p. 75.
6   JN, *Discovery of India*, p. 104.
7   JN, *Discovery of India*, p. 59.
8   JN, *Discovery of India*, p. 144.
9   JN, *Discovery of India*, p. 56.
10 JN to Krishna Menon, July 22, 1947, *SWJN II*, volume 3, p. 344.
11 Alan Campbell-Johnson, *Mission with Mountbatten*, entry for Wednesday, April 28, 1948.
12 *Jawaharlal Nehru's Speeches, volume one: September 1946–May 1949* (Ministry of Information and Broadcasting, Government of India, 2nd edition, November 1958), p. 10.
13 JN, *Discovery of India*, pp. 30–31.
14 Socialist Party programme, copy in AICC Papers, NML, File 27 (Part I)/1947, pp. 127–45; quotes from p. 127.
15 P. Thakurdas papers, NML, File 291 Part II: Post-War Economic Development Committee, pp. 265–6.
16 JN, *Discovery of India*, p. 398.
17 Speech at the AICC, New Delhi, September 24, 1946. *SWJN II*, volume 1, p. 6.
18 Speech in Assembly, October 28, 1946, *SWJN II*, volume 1, p. 533.
19 Speech broadcast from New Delhi, September 7, 1946, *Jawaharlal Nehru's Speeches, volume one*, p. 2. This was his first speech as a member of the Interim Government.
20 He described non-aligned countries as 'the proverbial clever calves that suck two cows'. Michal Kalecki, 'Observations on Social and Economic Aspects of "Intermediate Regimes"' (1964), reprinted in *Collected Works of Michal Kalecki, Volume V: Developing Economies* (Clarendon Press, 1993), pp. 6–12; the quote is from p. 10.
21 Speech in Constituent Assembly, January 22, 1947, *Jawaharlal Nehru's Speeches, volume one*, p. 22.
22 JN to Vijayalakshmi Pandit, November 14, 1946, *SWJN II*, volume 1, p. 539.
23 Nehru to Asaf Ali, Member for Communications, October 11, 1946, *SWJN II*, volume 1, pp. 516–18, p. 518.
24 Nehru to Asaf Ali in Washington, December 21, 1946, *SWJN II*, volume 1, pp. 556–7.
25 Nehru's note to Asaf Ali and KPS Menon, Ambassadors to the USA and China respectively, dated January 22, 1947, *SWJN II*, volume 1, pp. 575–577.
26 Press statement, January 20, 1947, *SWJN II*, volume 1, pp. 572–3.
27 JNP, NML, Part III, Sl No. 85, 28/10/40.
28 *SWJN*, volume 10, p. 87.
29 *Jawaharlal Nehru's Speeches, volume one*, p. 35.

30 JN to Asaf Ali, May 14, 1947, *SWJN II*, volume 2, pp. 148–50, quote from p. 149.
31 JN to Asaf Ali, May 14, 1947, *SWJN II*, volume 2, pp. 148–50, quote from p. 149.
32 *SWJN II*, volume 2, pp. 73–5
33 Note dated May 11, 1942, Lahore, to Colonel Louis Johnson, JNP, NML, volume 37, pp. 13–24, esp. pp. 22–3.
34 Quoted in S. Gopal, *Jawaharlal Nehru: a Biography*, volume 2 (Jonathan Cape, 1979), p. 53.
35 Nehru to Cripps, May 8, 1949, quoted in Peter Clarke, *The Cripps Version* (Allen Lane, 2002), p. 476 fn. 74.
36 Speech in the Constituent Assembly, May 16, 1949, quoted in S.L. Poplai (ed.), *India 1947–50: Select Documents on Asian Affairs*, volume 2, p. 71.
37 Pablo Neruda, *Memoirs* (Penguin, 1978), pp. 202–3.

5 CONSOLIDATING THE STATE, c. 1947–55

1 Press statement, August 15, 1947, *Jawaharlal Nehru's Speeches, volume one*, p. 27.
2 Figures are from Penderel Moon, *Divide and Quit: An Eyewitness Account of the Partition of India* (new edition, Chatto and Windus, 1998), Appendix; G.D. Khosla, *Stern Reckoning: a Survey of the Events Leading up to and Following the Partition of India* (Oxford University Press; new edition, 1989, 1950), p. 299; H.V. Hodson, *The Great Divide: Britain, India, Pakistan* (Hutchinson, 1969), p. 418; Mushirul Hasan, 'Introduction', *The Partition Omnibus*, (Oxford University Press, 2002), p. xxiv.
3 JN to Mountbatten, August 27, 1947, *SWJN II*, volume 4, pp. 25–6.
4 JN to Mountbatten, Lahore, August 31, 1947, *SWJN II*, volume 4, pp. 44–5.
5 JN to Rajendra Prasad, August 7, 1947, *SWJN II*, volume 3, p. 191.
6 Note to Cabinet ministers, September 12, 1947, *SWJN II*, volume 4, p. 65.
7 JN to Patel, September 30, 1947, *SWJN II*, volume 4, p. 114.
8 MK Gandhi, speech on January 12, 1948, *Delhi Diary* (Navajivan, 1948), pp. 330–3, reprinted in S.L. Poplai (ed.), *India 1947–50: Select Documents on Asian Affairs*, volume 1, p. 418.
9 Incident outside Birla House, January 24, 1948, *SWJN II*, volume 5, p. 31, note.
10 *Jawaharlal Nehru's Speeches, volume one*, p. 37.
11 Quoted in Bipan Chandra *et al.*, *India's Struggle for Independence*, p. 454.
12 Speech in the Constituent Assembly on February 2, 1948, reprinted in *SWJN II*, volume 5, p. 40.
13 Nehru to Mountbatten, December 26, 1947, cited in H.V. Hodson, *The Great Divide*, pp. 467–8.

14 Patel's broadcast, January 30, 1948, text reprinted in S.L. Poplai (ed.), *India 1947–1950: Select Documents on Asian Affairs*, volume 1, p. 433

15 J.B. Kripalani's speech on November 15, 1947, reprinted in S.L. Poplai (ed.), *India 1947–1950: Select Documents on Asian Affairs*, volume 1, pp. 438–42; quote from p. 438.

16 Resolutions of the Socialist Party, March 19–21, 1948, reprinted in S.L. Poplai (ed.), *India 1947–1950: Select Documents on Asian Affairs*, volume 1, pp. 450–1.

17 Resolutions of the Socialist Party, March 19–21, 1948, reprinted in S.L. Poplai (ed.), *India 1947–1950: Select Documents on Asian Affairs*, volume 1, p. 453.

18 Quoted in *SWJN II*, volume 3, p. 237.

19 JN to Vijayalakshmi Pandit, March 25, 1948, *SWJN II*, volume 5, p. 573.

20 JN to J.P. Narayan, August 19, 1948, quoted in S. Gopal, *Jawaharlal Nehru: a Biography*, volume 2, p. 67.

21 J.P. Narayan to JN, December 10, 1948, quoted in S. Gopal *Jawaharlal Nehru: a Biography*, volume 2, p. 69.

22 B.D. Graham, *Hindu Nationalism and Indian Politics: the Origins and Development of the Bharatiya Jana Sangh* (Cambridge University Press, 1990), esp. p. 20 ff.

23 Election figures taken from W.H. Morris-Jones, *The Government and Politics of India* (Hutchinson, 1964; edition cited 1967), pp. 163–4.

24 Objectives and Economic Programme Committee, text of resolution reprinted in S.L. Poplai (ed.), *India 1947–1950: Select Documents on Asian Affairs*, volume 1, pp. 445–6.

25 Speech to the Associated Chambers of Commerce, Calcutta, December 15, 1947, *SWJN II*, volume 4, pp. 563–4.

26 Speech at the All-India Manufacturers' Conference, April 14, 1947, *SWJN II*, volume 2, p. 585.

27 Speech to the Central Board of Irrigation, New Delhi, December 5, 1948, *Jawaharlal Nehru's Speeches*, volume 1, p. 90.

28 A.K. Shaha, *India on Planning: Planning for Liquidation of Unemployment and Illiteracy* (Calcutta, 1948), p. 108.

29 Quoted in Ashok Rudra, *Prasanta Chandra Mahalanobis: a Biography* (Oxford University Press, 1996), p. 432.

30 Quoted in (among other pieces: this is an oft-quoted statement) Simon R. Charsley and G.K. Karanth, 'Dalits and State Action: The "SCs"', in Simon R. Charsley and G.K. Karanth (eds), *Challenging Untouchability: Dalit Initiative and Experience from Karnataka* (Sage, 1998), p. 32.

31 Government of India, Planning Commission, *Gramdan Movement: a Handbook* (New Delhi, 1964), p. 2.

32 Jayaprakash Narayan, 'Letter to PSP Associates', *Towards a New Society* (Congress for Cultural Freedom, 1958), pp. 1–48; quotes from pp. 21, 26, 30, 32.

33 Ram Manohar Lohia, 'Preface' (1963), Marx, Gandhi and Socialism (2nd edition, Hyderabad, 1978, first published 1963), pp. xxxxiii–iv.

34 Foreign policy debate in the Constituent Assembly, December 4, 1947, *SWJN II*, volume 4, p. 600.

35 Apparently Krishna Menon cited this conversation with JN in his letter to JN of August 7, 1952 (S. Gopal, *Jawaharlal Nehru: a Biography*, volume 2, p. 59, fn. 77).

36 Talk to journalists, October 15, 1949, quoted in S. Gopal, *Jawaharlal Nehru: a Biography*, volume 2, p. 61.

37 William Foster, Administrator of the Economic Cooperation Association, quoted in Anita Inder Singh, *The Limits of British Influence*, (Pinter, 1993), pp. 92–3. See also George H. Jansen, *Afro-Asia and Non-Alignment*, (Faber, 1966), p. 105.

38 Quoted in Anita Inder Singh, *The Limits of British Influence*, pp. 107–8.

39 Girija Shankar Bajpai's telegram, May 1951, quoted in Tsering Shakya, *The Dragon in the Land of Snows: A History of Modern Tibet since 1947* (Penguin, 2000), p. 75.

40 Five Principles is the most commonly-used translation; Nehru himself translated the term as 'Five Foundations'. See Tibor Mende, *Conversations with Nehru* (Secker & Warburg, 1958), p. 73.

41 Frantz Fanon, *The Wretched of the Earth* (Penguin, 1967), pp. 195–6. Many Indian writers in CCF-funded publications, in contrast to those outside India, found the mysticism of the *bhoodan* movement not to their taste.

42 Quoted in Selig S. Harrison, *India: The Most Dangerous Decades* (Princeton University Press, 1960), p. 8.

43 Statement, August 12, 1947, *SWJN II*, volume 3, pp. 193–4.

44 JN to Abdul Huq, December 23, 1939, JNP, NML, volume 1, p. 7.

45 Speech, June 1952, quoted in K.S. Singh (ed.), *Jawaharlal Nehru, Tribes and Tribal Policy* (Anthropological Survey of India, 1989), p. 2.

46 Letter to Naga National Council, reprinted in the *National Herald*, October 2, *SWJN II*, volume 2, p. 604.

47 Speech, June 1952, quoted in K.S. Singh (ed.), *Jawaharlal Nehru, Tribes and Tribal Policy*, pp. 2–3.

6 HIGH NEHRUVIANISM AND ITS DECLINE, c. 1955–63

1 Nehru to K.M. Panikkar, November 12, 1953, quoted in S. Gopal, *Jawaharlal Nehru*, volume 2, (Jonathan Cape, 1979), p. 185.

2 Quoted in G.H. Jansen, *Afro-Asia and Non-Alignment*, (Faber, 1966), pp. 150, 159.

3 Quoted in G.H. Jansen, *Afro-Asia and Non-Alignment*, p. 117.

4 Quoted in G.H. Jansen, *Afro-Asia and Non-Alignment*, p. 120.

5 S. Gopal, *Jawaharlal Nehru*, volume 2, pp. 285–6.

6 Pranab Bardhan, *The Political Economy of Development in India* (Basil Blackwell, 1988).

7 Election figures taken from W.H. Morris-Jones, *The Government and Politics of India*, (Hutchinson, 1969), pp. 163–4.

8 Quoted in Francine Frankel, *India's Political Economy 1947–1977: the Gradual Revolution* (Princeton University Press, 1978), p. 160.

9 E.M.S. Namboodiripad, 'A Democrat in the Dock', in Rafiq Zakaria (ed.), *A Study of Nehru* (Times of India, 1959; 2nd edition, 1960), p. 223.

10 Krishna Menon, quoted in Michael Brecher, *Nehru's Mantle: the Politics of Succession in India* (Praeger, 1966), pp. 96–7.

11 S. Gopal, *Jawaharlal Nehru: a Biography*, volume 3 (Jonathan Cape, 1984), p. 122.

12 Quoted in G.H. Jansen, *Afro-Asia and Non-Alignment*, p. 298.

13 Nehru's memorandum, quoted in Neville Maxwell, *India's China War* (Jonathan Cape, 1970), pp. 80, 83.

14 Tsering Shakya, *The Dragon in the Land of Snows* (Penguin, 2000), p. 207.

15 Director of the Land Reforms Division of the Planning Commission, interview quoted from Francine Frankel, *India's Political Economy*, p. 167.

16 Quoted in Neville Maxwell, *India's China War*, p. 166.

17 Quoted in Neville Maxwell, *India's China War*, p. 169.

18 Ministry of External Affairs, Government of India, *Report of the Officials of the Governments of India and the People's Republic of China on the Boundary Question* (New Delhi, 1961), p. 5.

19 Quoted in Neville Maxwell, *India's China War*, pp. 171, 174, 175.

20 Michael Brecher, *India and World Politics: Krishna Menon's View of the World* (Oxford University Press, 1968), p. 131.

21 Election figures taken from W.H. Morris-Jones, *The Government and Politics of India*, pp. 163–4.

22 Quoted in Neville Maxwell, *India's China War*, p. 250.

23 Hiren Mukerjee in the Lok Sabha, November 8, 1962, in *Forward to the Defence of the Motherland under the Banner of Jawaharlal Nehru: Speeches by Communist Members in Parliament* (New Delhi: CPI, November 1962), p. 27.

24 Renu Chakrabarty in the Lok Sabha, November 10, 1962, in *Forward to the Defence of the Motherland under the Banner of Jawaharlal Nehru: Speeches by Communist Members in Parliament*, p. 35.

25 Details of the incident are in Neville Maxwell, *India's China War*, p. 410; S. Gopal, *Jawaharlal Nehru*, volume 3, pp. 228–9.

26 Tsering Shakya, *The Dragon in the Land of Snows*, p. 286.

27 Cited in Bertrand Russell, *Unarmed Victory* (Penguin, 1963), p. 105.

28 Speech in the Lok Sabha, intervening in the debate on the Official Languages Bill on April 24, 1963, reprinted in *Jawaharlal Nehru's*

Speeches, volume 5: 1963–64 (Ministry of Information and Broadcasting, Government of India, 1965), p. 29.

29 Speech in the Lok Sabha, intervening in the debate on the Official Languages Bill on April 24, 1963, reprinted in *Jawaharlal Nehru's Speeches, volume 5: 1963–64*, p. 31.

CONCLUSION: DEATH, SUCCESSION, LEGACY

1 Speech in the Lok Sabha on the No-Confidence Motion, August 22, 1963, reprinted in *Jawaharlal Nehru's Speeches, volume 5: 1963–64*, p. 76.

2 Quoted in S. Gopal, *Jawaharlal Nehru*, volume 3, p. 263.

3 JN to Ghulam Muhammad, March 4, 1962, quoted in S. Gopal, *Jawaharlal Nehru*, volume 3, p. 262.

4 *Jawaharlal Nehru's Speeches, volume 5*, p. 228.

5 JNP, NML, Part V, Sl No. 58, p. 84.

6 Nehru's will, dated June 21, 1954, text published in R.K. Karanjia's newspaper *Blitz*, quoted in Michael Brecher, *Nehru's Mantle*, (Praeger, 1966), p. 40.

7 Nehru's will, quoted in S. Gopal, *Jawaharlal Nehru*, volume 3, p. 269.

8 Hiren Mukerjee, *The Gentle Colossus: a Study of Jawaharlal Nehru* (Oxford University Press, 1986, 1st edition, 1964), pp. 5–6.

9 J.D. Bernal, quoted in Deepak Kumar, 'Reconstructing India: Disunity in the Science and Technology for Development Discourse, 1900–1947', *Osiris* 2001, p. 257

10 Tibor Mende, *Conversations with Nehru*, (Secker & Warburg, 1958), pp. 33–4.

FURTHER READING

There are innumerable books on Jawaharlal Nehru. Many are too hagiographic, or dominated by concerns with his personal life or his personality, to be useful. Most of them do not stand up to academic scrutiny. There are also several published memoirs of persons associated with Nehru at various points in his or their careers – of uneven quality and varying levels of usefulness. Much hard work has to be done on cross-checking sources used and finding out what level of access the writer had to Nehru or his circles, what axes he or she had to grind, and so on, before these works yield anything useful.

The three-volume official biography of Nehru by the late S. Gopal, *Jawaharlal Nehru: a Biography* (3 volumes, Jonathan Cape, 1975–84), is still the standard work, though it fails to be adequately critical. Gopal, son of the Sanskritist and later president of India, S. Radhakrishnan, was allowed privileged access to the Nehru papers, which are closed to ordinary researchers for the period after 1946. Gopal is also our main intermediary for the post-1946 period, having edited the published selections from the Nehru papers, the *Selected Works of Jawaharlal Nehru*, two series of which have appeared to date (Nehru Memorial Museum and Library, 1972–82; 1984–). It does not take a specialist to find that even these selectively published works are often at variance with the views expressed in Gopal's official biography – which does him credit as a scholar when he takes off his official hat. (Gopal has worn many official hats in his time – for instance, he was the head of the team of historians appointed to find archival evidence backing India's case on the Indo-Chinese border question that eventually led to the Indo-Chinese border war of 1962.) The first volume, dealing with the pre-1946 period, is the most reliable; thereafter, his narrative is sometimes clumsily partisan. Gopal's is, despite these defects, still the best account in existence.

There is a considerable body of work by B.R. Nanda, relating to Nehru himself, his father Motilal, the Nehru years, Gandhi, and the relationship between Gandhi and Nehru, which is generally reliable, if within a centrist and nationalist paradigm: see in particular *The Nehrus: Motilal and Jawaharlal* (Allen & Unwin, 1962) and *Jawaharlal Nehru: Rebel and Statesman* (Oxford University Press, 1995). Two older critical biographies still worth reading are those of Michael Brecher, *Nehru: A Political Biography* (Oxford University Press, 1959, recently reprinted) and Michael Edwardes, *Nehru: A Political Biography* (Allen Lane, 1971), although they are naturally not informed by the large amounts of recent research on India both in the late colonial and early post-independence period. A more recent biography, Stanley Wolpert's *Nehru: Tryst with Destiny* (Oxford University Press, 1996), is often anecdotal and involved in some speculations on the details of Nehru's sex life; it is an entertaining read, written by a man who met several of the main protagonists of his story. The most recent, Judith Brown's *Nehru: a Political Life* (Yale University Press, 2003), is good on personal details, especially on Nehru's life in prison and his relations with family members, but lacks an understanding of the wider political context or a knowledge of related new research, although the author has had privileged access to some of the post-1947 Nehru papers. Other projects now underway have as yet failed to produce any major surprises.

As to documentary sources, the Nehru papers for the period before 1946 are open to the public (with the requisite research permission; though even these have been ruthlessly culled – one may compare an earlier, published, index of the papers with the current hand-list to get a sense of the sorts of things the public is no longer allowed to see). The papers of the Indian National Congress and various of its committees and dependent bodies, and of Nehru's father Motilal, at the Nehru Memorial Museum and Library, New Delhi are also open to the public. Further material is available at the National Archives of India, New Delhi, and in the India Office Records at the British Library, London, but a directed research question is necessary in order for these archives to yield information. For the period after 1946, as mentioned before, the Nehru papers are closed to researchers without the requisite connections; those with the requisite connections have tended either to be official biographers whose work has consequently been suspect, or whose work has been suspected of being inaccurate by virtue of their having had such privileged access: Catch 22. Until the custodians of Nehru's reputation release him from their tenacious hold, many aspects of Nehru's life and politics will not be properly open to debate. Nonetheless, the *Selected Works of Jawaharlal Nehru* provides much material of value. Moreover, Nehru was a prolific letter writer and many of his letters have been published, continue to be published or can be traced in the papers of his correspondents.

It is of course important not to get too involved in the merely biographical details, and consequently to engage with the wider world in which Nehru lived and worked. General narratives of Indian history can be found in Sumit Sarkar, *Modern India* (Macmillan, 1983), still relevant reading although now twenty years old, and Sugata Bose and Ayesha Jalal, *Modern South Asia* (Routledge, 1998). For the post-1947 period, see also Paul Brass, *The Politics of India since Independence* (Cambridge University Press, 1990). A general narrative of the economic history of India is available in Dietmar Rothermund, *An Economic History of India* (2nd edition, Routledge, 1993). Published documents contained in the *Transfer of Power* series published by Her Majesty's Stationery Office, or the *Towards Freedom* volumes currently being published by the Indian Council for Historical Research (the present Government of India's attempts to censor some volumes of these collections, awaiting publication, will hopefully not be successful) are important sources for their respective periods. Contemporary newspapers are also useful. Works on specific themes and periods are dealt with below.

On British imperial *durbars* and the invented traditions of colonial rule in India, see Bernard Cohn, 'Representing Authority in Victorian India', in Eric Hobsbawm and Terence Ranger (eds), *The Invention of Tradition* (Cambridge University Press, 1983). On the question of the formation of 'Indian' identities, see Bernard Cohn, 'The Census, Social Structure and Objectification in South Asia', in *An Anthropologist among the Historians and other essays* (Oxford University Press, 1986); and Nicholas Dirks, *Castes of Mind* (Princeton University Press, 2001). On Indian nationalism, see Partha Chatterjee, *Nationalist Thought and the Colonial World: A Derivative Discourse?* (Zed Books, 1986); Sudipta Kaviraj, 'The Imaginary Institution of India', in Partha Chatterjee and Gyanendra Pandey (eds), *Subaltern Studies VII* (Oxford University Press, 1992); Sudipta Kaviraj, 'On the Structure of Nationalist Discourse', in T.V. Sathyamurthy (ed.), *Social Change and Political Discourse in India, Volume 1: State and Nation in the Context of Social Change* (Oxford University Press, 1994); Partha Chatterjee, *The Nation and its Fragments: Colonial and Postcolonial Histories* (Princeton University Press, 1993). For a different view, see Peter van der Veer, *Religious Nationalism: Hindus and Muslims in India* (University of California Press, 1994).

On the period of Gandhi's ascendancy, the ideological context is best provided by Gandhi's own writings: see his autobiography, *The Story of My Experiments with Truth* (Penguin, 1982), first published in two volumes in 1927 and 1929; and Anthony Parel (ed.), *Hind Swaraj and other writings* (Cambridge University Press, 1997). For work on the period, see Ravinder Kumar (ed.), *Essays on Gandhian Politics: the Rowlatt Satyagraha of 1919* (Clarendon Press, 1971); Gail Minault, *The Khilafat Movement* (Columbia University Press, 1982); Shahid Amin, 'Gandhi as Mahatma', in Ranajit Guha (ed.), *Subaltern Studies III* (Oxford University Press, 1984); Sumit Sarkar, 'The Logic of Gandhian Nationalism: Civil Disobedience and the Gandhi-Irwin Pact (1930–31)', *Indian Historical Review* III 1, 1976. See also Judith Brown, *Gandhi, Prisoner of Hope* (Yale University Press, 1989), the culmination of a career spent studying Gandhi. (Bizarre omissions include a proper discussion of the Jallianwalla Bagh massacre and Gandhi's role in the enquiry.) Basudev Chatterji, *Trade, Tariffs and Empire: Lancashire and British Politics in India 1919–1939* (Oxford University Press, 1992), deals with the political economy of the period between the two world wars, and Dietmar Rothermund, *India in the Great Depression 1929–1939* (Manohar, 1992), is on the political economy and social history of that period.

A good history of the internal workings of the left, to my mind, remains to be written. Some of this can be followed in the political journals and pamphlets of the time. For the period from the formation of the Congress Socialist Party to 1939 (when the journal collapsed due to financial difficulties) see *The Congress Socialist*. A line closer to Nehru was followed by the *National Herald* from 1938 – he was involved in its founding, and wrote regularly for it himself. Reba Som, *Differences within Consensus: The Left and Right in the Congress, 1929–1939* (Sangam, 1995), addresses the question of how the Congress left and right wings co-existed, to my mind not altogether satisfactorily. Leonard Gordon, *Brothers against the Raj* (Columbia University Press, 1990) provides a sympathetic perspective on the Bose brothers, Subhas and Sarat. There are now many documents in the public domain on the early history of the communist movement in India. M.N. Roy's works have appeared in print, and documentary histories of the Communist Party of India have been published by the original CPI and the breakaway (and now more successful) Communist Party of India (Marxist).

There is a huge literature on communalism, partition and independence: see Asim Roy, 'The High Politics of India's Partition: the Revisionist Perspective', *Modern Asian Studies* 24(2), 1990; Ayesha Jalal, 'Secularists, Subalterns and the Stigma of "Communalism": Partition Historiography Revisited', *Modern Asian Studies* 30(3), 1996; and David Gilmartin, 'Partition, Pakistan, and South Asian History: in Search of a Narrative', *Journal of Asian Studies* 57(4), 1998, for a helpful route through some of it. Alan Campbell-Johnson, *Mission with Mountbatten* (Hale, 1951); Penderel Moon, *Divide and Quit* (Chatto and Windus, 1961); and H.V. Hodson, *The Great Divide: Britain, India, Pakistan* (Hutchinson, 1969), are accounts by contemporaries; as is Maulana Abul Kalam Azad, *India Wins Freedom* (Orient Longman, 1988, first published with omissions, 1959). Ayesha Jalal, *The Sole Spokesman: Jinnah, the Muslim League and the Demand for Pakistan* (Cambridge University Press, 1985) is a crucial work. Among the regional studies are David Gilmartin, *Empire and Islam: Punjab and the Making of Pakistan* (University of California Press, 1988); Ian Talbot, *Provincial Politics and the Pakistan Movement: The Growth of the Muslim League in the North West and North East India 1937–1947* (Oxford University Press, 1989); Ian Talbot, *Freedom's Cry: The Popular Dimension in the Pakistan Movement and Partition*

Experience in North-West India (Oxford University Press, 1996); Shila Sen, *Muslim Politics in Bengal, 1937–47* (Impex India, 1976). Sulagna Roy, 'Communal Conflict in Bengal, 1930–1947', unpublished PhD dissertation (University of Cambridge, 1999), combines archival material and interviews to problematise the connections usually claimed between elite and popular politics. See also the essays in Mushirul Hasan (ed.), *Inventing Boundaries: Gender, Politics and the Partition of India* (Oxford University Press, 2000).

The work of R.J. Moore is useful on British imperial policy in the last years of empire: see his *Churchill, Cripps and India 1939–1945* (Clarendon Press, 1979); *Escape from Empire* (Clarendon Press, 1983); *Endgames of Empire* (Oxford University Press, 1988). On the Cripps-Nehru relationship, crucial to transfer of power negotiations, told from Cripps' point of view, see the relevant sections of Peter Clarke, *The Cripps Version: the Life of Sir Stafford Cripps 1889–1952* (Allen Lane, 2002). (No nuanced understanding of Indian politics should be expected from this book.) See also Ian Copland, *The Princes of India in the Endgame of Empire 1917–1947* (Cambridge University Press, 1997).

Some useful work on the transition from colonial rule to independence is now available. On the end of empire and the beginning of the Cold War, an overview of the imperial context is available in P.J. Cain and A.G. Hopkins, *British Imperialism: Crisis and Deconstruction 1914–1990* (Longman, 1993). On Indo-British relations, the Cold War and US and British concerns regarding regional politics in South and South-East Asia, see R.J. Moore, *Making the New Commonwealth* (Clarendon Press, 1987); Anita Inder Singh, *The Limits of British Influence: South Asia and the Anglo-American Relationship 1947–56* (Pinter Publishers, 1993); Philip Joseph Charrier, 'Britain, India and the Genesis of the Colombo Plan, 1945–1951', unpublished PhD dissertation (University of Cambridge, 1995).

On Kashmir, accounts of 1947–8 can be found in H.V. Hodson, *The Great Divide*, R.J. Moore, *Making the New Commonwealth* and, more recently, C. Dasgupta, *War and Diplomacy in Kashmir, 1947–48* (Sage, 2002). There is much material on Kashmir in general and on later events: a useful short account, arguing that Kashmir's autonomy within the Indian Union should have been respected and ought to be restored, can be found in Balraj Puri, *Kashmir: Towards Insurgency* (Sangam, 1993); and in a comparative and historical framework, although addressing current concerns, Suranjan Das, *Kashmir and Sindh: Nation-Building, Ethnicity and Regional Politics in South Asia* (Anthem, 2001).

For the post-independence period, not nearly enough historical research has been done, largely because of the problems of availability of archival evidence. Nehru's analyses and commentaries on Indian affairs in his published *Letters to Chief Ministers 1947–1964* (five volumes, Jawaharlal Nehru Memorial Fund, 1984–9) are usually quite insightful. On the foreign policy side, new evidence has now been drawn upon by some studies (see above). Some earlier work is still extremely useful: see for instance G.H. Jansen, *Afro-Asia and Non-Alignment* (Faber, 1966), which contains much material on India and on Nehru; Michael Brecher, *India and World Politics: Krishna Menon's View of the World* (Oxford University Press, 1968), provides extremely useful material in a series of interviews with Nehru's main ally and confidant in foreign policy matters.

For domestic politics, some general narratives exist; but newspaper reports, partisan political polemics or contemporary writings are often the best way into it. There is some material on the organisation of the Congress and the state machinery after independence: see for instance, Myron Weiner, *Party-Building in a New Nation: The Indian National Congress* (University of Chicago Press, 1967); Stanley Kochanek, *The Congress Party of India: the Dynamics of One-Party Democracy* (Princeton University Press, 1968); David C. Potter, *India's Political Administrators 1919–1983* (Clarendon Press, 1986); Suhit Sen, 'The Transitional State: Congress and Government in UP, c.1946–57', unpublished PhD thesis (School of Oriental and African Studies, University of London, 1998). On the question of language, see Robert D. King, *Nehru and the Language Politics of India* (Oxford University Press, 1997); on the Hindu Code, Reba Som, 'Jawaharlal Nehru and the Hindu Code Bill: A Victory of Symbol over Substance?' *Modern Asian Studies* 28(1), 1994. On the prime minister's role, see the essays in James Manor (ed.), *Nehru to the Nineties: the Changing Office of Prime Minister in India* (Hurst, 1994). Surveys of the reasons why India would eventually fall apart, outlining regional, linguistic, caste and communal tensions, appeared periodically: see Selig S. Harrison, *India: The Most Dangerous Decades* (Princeton University Press, 1960).

The central theme for post-independence India is development: it has generated much technical literature and much work in the political economy mode. On the corresponding social and intellectual history, see Benjamin Zachariah, 'British and Indian Ideas of "Development": Decoding Political Conventions in the Late Colonial State', *Itinerario* 3–4, 1999; Benjamin Zachariah, 'The Development of Professor Mahalanobis', review article, *Economy and Society* 26(3), 1997. Post-independence, A.H. Hanson, *The Process of Planning: A Study of India's Five-Year Plans, 1950–64* (Oxford University Press, 1966) and Francine R. Frankel, *India's Political Economy 1947–1977: The Gradual Revolution* (Princeton University Press, 1978) are detailed narrative accounts. Pranab Bardhan, *The Political Economy of Development in India* (Basil Blackwell, 1984); Sukhamoy Chakravarty,

Development Planning: The Indian Experience (Clarendon Press, 1987); Terence J. Byres (ed.), *The State and Development Planning in India* (Oxford University Press, 1994); Terence J. Byres (ed.), *The Indian Economy: Major Debates since Independence* (Oxford University Press, 1998), read together, provide a good sense of the debates.

On opposition parties and non-Congress politics, the largest literature relates to the main opposition party for most of the Nehruvian period, the Communist Party of India. The early narrative histories of the CPI, centrally concerned with its origins and development, were written in the 1950s at the height of Cold War paranoia and a lingering McCarthyism – funded by the American establishment, whose need for 'area studies' brought several academic departments into being. G.D. Overstreet and M. Windmiller's *Communism in India* (University of California Press, 1959) is a comprehensive account – but a serious left-winger reading this book might well have developed an over-optimistic picture of the communists' and the left's strengths in India. A companion piece, by David M. Druhe, *Soviet Russia and Indian Communism 1917–1947, with an Epilogue Covering the Situation Today* (Bookman Associates, 1959), attributes too much to Soviet conspiracy, but covers necessary ground for the pre-independence period. Early members of the Party, foreign organisers and breast-beating recanters have all written their memoirs. For the post-independence period, Party resolutions were routinely published and publicised, as were changes of line and reassessments. A history of the CPI in the Nehru years needs to be written.

For other parties: the socialists (of various description) were often their own publicists, most prominent among them being Jayaprakash Narayan and Rammanohar Lohia. On the continued importance of Hindu nationalism in the Nehruvian period, see B.D. Graham, *Hindu Nationalism and Indian Politics* (Cambridge University Press, 1990). See also Christophe Jaffrelot, *The Hindu Nationalist Movement in India* (Hurst, 1996); B.D. Basu *et al*, *Khaki Shorts, Saffron Flags* (Orient Longman, 1993); and Peter van der Veer, *Religious Nationalism*. The Swatantra Party is interesting in that it has been arguably the only secular (that is, non-sectarian or non-religious nationalist) right-wing party of any note in India. See H.L. Erdman, *The Swatantra Party and Indian Conservatism* (Cambridge University Press, 1967). Minoo Masani's *Congress Misrule and the Swatantra Alternative* (Manaktalas, 1966), a collection of his speeches and writings as a Swatantra member, is useful to get a sense of their own arguments.

On the Congress for Cultural Freedom and CIA funding in India, see the second volume of Minoo Masani's memoirs, *Against the Tide* (Vikas, 1981), in which he openly acknowledges receiving CIA funding, but denies it influenced anyone's political opinions. See also Margery Sabin, *Dissenters and Mavericks* (Oxford University Press, 2002), Chapter 6: 'The Politics of Cultural Freedom: India in the 1950s'. On the more directly political activities of the CIA in India, and on Tibet and Indo-Chinese relations, see Tsering Shakya, *The Dragon in the Land of Snows* (Penguin, 2000) and Neville Maxwell, *India's China War* (Cape, 1970). See also Bertrand Russell, *Unarmed Victory* (Penguin, 1963).

A number of the above works do not deal centrally with Nehru at all; but since Nehru was so central to the period under discussion, they have a strong bearing on understanding Nehru and Nehruvianism. They are also not necessarily in accord with the views expressed in this book, and are merely a representative sample drawn from a complex and extremely voluminous literature that in many of its aspects appears now to be in urgent need of revision.

INDEX

Abdullah, Sheikh Muhammad 178–9, 180, 211–12, 232, 255–6
Acheson, Dean 201–2
agriculture: cooperatives in 227, 242; failure of redistributive agenda and 'betting on the strong' 263; fall in prices 69; and Five-Year Plans 193–4, 224–5; limited income-generation potential of 152; Minister 'Kamarajed' 255
ahimsa 41, 45, 68
Ahmad, Z.A. 123–5
Aksai Chin 239–42
Ali, Mohammad (Prime Minister of Pakistan) 216–17
Ali, Mubarak 13
Ali brothers (Muhammad and Shaukat) 33, 39, 40, 42
All-India Hindu (Maha) Sabha 23, 62, 74, 90, 128, 172, 184, 187, 229; and concurrent membership of Congress 91, 124; members instigating riots 134; offices attacked after Gandhi's murder 174; opposes independent Bengal proposals 136; suspends explicitly political activities 175; and upper-caste Hindu opinion 148

All-India Muslim League 19, 31–2, 40, 43, 118, 128, 144, 156, 175; and 1937 elections 88–9; and 'atrocities' of Congress ministries 92–4; and Bose's presidency of Congress 98–9; and Cripps Mission 114–15; and Junagadh 176; League supporters and *Tebhaga* movement 154; and Nehru Report 61–2; opportunity of the Second World War: 105–6; 'Pakistan,' partition negotiations and violence 121–4, 129–35, 138; *zamindari* base 84
All-India Radio 180, 200, 209
All-India Trade Union Congress (AITUC) 47, 65–6, 75, 189
Ambedkar, Dr B.R. 73, 132, 148, 150, 195
Amery, Leo 106, 114, 117, 163
Andrews, C.F. 41
Arab states 179, 200, 203, 217
Arya Samaj 15, 23, 63
Aryan 9, 14
Asaf Ali 157, 162
Asian Relations Conference (1947) 159–60, 172, 238
Ataturk, Mustapha Kemal 209